A NATURAL HISTORY OF AMPHIBIANS

A NATURAL HISTORY OF AMPHIBIANS

Robert C. Stebbins and
Nathan W. Cohen

Illustrated by the Authors

PRINCETON UNIVERSITY PRESS   PRINCETON, NEW JERSEY

Library of Congress Cataloging-in-Publication Data

Stebbins, Robert C. (Robert Cyril), 1915–
A natural history of amphibians / Robert C. Stebbins and
Nathan W. Cohen; illustrated by the authors.
p. cm.
Includes bibliographical references (P.   ) and index.
ISBN 0-691-03281-5 (cl)
1. Amphibians.   I. Cohen, Nathan W., 1919– .   II. Title.
QL667.S84   1995
597.6—dc20   94-43931

Contents

Preface _____

THIS BOOK has been written for a general audience, for the pleasure and edification of anyone, anywhere, interested in learning about the ways of amphibians—the frogs, toads, salamanders, and caecilians (tropical snakelike amphibians) that grace our planet. Topics discussed follow closely the format of lectures given by the senior author over a period of thirty-three years of teaching vertebrate natural history and herpetology. They were selected because they related to the field experience of the authors and their students and were found to arouse student interest in amphibian natural history. An exception is the last chapter on "declining amphibians." The apparent worldwide collapse of many frog and toad populations has only recently come to the attention of scientists and, we believe, serves as an appropriate subject with which to end the book. The declining amphibian story is open-ended and represents a frame in an ongoing process, the outcome of which is uncertain. Some parts of it are speculative. However, it exposes the reader to the scientific process—the gathering of data, development of hypotheses, the importance of basic knowledge concerning the subject under study, and its ultimate integration with other fields of knowledge. All that has gone before in the book helps set the stage for understanding and evaluating the processes and events set forth in the chapter on declining amphibians. Its ecological message should be of concern to all of us.

We began our investigation of apparent amphibian declines in the spring of 1993, late in the writing of our book. In view of the international alarm among amphibian biologists over amphibian declines and what they might portend for the future of these and other animals, we felt we should include some information on the subject in this book. However, we were not fully prepared for the outcome. The results of our survey proved so disturbing that, upon its completion, we decided the topic warranted a full chapter in the book, even though many field studies were underway and new information was being reported almost daily in an international effort to assess the damage and its causes.

After nearly two lifetimes of devotion to the study, artistic representation, and protection of our esteemed subjects and our present effort to set forth their secrets for all to enjoy, we were profoundly sobered by the information we had obtained. If the senior author were now to redraw the distribution maps in his *A Field Guide to Western Reptiles and Amphibians* (Peterson series, 1985), he would be required to show many ranges with major gaps, sprinkled with question marks. Many of the gaps appear to represent out-right extinction of populations over large areas of former ranges.

It is our hope that by setting forth these findings in detail—as they existed, incomplete, at the time of our survey (spring 1993 to summer 1994)—against the backdrop of amphibian natural history information as presented in this book, amphibian conservation efforts will be promoted and studies of the causes of declines will be further stimulated. We fervently hope that the last chapter of the book will not become an epitaph for many members of a remarkable group of living beings.

Topics discussed in the book apply to amphibians worldwide[†] and deal with many important aspects of their lives. These draw upon the personal experiences, knowledge, and interests of the authors, who have studied many of these animals, both in the laboratory and field, for nearly a lifetime, and on the studies of many other biologists, extensively cited throughout the text. We have usually followed closely the wording of cited passages to avoid misconstruing the sense of the authors and have identified the sources of information that are not our own. Some information is considered to have become common knowledge and therefore citations are not included. Considerable older literature is included to provide historical perspective.

Scientific literature, including that on amphibians, grows exponentially, so we have had to be highly selective in our choice of references. We have made an effort to maintain a streamlined account for the general reader, but there is much in the book that will be useful to more advanced readers as well. At the end of some sections, additional references will guide readers who are interested in pursuing the subject under discussion in greater depth.

Often there are disagreements among scientists in their attempts to explain natural phenomena. This results from the nature of the scientific process. We have included a number of such controversies in the book to make clear the ongoing, self-correcting process that is the hallmark of science.

Conservation of wildlife is assuming a high priority as human pressures accelerate the process of wildlife decline and extinction. Amphibians have not escaped. In fact, they may be in the vanguard of decline (see chapter 20). It is our hope that the book will help further wildlife conservation goals by providing basic information on amphibians that is useful to government agencies that care for the land, to environmentalists, to the concerned public, scientists, developers, politicians, and to others who are addressing land-use issues.

Our selection of the title of the book, *A Natural History of Amphibians*, reflects our interest in individual animals and their populations, their taxo-

---

[†] The geographical distribution of each species mentioned in text is indicated in parentheses after the species name. See Frost (1985) for more detailed information on species ranges.

nomic relationships, how and where they live and reproduce, how they interact with one another and their environment, and the evolutionary processes that have made them what they are and that continue to shape their future. A natural history approach involves looking at not only the details of nature, but also seeing those details, perhaps often subconsciously, against the total backdrop of nature. It is this comprehensive worldview that now risks being blurred or lost in an age of scientific specialization and preoccupation with the needs and desires of humanity. Yet paradoxically, it is just such a broad view that is crucial to the present and future well-being of society.

In recent years teaching and research in natural history have declined in popularity, and greater focus is being given to cellular and molecular studies at many colleges and universities. On some campuses, natural history studies have never existed or have been eliminated completely. While the importance of studies at the level of molecules and cells is unquestioned, it is equally important to study life at the other end of the spectrum of biological organization—whole organisms and their interactions in nature. To paraphrase George Gaylord Simpson, knowing all there is to know about a lion's molecules and cells will not tell you why a lion roars. Like the science of ecology, this is what good natural history studies do—obtain direct, on-site knowledge of what is going on outdoors among diverse life forms, often including humans, and the environment. However, natural history studies tend to emphasize—perhaps more than ecological investigations—species identification, systematics and distribution, opportunistic observations of species behavior and interactions in nature, and observational techniques.

Many of the studies reported in this book are fine examples of the natural history approach. Often observations begin with no particular goal in mind—nature is allowed to be the teacher. Soon, however, questions arise and their answers call for the formulation of goals that may lead to field and laboratory experiments, sometimes including the use of biochemical techniques. Although almost any person has the potential of becoming a good field observer, training in observational techniques and methods of recording information in the field helps guide and quicken the process.

Given the rapid loss of species now occurring as the result of human actions, and society's related manifold social and environmental problems, training in natural history should receive high priority. A natural history orientation is needed now more than ever before—since "civilization" began severing humanity's ties with the natural world. Yet growing urbanization, which separates people from nature, and an academic mindset that nature study is old-fashioned and lacking in scientific rigor (sometimes justified) impede corrective action.

It is our hope that the information brought together in this book on amphibians will help increase interest in studies in natural history and show their importance to human well-being, and thereby contribute to an increase in public, educational, and governmental support for such research and teaching in our schools (see Greene, 1994).

Understandings derived from such studies will not only help us as individuals and as a society to recognize the implications of declining biological diversity, but also to see what remedial actions are necessary for restoration of a healthy planetary life-support system.

Acknowledgments

WE WISH to acknowledge the help of a number of people in the preparation of this volume.

Marvalee Wake reviewed the accounts of caecilians; her assistance greatly strengthened this part of the book.

Many people contributed information to the chapter on declining amphibians. It would have been impossible to have documented the species declines described therein without their help. They are as follows: Sandy Andelman, Stanley Anderson, Ronald Beiswenger, Andrew Blaustein,* David Bradford,* Bruce Bury, Cynthia Carey,* Lawrence Cory,* Stephen Corn, Martha Crump,* William Duellman, Gary Fellers,* William Gern,* John Harte, Mark Jennings, Randy Jennings, William Leonard, David Martin, Martin Morton, Charles Painter, Charles Peterson, Wayne Roberts, David Ross, Jay Savage, H. Bradley Shaffer,* Sam Sweet,* and David Wake.* We especially wish to thank Howard Bern,* colleague and friend, who suggested to us the possible role in amphibian declines of synthetic chemicals that mimic the natural hormone estrogen, and Theo Colborn* and Louis Guillette* for patiently helping us with many questions pertaining to exotic chemicals as endocrine disrupters. David Crews called our attention to the use of turtle eggs (obtained from species whose sex determination is temperature sensitive) in testing possible estrogenic effects of synthetic chemicals. Michael Tyler* provided information on Australian amphibians. (Those with an asterisk following their name also read a draft of the chapter and offered their critique.)

We wish to thank the following persons for allowing us use of their photographs: Martha Crump (Golden Toad, fig. 20.13), William Leonard (Cascades Frog, fig. 20.7), and Lu Ray Parker (Wyoming Toad, fig. 20.3). Katherine Milton provided the photograph of the Bicolored Tree Frog upon which the drawing was based (fig. 19.2).

Ingrid Radkey, reference librarian at the University of California, Berkeley, and David Kim helped with library work, and Jennifer Van Heuit and Melissa Martin brought the manuscript into final typed form. We particularly wish to express our gratitude to William Woodcock, editor-at-large for Princeton University Press, for his guidance in preparing this book for publication.

The senior author received a yearly U.C. Berkeley faculty research grant for part of the preparation of the book.

All drawings are by the senior author, unless otherwise noted. Many are original, but some have been adapted from the work of other illustrators (acknowledged in the figure legends). Many have been published before in his books and scientific publications, but are here gathered together for the first time in one place. A number of new drawings have been made for the book. Nearly all photographs are by the junior author. Exceptions are credited.

A NATURAL HISTORY OF AMPHIBIANS

Fig. 1.1 Representative amphibians. (A) Tiger Salamander (*Ambystoma tigrinum*), order Caudata. (B) Leopard Frog (*Rana pipiens*), order Anura. (C) Caecilian (*Ichthyophis gluti-nosus*), order Gymnophionia. (After Sarasin and Sarasin, 1887–90)

1

Introduction

The Major Groups of Living Amphibians
(Fig. 1.1)

The class Amphibia contains about 4550 described living species. At the rate that new species are being discovered, particularly in the tropics, the count is likely to go well above 5000. Approximately 44% of all frog species are known from the American Tropics alone (Duellman, 1988). More surely remain to be discovered if tropical deforestation doesn't eliminate them. Counts of new frog species are also increasing rapidly in Australia. In recent years, many new species of salamanders have been found in the Western Hemisphere, but they too are suffering habitat loss. Among living amphibians, some 390 are salamanders, order Caudata (Urodela); around 4000 are frogs and toads, order Anura (Salientia); and 163 are caecilians, order Gymnophiona (Apoda). Alternative names used for amphibian orders are in parentheses.

Most salamanders resemble a typical lizard in form but have a glandular skin, smooth or roughened with tubercles, lack true claws, and have a tail that is often somewhat flattened from side to side, especially when they are aquatic. They range in total length (TL) from around 1.5 inches (4 cm) (the Mexican lungless salamander, *Thorius pennatulus*) to over 5 feet (1.5 m) (the Giant Salamanders, *Andrias japonicus* and *A. davidianus* of Japan and China). Salamanders are widely distributed in the Northern Hemisphere but are scarce south of the equator except for New World members of the large family of lungless salamanders, the Plethodontidae, containing more than 250 species, which accounts for about 60% of all salamander species.

The frogs and toads are tailless (except as larvae), usually have long hind legs, webbed and unclawed toes, large eyes, and a smooth or warty moist, glandular skin. They range in snout-to-vent (SV) length from about three-eighths inches (1 cm) (Cuban Tree Toad, *Eleutherodactylus limbatus*), to around 12 inches (30 cm) (Goliath Frog, *Conraua goliath* of the Cameroons and equatorial Guinea). Frogs are worldwide in distribution except for polar areas. Since there are many families of tailless amphibians, varying in the extent to which their members resemble a typical frog or toad, we will hereafter use "anuran" as the group term.

Caecilians are limbless and worm or snakelike, lack or have a very short tail, vary as adults from around 3 inches (7.5 cm) to 30 inches (75 cm) TL for most (one species reaches about 5 feet [1.5 m] TL), have a furrowed moist skin with minute imbedded bony dermal scales in some species, lidless eyes covered by skin (and bone in some), reduced and of simple structure, probably responding mostly to light intensity, and a pair of short protrusible sensory tentacles on the head, olfactory and tactile in function. Most burrow in damp soil or decayed wood, but some are aquatic. Fertilization is internal by copulation. Some species lay eggs that hatch into free-living, aquatic larvae; others have direct development; and some are viviparous. Egg-laying species brood their eggs (Wake, 1986). Caecilians are widely distributed in the tropics. See Nussbaum and Wilkinson (1989) for a classification of caecilians.

The Place of Amphibians in Nature

The number of amphibians in an area can easily be misjudged and their ecological importance underestimated. Many species are secretive or are active at times when they are not readily observed. Gergits and Jaeger (1990b) reported that on a wet night in Shenandoah National Park (e US), Red-backed Salamanders (*Plethodon cinereus*) (See fig. 15.1), usually hidden by day, were found at a density of 7–10 individuals per square meter on the surface in some areas. Other species, when breeding, migrating, or transforming from the larval stage, may be readily seen in large numbers. In parts of the humid tropics and subtropics amphibians are the most abundant land vertebrates. Over eighty species, many notable by their voices, have been found at one locality in the upper Amazon basin. In many temperate and tropical woodland and forest habitats, amphibians may exceed in numbers and bulk per acre each of the other classes of terrestrial vertebrates—the reptiles, birds, and mammals.

In a study of Lesser Sirens (*Siren intermedia*), an eel-like aquatic salamander (se US) that reaches around 2 feet in length, Gehlbach and Kennedy (1978) found that the standing crop of this salamander in a Texas pond was greater than the total standing crop of seven species of fish in the same pond. In a hardwood forest (ne US), the total weight of the salamanders present was found to be about twice that of birds at their breeding peak and about equal to that of the small mammals. They produced more new tissue annually than either the birds or mammals, and of higher protein content, thus they provide a source of high-quality food for potential predators (Burton and Likens, 1975a,b). In a marsh in northern Michigan, amphibians were found to be the most important second- and third-level consumers in the food chain (Werner and McCune, 1979).

In a study of the terrestrial lungless salamander Ensatina (*Ensatina eschscholtzii*) in redwood forest habitat near Canyon in the Berkeley hills in California (January 1947 to April 1951), the senior author estimated adults at 170–200 per acre and total counts, including recently hatched young, at 600–700 per acre (Stebbins, 1954). In total number of individuals and, perhaps, in bio-mass (estimated at over 6 lbs per acre) this salamander, at the time of the study, was probably unmatched by any other vertebrate except the much smaller Cal-ifornia Slender Salamander (*Batrachoseps attenuatus*), which was more nu-merous. Including other salamanders present—the California Newt (*Taricha torosa*), and Arboreal Salamander (*Aneides lugubris*), salamander biomass per acre would probably have matched the findings of Burton and Likens. Stewart and Rand (1991) estimated average population size of the Puerto Rico Coqui (*Eleutherodactylus coqui*) (a 28–50 mm SV frog) at 20,570 adults per hectare (8325/acre).

What accounts for the great abundance and bulk of amphibians that exist in many habitats? They are the primary vertebrate predators on invertebrates in many freshwater and moist terrestrial environments, in particular the damp microenvironments beneath stones, within and beneath rotting logs, in leaf litter, underground, and in damp arboreal sites. All amphibians (with the ex-ception of many anuran larvae)—caecilians, salamanders, and anurans, aquatic and terrestrial—feed heavily on invertebrates. Their impact on this food source can be prodigious. Bruce and Christiansen (1976) estimated that small pond populations of one thousand individuals of the tiny Northern Cricket Frog (*Acris crepitans*) (e US) (studied in Iowa), under conditions similar to their study, would consume approximately 4.8 million small arthropods per year, mostly insects.

How does the amphibian biomass fit into ecosystem functioning? In many habitats amphibians are a major "conveyor belt" that provides for transfer of invertebrate energy sources to predatory animals higher up the food chain—to the many species of reptiles (particularly snakes), and some birds and mam-mals that prey upon them that are unable, or little able, to access directly the invertebrate food source. They also are a major food source for freshwater fish. The transfer is efficient because amphibians, in general, expend energy conser-vatively. As "cold-blooded," ectothermal (see chapter 11) vertebrates, they operate at generally much lower temperatures than the "warm-blooded" (endothermal) birds and mammals and, usually living in cooler, wetter envi-ronments, lower than most reptiles. Among terrestrial vertebrates, they thus exhibit low rates of energy expenditure for bodily maintenance. Terrestrial lungless salamanders, in particular, have low resting metabolic rates and spend long periods in inactivity. Although amphibians generally take longer to digest their food than the endotherms, they are highly efficient in biomass conversion (see Pough, 1983), as noted above, producing much new tissue and of high quality annually, which then becomes available to predators. In contrast to the endotherms, far less metabolic energy is lost as heat. In comparison with endo-therms of comparable size, many are slow to mature and long-lived, thus re-placement of individuals in populations is slow. Such populations, like plants, act as an energy reserve within ecosystems.

The grazing of anuran tadpoles, which in many freshwater ponds exerts important control over the growth of algae and other aquatic plants, transfers stored plant energy to tadpole-eating invertebrates, fish, and other vertebrates.

Amphibians thus have an important role in ecosystem energy flow and nutrient cycling in many ecosystems, including even many of those of arid lands, and through their foraging and death they participate importantly in decomposer food webs (Burton and Likens, 1975a,b; Scott and Campbell, 1992).

Amphibian Life Cycles and Modes of Reproduction

Most amphibians live both in fresh water and on land—they are *amphibious* (two-lived) (fig. 1.2). Some, however, are completely aquatic and others are wholly terrestrial. Most lay eggs—they are *oviparous*. The amphibious mode of life is presumed to represent the ancestral pattern—movement from terrestrial sites to water to breed and then return to land. The eggs, deposited at aquatic sites, hatch into free-living larvae that later transform to the land stage.

Many frogs and most salamanders of the family Plethodontidae, however, have abandoned aquatic life and lay their eggs in moist places on land. The larval stage is passed within the egg and the young emerge fully formed (fig. 1.3). Their eggs undergo *direct development*, circumventing the free-living larval stage. At the other extreme are strictly aquatic amphibians such as the Giant Salamanders (*Andrias*) of Asia (fig. 1.3B), the Hellbender (*Cryptobranchus alleganiensis*) (ne US), and mudpuppies (*Necturus*) (e US, se Can) (fig. 3.2) that lay their eggs in water. Caecilians lay eggs on land, except for the viviparous species. In some species, larvae wriggle to nearby streams where they are larval for about a year before metamorphosing and emerging on land. Others are direct developers.

Some amphibians are *viviparous*. The term, as used here (following Wake, 1982), refers to species that give birth to fully metamorphosed young that are nurtured by feeding on oviductal secretions produced by the mother. No placental attachment is involved. They undergo direct development. Viviparous species have arisen, independently, in all three orders of amphibians. They include many caecilians, but among salamanders only the Alpine Salamander (*Salamandra atra*) (Eur), and among anurans, so far, only the African livebearing toads, *Nectophrynoides occidentalis* and, by inference, *N. liberiensis* (Xavier, 1978, 1986). The Alpine Salamander, found in the Alps above about 2000 feet (700 m), gives birth to one or two transformed young on land after a period of 3–5 years, the duration evidently depending on weather conditions. The Mountain Viviparous Toad (*Nectophrynoides occidentalis*) (Afr, Mt. Nimbia region) is a diminutive (15–26 mm SV), high-altitude species (Xavier et al., 1970; Xavier, 1977). No water for tadpole development is found in its

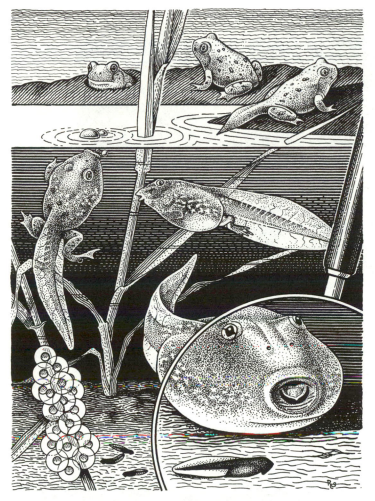

Fig. 1.2 Life stages of an "amphibious" amphibian, the Western Spadefoot Toad (*Scaphiopus hammondii*).

habitat, and sperm is transferred by cloacal contact. The gestation period is prolonged—around 9 months, the first 6 months or so of which occurs while the toads are underground during the dry season. The toadlets at birth are minute, around 7.5 mm SV. These high-altitude species (salamander and toads) live in cool, stressful environments, which probably accounts for their long periods of gestation.

Many amphibians (caecilians so far excepted) are *ovoviviparous*. They carry their developing eggs in the oviducts or, among anurans, on or within various parts of the body—stomach, skin pouches, etc., but the embryos *receive no nourishment* (or very little?—see Darwin Frog, chapter 18) from the parent.

Fig. 1.3 (A) A completely terrestrial amphibian, the salamander Ensatina (*Ensatina eschscholtzii*), guarding her eggs. (B) A Giant Salamander (*Andrias*), a completely aquatic Asian salamander that may reach over 5 feet in length.

They rely on their yolk supply for nutrients and, depending upon the species, hatch at various stages of development up to full metamorphosis. Intrauterine cannibalism, reported in *Salamandra salamandra* (Gasser and Joly, 1972), is an additional source of nutrients. A number of the members of the family Salamandridae are known to be ovoviviparous. They include the Fire Salamanders (*S. salamandra, lanzai, corsica, algira,* and *infraimmaculata*) (Eur, nw Afr, sw Asia) and perhaps *Mertensiella luschani* (se Turkey, Aegean Is) and *M. caucasica* (ne Turkey to Caucasus). These salamanders carry their developing embryos in the oviducts. In Fire Salamanders the young, often 10 to 40 in number, are usually born at an advanced larval stage with limbs well developed but gills still present. In populations of *S. salamandra* in northern Spain broods are smaller (often 4 or 5) and many young are born fully metamorphosed. Fire Salamanders are terrestrial after metamorphosis, but during birth, they enter water to release their young (Mario Garcia-Paris, pers. comm.).

Some anurans are ovoviviparous. Some, such as the Golden Coqui Frog (*Eleutherodactylus jasperi*) (Puerto Rico), carry the developing embryos to the transformation stage (Wake, 1978b). Others release their larvae at various stages of development, such as some of the marsupial frogs (Hylidae) (see chapter 18).

The African toad genus *Nectophrynoides* provides an overview (and summary) of amphibian reproductive modes, for within this small genus (eight species), all basic patterns are represented (Wake, 1982). In addition to the viviparous species mentioned, there are an egg-laying and a direct-developing species. See chapters 17 and 18 for further information on the great array of reproductive modes of amphibians.

Natural History Overview

In the following pages, we will look at a variety of aspects of the natural history of amphibians—anatomical features, sensory structures and their functioning, breathing, food habits, voice, how they protect themselves against predators, how they regulate their body temperature and body water levels, their home ranges and movements, their remarkable homing ability and migratory activities, their territorial behavior and fighting, and, finally, their reproductive behavior and their eggs and young. This constellation of topics will be full of surprises, for the animals described here have been molded in remarkable ways by the process of natural selection, and the rapidly advancing front of amphibian biology is creating a cascade of new discoveries.

2

Skin

THE SKIN of amphibians is water permeable, well supplied with glands, and often colorful, with the colors and patterns of many salamanders and anurans rivaling those of brightly colored birds (fig. 2.1). It performs many functions. It (1) protects against abrasion and pathogens, (2) serves as a respiratory membrane, perhaps marginally so in caecilians, (3) absorbs and releases water, (4) provides some dry-land species during droughts with a water-loss-resistant cocoon, and (5) through color change (in some species) (see chapter 11) and secretory activity may help control body temperature. In addition, (6) poisons in the skin help protect against predators, and (7) skin color and patterns in many species offer concealment and, sometimes, warn of noxious properties. Considered here are skin glands, coloration, and shedding. Other skin characteristics and functions are discussed in chapters 3 and 12. See Spearman (1977) for information on the comparative biology of skin, including that of amphibians.

The skin in the three major groups of amphibians—caecilians, salamanders, and frogs—is similar in structure. It is one of the anatomical features that supports a common origin for these animals, although an independent origin for caecilians has been proposed (Carroll and Currie, 1975). Fox (1986) points to skin features that caecilians and salamanders share which suggest relationship—large epidermal epithelial cell size and the presence of ampullary organs (see chapter 9) and Leydig cells. Nevertheless, caecilians are unique among living amphibians in having dermal scales. These mineralized structures are imbedded in the dermis within the folds between the skin furrows (Zylberberg and Wake, 1990). The function of the dermal scales is not fully understood. They are absent or poorly developed in aquatic and in a number of terrestrial species.

Glands

Granular (or serous) glands, whose secretion is often toxic or repellent, are scattered throughout the skin but are often abundant on the head, back, and tail, or are grouped, as in the "warts" and parotoid glands of toads (fig. 13.1) and the dorsolateral ridges on the back of frogs. They tend to be concentrated in the

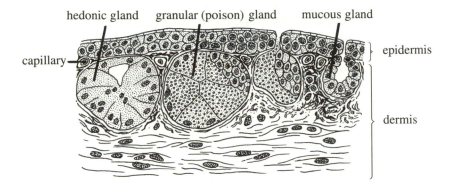

Fig. 2.1 Diagrammatic vertical section of the skin of an amphibian showing cell layers, glands, blood vessels, and other components. Thinning of the epidermis over blood vessels occurs in some lungless salamanders that rely heavily on skin respiration. (After Noble, 1931)

skin of the upper surfaces in caecilians. The granualr glands function primarily in defense. Their secretion is milky, yellowish, orange, or sometimes colorless and often sticky. It is distasteful to many animals and is frequently irritating to humans, "burning" the eyes or mouth. When swallowed, the poison of some species may cause generalized toxic symptoms, and volatile substances present in some, such as the spadefoot toads (*Scaphiopus*) (N Am), cause sneezing and nasal discharge.

Some amphibian poisons are highly potent, as in the North American newts (*Taricha* and *Notophthalmus*) (family Salamandridae), in the Neotropical poison-dart frogs *Phyllobates* and *Dendrobates* (family Dendrobatidae), in some harlequin frogs (*Atelopus*), and in the Sonoran Desert Toad (*Bufo alvarius*) (sw US, nw Mex) (family Bufonidae). Newt poison, "tarichatoxin," corresponds biochemically, or nearly so, to "tetrodotoxin" (TTX) found in pufferfish (family Tetraodontidae) and certain other marine animals. TTX is a powerful neurotoxin. The poison in newts and pufferfish is found primarily in the skin and gonads.

TTX is the most poisonous nonprotein substance known. In experiments, fish, frogs, reptiles, and birds have been killed quickly when force-fed sections of newt skin (Brodie, 1968b). TTX has the specific action of blocking sodium channels of excitable membranes (Fuhrman, 1986; Yasumoto et al., 1986), thus it acts on nerves and muscles. In mammals, poisoning can cause death by paralysis of chest muscles (Fuhrman, 1967). There have been several cases of human poisoning including at least one death (Brodie et al., 1974, and Bradley and Klika, 1981), but not from ordinary handling of newts. The poison must enter through the digestive tract or get into the blood stream. The poison may be bacterial in origin (Mosher and Fuhrman, 1984). *Alteromonas* sp. bacteria have been implicated in the production of TTX in pufferfish (Yotsu et al., 1987) and in the presence of TTX in certain other marine organisms (Yasumoto et al., 1986). Noguchi et al. (1986) have found TTX in a *Vibrio* sp. of bacterium isolated from the intestines of a xantid crab (*Atergatis floridus*), and Noguchi et al. (1987) discovered a TTX-producing bacterium (*Vibrio alginolyticus*) in the intestine of the tetraodontid fish (*Fugu vermicularis vermicularis*). Thuesen and Kogura (1989) have found TTX of bacterial origin in four species of arrow worms (chaetognaths). Little is known about the biosynthesis or natural analogues of TTX but studies are underway (see Yosumoto et al., 1988, 1989). See Scheuer (1990) for information on ecological aspects of marine microorganisms and comments on bacterial origin of TTX. *Alteromonas*, *Vibrio*, or some other TTX-producing bacteria may be involved in TTX toxicity in amphibians.

TTX has a wide distribution. It has been identified in animals from seven different classes in six phyla. In addition to newts and certain other salamandrids, atelopid frogs, a dendrobatid frog (*Colostethus inguinalis*) (Daly et al., 1994), xantid crabs, arrow worms, an annelid worm, and pufferfish, they include certain other marine fish, including some gobies, some marine gastropod mollusks, some cephalopod mollusks (including the deadly Australian Blue-ringed Octopus), and certain starfish. In the Blue-ringed Octopus, the poison resides in the salivary glands and is used to immobilize its prey.

Current theory is that TTX is first produced by bacteria and then reaches animals via the food chain, at least in coral reef environments. The red calcareous alga (*Jania* sp.) has been found to contain it (Yasumoto et al., 1986). The alga is eaten by certain crabs and fish. Its TTX content is so variable that the poison was presumed to be derived from symbiotic or epiphytic bacteria. Bacterial orgin has now been confirmed. *Altermonas* sp. TTX-producing bacteria have been isolated from the alga (see Yosumoto et al., 1989). How TTX reaches freshwater habitats and amphibians is unknown.

Another external source of amphibian poison has been discovered. Daly et al. (1994) have found that some of the skin alkaloids of the Green Poison-Arrow Frog (*Dendrobates auratus*) come from its diet. Their study strongly suggests a contribution from alkaloids of leaf-litter prey to the array of alkaloids in dendrobatid frogs. Among the poisons found in their study animals, the alkaloid precoccinelline is presumed to originate from the ingestion of small beetles and pyrrolizidine oximes from small millipedes. Other leaf-litter prey probably have also contributed skin toxins. The situation resembles that found in the larvae of some butterflies, such as the Monarch (*Danaus plexippus*), whose caterpillars get their toxicity, which helps protect them against bird predators, from the milkweed plants upon which they forage. Their toxicity is carried over to the adult butterflies.

The poisons of other dendrobatid frogs now need scrutiny in the light of these findings.

The steroidal alkaloids in the skin poison of *Phyllobates*, used to poison the blowgun darts of Indians in western Colombia, South America, are stronger than most curare mixtures. The skin secretion of the colorful gold to green frog, *P. terribilis* of western Colombia, is at least twenty times more toxic than that of other known poison-dart frogs and can be lethal to humans if it enters an open wound (Myers et al., 1978). In experiments performed by Brodie and Tumbarello (1978), Common Garter Snakes (*Thamnophis sirtalis*) (N Am) shook their heads and gaped when they bit or ate *Dendrobates auratus* (cen Am, Colombia). In some individuals convulsions, writhing, and rolling of the body occurred and in one case paralysis was followed by death. When American Toads (*Bufo americanus*) (e US) were eaten they caused no such symptoms.

For information on earlier extensive pharmacological studies of poison-dart frog poisons, see Albuquerque et al. (1971), Myers and Daly (1976), and Daly et al. (1978). See Habermehl (1971), Lutz (1971), and Daly et al. (1987, 1993) for general information on amphibian venoms.

Besides TTX and leaf-litter prey alkaloids contributing to the toxicity of amphibians, many amphibians are presumed to elaborate poisons of their own.

Secretions from mucous glands keep the skin moist, important in skin respiration and thermoregulation. They produce a film that protects against entry of bacteria and molds, reduces friction in swimming, and renders the body slippery, thus aiding escape from predators. The mucous gland secretions also protect the integument against desiccation, especially during terrestrial basking. Activity of the glands increases with temperature. In the Bullfrog (*Rana catesbeiana*) (N Am) increases have been observed over a range of body temperature of about 20°–28°C, and the frequency of synchronous discharge of the glands reached a level as high as seventeen times a minute (Lillywhite, 1971b). On land, the secretory activity of these glands results in considerable evaporative water loss through the skin, twenty to thirty times that of some lizards. However, water is replaced by dermal absorption when the amphibian returns to water or a moist place. Some water is also obtained from food.

During the breeding season some male salamanders develop, or experience enhancement of, "nuptial" skin glands whose secretions function in courtship as sexual attractants. Breeding males of many species of anurans may also exhibit glandular areas that appear to relate to reproductive activity. Depending on the species, swollen glandular areas may be present on ventral surfaces in various locations—on the throat, chest, abdomen, and base of the forearms and hindlimbs. Many species, however, lack such glandular areas.

Thomas et al. (1993) recognized sexually dimorphic (nuptial) skin glands in anurans as a unique gland type, set apart from mucous and serous (granular) glands. The study was based on fourteen species representing six families, and involved basic histological and histochemical tests. The nuptial glands are multicellular alveolar glands containing within their secretory cells granules that take up the stain eosin. The lumin (or chamber of the gland) contains a granular secretion, probably proteinaceous in nature. They include the "belly" glands of the round-bodied narrow-mouthed toads (*Gastrophryne*) (s US to Costa Rica) and certain other microhylids that secrete an adhesive mucus that binds a pair together during amplexus. Aside from these species, the function of the sexually dimorphic skin glands in anurans appears to be unknown, although they may well enhance the male's grip during amplexus or release chemical signals that may stimulate ovulation or egg laying in females.

Lipid-secreting glands (wax glands) are found in abundance in the skin of the uricotelic frogs (see chapter 12). These frogs live in semiarid environments. The waxy secretion is used to retard water loss through the skin, and is spread over the skin surface by a grooming action of the limbs.

Some glandular secretions appear to have antibiotic properties, retarding the growth of bacteria and molds.

Coloration (Fig. 2.2)

The darker tones of amphibians, the shades of brown and black, are produced by melanin, a dark pigment, usually found in skin melanophores in which the pigment can be dispersed or concentrated under hormonal action, resulting in darkening or paling of the skin. The bright-colored pigment cells of amphibians are the xanthophores, erythrophores, and iridophores. The latter contain reflecting platelets of guanine and related substances that give a whitish or silvery cast. The xanthophores and erythrophores impart yellow, orange, and red coloration and utilize pteridines and carotenoids as their basic pigments. Green coloration occurs when the light-reflecting platelets of the iridophores, which produce a light-scattering blue, a structural color, are filtered by the yellow pigment of overlying xanthophores (see Bagnara and Hadley, 1969; Bagnara, 1976).

Two kinds of color response occur in amphibians. Both involve movement of melanin in the melanophores, triggered by hormones. One is the primary color response of larval amphibians that blanch in darkness under the action of the pineal hormone, melatonin. The other adapts the amphibian to its surroundings, often entailing a shift in color to match background. It occurs under the action of the melanophore—stimulating hormone of the pituitary. In both cases the hormones are released into the general circulation and act directly on the melanophores (Bagnara and Hadley, 1970).

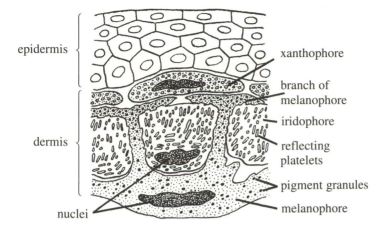

Fig. 2.2 Transverse section through the skin of the Green Treefrog (*Hyla ci-nerea*) (s and se US), showing pigment cell components and a dermal melano-phore with its melanic pigment dispersed into its branches, an action that occurs when the skin darkens. (After Bagnara et al., 1968, drawn with permission from the *Journal of Cellular Biology*)

Shedding

The surface of the skin (stratum corneum) is shed (or molted) periodically, sometimes at intervals of a few days to several weeks or longer. In anurans it often splits down the back, the limbs are pulled free, and the old skin is worked toward the mouth and swallowed (Larsen, 1976). In salamanders (Ensatina, *Ensatina eschscholtzii*, and others), the skin breaks around the mouth (fig. 2.3). The salamander then slides forward, forelimbs trailing at the sides until the skin reaches the chest region. The forelimbs are pulled free and a swelling of the body, which forms in front of the edge of the old skin, shifts backward, forcing the skin to the region of the hind limbs. The hind limbs are then pulled free and are used to push the skin backward on the tail. The clump of old skin is pressed against the ground and removed as the tail is drawn from it. The salamander may then turn and eat the slough—a source of moisture and some nutrients.

The shed skin of some amphibians can be used in distinguishing between diploid and polyploid individuals (Licht and Bogart, 1987). The nuclei of the cells of the cast stratum corneum of diploid individuals are consistently smaller than those of polyploids, presumably related to the amount of DNA present. The technique requires no living tissue or fluid and the animals need not be killed and can be maintained for other studies or released. In captives, skin samples can be obtained as shedding appears imminent or begins (as noted, some species are prone to eat their slough). A small sample, 3 mm square, can be stretched beneath a cover slip and examined directly. Formalin-preserved specimens can also be used in such studies.

For a comprehensive overview of molting, see Larsen (1976).

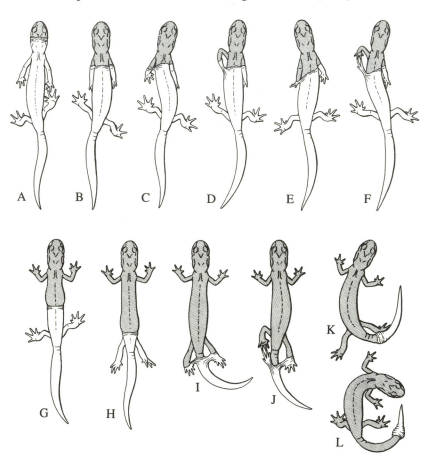

Fig. 2.3 Shedding in a salamander, Ensatina (*Ensatina eschscholtzii*) (w N Am). The sequence (A)–(L) shown is presumed to be common to many lungless salamanders (family Plethodontidae) and perhaps other salamanders (see text for details).

3

Breathing

As A GROUP, amphibians have a greater variety of respiratory structures than any other class of vertebrates. This is a consequence of the dual existence of many of them—living first as gilled and skin-breathing aquatic larvae and later as completely or partly land-dwelling lung and skin-breathing adults. At both stages, breathing appears to be augmented by pulsations of the throat, the movements of which create a flow of water or air over the vascular lining of the mouth and throat, as well as over the skin surface of the throat region. How important such mouth-throat (or buccopharyngeal) movements are in breathing is not yet fully clear. The subject is discussed further below. Thus, depending upon the kind of amphibian and its stage of development, breathing may be by means of the skin, gills, lungs, mouth-and-throat membranes or a combination thereof.

Gills

Larval amphibians (fig. 3.1) breathe primarily with gills that are usually lost at transformation, as lungs assume their respiratory role. Some amphibians, such as permanently larval forms, retain their gills throughout life. Examples are the mudpuppies (*Necturus*) (e N Am) (fig. 3.2) and neotenic individuals (see chapter 17) of species that usually transform.

In tadpoles, the gills ultimately lie inside the opercular or branchial chamber or chambers (fig. 3.1). Water flow over the gills is maintained by pulsations of the throat. With lowering of the throat region, which increases the size of the mouth cavity, water enters the mouth and/or nostrils. Then, by restricting outflow and contracting the throat, water passes through the pharynx across the food traps and gills, into the opercular chamber(s), and exits through the spiracle or spiracles. It does so in pulses, timed with gular movements (see fig. 3.3).

Lungs

The structure and size of the lungs in relation to body size vary greatly among amphibians (Czopek, 1962). In the torrent salamanders (*Rhyacotriton*) (fig. 3.4A), small (2.5–3.5 in TL) highly aquatic, cold-water species (nw US), the

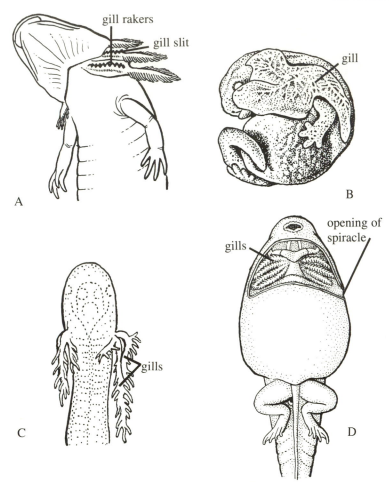

Fig. 3.1 Gill structure in larval amphibians. (A) Aquatic larva of a salamander. Gills are external. Water is drawn into the mouth and passes out through the gill slits. The gill rakers trap small objects (food particles, etc.) carried in the water flow. (B) Advanced embryo of Ensatina (*Ensatina eschscholtzii*) showing the large, membranous, highly vascular gills often found in terrestrial larvae of lungless salamanders that lay their eggs on land and undergo direct development (see text). The gills lie close to the egg capsule, where gaseous exchange occurs. Note the large yolk mass that nourishes the developing larva. (C) The external triradiate gills of a 40 mm fetal Mexican Caecilian (*Dermophis mexicanus*). The longest gill ramus is 8 mm. (After Wake, 1977b, redrawn, with permission from the author and D. H. Taylor and S. I. Guttman, from *The Reproductive Biology of Amphibians*, Plenum Press, New York, 1977.) (D) Gills of a tadpole (*Rana catesbeiana*) which lie inside the opercular chamber, here cut open at the level of the spiracular opening.

Fig. 3.2 The Mudpuppy (*Necturus maculosus*) (e US, se Can), a completely aquatic amphibian that has permanent gills.

Fig. 3.3 Gill-breathing in a Bullfrog tadpole. A drop of ink has been placed in front of the tadpole's mouth and is drawn in by pumping action of the tadpole's throat. After passing over the gills which lie encased inside the opercular chamber in the throat region, the ink emerges from the spiracle (in most tadpoles a single opening on the left side) in a series of pulses, timed with the tadpole's throat movements.

Fig. 3.4 (A) Torrent salamander (*Rhyacotriton*), a highly aquatic cold-water species with greatly reduced lungs. (B) A lungless salamander, the California Slender Salamander (*Batrachoseps attenuatus*). (C) Pacific Giant Salamander (*Dicamptodon*), a species with lungs.

lungs are very small (usually less than 10 mm long) and smooth-walled inside, whereas in the eel-like Lesser Siren (*Siren intermedia*) (se US) (to around 27 in TL), a completely aquatic, warmer water, permanently gilled species, ridges and folds (septation) within the elongate lungs may exceed by almost three times the total area of the lung sacs themselves (Czopek, 1962). In the Red-spotted Newt (*Notophthalmus viridescens*) (2.5–4.5 in TL) (e US, se Can), the lungs are smooth-walled elongate sacs lacking ridges.

Similar variation occurs among anurans. In the Tailed Frog (*Ascaphus truei*) (nw US, sw Can), a cold-water counterpart of the torrent salamanders, the lungs are considerably reduced. In toads (*Bufo*) they are generally complex, well septated, and vascularized. In the Old World Edible Frog (*Rana esculenta*) (cen Eur), the surface area of lung ridges may be eight times that of the lung sacs themselves (Czopek, 1962). The lungs of the African Clawed Frog (*Xenopus laevis*) are also complex. The number and surface area of the pulmonary ridges in amphibians may increase with body weight, as has been observed in some salamanders and frogs (*Rana*).

The capillary network of the lungs, often in the form of interconnecting meshes, more or less polygonal in shape, varies greatly, as does capillary diameter. Capillary meshes per square millimeter are few in torrent salamanders (*Rhyacotriton*), and capillary diameter varies greatly. The Red-spotted Newt has a much denser meshwork and capillary diameter is more uniform.

Caecilians are chiefly subterranean and thus live in an environment where oxygen levels are low. In general their skin appears to have little respiratory function (see Maina and Maloiy, 1988, and Toews and MacIntyre, 1978). It is perhaps not surprising, then, that septation of the lungs in these amphibians is extensive, particularly since studies by Wood et al. (1975) on, respectively, the Bluish-gray Caecilian (*Boulengerula boulengeri*) (Tanzania) and *Ty-phlonectes* (n S Am) (aquatic) indicate that in these caecilians blood volumes are large, haemoglobin concentrations are high, and the blood has a high affin-ity for oxygen and a high oxygen-carrying capacity. *Typhlonectes compressi-cauda* (n S Am) has remained submerged for up to 40 minutes in terraria and may burrow to depths of 2 feet (60 cm) (Moodie, 1978).

There is considerable diversity in the general form of the lungs in caecilians. *Ichthyophis orthoplicatus* (Sri Lanka) has paired lungs, but the left is a quarter the size of the right. In *Typhlonectes compressicauda*, both lungs are well developed; thus, in addition to functioning in respiration, they may also be hydrostatic in function in this aquatic species. *Hypogeophis rostratus* (Sey-chelles Is) is reported to have a well-developed right and a rudimentary left lung, whereas in *Boulengerula taitanus* (Kenya) only a single lung has been found (Maina and Maloiy, 1988). Terrestrial species, as a group, usually have an elongate right lung which may be 50%–75% of total body length (Wake, 1974) and a left lung that is no more than 10% of body length.

Contraction of the body wall and of smooth muscle fibers connecting sepa-rate cartilaginous half-rings supporting the wall of the lung appears to provide for exhalation. Inhalation occurs with relaxation of the body wall and muscle fibers connecting the rings. The lung recoils to its original form (see Wake, 1974).

Such great variation in the lungs of amphibians suggests considerable dif-ferences in their importance among species in gas exchange and metabolism. Factors to be considered in interpreting species lung structure are (1) the im-portance of the lungs in respiration relative to other respiratory structures; (2) species thermal characteristics; (3) activity levels; and (4) habits and evolu-tionary relationships. Anurans tend to have more elaborate lungs than sala-manders, and caecilians perhaps have more advanced lungs than most other amphibians (Prattle et al., 1977). Increased septation of the lungs seems to be associated with increasing levels of metabolic activity. Anurans tend to be more active and to operate at generally higher body temperatures than salamanders.

Although lungs function in breathing in most amphibians, they also serve as hydrostatic organs and aid in the control of buoyancy. By changing the amount of air in the lungs, an amphibian increases its ability to sink or float. In fast or turbulent well-oxygenated waters, where breathing needs can be met primarily by skin respiration, lungs may be a handicap. Control of body movements in fast waters may be improved by reducing buoyancy. Thus lungs are sometimes reduced or absent in stream-dwelling amphibians. Low water temperature, imparted also to amphibians living in such waters, may also reduce respiratory demands. The lungless salamanders (Plethodontidae), many of which are completely terrestrial, may have arisen from ancestors that lost their lungs during life in the turbulent waters of cold brooks and streams of eastern North America. Once lost, lungs were never regained.

However, this long-accepted explanation has been challenged by Ruben and Boucot (1989) and Ruben et al. (1993). They cite geological and paleontological evidence that indicates that the area of presumed origin in the Appalachian region (e N Am), in the latter half of the Mesozoic, had been eroded to a nearly level surface (peneplane), where swift cool streams likely would have been absent. Further, Reagan and Verrel (1991) suggest that loss of lungs may have resulted from a shift from an energetically expensive amphibious life (involving migration and aquatic courtship and mating) to a less energetically demanding courtship and mating pattern on land and a generally more sedentary life. Land life was accompanied by modifications of the hyoid apparatus, perhaps entailing narrowing of the head, in the development of a more effective tongue-protrusion mechanism used in catching terrestrial prey. Head narrowing, accompanied by a concomitant decrease in lung tidal volume and existence in an oxygen-rich land environment, may have set the stage for lung loss.

The foregoing hypotheses should be carefully considered. However, we are not ready to completely abandon the earlier explanation. We are impressed by the considerable number of cold-stream amphibians, some distantly related, that display varying degrees of lung reduction. There are also uncertainties concerning the physical characteristics of possible Mesozoic sites of origin. See Beachy and Bruce (1992) for a response to Ruben and Boucot (1989).

Skin

Breathing involves both uptake of oxygen and release of carbon dioxide. Gatz et al. (1974) found that in the lungless Dusky Salamander (*Desmognathus fuscus*) (e US), 85% of total gas exchange took place through the skin. Much of an amphibian's carbon dioxide may be released through the skin—about 80% in some mole salamanders (ambystomatids) and in torrent salamanders (*Rhyacotriton*) (w US) (fig. 3.4A) (Whitford and Hutchison, 1966).

Various modifications of the skin have occurred in relation to the breathing needs of amphibians. There is great variation in the intricacy of the blood vessel network and in the amount of overlying epidermal tissue. As in the lungs, capillary meshes in the skin tend to be polygonal in shape. The vascular

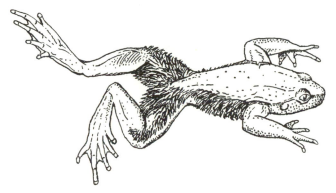

Fig. 3.5 During the breeding season, when its oxygen demands are high, the male Hairy Frog (*Trichobatrachus robustus*) develops vascular hairlike filaments on its body that act like an external lung. (After Noble, 1931)

net in torrent salamanders is sparse. They are small and live in cold, well-oxygenated waters. It is dense in many terrestrial lungless salamanders that depend greatly on skin respiration, and the epidermis may thin down where capillaries come close to the surface. However, slender salamanders (*Batrachoseps*) (w US, nw Mex) (lungless) (fig. 3.4B) generally have a poorly developed skin capillary network, possibly compensated for by their small size (thus much skin surface in relation to body mass) and high percentage of nonnucleated red blood cells in the more attenuate species. It is presumed that in the absence of nuclei, there can be more hemoglobin in each red cell to trap oxygen, but this issue has not been fully settled (see Villolobos et al., 1988). Other diminutive members of the bolitoglossine salamander group also have high levels (80%±) of nonnucleated red cells.

The number of skin capillary meshes and diameter of the capillaries may vary in different parts of the body. In the Marbled Salamander (*Ambystoma opacum*) (se US), for example, the capillary network is somewhat better developed anteriorly than posteriorly, and the posterior ventral sides are least vascularized (Czopek, 1962). In the Southern Giant Salamander (*Dicamptodon ensatus*) (Cal) (fig. 3.4C), the diameter of the capillaries on the dorsum is almost twice that on the lower sides (Czopek, 1962). The significance of these variations is not well understood.

In some amphibians, skin breathing may be enhanced by the presence of vascular folds or appendages. The wholly aquatic Hellbender (*Cryptobranchus alleganiensis*) (ne US) and the Asiatic Giant Salamanders (*Andrias*) (Japan and w China) have a wrinkled, fleshy fold of skin on each side of their bodies. Skin capillaries penetrate their rather thick epidermis, to lie just under the skin's surface. Breathing is aided by swaying the body from side to side (Harlan and Wilkinson, 1981).

In the African "Hairy" Frog (*Trichobatrachus robustus*) (w Afr) (fig. 3.5), a species with reduced lungs, the skin is well supplied with capillaries. During the mating season, when oxygen demands are high for the muscular males, hairlike filaments (resembling the finer branches of gills) appear on the thighs and sides of the body, in response to the increased respiratory requirements.

See Feder and Burggren (1985), Burggren (1988), and Malvin (1988) for reviews of skin respiration in amphibians.

Buccopharyngeal Respiration

There has been controversy over the extent to which the throat pulsations of amphibians are important in breathing. Foxon (1964) regarded such movements as "sniffing," thus serving primarily an olfactory function. Doubts as to the importance of buccopharyngeal breathing arise because of the relatively small area of moist vascular surface involved (see Czopek, 1962), the meager vascularity of the region in many species, and the dearth of information on the amount of buccopharyngeal activity that occurs in undisturbed amphibians. However, it is difficult to watch the rapid, nearly continuous throat flutter of some of the smaller lungless salamanders, such as the slender salamanders (*Batrachoseps*) (w US, nw Mex), without feeling that a significant respiratory role is served. The movement can be seen at almost any time the animals are viewed and in captives long accustomed to human presence. These animals are fanning the air at high speed with a moist vascular sheet of tissue that is exposed to the air both in and outside the mouth. A respiratory interpretation, of course, does not rule out an olfactory one.

There is now evidence that buccopharyngeal movements, in themselves, are important in breathing for at least some species (if not all) and that the importance of this breathing mechanism may vary with temperature. Such pulsations have been shown to play a significant role in the respiration of torrent salamanders (*Rhyacotriton*), nearly lungless species noted earlier as having scant skin vascularity (Whitford and Hutchison, 1966). In the Spotted Salamander (*Ambystoma maculatum*) (e US), these authors (1963) showed that buccopharyngeal pulsations increased greatly at higher temperatures, whereas the rate of lung inspirations remained relatively constant, suggesting that such respiration was most important at higher temperatures.

The Lung-breathing Mechanism

On land, amphibians use movements of the throat not only to move air in and out of the buccopharynx, but also to force air into their lungs. They breathe with the mouth closed and use valvular nostrils to control the flow of air. To draw air into the buccopharynx, the throat is lowered, thereby increasing the size of the buccopharyngeal cavity and creating a partial vacuum. Air moves in through the nostrils. In expelling air from the buccopharynx, the nostrils are opened and the throat contracts, forcing the air to the outside.

To force air into the lungs, the nostrils narrow or close, the throat contracts and the glottis, or opening to the lungs, is opened. Air is forced back into the elastic lungs, which stretch and expand under pressure. With expiration, the glottis opens, and the air moves out of the lungs under the elastic recoil of these organs, aided by movements of the body wall.

However, if you watch the breathing movements of a frog or toad on land, you will usually note more frequent movements of the throat than the body wall. You can also see that the mouth is kept closed and that movements of the nasal values are synchronized with the throat pulsations. Intake and expulsion of air from the lungs occurs less frequently, and less regularly, than the ventilation movements of the buccopharynx, and are evidenced by a deeper depression of the throat.

The difference in frequency can be explained as follows. In a typical breathing cycle in a frog, the buccopharyngeal chamber is filled with air just before the air in the lungs from the previous cycle is expelled. This is accomplished by lowering the throat, with glottis closed. The air taken in resides mainly in a depression in the floor of the buccopharyngeal cavity. Air is now expelled from the lungs at high velocity through the nostrils. Movement of the body wall occurs at this time. The air is thought mostly to pass over that just taken in and residing in the floor of the buccopharynx; presumably there is little mixing. Upon completion of exhalation, the nostrils close and the throat is contracted, forcing the bypassed air in the buccopharynx into the lungs. The glottis now closes and throat pulsations occur, clearing the buccopharynx of any residual unexpired air and filling the buccal chamber with outside air in preparation for the next breathing cycle. Thus in a single breathing cycle a number of throat pulsations occur each time the lungs are filled and emptied (Gans et al., 1969; Gans, 1970). See also de Jongh and Gans (1969) and Jones (1982).

The efficiency of the buccopharyngeal pump, as it is used to force air into the lungs, may vary with the size of the buccopharyngeal chamber. The size of this chamber can affect the amount of air movement to and from the lungs. One measure of its size is the distance between the jaw articulations. Thus head width should be considered in assessing the relative importance of buccopharyngeal, lung, and skin respiration in amphibians. Relative head width may be as important, or more so, than the degree of vacularity of the lung surfaces in determining the role of the lungs and buccopharyngeal lining in breathing (Whitford and Hutchison, 1966). The buccopharyngeal pump is also important in sound production.

4

Limbs and Locomotion

SALAMANDERS and anurans typically have four limbs. The hind ones are enlarged in most anurans, an adaptation for jumping (Zug, 1972, 1978) and
swimming. In anurans the relative length of the fore- and hind limbs and body
form are predictive of the probable mode of locomotion (see Emerson, 1988).
Species with long hindlimbs are generally jumpers or swimmers; species with
short hindlimbs walk, run, or hop (Pough et al., 1992); and walker-burrowers
are often stout bodied and short limbed.

In salamanders, the limbs are greatly reduced in mud eels (*Amphiuma*) (fig.
4.1A) and the hind pair is missing in sirens (*Siren* and *Pseudobranchus*) (all se
US). Caecilians are limbless (fig. 4.1B). There are usually 4 toes on the fore-
foot and 5 on the hind (fig. 4.2A), but the toes may be reduced in salamanders
to 4–4 or, less commonly, to 3–3, 2–2, or 1–1, as in the amphiumas. The tips
of the toes are sometimes horny, but true claws are absent.

The amount of webbing of the toes in anurans (usually little or not at all
developed on the front feet) varies with the species, the extent of aquatic habits, and with time of year, usually increasing during the breeding season, particularly in males. The undersides of the feet in some anurans are shod with
horny tubercles at the joints and on the palms and soles (fig. 4.2G). Foot tubercles protect against abrasion and increase the gripping power of the feet. One
or two enlarged tubercles on the hind feet of toads and other burrowing anurans (fig. 4.2H,I) are used in digging backward into the soil, the method of
burrowing used by most anurans.

Salamanders and tadpoles can regenerate lost limbs and toes but most transformed anurans cannot or, at most, produce nonfunctional "stump tissues"
(Goode, 1967). However, Ovaska and Hunte (1992), in a study of a population
of *Eleutherodactylus johnstonei* (West Indies), marked by toe clipping, found
that regeneration of the toes was so rapid they had to be reclipped every few
months during the rainy season.

Locomotion in caecilians is primarily by worm-like regional contractions of
the body ("vermiform" locomotion), or by eel-like lateral undulations. Gaymer
(1971) studied locomotion in *Hypogeophis* from the Seychelle Islands. The
following comments are based in part on his study and information from Marvalee Wake. Vermiform locomotion, in outward form, resembles that of earthworms. It is used by caecilians in burrowing where lateral undulations of the

A

B

Fig. 4.1 (A) The Mud Eel or Two-toed Amphiuma (*Amphiuma means*) (se US). This salamander may reach over 3 feet in length. It is mostly aquatic but may move over land in wet weather. Note the minute forelimbs which bear only two toes. Hind limbs are lacking. (B) A caecilian (*Dermophis*), a limbless burrowing amphibian.

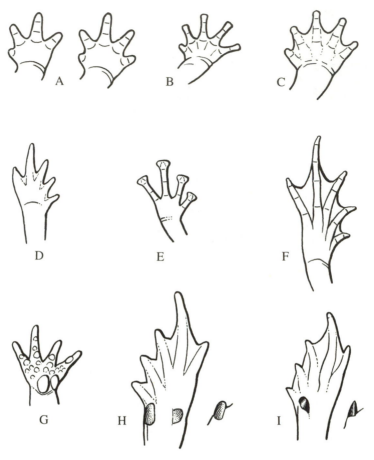

Fig. 4.2 Variations in the foot structure of amphibians. (A) to (F) are upper surfaces of feet, and (G) to (I) are under surfaces. (A) The typical amphibian toe arrangement, four toes on the front feet and five on the hind feet (*Plethodon*). (B) The elongate toes with squarish tips of a climbing salamander (*Aneides ferreus*). (C) The spatulate foot of a rock-dwelling salamander (*Hydromantes*). (D) The hind foot of the Tailed Frog (*Ascaphus truei*), with an enlarged outer toe. (E) Toe pads of a hylid frog, an adaptation for clinging and climbing. (F) Hind foot of a ranid frog showing extensive webbing. (G) Underside of the front foot of a toad showing horny tubercles that reduce abrasion. (H) Underside of the hind foot of a toad (*Bufo*) showing metatarsal tubercles. (I) The sharp-edged black horny spade of spadefoot toads (*Scaphiopus*) used in burrowing.

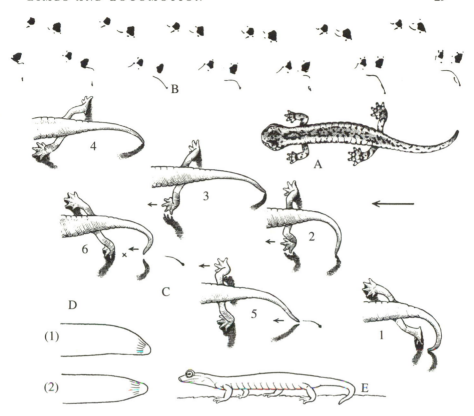

Fig. 4.3 Locomotion in a web-toed salamander (*Hydromantes*) (Cal), the Mount Lyell Sala-mander (*H. platycephalus*) of the high Sierra Nevada of California. The three California species use the tail as an aid in crawling. (A) Adult showing granite-matching pattern and flattened form. (B) Track of the salamander. (C) Stages 1 to 6 and back to 1 showing successive stages in a single completed tail movement. The *x* in stage 6 indicates where the tip of the tail will touch the ground. (D) Side (1) and top (2) views of the tail tip. (E) Posture when crawling.

body may be restricted. The axial (vertebral) musculature contracts, forming alternating lateral curves within the sheath of the body wall musculature and skin. The alternating axial contractions cause acceleration within the sheath, then each axial contraction is followed by a contraction of the body wall mus-culature. As the series of coordinated contractions passes down the body in waves, locomotor progression occurs. The annuli (body rings) of the skin may help in maintaining position. In burrowing, the head is moved up and down. This form of locomotion makes possible a strong ramming action of the head. Lateral undulatory locomotion is usually employed when caecilians swim, or crawl on the ground surface.

Many amphibians have feet modified for climbing (fig. 4.2E). Webbing and shortening of the toes has occurred in some bolitoglossine lungless salamanders (fig. 4.3). Some have the toes completely enclosed in the web, forming a spatulate or platelike foot that maximizes contact with the locomotor surface. The smooth, glandular surfaces adhere by suction and surface tension (Green, 1981). *Bolitoglossa occidentalis* (cen Am), a small Neotropical arboreal species often found on smooth leaf surfaces, has platelike feet in which the central toe tip extends slightly beyond the general contour of the web. Just before a foot is lifted, the toe is raised, thereby evidently helping to remove surface tension between the foot and the substratum. In the web-toed salamanders (*Hydromantes*) of California, rock-climbing animals, the toes are short and enclosed in a fleshy web (fig. 4.2C). They use their tail as an aid in climbing (fig. 4.3). Just before the down-slope hind foot is lifted, the tail tip is placed against the substratum, providing support while the foot moves forward to its next position. When crawling directly upslope, the tail often swings like a pendulum, alternately providing support as first one foot and then the other is moved.

Many climbing anurans have adhesive toe pads or disks (see Emerson and Diehl, 1980). The structures have appeared independently in several families. The friction surface of the pad is typically covered with elongate columnar cells with free flat-topped ends (fig. 4.4). Mucous glands open among these cells. The flat cellular surfaces and the mucus, along with surface moisture, provide the adhesive properties of the pads. Adhesion in treefrogs appears to be primarily by surface tension (Green, 1981). Two flat surfaces will adhere if they are sufficiently wettable and their contact angle is sufficiently low. Adhesion is caused by surface tension at the air-liquid surface, producing a concave meniscus (Green, 1981) (see fig. 4.4C). A detergent applied to the toe pads will prevent adhesion, but when removed adhesive properties are restored. In the more advanced treefrogs such as *Hyla* and others, a small bone or cartilage is intercalated (lies between) the terminal toe bone that supports the pad and its neighbor, giving greater flexibility of the toe tip and reducing the angle of contact of the pad with the substratum for a more effective grip (Green, 1979).

Some arboreal anurans parachute (sometimes called "plopping") by spreading their broadly webbed and enlarged fore and hind feet and deflecting their descent (fig. 4.5). The angle of descent is usually steep, far less than 45°, thus such excursions cannot be considered a glide as defined by Oliver (1951). However, these frogs are often capable of considerable maneuverability during descent, which may be of greater importance than horizontal distance traveled (Emerson and Koehl, 1990). Notable examples of "ploppers" are Old World forest tree frogs of the family Rhacophoridae (Wallace Tree Frog, *Rhacophorus nigropalmatus*, the Borneo Flying Frog, *R. pardalis*, and others), and the Neotropical hylid Spurrell Tree Frog (*Agalychnis spurrelli*). The latter is able

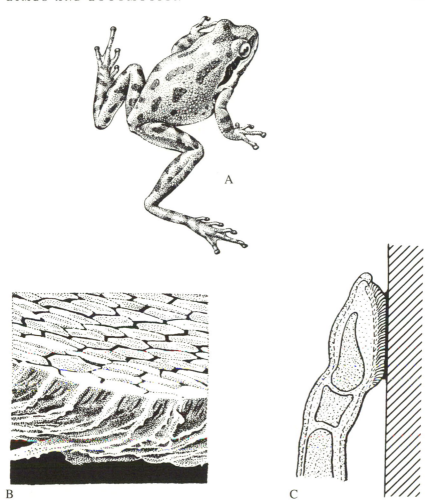

Fig. 4.4 (A) A frog with toe pads, the Pacific Treefrog (*Pseudacris regilla*). (B) Scanning electron micrograph of toe-pad epidermal cells of the Gray Treefrog (*Hyla versicolor*). Note the flat-surfaced hexagonal shapes of the individual cells, which come into contact with the substratum (X1, 200). (C) Diagrammatic section through a toe pad in contact with a glass surface, illustrating the proposed mechanism of adhesion by surface tension. Note the adhesive epidermis and the meniscus associated with the interposed fluid layer (in black). (After Green, 1981, illustrations B and C, redrawn with permission from *Copeia*)

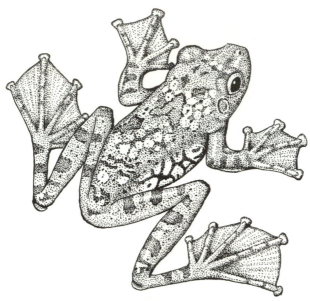

Fig. 4.5 The Borneo Flying Frog (*Rhacophorus pardalis*) with
limbs and webs extended as the frog parachutes. Note the skin
flaps at the sides of the forelimbs and on the heels.

to land as much as 35° to right or left and facing 180° from its original direction of descent, indicating considerable maneuverability when airborne (Scott
and Starrett, 1974). The subtropical forest frog, the Puerto Rican Coqui
(*Eleutherodactylus coqui*), is able to deflect its fall, landing 3–10 feet (1–3 m)
horizontally from the point directly below the departure point (Stewart, 1985).
Wallace Tree Frog, observed by Ilya Darevsky (pers. comm.) in central Viet-
nam, may land as much as 5 meters beyond its launch point at a height of
around 6 meters. Its glide angle can thus be quite close to 45°. The body is
concave when parachuting.

Parachuting is thought to aid these arboreal frogs in escaping predators, in
quickly avoiding unfavorable conditions in the tree canopy and returning to
protective cover on the ground, and perhaps in capturing prey. Stewart (1985)
believes plopping may occur in many tropical arboreal frogs, but perhaps only
becomes obvious at high population densities.

5

Tail

SALAMANDERS, some caecilians, and larval amphibians have a tail, but anurans lose theirs at metamorphosis. The tail in caecilians may be very short or absent. The "tail" of the Tailed Frog (*Ascaphus truei*) (nw US, sw Can) is a copulatory organ, not a true tail (fig. 17.8). In amphibian larvae and aquatic salamanders, the tail has dorsal and ventral fins, is laterally flattened, not readily lost, and is the chief organ of propulsion in swimming. In most salamanders of the families Ambystomidae and Salamandridae, it is longer and broader in males than in females. During amplexus, the male often clasps the female from above in piggyback fashion and transports her by the sculling action of his tail—usually away from other individuals.

In terrestrial salamanders the tail may also be used in locomotion. Its lateral undulatory movements help propel these animals (especially when they move rapidly) through leaf litter, among rocks, and over the ground surface. In the Arboreal Salamander (*Aneides lugubris*) (Cal) and in most climbing bolitoglossines, it is prehensile (fig. 5.1). It is used like a cane or fifth leg in the climbing web-toed bolitoglossines (*Hydromantes*, fig. 4.3; and others). Tail movements are also employed in jumping, a form of locomotion well developed in some plethodontid salamanders, which can leap several times their total length.

In many salamanders the male uses his tail in courtship, wafting glandular secretions toward the female or, as in some plethodontids, stroking her with it. In some lungless salamanders it is an important storage organ for proteins and lipids which can be drawn upon when food is short or when metabolic demands are high during periods of growth or reproduction (Maiorana, 1977). Its dissolution at the time of tadpole transformation to the frog stage presumably provides energy and nutrients required for this dynamic process at a time when, with rare exceptions, feeding is suspended.

Many salamanders use the tail in defense. It is usually well supplied with mucous and granular glands and may be lashed at the attacker (fig. 5.2). The sticky, often acrid secretion of the granular glands may irritate the eyes and mouth or gum up the jaws of predators. In some species the tail is cast off when seized and, if sticky and held in the mouth, may in some cases delay or even prevent a follow-up attack (Beneski, 1989). If dropped, its often violent movements may distract the attention of the predator, permitting the prey to escape (Ducey and Brodie, 1983). Movements may last for 10–15 minutes, depending on environmental temperatures.

Fig. 5.1 The plethodontid salamander (*Bolitoglossa rostrata*) (from Gua-
temala) using its prehensile tail in climbing.

Fig. 5.2 Ensatina (*Ensatina eschscholtzii*) in defense pose. The tail is waved from side
to side, and a whitish sticky secretion may exude from batteries of large poison glands
over its upper surface.

Some species have a predetermined zone of breakage at the base of the tail, marked by a constriction, an area of weakness in the skin. Examples are found in the family Plethodontidae and include all members of the neotropical genus *Bolitoglossa* (cen and S Am), the Four-toed Salamander (*Hemidactylium scutatum*) (e US), and Ensatina (*Ensatina eschscholtzii*) (w NA). When the tail breaks free, rupture occurs at this zone and between, rather than through, the vertebrae as in lizards. Segmental muscles pull out, leaving behind a hollow cylinder of skin on the tail stump that closes over the wound. Contraction of sphincter muscles on the blood vessels minimize bleeding. Other salamanders, such as those with slender tails (slender salamanders, *Batrachoseps*, and others), which lack tail-base constrictions, may sever the tail almost anywhere, but the mechanics are similar. Still others with thick tail bases such as *Pseudotriton* and the dusky salamanders (*Desmognathus*) (both e US), capable of losing their tails, evidently lack specializations for tail loss (Wake and Dresner, 1967).

The importance of tail autotomy is indicated by the high frequency of regenerating tails in some species—50%–80% in some populations of California Slender Salamanders (*Batrachoseps attenuatus*) studied by Maiorana (1977). Experiments with the Mountain Dusky Salamander (*Desmognathus ochrophaeus*) (e US) show that tail-loss in this salamander in response to the attack of a predator (chickens) can be highly protective (Labanick, 1984), especially when the predator is learning to cope with the tail loss ruse. The tail is readily autotomized, its wriggling motion attracts the predator's attention, and the tail is eaten exclusively, or before the body. The delay thus extends the salamander's escape time.

"Autotomy" of the tail, however, is usually resorted to only when the animals' life is threatened, for the tail has other important functions. Ensatinas (w NA), although specialized for tail loss, do not readily shed their tails (Beneski, 1989). Although a tail can be regenerated, its loss temporarily reduces chances for survival because of locomotor impairment, reduced protection against predators, and loss of energy reserves. In Ensatina, adults may require around one to two years for complete regeneration of the tail (Stebbins, 1954), probably depending on age, nutrition, thermal experience, and energy levels. There is some evidence that in the California Slender Salamander, which may store as much as 60% of its lipids in the tail, tail loss may delay maturity and inhibit reproduction (Maiorana, 1974, 1977). These salamanders may reduce the size of their egg clutch or even forgo annual reproduction in favor of regenerating a lost tail. Jamison and Harris (1992) have found that in the Red-backed Salamander (*Plethodon cinereus*) a higher priority is placed on regenerating tail length than on restoration of its fat-storing role when food reserves are low.

Because male plethodontid salamanders actively use their tails in courtship, tail loss in males might be expected to reduce their reproductive success in inseminating females. However, Houck (1982) found no significant differences in courtship and insemination effectiveness between tailed and tailless male Mountain Dusky Salamanders. Further study, however, is needed. There is also the possibility that loss of the tail may reduce success in male-male encounters over females. In some lizards a lowering of position in male peck orders occurs with tail loss.

See Wake and Dresner (1967) for information on tail loss and its evolution in salamanders. Antipredator functions of tail loss are discussed further in chapter 13.

6

The Nose and Chemoreception

AMPHIBIANS have two sensory areas in the nose that respond to the chemistry of the environment—the olfactory epithelium and the epithelium of the vomeronasal organs (Jacobson's organs). The vomeronasal organs are usually located near the internal nostrils, but in plethodontid salamanders they may extend from near the nostrils, laterally, well back toward the internal nostrils (fig. 6.1B). Nerve fibers from each sensory area connect with the olfactory lobes of the brain, but they terminate in different parts of the lobes, those of the vomeronasal organs in the accessory olfactory bulb. Airborne and aquatic odors are apparently detected chiefly by the olfactory system, and substances in the mouth or, in lungless salamanders, picked up from the external environment (substrate, contact with other individuals) by the nasolabial grooves (see below) are detected by the vomeronasal system.

Caecilians have an opening on each side of the head between the eye and nostril (see fig. 1.1) through which a tentacle can be protruded that functions primarily in conveying airborne chemoreceptive information to the vomeronasal organs and thence to the accessory olfactory bulb. The tentacles also have a tactile function. The structures are unique among vertebrates. Upon decline in visual function in these primarily subterranean animals, the tentacles appear to have evolved through modification of muscles and other structures associated with the eyes (see Billo and Wake, 1987; Schmidt and Wake, 1990). The tentacular-vomeronasal system evidently makes possible nasal chemoreception in caecilians when the nostrils are closed during burrowing and swimming.

The tentacle contains a duct that opens to the exterior. The organ is extruded by hydrostatic pressure created by contraction of smooth muscle fibers around the Harderian gland and its fluids in which the organ lies. A slender muscle, originating on the neurocranium and inserting on the base of the tentacle, returns the organ to its resting position.

Dawley (1987a) notes that the vomeronasal epithelium in vertebrates appears to be stimulated only by large complex molecules of limited volatility (see also Sheffield et al., 1968; Halpern, 1983) and that vomeronasal detection (via the nasolabial grooves) may be possible when lungless salamanders are in close proximity to the odor. Stimulation of the vomeronasal system has been shown to be necessary in sex-related social behaviors in mammals and snakes (Halpern, 1983). In snakes it has been associated with prey identification, courtship, and aggregation behavior. Through recognition of species-specific

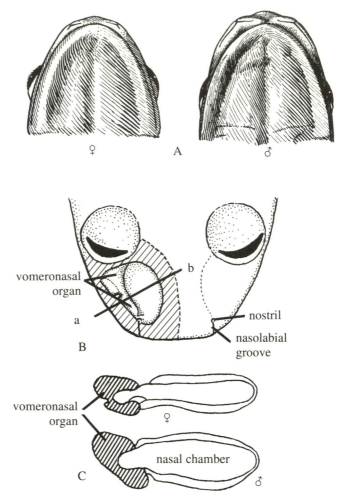

Fig. 6.1 The nasolabial groves and vomeronasal organ of lungless salamanders (Plethodontidae). (A) Sex difference in forking of grooves at
the edge of the upper lip in a female (left) and male (right) Ensatina
(*Ensatina eschscholtzii*). (B) The right-hand nasal passage of a Red-
backed Salamander (*Plethodon cinereus*), exposed to show the position
of the vomeronasal organ. (C) Cross section through female (top) and
male (bottom) nasal passages at line a-b in (B), showing differences in
size of the vomeronasal organ. (B and C after Dawley, 1992, redrawn
with permission from *Copeia*)

cues, this system probably plays an important role, at least in plethodontid salamanders, at the boundaries of species ranges in preventing or permitting varying degrees of hybridization (see Dawley, 1987b; Houck et al., 1988). In some cases it may help protect against predation. Detection of chemical cues by the Seal Salamander (*Desmognathus monticola*) (e US) may lower its risk to predation from the Black-bellied Salamander (*D. quadramaculata*), which shares much of its range (Roudebush and Taylor, 1987; Jacobs and Taylor, 1992).

Since in any given situation, it is usually unknown whether the olfactory or vomeronasal sense, or both, are being used in amphibian nasal chemorecep-tion, when there is uncertainty we lump them together under the "olfactory sense" or "chemoreception."

The olfactory sense is well developed in most amphibians but is, perhaps, best developed in burrowing toads, in newts, and certain other salamanders (Kauer, 1974; Kauer and Moulton, 1974), and in caecilians. In salamanders it often plays a part in courtship and in species, sex, and individual recognition, in finding and recognizing mates (Dawley, 1986), sometimes in avoiding ene-mies, in egg-clutch recognition (Forester, 1979; Forester et al., 1983), and in the detection of territorial boundaries, but in feeding it is usually inferior to sight. However, in experiments, web-toed salamanders (*Hydromantes*) and some other plethodontids were able to locate and feed on prey in total dark-ness, detecting it apparently by the sense of smell (Roth, 1976) or, perhaps, through vibrations caused by movements of the prey.

Olfaction (probably the vomeronasal sense) appears to be used by gravid female Red-backed Salamanders in assessing the food resources of male terri-tories. The male's feces and his territory bear his odor and his feces the odors of consumed prey. The level of interest of females is shown by the frequency with which they nose-tap the male's territory and squash his feces (with their noses). Experiments by Jaeger and Wise (1991) have shown that, in this way, females determine the quality of the male's food supply. Walls et al. (1989) have also shown that gravid females prefer territories of males in natural forest habitat that have access to high-quality prey.

In both salamanders and anurans (Grubb, 1975), olfaction has also been implicated in the recognition of breeding sites and in homing orientation.

Function of the Nasolabial Grooves

The nasolabial grooves of lungless salamanders (family Plethodontidae) are unique structures found in no other postembryonic terrestrial vertebrates. They are used in obtaining information on the chemistry of the environment and as an aid in individual, species, and sex recognition. A groove is present on each side of the snout—a hairline nonciliated furrow that extends from the edge of the upper lip to the nostril (figs. 6.1B and 7.2A). Plethodontids often tap the substratum with their snouts when they crawl, and they sometimes lightly probe other individuals. If the surface is wet, fluid (bearing chemoreceptive information) passes rapidly up the grooves by capillary action to the external nares, where it is drawn into the nose by ciliary movements within the nasal cavity and then over the chemoreceptors of the vomeronasal organs (Brown, 1968; Dawley, 1987a; Dawley and Bass, 1989). It then passes through the internal nares into the mouth and pharynx.

The distal end of the groove in males of some species extends onto a nipple-like palp that projects downward from the upper lip. In others it may divide into two long branches (*Ensatina eschscholtzii*) (fig. 6.1A) or break up into a capillary network on the swollen anterior edge of the lip. Although females have nasolabial grooves, they lack such elaborate modifications. The modifications in males suggest that they use the grooves especially during reproductive behavior—in tracking and identifying females. Dawley (1992) has shown that male Red-backed Salamanders (*Plethodon cinereus*) (ne US, se Can) have significantly larger vomeronasal organs than females (fig. 6.1C). Nose-tapping, a method of vomeronasal stimulation (often applied to the body of the female) is used repeatedly by male plethodontid salamanders during the initial stages of courtship. In addition, recognition of conspecific and individual (including self) odors are probably important for both sexes in acquiring familiarity with an area, recognizing home range, intruders, and territories of other individuals (Tristram, 1977; McGavin, 1978).

Larval Amphibians

Chemoreception is also important to larval amphibians. Like salmon smolt, aquatic larvae of many amphibious species appear to become imprinted on the chemistry ("odor"?) of their natal site and often return to it when ready to breed. Chemoreception is used by bufonid tadpoles in the detection of alarm substances released from the skin of injured individuals (see Hews, 1988). They respond by fleeing the area. It is also employed in the detection of food and, sometimes, predators. Many amphibian larvae use chemoreception to detect predatory fish and respond by fleeing and by increasing their use of cover (Petranka et al., 1987; Kats, 1988; Kats et al., 1989).

Control of Nasal Water and Air Flow

Movement of air and/or water through the nose is controlled by valvular nostrils. Closure of the nostrils in frogs is accomplished by an upward movement of the lower jaw while the mouth is closed. This elevates the tip of the upper jaw and compresses the nostrils. The action is required in lung respiration, for the mouth and nostrils must be closed when air in the mouth is forced back into the lungs by contraction of the throat.

Snorting and sniffing actions are achieved by compressing and lowering the gular region (perhaps also involving tongue movements), resulting in air pressure changes in the nasal cavities.

7

Eyes and Vision

MUCH of the information on amphibian vision is based on studies of only a few kinds of anurans and salamanders—such as the Leopard Frog (*Rana pipiens*) (N Am), Bullfrog (*Rana catesbeiana*) (e NA), the Common Toad (*Bufo bufo*) (Eur, Middle East, nw Afr), the Tiger Salamander (*Ambystoma tigrinum*) (N Am), Old World newts (*Triturus*) (Eur to Ural Mts) and salamanders (*Salamandra*) (Eur, nw Afr, w Asia), and plethodontid salamanders (N and S Am). This must be kept in mind in considering the remarks that follow.

There is great variation in the visual capabilities of amphibians. Most frogs have large, protuberant, well-developed eyes that, together, see in virtually all directions at once, encompassing the most extensive visual field among vertebrates, with perhaps the exception of a few fishes. Many appear to have good depth and color perception and great acuity for detecting both small and larger prey at close range. They also see well moving distant objects, as anyone who has tried to stalk a frog has discovered. Other anurans such as most toads (*Bufo*) and most salamanders have eyes adapted primarily for vision at night or under conditions of dim light, but many also see quite well in lighted surroundings. Vision is often assisted or supplanted by a well-developed sense of smell (chemoreception) in salamanders, in general more so than in most anurans. Even so, many salamanders make extensive use of sight, including many species that have marked light-shunning habits. Salamanders that rarely expose themselves by day may be seen looking toward the lighted opening of their shelters, perhaps to more easily detect prey or predators. Caecilians, chiefly burrowing, crepuscular amphibians, have variously reduced eye structure and a few are blind, or perhaps detect only changes in light intensity.

Most amphibian larvae have the eyes located at the sides or toward the top of the head, but with metamorphosis the eyes become more forward in position, the shift probably relating to the nearly universal feeding on small animal prey of postmetamorphic individuals. The overlap in visual fields of the two eyes aids depth perception in targeting prey. Binocular vision reaches its peak in the lungless salamanders (family Plethodontidae).

There may be great differences in spectral sensitivity of amphibian eyes depending on the extent of diurnality, nocturnality, and/or fossorial behavior (Hailman and Jaeger, 1974). Light-intensity preferences, daily activity rhythms, and choice of habitat all influence the often relatively narrow range of light levels during a day at which an amphibian is active. This is presumably the range within which its eyes are best adapted, the optimum ambient illumination (OAI) level for the species (Jaeger and Hailman, 1981). The bimodal activity pattern of some species may reflect such adaptation. Buchanan (1992) found that individual male Squirrel Treefrogs (*Hyla squirella*) (se US), a nocturnal species, studied in Louisiana in their natural habitat (June 2–August 3, 1987) were most active after sunset (8–11 P.M.) and before sunrise (3–5 A.M.). Temperature and humidity changes could not explain the activity pattern; therefore, it was inferred that the response was to two periods of similar illumination (less that 0.003 lux), which may coincide with the OAI level for the species.

Species differences in light sensitivity probably contribute to partitioning of habitat use among coexisting species and thereby reduce competition. In addition, shifts in sensitivity may occur upon metamorphosis and with changes in seasonal activity, as when a terrestrial species that is chiefly nocturnal during most of the year becomes active by day in the aquatic environment of its breeding site. Retinal sensitivity may then shift from that adapted to low levels of light intensity to far higher levels.

Differences in species sensitivity to light are usually reflected in the proportion of rods and cones in the retina. The rods are sensitive to light intensity, the cones to color. In a study of Old World salamandrids the percentage of rods was found to vary directly with the extent of crepuscular and nocturnal activity (Möller, 1951).

In highly aquatic amphibians (pipid frogs [S Am, Afr], permanently aquatic gilled salamanders, and others), the eyes are small, and there may be varying degrees of retinal simplification. Mudpuppies (e US) have such simplified retinas. Loss of the eyes has occurred in some aquatic cave dwellers such as the Georgia Blind Salamander (*Haideotriton wallacei*), Texas Blind Salamander (*Typhlomolge rathbuni*), and the Olm (*Proteus anguinus*) of Adriatic Europe. Caecilians are said to have "vestigial" eyes. However, in species studied by Wake (1980b, 1985) the eyes appeared to be functional, based on the presence of an intact retina and optic nerve.

Vision in Water and on Land

The amphibious life cycle of many amphibians requires them to see underwater and on land. A compromise is called for because vision cannot be equally acute in both environments. Life patterns must be considered in assessing and interpreting visual capabilities that must cope with such different conditions.

A change from vision in air to water decreases the refractive power of the eyes. In water, there is no light refraction at the corneal surface because the cornea and water have the same refractive index. Focusing depends on the lens only, which, in amphibians, is moved rather than changed in shape (see below). A terrestrial salamander, for example, becomes more farsighted when it enters water, and an aquatic one more shortsighted (myopic) in air (Grüsser-Cornehls and Himstedt, 1976). Predominantly to completely aquatic species tend to have flatter corneas and more spherical lenses ("aquatic optics") than do terrestrial species, which have more rounded corneas and flatter lenses. The Old World newts (*Triturus*), more aquatic than terrestrial, have spherical lenses. In water, the visual acuity of the European Smooth Newt (*Triturus vulgaris*) (Eur, w Asia to Asia Minor) appears to be about the same at very close range (1-1/4 in, or 3 cm) as it is at greater distances. However, newts are shortsighted on land and they have weak powers of visual accommodation. Since they chiefly detect their prey at close range, and often within reach, this is evidently not a serious disadvantage. The behavior of western newts (*Taricha*) (w US, w Can) suggests that they are similar to *Triturus*. On the other hand, the flatter lens of the Fire Salamander (*Salamandra salamandra*), a terrestrial species, evidently provides focus over a considerably greater distance. In the larval stage it has "aquatic optics" (a spherical lens close to a flattened cornea). During metamorphosis and later development to the adult stage, the lens flattens, moves toward the retina, and the corneal curvature increases (Sivak and Warburg, 1980).

Some Additional Anatomical Aspects

Amphibians focus their eyes by a change in position of the lens, rather than by a change in its shape as in reptiles, birds, and mammals. In anurans, dorsal and ventral protractor muscles move the lens outward, toward the cornea. In salamanders only a ventral muscle is present, thus during accommodation only a slight tilting of the lens is possible. In plethodontid salamanders, animals in which the lens is very large (in some species almost filling the space between the pupil and the retina) (fig. 7.1), accommodation may play only a minor role in object identification and distance estimation (Roth, 1987).

The pupil varies in shape: round in most salamanders (fig. 7.2B); round, horizontally oval (fig. 7.3), or vertically elliptical in anurans. The vertical pupil is capable of great contraction and dilation, going from a hairline slit in some species in bright light to near disappearance of the iris when fully dilated at night. Vertical pupils are associated with nocturnality, but many nocturnal species lack them. Reflective pigment cells in the iris of some amphibians may help cut down dazzle when the animals are exposed to bright light (fig. 7.2A).

In most amphibians the adult retina contains four kinds of photoreceptors, "red" and "green" rods (named for their appearance in fresh tissue), differing in the wavelengths of light that they maximally absorb, and single and double cones. The "red" rods contain rhodopsin (rods of this kind are found in all vertebrates) and have a peak absorption of light at a wavelength of 502 nm.

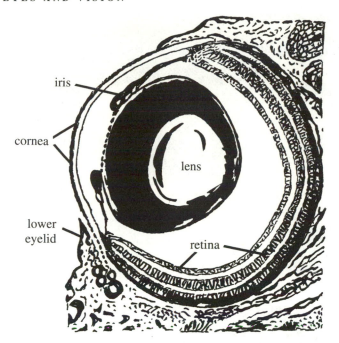

Fig. 7.1 Horizontal section through the eye of the neotropical Palm
Salamander (*Bolitoglossa subpalmata*), a lungless salamander, family
Plethodontidae. Note the strongly curved cornea, large lens, and the
thick retina. (After Linke et al., 1986, with permission from John
Wiley and Sons, Inc.)

They respond best to yellow-green light. "Green" rods have a peak absorption
at 433 nm and respond best to blue light. "Green rods" are specific for amphibians and may be involved particularly in hue discrimination. In toads they are
highly sensitive receptors that respond to low light intensities (Matthews,
1983). Single cones (yellow sensitive) maximally absorb light with a wavelength of 580 nm. Double cones are pairs of receptors in which the membranes
of the inner segments are fused. They consist of a "principal cone" with the
same pigment as the single cone and an "accessory cone" with the same pigment as the red rod (Wilczynki, 1992). The red rods presumably respond to
low light levels as do the rhodopsin-bearing rods of other vertebrates. The
remaining photoreceptors are involved in color vision.

  Oil droplets are present in anuran cones. While they probably filter out damaging ultraviolet radiation, they appear not to contribute to acuity of vision, as
evidently occurs in reptiles (Hailman, 1976). Their function may be chiefly
chemical storage, perhaps in relation to the visual pigment cycle.

  Retinal ganglion cells respond to boundaries, convexities, changing con-
trasts, light intensities, and moving objects. The optic tectum seems to be the

A

B

Fig. 7.2 (A) Ensatina (*Ensatina eschscholtzii xanthoptica*), a salamander with a reflective eye patch in the upper iris. (B) California Tiger Salamander (*Ambystoma californiense*) (Cal), a strictly nocturnal species, showing the round pupil characteristic of many salamanders.

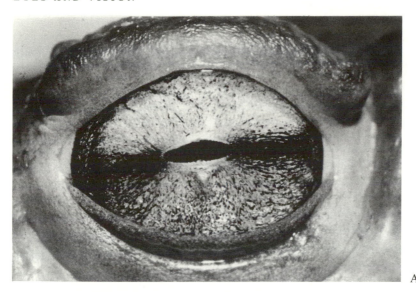

A

B

Fig. 7.3 (A) Eye of the Sonoran Desert Toad (*Bufo alvarius*) (sw US, Mex). The gray crescent-shaped tissue is the nictitating membrane just emerging from behind the lower lid. Note the horizontally oval pupil common among toads. (B) Nictitating membrane nearly covering the eye of the Southwestern Toad (*Bufo microscaphus*) (sw Cal).

highest brain "center" for visual motor control mechanisms and is involved in triggering prey-catching behavior. Roth's studies (1987) indicate that the cell types and secondary and tertiary visual pathways of the tectum are essentially similar in salamanders and frogs.

Roth (1987) proposes that prey recognition in amphibians results from the integrated output of many different tectal neurons functioning as a prey recognition network. He thus moves away from earlier explanations that called for activation of populations of retinal "detector neurons" ("bug" detectors) with response properties that corresponded to particular types of prey items in the environment. Although signals from these "bug" detector neurons may predispose the brain to deal with a potentially important object in the environment, the brain must process and compare this information with other input before calling for action (see Wilczynski, 1992). Prey recognition by amphibians appears to be more complex, and more like that of the "higher" vertebrates (the reptiles, birds, and mammals) than had been previously thought (see Nishikawa, 1989).

Distance Perception and Visual Acuity

Laboratory experiments and field observations reveal that many amphibians are able to determine accurately distances between objects and distances to their prey. Some anurans can judge the distance to their prey with precision using either monocular or binocular vision (see Douglas et al., 1986). Although when startled or forced into unfamiliar terrain a frog or salamander may appear clumsy in its efforts to escape, close watching of individuals on their home ground indicates familiarity with surrounding features such as rocks, branches, animal burrows, and crevices, and the spatial arrangement of these objects in the habitat. Olfactory and kinesthetic information may be involved, as well as sight. Prey-catching behavior indicates good depth perception, in some species even under conditions of very low illumination. The plethodontid Italian Cave Salamander (*Hydromantes italicus*) (se France to cen Italy) is able to catch small insects on the tip of its "projectile" tongue in almost total darkness (Roth, 1976) (see also chapter 8). Toads (*Bufo bufo*) (Eur) also snap at prey or experimental dummies at very low light intensities, at light levels at which humans can no longer see (Larsen and Pedersen, 1982).

Linke et al. (1986) calculated visual acuity in plethodontid salamanders based on morphological information. They determined that under night or twilight conditions (rod vision), an object 0.5 mm in length (collembola size) should be detectable at a maximum distance of 2.3 inches (57 mm) by the Mountain Dusky Salamander (*Desmognathus ochrophaeus*) (ne US) and 3.3 inches (82 mm) by the Northern Two-lined Salamander (*Eurycea bislineata*) (e US, se Can). Under sufficient light, optical resolution, based on pupil aperture of the eye, would permit detection of an insect 0.5 mm in length at a distance of 31 inches (78 cm) in *Hydromantes italicus*, 16 inches (41 cm) in the California Slender Salamander (*Batrachoseps attenuatus*), and 79 inches (147 cm) in the Northern Two-lined Salamander.

Plethodontid salamanders are the only amphibians with forward-looking eyes and binocular vision that closely parallels the well-developed binocular vision of many reptiles, birds, and mammals (see Roth, 1987).

Use of Vision in Feeding

Transformed amphibians, larval salamanders, and a few tadpoles feed on insects and other invertebrates, and transformed individuals occasionally feed on small vertebrates. Vision is the chief sense used, and movement of prey is usually, but not always, necessary to trigger the feeding response.

In orienting on prey, amphibians move their eyes very little, often seemingly not at all. Rather, since their retinal receptive field is relatively fixed in relation to their body axis, they usually bring their eyes into position for focusing by aiming their body or by turning the head. Head turning is generally more common in salamanders than in anurans.

What are visual characteristics of prey that trigger the feeding response of an amphibian? As a general rule, the prey must move (but not too slowly or fast) and must be of proper size (not too small or large) and appropriate shape (not stand too high). Degree of contrast with background is also important. With respect to size, for example, in experiments with *Hydromantes italicus*, a small, actively moving prey specialist, Roth (1976) found optimum prey size to be between 2.5 and 5 mm^2, with an acceptable range of 0.5 to 10.0 mm^2.

Models of varying shape (disks, squares, rectangles) and size, often moved at different speeds, degree of jerkiness, direction, and sometimes against different backgrounds, have been used to investigate the kinds of stimuli that elicit feeding responses. Such responses are often measured by orientation toward or away from the stimulus, or by tongue slaps at the target offered. Such studies are most meaningful when viewed in the light of the natural foraging behavior and prey selection of the species chosen for study.

Some sample investigations follow. In a study of the Common Toad (*Bufo bufo*), of the paired alternatives listed below, the first in each case had the greatest "releasing" value for the feeding response: (1) small, moving white objects on a black background vs. small black objects on a white background (Ewert, 1976); (2) horizontal lines vs. squares or bars; (3) expansion of the models in the direction of their movement vs. no expansion; (4) retreating models vs. approaching ones (Beck and Ewert, 1979); (5) stepwise or jerky movements vs. steady movement (Borchers et al., 1978). Horizontal lines and elongation of models in the direction of movement are features that suggest worms. Vertical expansion of models decreased releasing values. For toads, "there are no worms walking on their heads" (Ewert, 1976; Ewert et al., 1978).

In the Green Treefrog (*Hyla cinerea*) (se US), Freed (1982) found that prey size (length and dorsal surface area), shape (length/width ratio), speed, and distance from the predator at the time of prey detection were all positively correlated with feeding responsiveness. Green Treefrogs respond more slowly to distant food items and more quickly to prey that exhibit large length/width ratios and high crawling speeds. Moving, elongate stimuli with ratios greater than 3:1 have been found most effective in eliciting feeding responses in toads (Ewert et al., 1979); and Green Treefrogs (from Florida) were found to select natural foods (wormlike larvae) characterized by length/width ratios in excess of 5:1 (Freed, 1982).

The plethodontid Sardinian Cave Salamander (*Hydromantes genei*), a species that commonly feeds on small, compact, active prey, was more attracted to a moving 5 × 5 mm black square than to a 2.5 × 10 mm rectangle moving horizontally. The latter, when moved vertically, was the least effective in triggering a feeding response (Roth, 1987).

In a study of the Fire Salamander (*Salamandra salamandra*), Luthardt and Roth (1979) found that jerkiness, speed of movement, and orientation of models could influence feeding attempts. A black rectangle (32 × 4 mm), seen against a white background, was moved at different velocities (0.5, 1.25, and 3.125 cm/sec) and different step frequencies or degrees of jerkiness (0.25, 0.5, 1, 2, 4, and 8 steps/sec). When the rectangle was moved continuously with its long-axis parallel to the direction of movement at low velocity (0.5 cm/sec), or stepwise at 4–8 steps/sec (a high level of jerkiness), prey-catching behavior (snapping at the model) occurred in 80% of all cases. On the other hand, at high velocity (3.125 cm/sec) and moving continuously or stepwise regardless of degree of jerkiness, the model was relatively inefficient in eliciting a response (25% of cases). When the model was oriented perpendicular to movement direction and moved rapidly, whether continuously or stepwise, it was found to be relatively efficient (48% of cases) in causing a feeding response. It also displayed this efficiency when moving slowly and stepwise at a frequency of 2–4 steps/sec. The vertical model was less efficient (26%) when moving slowly, continuously, or stepwise at 0.25–0.5 or 8 steps/sec.

It is of interest to consider the movements of actual prey in relation to their findings. Elongate prey such as mealworms and earthworms move slowly and continuously, or discontinuously at low step frequencies. Prey of compact shape such as crickets, beetles, and flies move fast and jerkily. Thus the horizontal orientation experiments relate well to the behavior of elongate prey. However, the results obtained with vertical orientation of the model are not easily explained in relation to compact prey behavior.

Roth (1987) notes that in some salamanders there seems to be a tendency for elongate stimuli oriented parallel to the direction of movement to decrease in effectiveness with increasing velocity, whereas the opposite seems to be the case for elongate stimuli oriented perpendicular to the direction of movement. Possibly the edge of a vertical bar, when moving rapidly, is interpreted by the animal as the leading edge of a compact object.

In some larval salamanders tested, shape does not appear to be a crucial factor in triggering the prey-catching response. However, after metamorphosis it becomes more important, and wormlike models become more attractive. As in toads, shapes that are elongate in the direction of movement and do not extend perpendicular to movement too much are most effective.

Luthardt-Laimer (1983) found a slowly moving horizontal bar was very effective in evoking food-catching behavior in larval and transformed Fire Salamanders. Larvae at an age of one or two days, with no experience with actual prey, were especially attracted to the moving bar. Evidently there are innate preferences in this salamander that are effective immediately after birth. Evidence was also found for an imprinting-like process during early life, following transformation. Animals fed tubifex worms and earthworms continued to prefer the slowly moving horizontal bar, whereas those raised on crickets showed no such preference. Apparently the two months following metamorphosis are a sensitive period for imprinting of visual prey preferences, during which such preferences are established and after which they are no longer "learned."

Large moving objects, chiefly in the air, represent a potential enemy. Ewert (1976) found an optimal size for a black disk in releasing maximal escape behavior in toads. There was less reaction to smaller or larger disks.

Prey-catching behavior of toads was generally inhibited by a group or swarm of simultaneously moving prey (mealworms) (Ewert, 1976). When frightened, a toad may duck and jump (enemy approaching from the air) or turn away and run (enemy approaching on the ground).

During the breeding season, the reaction to moving objects shifts. Prey-catching and avoidance responses to models decrease. The relevant visual stimulus for the male in spring is the female, and he responds to her large size as a first step in the signals that ultimately lead to clasping. At this season the male response to moving objects may be encompassed by the phrase, "If it's not too large or too small, mate with it."

Color Vision

Many amphibians evidently have good color vision, as may be inferred from their habits and the proportion of retinal cones. This is evident during prey-catching behavior in frogs and toads (Birukow and Meng, 1955). It can be expected to be best developed in diurnal forms, especially those in which the sexes differ in color.

When responding positively to light, frogs have a preference for blue light, and they will jump toward it rather than to green or other longer wavelengths. This represents true color perception and not merely an intensity preference. Muntz (1964) has suggested that the response promotes escape toward water where there tends to be more blue light than on land. However, in an extensive survey of anuran families, Hailman and Jaeger (1974) failed to find ecological evidence for this. They note that aquatic species moving toward water surfaces, terrestrial species moving toward breaks in a forest canopy, and arboreal species moving toward the crowns and branch tips of trees all achieve a higher ambient illumination by moving toward the blue light of the sky. Transformed salamanders have also been shown to have somewhat similar preferences for the light of shorter wavelengths.

Herbivorous tadpoles appear to have a preference for green or yellow-green, the color of plants on which they feed and in which they shelter, a preference that shifts toward a short wave "blue" at metamorphosis (Jaeger and Hailman, 1976). Kasperczyk (1971), working with the Common Frog (*Rana temporaria*) (Eur e to Urals), the Fire Salamander (*Salamandra salamandra*), and the Warty Newt (*Triturus cristatus*) (Eur to cen Russia), reported that they have a range of color vision that corresponds well with that of humans. In experiments, these amphibians were able to recognize eight basic colors—red, orange, yellow, yellow-green, green, blue-green, blue, and violet, and they could distinguish them from shades of gray. In an ingenious experiment, Himstedt (1972), using colored filters and a worm-shaped dummy, demonstrated that the Fire Salamander, Smooth Newt (*Triturus vulgaris*), Alpine Newt (*T. alpestris*), and Warty Newt (*T. cristatus*) could distinguish blue, green, yellow-green, yellow, and red from gray. The green dummy had less releasing value than blue, yellow, or red in all species. Newts are sexually dimorphic in color, and their color discrimination corresponds well to just those colors—blue and red—which predominate in the body coloration of the male.

Eye Protection

The eyes of most salamanders and frogs are protected by movable eyelids. The upper lid is moved mainly by retraction and protrusion of the eyes. The lower, however, has more inherent mobility. Anurans have a thin, translucent to transparent nictitating membrane, continuous with the lower eyelid, which, when at rest, is retracted behind it. The membrane is drawn over the eyes when an anuran swims and dives and protects, cleans, and moistens the eyes on land (fig. 7.3A,B). Caecilians, permanently aquatic salamanders, amphibian larvae, and pipid toads (fig. 9.4A) lack movable lids.

Use of Amphibians in Studies of Vision

Amphibians have contributed enormously to an understanding of vertebrate vision, including that of humans. They have been indispensable in research on the anatomy, photochemistry, and physiology of the vertebrate retina and in recent years have been favored animals in neuroanatomical and neurophysiological studies of vertebrate visual systems.

The Tiger Salamander (*Ambystoma tigrinum*) (N Am) has been a valuable subject in retinal research. Its large, easy to handle, retinal photoreceptors, possibly a reflection of the salamander's large DNA molecules which confer large size on all its cells, are of special interest. Its rod cells are used to determine what substance in the rods transmits the light-evoked electrical message to the optic nerve.

See Fite (1976), Linke et al. (1986), Roth (1987), and Wilczynski (1992) for more comprehensive information on amphibian vision.

8

Food Habits

Kinds of Food and Their Detection

Most amphibians feed on a variety of live animals, often seemingly taking whatever they can swallow. Some species are cannibalistic, especially when the production of young is prodigious. Exceptions are the many herbivorous tadpoles and those species that occasionally scavenge or rarely feed (after metamorphosis) on plant materials or other nonmoving food items. The sirens (*Siren*) (se US), aquatic eel-like salamanders lacking hind limbs, apparently feed more than incidentally on aquatic plants, as they forage for invertebrates and fish. The Arboreal Salamander (*Aneides lugubris*) (w US) appears to feed to some extent on fungus, judging by the large numbers of fungal spores found in digestive tracts of some individuals. The Mexican Burrowing Toad (*Rhinophyrnus dorsalis*) (s Tex to Costa Rica), in a family of its own, is one of few anuran feeding specialists, highly modified in structure to feed on ants and termites. In contrast with other anurans, it projects its tongue with the tip foremost, rather than flipping the rear part forward (Trueb and Gans, 1983). Such action is well suited for catching small prey in nooks and crannies.

Little is known about the kinds of food eaten by caecilians. Dentition and fragmentary stomach contents of the aquatic *Typhlonectes obesus* (Brazil) suggest that this species probably forages occasionally at the water's surface, scraping prey such as insect pupae from rocks and logs (Wake, 1978a). Moodie (1978) reports that fifty individuals of the aquatic *T. compressicauda* near Manaus, Brazil, had mostly empty stomachs. They may have been caught (by local fishermen) before or at the beginning of feeding. However, one individual had fed on arthropods and another on shrimp (about 20 mm long). Local fishermen confirmed that this caecilian fed on shrimp and said they also ate small fish. They live in water-filled burrows and enter water to forage. Examination of stomach contents of two terrestrial Costa Rican species by Wake (1983) indicated a diet chiefly of invertebrates—several species of earthworms, termites, coleopteran and hemipteran larvae, and occasional larger prey, including orthopteran instars. Terrestrial forms may occasionally eat lizards (Moll and Smith, 1967) and small snakes. Prey is sought both below ground and on the surface. The tentacles (see chapter 6) are used in detecting prey.

Some amphibians feed on immobile food items—dead animals, their own (Kaplan and Sherman, 1980; Marshall et al., 1990) or the eggs of other amphibians, insect pupae, and even food scraps. The Southern Toad (*Bufo ter-restris*) (se US) will eat pet food and the widespread Marine Toad (*Bufo marinus*) garbage, both raw and cooked (lettuce, avocado, carrot peelings, rice, peas, etc.) (Alexander, 1964), and carrion, feces, rotting vegetation, and dog food (Rossi, 1983). Tiger Salamanders (*Ambystoma tigrinum*), and probably other ambystomatids, will eat nonmoving prey when appropriate odor cues are present (Lindquist and Bachmann, 1982). Some plethodontid salamanders also eat nonmotile prey. A small Brazilian frog, *Hyla truncata*, includes in its diet fruits of *Anthurium harrisii* (Araceae) and *Erythroxylum ovalifolium* (Erythroxylaceae). The fruits taken (swallowed whole) ranged from 3 to 10 mm in length. Defecated seeds of *A. harrisii* germinate and thus the frog may play a part in the seed dispersal of this plant (da Silva-Helio et al., 1989).

Tremorlike eye movements in the Fire Salamander (*Salamandra salamandra*), of sufficient magnitude to displace the retinal image over several photoreceptors, appears to provide a mechanism for the perception of stationary objects (see Manteuffel et al., 1977). How widespread such movements are among amphibians is presently unknown.

Visual Prey Detection

Sight is usually the dominant sense in detecting prey (caecilians excepted), and it is used by the majority of amphibians, sometimes even under conditions of extremely dim light. Movement of the prey is the stimulus that usually triggers the feeding response. The reaction to movement of an object of appropriate size is so strong that many amphibians can be induced to snap at moving inanimate lures, and there are a few records of amphibians feeding on unsuitable and even lethal objects. Frogs have been caught on a fish line with hook baited with a piece of conspicuously colored flannel, cast nearby. Hamilton (1948) reported two large Green Frogs (*Rana clamitans*) (e N Am) with stomachs laden with elm seeds they had plucked from a stream as the seeds floated by; and the senior author collected a large *Bufo* in South America that had crammed its stomach with floating rice hulls. Oliver (1955) reported that Marine Toads in the Hawaiian Islands experienced a seasonally fatal epidemic from feeding on the falling poisonous blossoms of strychnine trees!

Role of Olfaction

Detection of food by olfaction is widespread among amphibians but is usually secondary to vision. It is relied upon especially when light is weak or absent and/or the food is immobile. Importance of olfaction in food detection varies with the species. Caecilians, many salamanders, and toads seem especially to rely upon it. It has been shown to enhance prey detection in Tiger Salamanders (Lindquist and Bachmann, 1982) and other salamanders. The Italian Cave Salamander (*Hydromantes italicus*) is able to localize prey so precisely by olfaction that it can shoot its tongue toward the prey (2–3 cm away) in total darkness (Roth, 1987).

However, in lighted surroundings, where sight can predominate, inhibition of the olfactory feeding response to motionless odoriferous prey may occur. This can be observed in salamanders that in darkness or dim light would ordinarily feed, yet in lighted surrounding wait for the prey to move and may stare at it for long periods without, or only occasionally, engaging in feeding behavior. Experiments have shown that some salamanders can learn to recognize immobile prey (Roth, 1987).

Olfaction appears to be a primary sense used by blind subterranean salamanders living in total darkness, and by sighted species, especially on overcast nights, in caves, animal burrows, and in the depths of leaf litter. Detection of vibrations produced by mobile prey may also be involved. The Red-backed Salamander (*Plethodon cinereus*) of the forest floor (e N Am) sometimes feeds in almost complete darkness and on motionless prey. Chemoreception is used (David and Jaeger, 1981). These animals seem to follow chemical gradients on moist surfaces in finding food such as dead fruit flies (*Drosophila*) offered them. They tap the substratum and the flies with their nasal cirri, evidently using the capillary action of the nasolabial grooves (see chapter 6) in picking up the scent. Although movement is important in feeding behavior in these salamanders, it is not necessary to elicit a feeding response. Visual cues enhanced feeding on motile prey whereas chemical cues stimulated feeding on nonmotile prey.

David and Jaeger (1981) found that long-term exposure to a particular type of prey elevated the feeding response to that prey type. Conditioning of this sort has also been shown in Western Toads (*Bufo boreas*) (w N Am) by Shinn and Dole (1979 a,b) and Dole et al. (1981). In experiments, the toads were attracted to the odor of insects (mealworms, crickets) upon which they habitually fed and even directed tongue "slaps" at the odor source when their accustomed prey was not in sight. A similar response to an odor source (dog food extract) was observed in the Marine Toad (*Bufo marinus*) (s Tex to n S Am; widely introduced) by Rossi (1983). Olfaction may also be used by amphibians in avoiding noxious food (Shinn and Dole, 1978).

In addition to sight and olfaction, some amphibians respond to terrestrial vibrations created by prey. Some aquatic adults and most aquatic larvae may detect prey by mechanoreception and some by electroreception via the lateral line system in the manner of some fishes (see chapter 9 for further discussion). Aquatic adult caecilians appear to have only electroreceptors.

A classical study by Martin et al. (1974) established the relative importance of visual, chemical, and tactile stimuli for food intake in the Red-spotted Newt (*Notophthalmus viridescens*) (e N Am). Additional studies of this type are desirable.

Food Preferences

Although it often may appear that many amphibians have a low level of discrimination in feeding, it must not be assumed that they are wholly lacking in food preferences. Prey attributes of size, movements (orientation and speed), palatability, and nutritive value can affect food choice and are subject to learning. Hunting procedure (high-energy pursuit versus low-energy ambush) may change in the light of experience with prey of different sizes, as shown in studies of the Red-backed Salamander (ne US, se Can) by Jaeger and Rubin (1982). Large flies (*Drosophila*) were captured more often than small ones by pursuit rather than ambush, if the salamanders had experience with the two types of flies. They evidently learned that the larger flies were more worthy of pursuit than the smaller ones. Maiorana (1978) found that California Slender Salamanders (*Batrachoseps attenuatus*) at times seemed selectively to ignore small prey, and when feeding on small prey preferred collembolans to oribatid mites of similar size, perhaps because of the thick indigestible exoskeletons of the latter. Plethodontid salamanders (bolitoglossines), which greatly extend the tongue when feeding, commonly eat small prey even though their gape would allow them to take much larger prey. The prey, caught on the sticky tongue pad with a tongue flick of great speed, must usually be taken completely within the mouth when the tongue is returned (see Roth, 1987). Availability and abundance of prey can greatly influence what is ingested and may tend to conceal preferences.

In studies of foraging behavior, a number of factors must be considered, such as different nutritional needs between the growing young and adults; sex-related requirements such as energetic needs of males engaged in courtship, vocalization, and defense of territories; females involved in yolking eggs and/or nurturing young; and seasonal shifts in composition and abundance of prey (see Donnelly, 1991).

The Feeding Mechanism

One of the few characteristics that the three living orders of amphibians share in common is "jointed" or "hinged" pediceled teeth. The tooth base or pedicel is attached to the jaws, and the tooth crowns are loosely bound or fused with the crown. Crowns are typically conical, bicuspid, and usually more or less

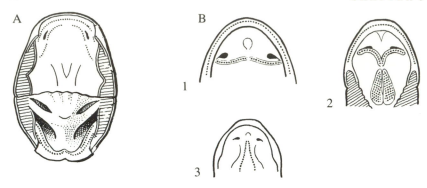

Fig. 8.1 Tooth arrangements in salamanders. (A) Teeth in larval salamander. The jaws have been severed (cut surfaces are represented by horizontal hatching) to more fully open the mouth. (B) Tooth arrangement in the upper jaws of adult salamanders, an ambystomatid (*Ambystoma*) (1), plethodontid (*Ensatina*) (2), and newt (*Taricha*) (3) (all w N Am).

recurved in the direction of the rear of the mouth. Teeth are shed and replaced throughout the life of the amphibian. Caecilians, salamanders, and some anurans have teeth in one or two rows margining both the upper and lower jaws. Frogs (*Rana*) typically lack teeth in the lower jaw (fig. 8.3), and toads (*Bufo*) lack them entirely. In many amphibians there are also teeth in the roof of the mouth, such as the vomerine and palatine tooth patches of many salamanders (fig. 8.1).

Depending upon the species, the teeth are used largely in holding, crushing, and sometimes shredding prey, and in handling the prey as it is being worked into the throat. There may be little or no mastication. Fetal viviparous caecilians develop special teeth that are used to scrape the lining of the oviduct, thus stimulating the secretion of a nutrient substance, which they ingest by mouth. There is no placental attachment. Viviparous caecilians differ from one another in their fetal dentition, which varies in tooth size, shape, and arrangement (Wake, 1976) (fig. 17.13). Tooth crowns are modified for scraping and may bear spikes, cusps, or denticles.

The tongue of many salamanders and anurans can be extended well beyond the opening of the mouth (fig. 8.2) and is used in catching insects and other small animals on land. It impacts on, adheres to, and pulls prey into the mouth (Regal and Gans, 1976). The tongue in caecilians, however, is not extensible. It remains in the floor of the mouth when engulfing prey. In many anurans and some salamanders, the tongue is free behind and flipped out, hind part foremost (figs. 8.2, 8.3).

In most salamanders, the tongue is thrust forward by contraction of muscles associated with the hyoid apparatus to which the tongue is attached. Some salamanders have the tongue attached broadly to the floor of the mouth and

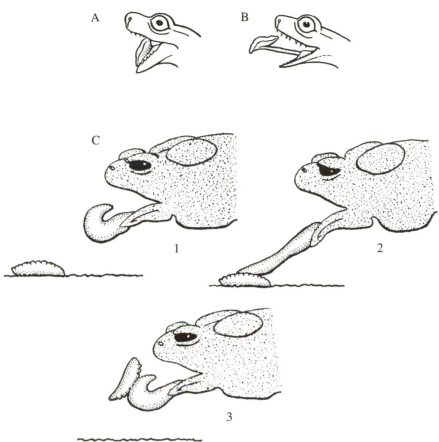

Fig. 8.2 Amphibian tongues. (A) Partly protruded tongue of a "tied-tongue" lungless salamander. The tongue is attached in front, but the tongue pad is protrusible from behind.
(B) "Projectile tongue" of a bolitoglossine lungless salamander. The tongue pad is free all
around and attached to a highly extensible base. (C) Tongue action in the American Toad
(*Bufo americanus*) typical of most anurans. Note resting position of the tongue in figure 8.3,
its sticky surface uppermost. As the tongue is thrust outward, this surface impacts the prey,
adheres to it, and carries it into the mouth. (Drawings based on time-lapse photographs,
courtesy of Kiisa Nishikawa)

anteriorly (fig. 8.2A), but others have it free all around and attached to a pediceled base (fig. 8.2B). This mushroomlike structure can be protruded in some
species (bolitoglossine lungless salamanders) for over one-third the snout-vent
length and can be fired both directly forward and to the side. In capturing prey,
the action of this "projectile-like" tongue may be so quick (in the range of 10
milliseconds) as to be nearly undetectable by human eyes. Such salamanders,

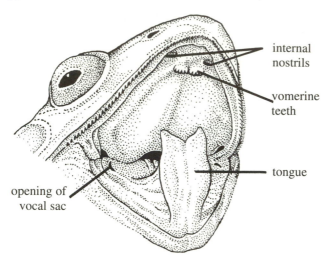

Fig. 8.3 Mouth of a frog (*Rana catesbeiana*) (e N Am), showing teeth in the upper jaw (absent in the lower jaw); tongue partly elevated, the pad attached in front, but free behind; and openings of the vocal sacs (in male only). (After Storer et al., 1979, with permission from McGraw-Hill)

when close to their prey, may simply wait until the prey comes within firing range. The projectile tongue is especially effective in catching small, highly motile prey. For additional information on salamander tongues, see Özeti and Wake (1969) on salamandrids and Lombard and Wake (1976) on plethodontids.

In a typical terrestrial feeding sequence in the Tiger Salamander (*Ambystoma tigrinum*), and apparently in other ambystomids, the salamander rises and rocks forward on its forelimbs as its mouth gapes and the tip of its lower jaw contacts the substratum. The cranium is elevated and is held more or less horizontally. The tongue is extended and its posterior glandular portion becomes the tip of the fully protruded tongue. At this stage the tongue has a deep central depression and elevated rims. The anterior rim collapses upon contact, engulfing the prey in a sticky trough, and the prey is drawn into the mouth. The neck of the animal is then flexed and the cranium snaps downward. The entire action may occur in a little over one-tenth of a second (Larsen and Guthrie, 1975). The salamander may lunge or bound forward following capture of the prey, thereby ensuring its hold and inflicting further damage with its teeth. Elongate prey may be swung violently from side to side before being ingested. In a more recent study, Larsen and Beneski (1988) have detailed, with cinematography, the feeding movements of the Dusky Salamander (*Desmograthus fuscus*) and Black-bellied Salamander (*D. quadramaculatus*) (both e US), which follow closely the movements described above. The authors conclude that probably most, if not all, terrestrial salamanders capture prey in a fundamentally similar manner.

In anurans, based on studies of *Rana* and *Bufo*, a complicated system of muscles is involved in protrusion of the fleshy tongue. The projectile part of the tongue is separated from the hyoid system although there is some forward movement of the hyoid in the tongue action. As the tongue is rotated over the front of the lower jaw, muscular contraction stiffens it into a rod, and inertial travel of the tongue pad carries it forward to the point of impact on the prey. At the end of the strike, the rear part of the tongue containing the tongue pad has rotated 180° from its resting position (Gans and Gorniak, 1982a,b) (see fig. 8.2).

The tongue of many salamanders and anurans is kept sticky by mucous glands in the tongue pad and by pressing it against glands that produce adhesive secretion in the roof of the mouth; a sticky surface is essential for the adhesion of small prey when feeding on land.

Some amphibians, especially certain completely or nearly completely aquatic kinds, have the tongue reduced or absent. When feeding under water, some anurans, permanently or temporarily aquatic salamanders, and many aquatic larvae use a "gape and suck" method. This consists of rapidly opening the mouth while expanding the throat and, in gilled forms, restricting the openings of the gill slits, causing a rapid inflow of water, which carries the prey into the mouth. Following seizure of the prey, in aquatic larval forms the water passes out through the gill slits, but after metamorphosis, and closure of the slits, it exits through the mouth. Thus in those salamanders that do not retain gill slits at metamorphosis and in transformed anurans that use gape and suck foraging, a bidirectional movement of water occurs. Water passes into and out of the mouth, in contrast to the more efficient unidirectional flow associated with the presence of gill slits. See Shaffer and Lauder (1985), Lauder (1985), and Lauder and Shaffer (1986) for details concerning this method of feeding.

In swallowing, many salamanders and anurans depress their eyes and, since eyeballs are firm and their lower surfaces extend into the mouth, they may aid in crushing the prey and in forcing food into the throat. Some anurans use the forelimbs to cram food into the mouth, and many wipe the mouth and eye regions with their forefeet after ingestion or feeding attempts.

Methods of Catching Prey

Some amphibians are primarily "sit-and-wait" predators, lurking beneath objects or in other shelters, or sitting quietly exposed, seizing their prey as it comes into range. The Tiger Salamander (*Ambystoma tigrinum*) seems to be essentially such a predator. Others, such as some toads (*Bufo*) and dendrobatid frogs, may spend much of their time actively searching for prey. The two methods are not mutually exclusive, and a given species may use both depending upon innate tendencies, degree of hunger, and other factors. Terrestrial caecilians often retreat into their burrows with their prey, spinning around and around, in corkscrew fashion as they descend, which causes the prey to be sheared to the width of the jaws. The prey is engulfed by a series of gulps (Wake and Wurst, 1979).

In contrast to most salamanders and anurans, caecilians are "jaw feeders" (Bemis et al., 1983), seizing their prey directly with a strong bite, without tongue protrusion. The hinged teeth in the Mexican Caecilian (*Dermophis mexicanus*) (cen Am), studied by Bemis et al. (1983), fold inward slightly but not outward, thus they act like a ratchet during feeding. The struggles of the prey and jaw movements result in prey shifting inward, rather than out of the mouth. Since hinged teeth are characteristic of amphibians, this ratchet action may be widespread in the group.

A few amphibians lure their prey. Some of the Neotropical horned frogs (*Ceratophrys*) (S Am)—squat, sedentary, camouflaged animals of the forest floor—move their toes to attract small frogs and perhaps other animals upon which they feed (Wickler, 1968). Murphy (1976) observed a captive Colombian Horned Frog (*C. calcarata*) (Colombia and Venezuela) (fig. 8.4) vibrating and undulating its toes while lifting its hind foot upward and forward, apparently to draw prey near its mouth (fig. 8.5), and Radcliffe et al. (1986) observed young Ornate Horned Frogs (*C. ornata*) (Argentina, Uruguay, Brazil) in captivity using hind toe movements in luring prey. Both hind feet were often lifted together and held upward so that the toes (bright yellow) were visible over the frog's hindquarters when viewed from the front.

Toft (1981) studied the foraging habits of leaf-litter frogs in Panama. A range in dietary habits was observed. Extremes were represented by (1) typical sit-and-wait species, stocky wide-mouthed anurans that caught small numbers of large mobile prey and had little locomotor endurance (*Eleutherodactylus*), and (2) widely foraging species, slim and narrow-mouthed, that caught large numbers of small, sedentary prey and were able to sustain long periods of activity (*Atelopus* and *Dendrobates*). The sit-and-wait species were concealing-colored, whereas the latter were mostly toxic and some were warningly-colored. Species that walk or hop and sit-and-wait for prey are less dependent on aerobic capacity than those that jump and forage widely.

Competition for Food and Partitioning of Food Resources

Competition for food usually occurs among members of a species rather than between species. Within a species, individuals of similar size living in the same area are most likely to be in conflict. Members of different species are less likely to compete for food because they often live in different environ-

Fig. 8.4 The Colombian Horned Frog (*Ceratophrys calcarata*) (S Am), a forest-floor dweller that lures its prey.

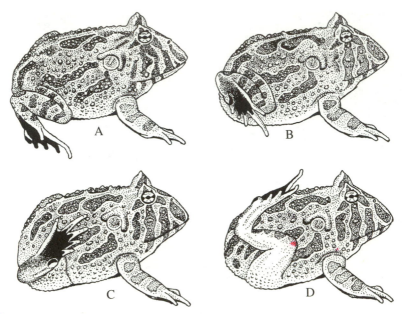

Fig. 8.5 A Colombian Horned Frog (*Ceratophrys calcarata*) in the act of prey-luring. The frog lifts its hind limbs (sequence A–D) and vibrates and undulates its toes held up behind its head to attract prey close to its mouth (see text for details). (After Murphy, 1976)

ments, feed at different times, or eat different foods. The food source thus is "partitioned" (parceled out) among the various species. Intraspecific competition for food (Burton, 1976) and partitioning of food resources among coexisting species (Toft, 1981) have been observed among both transformed and larval amphibians.

Intraspecific Competition

Generally, within a given species, the larger individuals have a greater impact on the feeding opportunities of the smaller ones than the reverse, because they can eat small as well as large prey. Furthermore, when a food source is circumscribed and limited and individuals gather to exploit it, the larger animals, by virtue of size and sometimes aggressive behavior, may obtain more food than the smaller ones. The latter has often been seen among species of captive frogs and toads when groups of individuals are fed together. Feeding hierarchies commonly form, with the smaller animals tending to wait in the background while the larger ones feed. Wrestling, butting, tongue slaps, and nipping, separately or in combination, may be seen among the competing individuals (Boice and Witter, 1969; Boice and Williams, 1971).

Interspecific Competition

At certain times and places, competition for food may exist among coexisting species. Factors that may reduce such competition are differences in selection of microenvironments or habitats, life histories, body size, gape or mouth size (often reflected in head size), tongue structure (Sites, 1978; Roth, 1987), and manner and timing of feeding (Fraser, 1976). As with intraspecific competition, small species of amphibians tend to feed on a smaller range of prey size than larger species, which in addition to being able to take much larger prey may sometimes also eat many small animals. However, in a study of plethodontid salamanders in northwestern California (Black Salamander, *Aneides flavipunctatus*; Arboreal Salamander, *A. lugubris*; California Slender Salamander, *Batrachoseps attenuatus*; and Ensatina, *Ensatina eschscholtzii*), Lynch (1985) found that the larger species appeared not only to select larger prey, but also to ignore most small prey. When, in addition to large size, gape is also relatively large, use of large prey tends to be maximized, as has been observed in *Aneides*. Similar results have been obtained by Christian (1982) in the Striped Chorus Frog (*Pseudacris triseriata*) (N Am). Average maximum prey size increased with increasing frog size but leveled off for the larger frogs, whereas average minimum prey size continued to increase with increasing frog size.

Eating large prey can be energetically favorable because the energy derived from the prey item is often much greater than that derived from a small one and outweighs the minor difference in energy expenditure involved in the two levels of feeding effort required.

Competition among Larvae

Usually more than one amphibian species is found breeding at any given aquatic site and at some localities a dozen or more species may use the same site. Feeding competition among their larvae might be expected. In such locations (1) the time of hatching of larvae of the different species is often staggered, reducing their temporal overlap; (2) larvae may grow at different rates before they begin to feed, thus they vary in size and feed on different sizes of prey. Such variation may be related to yolk supply (Orr and Maple, 1978) or other factors; (3) larvae may feed at different locations in the pond—some at the surface, others at the bottom, and still others at intermediate depths. In these and other ways the habitat is "partitioned" among the species. Heyer (1976) and others suggest, however, that at many aquatic sites plant growth is so exhuberant that there is little competition for food among larvae and that partitioning of the habitat among the several species primarily reflects temporal and microhabitat differences associated with the evolutionary history of each species.

Metabolic Reserves

In amphibians, abdominal fat bodies are an important depot for fat storage but some fat (carcass fat) is stored elsewhere, often in and beneath the skin (some exceptions? See Wygoda, 1987), in the liver, and in the tails of some salamanders. These energy reserves are drawn upon for metabolic maintenance during dormancy (Fitzpatrick, 1976), coping with food shortages, yolking of eggs, and the metabolic demands of metamorphosis.

Fat bodies may fluctuate greatly in size, sometimes packing the abdominal cavity prior to hibernation and being greatly depleted at the end of the reproductive period. However, in the Skipper Frog (*Rana cyanophlyctis*—in southern India), which breeds throughout the year, fluctuation in fat body size seemed to indicate nutritional status, more than reproductive demands (Saidapur et al., 1989).

The liver in some species may also undergo changes. For example, in the Yosemite Toad (*Bufo canorus*), a high-mountain species that has an active period of only around four months (May or June to September), the liver increases in weight during postbreeding foraging, becomes largest just before hibernation, and decreases during hibernation and the breeding season. It then increases gradually thereafter (Morton, 1981). Changes evidently relate to carbohydrate and fat storage and the metabolic demands of reproduction. The cost of breeding activities in males, a time when they apparently do not feed, is presumed to be high.

It is of interest that some females emerge from hibernation with considerable fat. Females sometimes skip a year in reproduction.

Some individuals of desert-dwelling spadefoot toads (*Scaphiopus*) may also emerge with considerable fat. This may relate to the uncertain opportunities for breeding in these animals (Seymour, 1973), and may be an adaptation for surviving periods of food shortage and making possible yolking of eggs upon the advent of favorable conditions for reproduction (Seymour, 1973). See Jørgensen (1992) for further discussion of fat storage in amphibians. See Larsen (1992) for a comprehensive review of feeding in amphibians.

9

Ears and Hearing

THE INFORMATION available on auditory structure and hearing capabilities of anurans, salamanders, and caecilians varies greatly. Most attention has been given to anurans, usually highly vocal animals, which clearly communicate by voice. Salamanders, caecilians, and amphibian larvae have been considered mute or to have very limited capabilities for sound production. We will give most attention therefore, to anurans, which we consider first.

Anurans

Most anurans have well-developed ears, including an eardrum, a middle ear cavity with sound-transmitting ossicles, and an inner ear with auditory sensory areas. Eardrums are conspicuous in many species (fig. 9.1). A primary function of hearing in anurans is the detection of species vocal signals, important in establishing territories and in attracting and finding mates. Anurans not only recognize the characteristic advertisement call (see chapter 10) of their species but they also recognize distinctive sounds directed toward the same or the opposite sex, important in territorial behavior or mating. In some species, whose voice varies geographically, members of a population can distinguish between their own and other dialects (see chapter 10). In addition, some anurans evidently detect sounds made by storms and/or certain predators and prey. The sound (or ground vibration) of rainfall and/or thunder is thought to trigger emergence from underground retreats in some species of arid lands (Dimmitt and Ruibal, 1980), and the Marine Toad (*Bufo marinus*) evidently finds some of the frogs upon which it feeds by their voices (Jaeger, 1976). Australian aborigines obtain various species of the burrowing frog genus *Cyclorana*, which they use for food, by stomping on the ground. The Water-holding Frog (*C. platycephala*), found in the drier inland regions in central Australia, is most significant in this regard (M. Tyler, pers. comm.).

The reception of sound in amphibians is primarily by means of two sensory areas in the inner ear—the basilar papilla (BP) and the amphibian papilla (AP), each containing auditory hair cells (fig. 9.2). The AP is unique to amphibians and the only auditory sense area in some salamanders that lack a BP. High frequencies, mostly above 1000 Hz (cycles per second) (1k Hz), are received by the BP; middle and low frequencies, mostly below 1k Hz, are received by

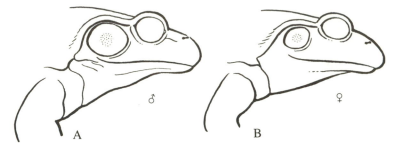

Fig. 9.1 External ear structure of an anuran, the Bullfrog (*Rana catesbeiana*) (e N Am). The eardrum is much larger in males than in females.

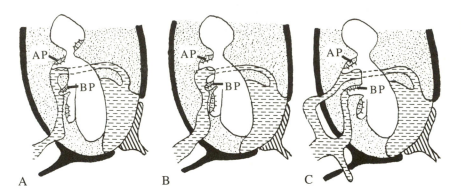

Fig. 9.2 Schematic drawing of left inner ear structure of (A) a caecilian, (B) a salamander, and (C) an anuran, showing the position of the amphibian papilla (AP) and basilar papilla (BP). The columella footplate is shown in diagonal hatching, the fluid-filled perilymphatic system in horizontal broken lines. (After Fritzsch and Wake, 1988, with permission from *Zoomorphology* and the authors)

the AP. In the Bullfrog (*Rana catesbeiana*) and in many other anurans, there are separate populations of nerve fibers in the auditory nerve that respond to each of these frequencies. BP fibers in the Bullfrog are most sensitive to frequencies of about 1400 Hz, and AP fibers to frequencies of about 700–800 Hz and around 200–300 Hz (Capranica, 1977). The overall effective band width for long-range aerial signaling in anurans is about 400 to 4000 Hz (Littlejohn, 1977).

Study of the neuroanatomy of the sensory epithelium of the AP of anurans has revealed considerable variation in its size and configuration in different anuran lineages (see Lewis, 1981a,b, 1984), and a possible influence of such variation on the rate of species formation (Ryan, 1986). Primitive anurans (Ascaphidae, Leiopelmatidae, represented by only four species) have a much less elaborate neuroepithelium (single patch) than the more advanced lineages represented by some eight families and over two thousand species, which have two neuroepithelial patches apparently corresponding to spacial separation of frequency sensitivity. In between are intermediate structural character states found in the less advanced Discoglossidae (nine species) and the Pipidae and Pelobatidae (sixty-six species) (Ryan, 1986).

If, indeed, AP neuroanatomy has influenced the rate of species formation, how may it have done so? Perhaps by affecting the extent to which vocalizations of a given lineage can diverge. Differences in voice are recognized as one of the most important isolating mechanisms in the speciation of anurans. In anurans, the preferential responses of females to the mating call of males of their species often maintains reproductive isolation among populations. Elaboration of the AP neuroepithelium, accompanied by an increased range in auditory frequency sensitivity, may have provided the basis for the vocal divergence that appears to have been so important in anuran speciation (Ryan, 1986).

In salamanders and caecilians, the AP is relatively simple, much like the primitive anuran condition (Wilczynski, 1992).

The Opercularis System

Frogs and salamanders are unique in having within the middle ear two ossicles, the columella (the homologue of the stapes of higher vertebrates) and operculum (fig. 9.3). In anurans, the ossicles are involved in sorting out low and high frequencies and transmitting them via the columella to appropriate sensory areas, respectively, the low frequency AP and the high frequency BP (Lombard and Straughan, 1974). The columella, including its distal plectrum, which attaches to the eardrum, carries airborne vibrations received by the eardrum across the middle ear cavity to the oval membrane, where vibrations are transmitted via the fluids of the inner ear to tectorial membranes that move the auditory hair cells. There the vibrations are translated into nerve signals that pass to the brain via the auditory (eighth) nerve. The operculum is loosely articulated with the foot plate of the columella near its contact with the oval membrane, and at its other end it is connected to the shoulder blade (suprascapula) by the opercularis muscle. This connection places it in a position to be affected by vibrations transmitted to the scapular area via the forelimbs. When the opercularis muscle contracts, the operculum couples or "locks" to the columella foot plate, thereby adding to the mass of the plate in the oval window and "stiffening" the sound-transmitting mechanism of the middle-ear complex. This creates a mechanically more efficient system for transmission of low frequencies (received by the AP) from the eardrum to the inner ear.

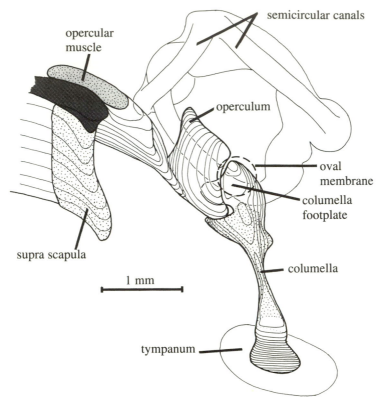

Fig. 9.3 Right middle ear of the Pacific Treefrog (*Pseudacris regilla*) (w N Am), showing the structures that permit a frog to focus its hearing either on general environmental sounds or on the calls of its species. (Courtesy of the *Journal of Experimental Biology*, 1974, and Company of Biologists Limited, Cambridge, U.K.)

When the muscle relaxes, the operculum uncouples, and the ear, via the tympanum and columella alone, is responsive to high frequencies received by the BP. Thus the tympanum-columella complex and the opercular complex provide a two-unit system for both high- and low-frequency transmission.

High-frequency perception appears to be involved primarily in species communication by means of advertisement calls directed toward prospective mates or rivals. The advertisement call of a majority of anuran species has a sound spectrum with an energy peak matching the best frequency of BP reception, and for many anurans the BP is the only organ capable of responding to call frequencies (Wilczynski, 1992). However, some species depend on stimulation of both the AP and BP for recognition of species-specific calls. Examples are the Bullfrog, Northern Leopard Frog (*Rana pipiens*), and the Green Treefrog (*Hyla cinerea*) (see Wilczynski, 1992.)

The uncoupling mechanism that inactivates the low-frequency, or opercularis, system (OPS) appears to be especially important during reproductive chorusing. By dampening the low-frequency (AP) system, reception of environmental "noise" is reduced and the auditory system can focus on the vocal signals of the species. The ear in this sense behaves as a filter, tuned to particular frequency band widths, and the dominant frequency of the call has a function similar to that in human-engineered communications systems, for it provides each species with its own channel over which messages can be sent (Straughan, 1973). The importance of such channeling is apparent since it is quite common for a half dozen or more species to call simultaneously at the same breeding site in choruses involving hundreds and even thousands of individuals. An estimated 6000–7000 males of five species (*Bufo* and *Scaphiopus*) have been heard calling together at a playa near the Dona Ana Mountains, Dona Ana County, New Mexico (Creusere and Whitford, 1976).

Low-frequency perception (often less than 500–600 Hz), on the other hand, seems to be directed more toward general environmental sounds in terrestrial situations, probably including those made by the approach of predators. Such frequencies may be transmitted through the substrate and via the forelimbs and the suprascapular-opercular link to the inner ear when the amphibian is in contact with the ground. The opercularis muscle of the Bullfrog (*Rana catesbeiana*) (N Am), for example, has been found to be active only when the frog emerges, is exposed to the air, and is actively respiring (Hetherington and Lombard, 1981). Further study by Hetherington (1988a) has shown that the OPS functions especially effectively when the frog is in the typical sitting posture with the head held off the ground, and that the OPS is evidently specialized primarily for reception of vertical motions of the substrate of low frequency. The effectiveness of the OPS appears best at about 50–75 Hz. Opercular movements produce waves in the inner ear fluids which then stimulate end organs, such as the saccule, which appears to be primarily a seismic (ground-vibration) receptor (Lewis et al., 1982; see also Eatock et al., 1987).

There is evidence that the low-frequency system in anurans is also involved in the detection of "release signals"—the sounds and/or body vibrations that may be given when an individual experiences unwanted amplexus (see chapter 17). Body vibrations that accompany the release call may have the same pulse rate as the airborne call but at a low energy level—in the American Toad (*Bufo americanus*) (e N Am), below 500 Hz (Brown and Littlejohn, 1972). In females (usually voiceless), body vibrations alone may signal release. Release vibrations are widespread in anurans. They perhaps reach the recipient's inner ear by conduction directly through the body or via the suprascapular-opercular link (Capranica and Moffat, 1975).

In view of the foregoing information on the seemingly terrestrial role of the opercularis system, it is not surprising to find that it is absent or incomplete in amphibian larvae, neotenic and completely aquatic salamanders, in the highly aquatic pipid frogs and certain other frogs, and evidently in the presumably voiceless Tailed Frog (*Ascaphus truei*).

For a review of anuran auditory capabilities, see Narins (1992).

Salamanders

These amphibians lack eardrums and a middle ear cavity but have functional sensory reception areas in the inner ear. The columella can be moved in larvae but in adults it is fused to the skull. The basilar papilla (BP) and amphibian papilla (AP) are both present in primitive salamanders but the BP declines, or may be absent, in more "advanced" (derived) species. Regression of the BP appears to be related to the lack of a tympanic-middle ear sound transmission system and the evident lack of communication by airborne sound in these animals. Caecilians (see below) also lack this system.

Little is known about salamander hearing. The morphology of the inner ear is diverse and complex, indicating that the ear must have an important role (Lombard, 1977). However, the uncoupled opercular plate of these animals appears to be suitable only for low-frequency transmission via the suprascapular-opercular link.

Wever (1978) has shown (based on work with *Ambystoma* and *Taricha*) that sounds applied to the oval membrane of one ear produce a path of vibratory motion that passes through the brain cavity in the cerebrospinal fluid beneath the brain to the oval membrane on the opposite side. Enroute, the vibrations stimulate both right and left amphibian papillae (and basilar papillae, when present). Sound must literally "go in one ear and out the other." Wever suggests that perhaps salamanders are mainly sensitive to "incident" sounds or sudden changes in sustained sounds and largely fail to hear steady tones. The ability to localize sounds in space may be poorly developed.

Ross and Smith (1978) have demonstrated auditory sensitivity of prostrate salamanders (*Notophthalmus*, *Plethodon*, and *Ambystoma*) to vibrations of the substratum.

Caecilians

These animals also lack eardrums and middle ear cavities. The amphibian papilla is the primary auditory sensory area. Like salamanders, caecilians may have both the BP and AP, but the BP is absent in all derived forms (Fritzsch and Wake, 1988) and perhaps deteriorated as a result of subterranean habits. Results of sound tests obtained from the few species studied suggest that they detect low-frequency sound vibrations through water and mud rather than air. The unmodified head skin and head musculature and the single columella serve in sound reception and conduction (Wever and Gans, 1976).

Amphibian Larvae

Hearing in larval amphibians has been less studied than in postmetamorphic individuals. In tadpoles, an otic capsule with oval window is present beneath the skin on each side of the head, but middle ear structures are absent. Sound waves in water evidently transmit directly to the tissues of the larva. Weiss et al. (1973) found the range and sensitivity of Bullfrog tadpoles to be similar to those of adult Bullfrogs except that the typical secondary sensitivity peak in the higher frequencies of the hearing range of adult frogs was absent. Responses extended from 100 to 4000 Hz with best sensitivity in the lowest portion of the range. Larval ranid frogs have "columellar connections" between the lungs and the round window of the the inner ear, an arrangement that parallels that of ostariophysian fishes with their Weberian ossicles. After metamorphosis this system becomes a pressure-release mechanism for the inner ear (Hetherington, 1988b).

For a more comprehensive discussion of the auditory system in amphibians, see Wilczynski (1992).

Lateral Line System

In addition to auditory hair cell mechanoreceptors, highly aquatic adults and larval amphibians (see fig. 9.4) usually have mechanoreceptive neuromasts. These are hair cells, usually in pitlike depressions in the skin, that resemble those of fishes and through which changes in water currents and pressure are registered. These organs are associated with the lateral line system and are usually arranged in rows on the head and along the sides of the body (fig. 9.4). They inform the amphibian of current flow, including wave direction, assist in spatial orientation, and, at close range, detect the presence of other individuals, enemies, and sometimes prey. The aquatic African Clawed Frog (*Xenopus laevis*) (s Afr) has been observed to swim in the direction of water waves, where it may engage in prey-catching behavior and is reported to recognize wave frequencies at an "absolute pitch" level of discrimination (Elepfandt, 1986).

In many aquatic salamanders and some caecilians, ampullary organs are also present in the lateral line system. Their sensory cells lie at the base of a pit or canal. Ampullary organs function as electroreceptors. For example, in the

A

B

Fig. 9.4 The lateral line system in aquatic amphibians. (A) African Clawed Frog (*Xenopus laevis*); note the "stitchery" on the side of the body. (B) Amphiuma (*Amphiuma means*) (se US); note the pits on the head and body.

aquatic larvae of the caecilian *Ichthyophis*, ampullary organs concentrated in the head region may be capable of detecting prey and predators and perhaps the location of the water surface (Hetherington and Wake, 1979). Larval vision is apparently reduced and they forage at night. The larvae have lungs and they probably rise to gulp air at the surface.

Fritzsch and Wake (1986) suggest three lines of modification of the lateral line system in amphibians: (1) anurans, which have lost ampullary organs completely and may or may not lose the neuromast system during metamorphosis; (2) salamanders, which have both ampullary organs and neuromasts or lack both; and (3) gymnophiones (caecilians), which have both as larvae and lose them during metamorphosis, or possess only ampullary organs as embryos and as adults, or lack both entirely.

Reception of Seismic Signals

Anurans are highly sensitive to vibrations of the ground. Response is primarily to Rayleigh waves, substrate surface waves with a strong vertical energy component. The mechanism involved appears to be as follows: Lewis and Narins (1985) note that the saccule portion of the ear of frogs contains a large calciferous mass. As ground vibrations are transmitted via the forelimbs and the suprascapular-opercular link, the mass is displaced less than surrounding tissue and thus motions are created between it and its associated hair-cell receptors.

White-lipped Frogs (*Leptodactylus albilabris*) of Puerto Rico respond to seismic signals of their own (see Lewis and Narins, 1985). When they are prone, with their gular region pressed against the ground surface, a typical calling position, their vocal sac thumps the ground as they chirp. Frogs up to several meters away evidently are able to detect the thumps because they respond with chuckling sounds (which appear to be involved in male-to-male interactions), not only to the thumps but also to tapping with a fingertip or a rubber mallet. The vocal sac thumps propagate through moist soil at about 100 m per second, or about a third the speed of sound in air. Thus the delay between the chirp and the accompanying seismic signal might indicate to other males the distance of the signaler, thereby aiding in the spacing of territorial claims. Perhaps the opercularis system is involved in the detection of these signals.

10

Voice

AMPHIBIANS were the early vertebrate communicators by voice on land and now, at some localities in season, the calls of frogs dominate all other natural sounds at night. Males are the strong-voiced vocalizers and their voices have been studied at length, but possible sound communication in caecilians and salamanders has been given far less attention because they have been regarded as voiceless or as producing only weak or incidental sounds. Female anurans have also been little studied.

Caecilians

Thurow and Gould (1977) reported soft yelps or squeaks, almost inaudible smacking sounds, and clicks produced by a Neotropical caecilian (*Dermophis*), a burrowing animal. They suggest that the clicking sounds may be produced by an abrupt contact between the floor of the mouth and the openings of the internal nares, and that the sounds may be used as an aid in orientation, as in bats, or in species communication. It is speculated that the nasal canals serve to transmit airborne vibrations back to the vicinity of the otic capsules. The clicking sound can be imitated by snapping the edges of two finger nails past each other. *Typhlonectes* (n S Am) occasionally squeaks when it pokes its nostrils above the surface of the water to breathe (M. Wake, pers. comm.).

Salamanders

Most salamanders have been considered voiceless or at best capable of making only faint snapping, ticking, or popping noises, perhaps with the opening and closing of the nasal valves or the glottis. A few can squeak by means of gular contractions, which cause air movements, possibly between the jaw margins and through the nose. At least one species, the Southern Giant Salamander (*Dicamptodon ensatus*) (Cal), has "vocal cords" and can bark or rattle. Its sounds are thought to startle predators. Whether other members of the genus vocalize is apparently unknown.

The Arboreal Salamander (*Aneides lugubris*) (w US), despite its lunglessness, may squeak repeatedly when first caught, retracting its eyes into their sockets each time a sound is produced. When the eyeballs are depressed, their undersides protrude into the mouth cavity, thereby compressing the air in the mouth, and forcing it outward. It is this movement that appears somehow to cause the sounds produced. Ensatina (*Ensatina eschscholtzii*) (w US, sw Can) occasionally makes a snakelike hissing sound (Brodie, 1978), which might put off an animal like a shrew that uses hearing in hunting. The Lesser Siren (*Siren intermedia*) (se US) produces faint clicking sounds that may influence species behavior (Gehlbach and Walker, 1970) and, when attacked, sometimes shrill cries of distress (Conant and Collins, 1991). When disturbed, Dwarf Sirens (*Pseudobranchus striatus*) (se US) may yelp faintly. Faint, brief sounds have been described for the Red-spotted Newt (*Notophthalmus viridescens*) (e US, se Can) characterized as "tic-tic-tic" (Christman, 1959), for the Spotted Salamander (*Ambystoma maculatum*) (e US, se Can) (Wyman and Thrall, 1972), and California Newt (*Taricha torosa*) (Davis and Brattstrom, 1975). The Northwestern Salamander (*Ambystoma gracile*) (w N Am) produces a "tic" sound, constant in character, when engaging in aggressive or defensive behavior (Licht, 1973).

Anurans

Method of Sound Production

A few anuran species appear to be voiceless, but most produce sounds usually made by forcing air from their lungs over vocal cords in the larynx and into a sac or sacs in the throat region, which modify and amplify the sound. The air enters the vocal sac(s) through an opening on each side of the mouth cavity (see fig. 8.3). The vocal sac or sacs swell out balloonlike when distended with air (Fig. 10.1). Depending upon the nature of the call, the air may be moved steadily forward from the lungs by contraction of muscles of the body wall, or a smaller quantity may be propelled back and forth through the larynx with the aid of contractions of the throat and/or vocal sac. The vibrating inflated sac, with its resonant qualities, aids transfer of sound energy from the animal to the atmosphere, and sometimes to water and/or the ground. Some anurans have internal vocal sacs. Fire-bellied toads (*Bombina*) (Eur to China) are unusual in producing their vocalization on inspiration (Lörcher, 1969). When deflated, the vocal sac or sacs of many anurans are pleated and dark-colored (fig. 10.1D). This characteristic, along with darkened toe pads (see fig. 17.1F), aids an observer in distinguishing sex.

In the pipid frogs (African Clawed Frog and relatives), vocal cords are absent. Their voice box contains a pair of longitudinal bony rods that articulate anteriorly by means of cartilaginous disks. The rods can be moved by muscu-

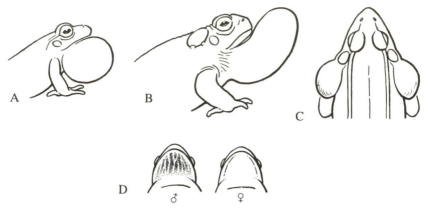

Fig. 10.1 Distended vocal sacs of anurans, showing variation in shape and position. (A) Pacific Treefrog (*Pseudacris regilla*) (w N Am). (B) Great Plains Toad (*Bufo cognatus*) (cen US, Mex). (C) Northern Leopard Frog (*Rana pipiens*) (N Am). (D) Throat region of male and female Pacific Treefrog, showing differences in coloration associated with the vocal sac in the male, which when deflated is dark colored.

lar contraction. The metallic clicking sounds made by these frogs are presumed to result from the articular joint opening and the disks slipping by one another (Rabb, 1960).

Sound production in anurans is discussed at length by Gans (1973). See Wells (1977b), Emerson and Inger (1992), and Emerson and Berrigan (1993) for information on voiceless species.

Voice Intensity, Volume, and Directionality

There is great variation in vocal intensity. In some species voice is geared for a maximum species hearing range of only a few yards, whereas in others voice is used to attract other individuals from afar. In a study of Australian frogs, Loftus-Hills and Littlejohn (1971) estimated maximum effective sound propagation distances for two species as 4 meters and 100 meters. Many species, such as the spadefoot toads (*Scaphiopus*) (N Am) and others, with very loud voices, probably hear one another over distances measured in kilometers. Martof (1953a) reports that the advertisement calls of Green Frogs (*Rana clamitans*) could be heard at a distance of more than a half mile. Species such as spadefoots that breed at temporary sites that often vary in location (depending on the vagaries of rainfall), in particular require a long-distance communication system (see also Gerhardt and Klump, 1988—Barking Treefrog).

In some loud-voiced species, sound pressure levels may be around 90 to 120 decibels (dB) (measured at 25 cm from source) (Passmore, 1981) and males may expend much energy in sending such intense signals. Since many anurans call from ground level, a strong voice helps to overcome the effect of attenuation of sound caused by the ground surface. It is not surprising then to find that the trunk muscles of male anurans, which propel air from the lungs during vocalizations, are specialized for this purpose and differ in their aerobic capacity from that of females (Given, 1990). For example, Taigen et al. (1985) found that the trunk muscles in male Spring Peepers (*Pseudacris crucifer*) accounted for 15% of total body mass in contrast with 3% in females. Citrate synthase (CS) activity, indicative of oxidative capacity, was six times that of leg muscle and seventeen times the CS activity in female trunk muscle.

Taigen and Wells (1985) note that in the Gray Treefrog (*Hyla versicolor*) (e US) advertisement calling is among the most energetically expensive activities regularly undertaken by any anuran and, indeed, is the most demanding yet measured in an ectothermic (see chapter 11) vertebrate. The tiny (1 to 2.5 g) Central American frog (*Physalaemus pustulosus*) (Mex to Colombia and Venezuela), when calling, has been recorded as consuming oxygen at a rate of about seven times that of individuals at rest in the daytime, and four times that of noncalling frogs at night. Energy expenditure goes up with rate of calling (Bucher et al., 1980). The energy cost of vocalization has also been noted in weight loss of the small (< 38 mm), actively calling territorial males of the Red-groined Toadlet (*Uperoleia rugosa*) (se Aus) (Robertson, 1986). In some species, calling may be persistent and prolonged. The Marsupial Frog (*Gastrotheca marsupiata*), a Neotropical species, has been recorded as producing about 250 advertisement calls an hour (about 4 per minute) during the entire night (Sinsch, 1988). Ovaska and Hunte (1992) found that *Eleutherodactylus johnstonei* (Barbados, W. Indies) called for no more than 30 minutes at a time, after which they left their calling site to forage or remain immobile, perhaps to rest.

At close range, voice intensity may be involved in spacing of males within a chorus. Fellers (1979a) observed that male Gray Treefrogs (*Hyla versicolor*) (e US) have a threshold intensity above which one male will not tolerate another's mating call and will move away or stop calling. Brenowitz et al. (1984) found that Spring Peeper (*Pseudacris crucifer*) males tended to stay just within the auditory threshold of one another, thus maximizing the distance between males while, at the same time, ensuring they remained within the chorus.

Bullfrogs (*Rana catesbeiana*) recognize calls of neighboring frogs from those of strangers and can detect the sound-source direction of their neighbor's call. They respond with aggressive behavior to a stranger that has replaced a familiar neighbor. Such behavior prevents unnecessary conflicts between neighbors once a territorial boundary has been established (Davis, 1987) (see also chapter 15).

In addition to volume and intensity, a variety of factors can affect sound propagation and projection such as perch height, timber and pitch, sound frequency, reflective surfaces, and environmental impediments to sound radiation (density of plant growth, rocks, etc.). Air currents and reverberations caused by reflective surfaces, can distort vocalizations. Some species vocalize under water. This has been observed, through hydrophone recordings, in the Red-legged (*Rana aurora*) and Foothill Yellow-legged (*R. boylii*) Frogs (w N Am) and in the Surinam Toad (*Pipa pipa*) (S Am).

To what extent do male anurans position themselves to achieve directionality of their calls? Some species produce a directional sound field and might benefit by "aiming" their calls. In many species, however, the sound field is nondirectional. Might some frogs use reflective surfaces such as large leaves, rocks, and logs to direct their calls? In their study of the Puerto Rican Coqui (*Eleutherodactylus coqui*), Narins and Hurley (1982) found eleven of fourteen males had nondirectional sound radiation patterns, whereas in three the sounds were directional.

Whether male anurans choose calling sites because of their acoustic properties has not yet been shown convincingly, but certainly physical characteristics of such sites differ and affect sound propagation and directionality (see Wells and Schwartz, 1982).

The "Advertisement" Call

FUNCTION AND CHARACTERISTICS

A basic function of voice in anurans is to bring the sexes together for mating, and it is the vocalization of males that usually achieves this goal. Males produce a distinctive "advertisement call" (Wells, 1977b) that serves to identify the species, sex, reproductive state, and location of the individual and often has the dual function of establishing territories and attracting females. Since it is a species identification signal, it is not surprising to find that the ears of both sexes are usually "tuned" to recognize it. The advertisement call may be considered a form of long-range courtship. Because the call is broadcast at large and is ordinarily not directed exclusively toward one sex or the other, it is appropriate to refer to it as an advertisement call rather than a mating or sex call, as has been customary in the past.

As noted above, an advertisement call may have separate components, one directed primarily toward males, the other toward females. An example is the diphasic (two-parted) "co-qui" call of the Puerto Rican Coqui. The "co" portion apparently is important in maintaining spacing among neighboring males, whereas the "qui" note attracts females (Narins and Capranica, 1976; Capranica, 1977). Narins (1976) observed that if one male approached to within about 20 inches (50 cm) of another calling male, the latter dropped the "qui" note and engaged the intruder in a bout of "co" notes. This was followed by biting and butting attacks if the intruder did not retreat. Females, when given a choice between the two notes broadcast over a speaker, prefer the "qui" note and moved in its direction. The difference in sexual response is reflected in the excitability of their primary auditory neurons.

Stewart and Rand (1991) have added further details on Coqui vocalizations. Both sexes produce aggressive calls in antagonistic interactions. These are multinote calls, with those of the female being softer and shorter than those of the male. The aggressive call of the male differs from the two-noted "co-qui" advertisement call in having a rapid succession of "qui" notes with more "notes" added in defense of retreats and still more in defense of nests (up to thirty-seven).

When an intruding male comes close, the Pacific Treefrog (*Pseudacris regilla*) (w US, sw Can) changes from a two-parted (diphasic) to a monophasic "encounter" call, and the Spring Peeper (*Pseudacris crucifer*) (e US), named for its "peeping" advertisement call, emits a "trill" (Rosen and Lemon, 1974).

The European Green Treefrog (*Hyla arborea*) (Eur e to Caucasus, nw Afr), which closely resembles the Pacific Treefrog, also gives aggressive calls when "challenging" another calling male (Márquez-M. de Orense and Tejedo-Madueño, 1990). On several occasions a calling male was seen to displace a rival simply by walking toward him to within 12–16 inches (30–40 cm).

In the tiny African Leaf-folding Frog (*Afrixalis delicatus*) (15–22 mm SV), a diphasic species (a "trill" call for females and a "zip" for males), the frequency of male and female call components may shift with chorus size and arrival of females. The larger the chorus (thus heightened male interactions), the greater the frequency of male-directed "zip" calls. The presence of a female resulted in a higher proportion of female-attracting trills (Backwell, 1988). Probably many advertisement calls, both diphasic and monophasic, serve such dual functions.

DIFFERENCES IN ADVERTISEMENT CALLS AND THE
PROBLEM OF ACOUSTICAL INTERFERENCE

Because favorable amphibian breeding sites are often quite limited, many individuals of a number of different species may use the same restricted area, and a premium is placed on the evolution of mechanisms for avoiding acoustical interference that might cause jamming or swamping out of their calls. Species have diverged in the sound and temporal characteristics of their calls (in pitch, timber, pulse frequency, duration, cadence, volume, etc.), in their spatial separation at breeding sites (Ptacek, 1992), in their time of spawning, and in other ways (see also Etges, 1987; Penna and Veloso, 1990). Vocal divergence helps to ensure species recognition and reduces the chances for mismatings between closely related species and wasted reproductive effort or a breakdown (through interbreeding) in their established, usually well-adapted genetic systems. Thus the advertisement call is an important premating isolating mechanism (see Duellman and Pyles, 1983).

It is of interest in this connection that in some species (particularly closely related ones) with similar voices, vocal differences are greatest in areas where they coexist (are in sympatry) (Blair, 1955, 1974; Littlejohn, 1965a,b; Ball and Jameson, 1966; Fouquette, 1975; Duellman and Pyles, 1983). Examples are the Narrow-mouthed Toads (*Gastrophryne carolinensis* and *G. olivacea*) (se and cen US, s US, Mex), Cricket Frogs (*Acris gryllus* and *A. crepitans*) (se US, se and cen US), and Chorus Frogs (*Pseudacris nigrita* and *P. triseriata feriarum*) (both se US). In the Narrow-mouthed Toads call duration and pulse rates are more distinctive in sympatry; in the Cricket Frogs there is a difference in pulse rate of such magnitude that the species ranges of variation are not known to overlap (Littlejohn, 1977); and in the Chorus Frogs pulse rate and pulse number appear to be critical in premating reproductive isolation. Pulse repetition rate or frequency has been shown to be crucial for call discrimination in some species (Loftus-Hills and Littlejohn, 1971).

GEOGRAPHIC VARIATION IN ADVERTISEMENT CALLS: "DIALECTS"

Often in a widely ranging species or those with a spotty distribution, the advertisement call varies from place to place. Such shifts in vocal characteristics or "dialects" sometimes correspond to subspecies distributions based on color or morphology, a situation comparable to that found in birds. A variety of selective factors is probably involved in the production of dialects; however, sometimes they seem to be simply the side effect of geographic variation in size. Nevo and Schneider (1975) noted that variation in the fundamental frequency (pitch) of the mating call in Old World Green Toads (*Bufo viridis*) (Eur to w China, n Afr) was an incidental by-product of adaptation of body size to environmental humidity. Israel Green Toads, living in a relatively dry environment, are larger, and the fundamental frequency of their call is distinctly lower than that of the smaller central European green toads that live in more humid environments. In other respects the voices are almost identical.

The hearing of the females in some vocally divergent species populations is closely coupled with the local dialect, and they are indifferent to the calls of males with a different dialect. Female Cricket Frogs (*Acris crepitans*) from New Jersey and South Dakota (different subspecies) chose the sounds of the males from their respective areas when offered a choice. Males from New Jersey have higher pitched voices (energy peak at around 3500 Hz) than those from South Dakota (peak at around 2900 Hz).

Two types of medullary cells have been identified (Capranica et al., 1973; Capranica, 1977)—one sensitive to high-frequency tones and the other to low-frequency tones. The high-frequency cells presumably receive input from the basilar papilla (BP) and the low-frequency ones from the amphibian papilla (AP). Such a dichotomy is probably widespread among anurans (Loftus-Hills and Johnstone, 1970). The BP plays the principal role in detecting mating calls in the Cricket Frog (*Acris crepitans*), since there are no lower frequency elements in the call that would excite the AP. Capranica found that the frequency sensitivity of the BP varied over the geographic range of the species, matching the spectral peak of local dialects. Frequency sensitivity of the cells in the auditory nucleus in the medulla of the brain in frogs from New Jersey was most pronounced at around 3500–3550 Hz, whereas in frogs from South Dakota it was around 2900 Hz. A neural basis for the behavioral differences in these frogs has thus been established. Females not only recognize the voices of males of their own species but they also discriminate between the calls of males with different dialects.

Chorus Formation and Pairing

In a typical anuran breeding sequence, males of a given species congregate in large numbers at the breeding site and begin broadcasting their advertisement calls. First arrivals attract other males by their calls. Later, females come to the male chorus, often intermittently over a sometimes protracted period. Males often alternate their calls when near one another, particularly in those species that have a prolonged breeding period and in which males are territorial. This results in accentuating the distinctiveness of each individual's call so that it is not lost in the din of other voices and aids the process of pairing, usually initiated by the females. Such frog choruses thus often have a syncopated quality. If the sounds associated with a breeding assemblage are not overly complex, the reproductively "ripe" female may be able to respond to the voice of a male of her choice and move in his direction, often ignoring other callers enroute. She may promptly be seen by him, or she touches him and amplexus may immediately occur. On the other hand, she may spend some time within areas occupied by several different males, perhaps assessing the males and the quality of their territories before mating. The latter seems to be true in the Green Frog (*Rana clamitans*) (Wells, 1977a).

In some species males seem to require considerable physical contact by the females before they are aroused. Márquez-M. de Orense and Tejedo-Madueño (1990) noted that European Green Treefrog (*Hyla arborea*) (Eur to Caucasus, nw Afr) females swam toward calling males and literally "walked over" them before the males reacted to their presence.

THE ROLE OF VOICE IN MATE SELECTION

The tendency for males to call in groups, with the same male (the "chorus master") usually initiating a calling sequence, may aid females in selecting a mate. Such groups may contain two, three, or more individuals, with the timing of their calls reflecting a call peck order, with the chorus master often the dominant individual. Individual differences in voice among the members of a group often are recognizable by humans (see Mauger, 1989) and may be related to size, age, vigor, and perhaps other factors. Male Spring Peepers (*Pseudacris crucifer*), for example, frequently form duets and trios giving their calls alternately and at different pitches (Goin, 1949). Choruses of the Pacific Treefrog (*Pseudacris regilla*) often contain subgroups made up of duets, trios, and quartets. Within the subgroups the members typically call in a repetitive sequence and the same frog usually initiates calling. Chorus leaders and calling hierarchies have been observed in other species as well (Wickler and Seibt, 1974).

In prolonged breeders (see chapter 17), vocal characteristics seem to be of special importance in mate selection by females. As noted, voice may indicate size, vigor, and peck-order position among males. Chorus masters are often the larger, older, and often the more vigorous individuals. Their voices may be louder, deeper, or in other ways reflect their status. Since they often initiate choruses, their voices stand out from the rest. However a cautionary note is in order: Halliday and Verrell (1988) argue that female choice that favors larger males may not, as has frequently been suggested, mean that females invariably mate with older males, but with males that have shown rapid juvenile growth. Although there is a positive relationship between age and body size in amphibians, it is usually quite weak. There is much variability in body size at any given age.

In the Wood Frog (*Rana sylvatica*), the quantity of sperm produced, and thus expected fertilization success, was found to be related to body weight. Thus in this species the larger males appear to have a greater ability to produce offspring than the smaller ones (Smith-Gill and Berven, 1980). In experiments with the Southern Spadefoot Toad (*Spea multiplicata*) (sw US, Mex) in New Mexico, Woodward (1986) obtained evidence that the larger males transmit genes that enhance juvenile growth, and Mitchell (1990), in a field study in New Mexico of the Woodhouse Toad (*Bufo woodhousei*), found that the larger males produced offspring that were 10% heavier at transformation than those sired by small males.

Vocalizations vary in pulse rate, length, cadence, loudness, and dominant frequency, depending on the species. There are sometimes species differences in the particular element(s) among this suite of characteristics to which females respond. In a study conducted by Wagner (1989) on Blanchard Cricket Frog (*Acris crepitans blanchardi*) (cen and e US), dominant frequency was the only vocal characteristic that consistently correlated with male snout-vent length. The larger males tended to have the lower-pitched voices. In a later study, Wagner (1992) found that males may give a deceptive signal of their size by lowering the dominant frequency of their calls, thereby repelling other males in contests over calling sites. However, he concluded that the primary function of a change in call frequency was to signal fighting ability, not to bluff size. In the Woodhouse Toad (*Bufo woodhousei*) (from e US), pulse rate was the only characteristic that varied predictably with body size and appeared to be the means whereby females were able to select the largest males as mates (Fairchild and Kandel, 1980). Dominant males, when older, have genetic traits that have stood the test of time.

That there are, indeed, measurable differences in male vocal characteristics within a species has been shown by a number of studies (Gerhardt, 1975; Haas, 1976; Licht, 1976; Wilbur et al., 1978), and females, in both the laboratory and field, have been observed to ignore all callers but the male of their choice. Passmore (1981), however, points to a possible trap in interpretation. Since calling males of some species produce an asymmetrical, directional sound field, rather than one that extends in all directions, the nature of the sound field and the orientation of the callers must be considered in assessing female behavior. A female may not have entered the asymmetrical sound field of males that were bypassed. Rather than selecting a particular mate, she may simply be responding to the loudest call she perceives.

OTHER FACTORS IN MATE SELECTION

Voice and size, as often indicated by voice, however, may not always be the most important factors in pairing and mating success. Indeed, voice may not always be a reliable indicator of size (Sullivan, 1984; Asquith and Altig, 1990). In the American Toad (e US, se Can) mating success appears to be independent of size (Kruse, 1981). Licht (1976) speculates that females of this species select a mate of a size most effective for successful amplexus. Females have been seen to shake off males that seemed to be either too large or too small. Size was not found to be important in male mating success in Painted Reed Frogs (*Hyperolius marmoratus*) (s Afr) (Dyson et al., 1992).

In the Gray Treefrog (*Hyla versicolor*) (e US), perch site appears to be critical (Fellers, 1979b). The quality of a male's territory may also be more important than his voice. Some tropical Central American Poison-Arrow Frogs (*Dendrobates*) establish large territories on the ground and call from usually elevated perches on logs and leaves. Females seek suitable egg-laying sites on the ground where they deposit their eggs in areas of moist soil. Selection of their mate appears to depend primarily on the quality of his territory. In the Blacksmith Treefrog (*Hyla faber*) of the Neotropics, males build shallow mud basins along the edges of streams to serve as nurseries for developing eggs and larvae. They call from the vicinity of the nests. Gravid females move along the stream borders and inspect the nests, sometimes spending as long as 15 minutes in a nest examining its edge, bottom, and general characteristics. During amplexus the pair may renovate the nest (Martins and Haddad, 1988). Females evidently choose their mate on the basis of the quality of his nest, rather than the sound of his voice (Wells, 1977b).

In experiments with vocalizations of male Painted Reed Frogs (Afr), an arboreal species, Backwell and Passmore (1990) obtained evidence that females favored calls (emitted from loudspeakers) associated with suitable perches, allowing them an elevated approach to the site of the calling male.

In a study of glass frogs (*Hyalinobatrachium fleischmanni*) (Mex to Ecuador) and *Centrolene prosoblepon* (cen to n S Am) in Costa Rica, Jacobson (1985) found that the number of nights a male occupied a given site seems to be the important factor in male mating success, rather than size, call pitch, or duration.

In "explosive" opportunistic breeders (see chapter 17), those that congregate quickly, often at temporary and sometimes short-lived and unpredictable breeding sites, vocalizations may be a din of voices and syncopation of calls absent or obscure. In such species females may perhaps exercise little or no choice in mate selection. Although Woodward (1982b) found that males in amplexus averaged slightly larger size than nonamplexing males in some anuran populations in New Mexico, he had no evidence that this resulted from female choice. The species in question, Couch Spadefoot (*Scaphiopus couchii*), Southern Spadefoot (*Spea multiplicata*), and Woodhouse Toad (*Bufo woodhousei*) (at times), are high-density explosive breeders. Males are considered to be nonterritorial and they engage in "scramble competition" for females. There are frequent male-male interactions involving wrestling bouts. These male interactions are as likely to result in a greater mating success of the larger males as is female choice.

The Costa Rican Treefrog (*Hyla pseudopuma*) (Costa Rica, w Panama) is an explosive breeder in ephemeral ponds following heavy rains. Crump and Townsend (1990) found that mating was random with respect to body size in the populations they studied, but cautioned that less dense populations with different sex ratios, and more prolonged favorable breeding conditions, might yield a nonrandom result.

The foregoing examples indicate that attempts at generalizations concerning the factors involved in anuran mate selection must be made with caution. Although there is considerable evidence for nonrandom mating based on body size and associated vocal characteristics of males, this evidence must be considered in the light of variation among species and among and within populations. Future studies should focus on the structural and behavioral characteristics of species populations in a variety of locations and under varied habitat conditions.

Vocalizations at Short Range: Courtship Calls

As another individual approaches, the call of male anurans may be modified. With females, which usually approach silently, a form of short-range vocal courtship may be employed. The call rate or intensity may change, special courtship calls may be given, or tactile or visual signals may be employed, which aid the female in finding individual males. Often short-range courtship calls are softer than advertisement calls, perhaps enabling a male to attract a female without eliciting similar courtship calls from competing males (Wells, 1976a).

Vocal Responses to Approaching Males

If an approaching individual vocalizes and is identified as a male, a number of possible responses may occur (Wells and Greer, 1981). If far away, the male may time his calls to avoid overlap with the intruder. With closer approach, he may increase his repetition rate or number of notes per call, apparently attempting to outsignal the intruder. With still closer approach, encounter calls (aggressive notes) (Allan, 1973; Robertson, 1986; Wells, 1989; Wagner, 1989) may be given, with the increasing sound pressure level of the intruder's voice perhaps acting as the trigger. Aggressive notes may be escalated if the intruder gives aggressive notes, and finally any female-attracting components of the call may be abandoned in favor of aggressive notes if the intruder comes very close.

In studies to date, emphasis has been placed on male vocalizations and their role in courtship and aggressive behavior. Far less attention has been given to vocalizations of females. Females of a number of anuran species, including the Bullfrog (*Rana catesbeiana*) (N Am) and Edible Frog (*R. esculenta*) (Eur), are known to give aggressive calls. Female Puerto Rico Coquies (*Eleuthero-dactylus coqui*) do so in defense of their retreats against conspecifics, both male and female (see chapter 15). Female Bullfrogs may give soft calls during reproductive chorusing, and female Carpenter Frogs (*R. virgatipes*) (e US) a "chirp" during courtship (Given, 1987). Females of the common Bornean Frog (*R. blythi*) gave a low, soft tonal call that seems to signal to the male an invitation to amplexus. It is given when the pair is at the male-constructed shallow gravel nest in a stream where the partners may work seemingly to "finish" a nest begun by the male. The male, who lacks an advertisement call, sometimes responds with the same soft call (Emerson, 1992).

In future studies, more attention should be given to the voices of females, and their role in anuran communication.

Vocalizations and Predation

Vocalizations may cease or be modified under threat of predation. For example, the Central American Narrow-mouthed Toad (*Physalaemus pustulosus*) is preyed upon by the Fringe-lipped Bat (*Trachops cirrhosus*) which detects the frogs by sound and sight as they call along pond and stream banks (Tuttle and

Ryan, 1981). The more complex calls of the frogs, which are most attractive to females, are also more attractive to their bat predator, which may, in part, explain why the frogs do not maximize their use of complex calls (Ryan et al., 1982).

Da Silva Nunes (1988a) observed that males of *Smilisca sila* (cen Am), under moonlight in the field when the frogs could see their bat predators, called more frequently and longer, used more complex calls, and were less likely to call from under leaves than on moonless nights. Males also called more frequently at dusk on moonless nights than on moonlit nights.

The sexual calling of explosive breeders (see chapter 17) that engage in "scramble competition" for females typically produces a cacophony of sound because of the overlapping of the calls of individual males. Predators hunting by sound presumably have greater difficulty in singling out calling individuals for attack in such choruses compared to those in which calls are syncopated (Zimmerman and Bogart, 1988). Another advantage of explosive breeding, particularly in environments where predators are numerous, is the short time the frogs are exposed to predators compared to prolonged breeders.

Other Vocalizations

Anuran vocalizations are not limited to the advertisement call with its sexual and territorial components. Other sounds are produced: release calls, given primarily by females to thwart or terminate amplexus; amplexus calls, faint sounds emitted by males of some species during amplexus (Price and Meyer, 1979); reciprocal calls given by females in response to the advertisement call of the male, allowing a pair to converge through alternation of their vocalizations and orientation on each other's voices, as in pipid and dendrobatid frogs (Littlejohn, 1977); rain calls given with a rise in humidity; and distress or fright calls produced when a frog is threatened, injured, or attacked. Tyler (1989) reports the "fright" call given in the presence of a dog or cat, which responded by watching the frog closely, sometimes pawing it and so eliciting "another burst of screams." Schuett and Gillingham (1990) report that the playback in the field of the screams of the Northern Leopard Frog (*Rana pipiens*) attracted a variety of predators. Perhaps during disputes among predators over who shall have the prey, the prey's chances of escape are increased. Screams may also startle predators into loosening their grip. All vocalizations except the distress call are given with the mouth, and usually the nostrils, tightly closed.

11

Temperature Characteristics

AMPHIBIANS, like nearly all animals other than the birds and mammals, are ectotherms. They have little metabolic control of their body temperature and derive their temperature chiefly from their surroundings—air, water, substrate, and, in some species, through direct exposure to the sun. The term "ectotherm" means temperature from the outside, in contrast to "endotherm," temperature generated and controlled from within, as in "warm-blooded" birds and mammals. Amphibians are able, however, to exercise some thermal control, often within rather broad limits, by their behavior and physiological mechanisms.

Behavioral temperature control involves movements from place to place within the temperature mosaic of the environment, and sometimes the positioning of the body to increase or reduce exposure of surfaces to environmental temperature sources. Daily movements to adjust body temperature may be frequent, few, or absent, depending on the thermal sensitivity of the species, stage of life, competing physiological demands (such as food or moisture requirements), and other factors.

The rate at which an amphibian warms and cools and the temperature at which its own temperature stabilizes (equilibrates) upon reaching a constant thermal environment depends on a variety of factors—in particular, the animal's size (or mass), behavior, and physiological controls. Other things being equal, a large amphibian will warm and cool more slowly than a small one because of differences in the surface-mass ratio. The amount of basking and exposure of body surfaces to temperature sources through body and limb-positioning can also play a part. Basking frogs often have a portion of their body in contact with water or a moist surface and may vary the amount of exposure. Physiological mechanisms include control of the rate and amount of evaporative water loss from the skin, important in lowering body temperature; skin color changes affecting the absorption and reflectance of solar radiation; and perhaps also cardiovascular effects that may influence the rate of heat gain and loss through changes in the blood flow to the skin. The latter, however, has been little studied.

Wygoda (1989) studied (in Louisiana) rates of temperature change in frogs, relating it to levels of evaporative water loss (EWL). He subjected similarly sized Green Treefrogs (*Hyla cinerea*) (se US) and Southern Leopard Frogs (*Rana utricularia sphenocephala*) to step changes in environmental temperature from 15° to 30°C. Whereas starting temperatures of the frogs were the same (15°C), equilibration body temperatures were significantly higher in the Green Treefrog (26.6°C) than in the Southern Leopard Frog (18.1°C) after about half an hour in an environment of 30°C. Rates of temperature change were 2.5 times higher in the former and can be explained by reduced evaporative heat loss from the skin. The Green Treefrog is an arboreal species. In the aerial locations of its habitat it is more subject to desiccation than is the ground-dwelling Leopard Frog. It thus appears to be more conservative in spending body water in thermoregulation than the Leopard Frog. Reduced evaporative water loss in the Green Treefrog and other arboreal frogs that derive their body temperature from exposure to the sun appears to be an adaptation that permits such frogs to spend considerable periods of time aloft (see Wygoda and Williams, 1991).

Shoemaker et al. (1989) have also shown a relationship between body temperature levels and EWL in the arboreal frogs *Chiromantis* and *Phyllomedusa* (see chapter 12). These frogs generally have low EWL levels. Extent of EWL control was related to body water levels. When well hydrated, these frogs, in a warm environment, could maintain their body temperature at about 40°C. They did so by employing EWL rather than moving away from the high ambient temperature. However, when deprived of water they maintained a lower body temperature and seldom employed evaporative cooling.

Skin color changes can affect the absorption of solar radiation. Amphibians usually darken when cold and become lighter when warm, but the color observed by humans may not always indicate accurately spectral absorption. For example, in the Striped Chorus Frog (*Pseudacris triserata*), green individuals actually absorb more light than brown ones (to human eyes, the darker frogs) (Hoppe, 1979). In general, however, darker skin (to human eyes) absorbs more solar radiation than lighter skin.

The Kenyan Reed Frog (*Hyperolius viridiflavus*) (cen Afr), a species of African savannas, during the long dry season deposits large amounts of nitrogenous wastes (chiefly in the form of platelets of guanine) in the skin iridophores which greatly increase in number. During the heat of the day, the reflective waste pigment is dispersed, increasing skin reflectance and reducing heat gain. Since the frogs are ureotelic (see chapter 12)—eliminating their nitrogenous wastes in the form of urea which is water soluble—such skin deposition of metabolic wastes also conserves water. In experiments, froglets have tolerated over thirty-five days of dryness (see Schmuck et al., 1988, and Kobelt and Linsenmair, 1992).

Certain Neotropical leaf-sitting glass frogs (*Centrolenella*) (Mex to Argentina) and hylid treefrogs, Morelet Frog (*Agalychnis moreletii*) (cen Am) and the Mexican Giant Treefrog (*Pachymedusa dacnicolor*) (Mex), green in color, reflect light in the near infrared which may play a part in thermoregulation (Schwalm et al., 1977).

Tracy et al. (1992) compared rates of heating and cooling in a reptile and a frog—the Common Chuckwalla (*Sauromalus obesus*) and Northern Leopard Frog (*Rana pipiens*)—immersed in water. The former warmed 32% faster than it cooled, a ratio of heating and cooling rates similar to that found in many species of lizards, but the frog displayed no control over heating and cooling rates. Regulation of blood flow to the skin and appendages appears to be the mechanism involved in controlling such rates in lizards. Differences in body shape, surface areas through which heat can spread, blood flow control to the skin, and/or other factors may account for the differences noted between the two species. However, the role of cardiovascular changes in influencing rates of warming and cooling requires more study.

Basking

Basking is often important in body temperature regulation in diurnal ecto-therms. However, there has been some controversy over the extent to which amphibians thermoregulate by this means. It is now clear that some do. Brattstrom (1963) observed that the Cascades Frog (*Rana cascadae*) (nw US), Northern Leopard Frog (*R. pipiens*) (s Can, n and cen US), and Green Frog (*R. clamitans*) (e US, se Can) were able to maintain their body temperatures above their surroundings by exposing themselves to the sun. Lethal temperature levels were avoided by evaporation of water from their skins, the rate of which these frogs can evidently regulate.

Bradford (1984) noted that the Mountain Yellow-legged Frog (*R. muscosa*), a diurnal high-mountain species in California, regularly elevated its body temperature by basking, as does the Andean Toad (*Bufo spinulosus*), which on clear days elevated its core body temperature up to 15°C above air temperature in the shade and reached a maximum of 32°C. At air temperatures in the sun exceeding 29°C, this toad maintained its body temperature below 32°C by evaporative cooling (Sinsch, 1989).

Lillywhite (1970, 1971a, 1974) demonstrated thermoregulation in the Bull-frog (*Rana catesbeiana*), including basking and posturing to control the flux of heat to and from its body. When heat stressed, Bullfrogs sat increasingly more erect and finally held the body off the ground. They lay prostrate when it was cool. Diurnal juvenile Western Toads (*Bufo boreas*) (w N Am) elevated their temperature by basking beneath incandescent lamps in a photothermal gradient (Lillywhite et al., 1972).

Recently metamorphosed anurans seem especially prone to expose themselves to the sun when there is adequate soil moisture or opportunity to enter water to make up water losses entailed in keeping the skin moist. Some young toads (*Bufo*) and toad tadpoles are notably diurnal compared with the adults.

They elevate their body temperature by basking and thereby accelerate feeding, digestion, growth, and, in transformed individuals, deposition of fat prior to winter dormancy (see Seymour, 1972, on juvenile Green Toads [*Bufo debilis*] [sw US, Mex], and Brattstrom, 1979). Freed (1980) has observed an increase in growth rates of juvenile Green Treefrogs (*Hyla cinerea*) (se US) associated with random basking.

Temperature Preferences

Most amphibians are capable of activity over a fairly broad range of temperatures between their lethal extremes and in general do not have as narrow thermal limits for normal activity (feeding, breeding, etc.) as do most reptiles (fig. 11.1). There is increasing evidence, however, that many species, including their larvae (Beiswenger, 1978), have thermal "preferenda," or a range of preferred temperatures, and that they exercise considerable behavioral temperature regulation within the constraints imposed by the environment and their niche requirements. Such constraints vary greatly. Thus, in light-avoiding terrestrial salamanders that live in cool, moist environments, they may be great, but in some amphibious diurnal frogs they are far less, and the animals can more fully realize their thermoregulatory potential.

Many factors influence the choice of temperatures at any give time—species differences, age or stage of development, an individual's recent thermal experience (acclimation effects; see below), seasonal and daily shifts in preferenda, and needs that downplay thermal selection in favor of other biological drives—procuring food and shelter and regulating body water levels (Spotila, 1972).

Although one can describe the "preferred temperature" of an ectotherm under controlled conditions in a laboratory thermal gradient, the concept is of more limited usefulness in the field because of restrictions imposed by the environment. For example, despite its ability to thermoregulate, in the field the high altitude Mountain Yellow-legged Frog (*Rana muscosa*) (Cal) rarely achieves the average selected temperature that is obtained for it in a laboratory thermal gradient (Bradford, 1984).

Recent thermal experience can affect thermal preferences. In a study of the Red-backed Salamander (*Plethodon cinereus*) (ne US, se Can), animals acclimated to warm temperatures sought cooler locations in a thermal gradient than unacclimated controls, and those acclimated to cool temperatures sought warmer locations (Feder and Pough, 1975). The latter response would facilitate rapid feeding and digestion following a period of cold weather and possible starvation (Brattstrom, 1979). Bullfrog (*Rana catesbeiana*) (N Am) tadpoles at later stages of development, and especially when acclimated to high temperatures, preferred higher temperatures in gradient tests (Hutchison and Hill, 1978).

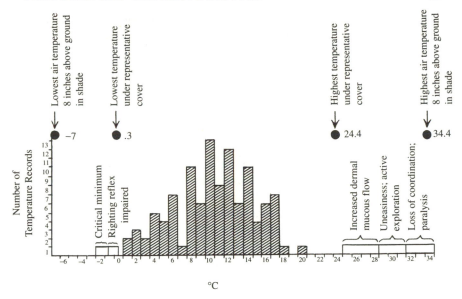

Fig. 11.1 Body temperatures (hatched bars) of adult individuals of the salamander Ensatina (*Ensatina eschscholtzii*), recorded over a 4-year period in its natural habitat in the Berkeley hills, California, shown in relation to the extreme temperatures that occurred in its microenvironment during that period. Body temperatures at which individuals are incapacitated are shown.

Some ectotherms undergo a daily shift in thermal preferences. Diurnal species may seek lower temperatures at night and nocturnal ones in the daytime. Such behavior in reptiles has been referred to as "voluntary hypothermia" (Regal, 1967) and has been regarded as a precursor to the daily depression in body temperature associated with sleep and inactivity in endotherms, the birds and mammals. It has been shown in the Mudpuppy, a completely aquatic, nocturnally active animal (Hutchison and Spriesterbach, 1986). Mudpuppies (*Necturus maculosus*) (e US, se Can), after "acclimatization" at 15° ± 1°C and placed in a thermal gradient on a daily cycle of 12 hours light to 12 hours dark, selected considerably higher temperatures (to around 6°C higher) at night, their usual time of activity.

Behavioral control of body temperature permits the amphibian, at its various stages of development, to adjust the mean of its preferred body temperature to fit its needs. By seeking somewhat higher temperatures within its preferred range, larval development and growth can be accelerated, growth of juveniles can be sped up, digestion and other physiological processes enhanced, and some diseases combated (see chapter 11). On the other hand, by seeking lower temperatures, recovery from daily or seasonal high metabolic demands can be promoted, and prolonged periods of deprivation and unfavorable environmental conditions, tolerated. Acclimation and acclimatization shifts in temperature preferences (discussed below) may also aid these processes.

Tolerance of Temperature Extremes

Most amphibians cannot tolerate temperatures above about 100°–110°F (38°–43°C), and some cold-water species, such as torrent salamanders (*Rhyacotriton*) (nw US), may die in a state of heat rigor at temperatures as low as 83°F (28°C). However, many species can tolerate temperatures at or slightly below freezing for varying lengths of time. Anurans as a group have higher operating and tolerance temperatures than salamanders. Body temperatures recorded in anurans ranged from 38° to 96°, mean 81°F (3°–36°, mean 27°C) and in salamanders from 28° to 80°, mean 67°F (2°–27°, mean 19°C) (Brattstrom, 1970; see also Roth, 1987).

The senior author found an Ensatina (*Ensatina eschscholtzii*) (w US, sw Can) crawling slowly across a paved road during a sleet storm. Its cloacal temperature was 1°C. Jones (1985) found an adult male Northwestern Salamander (*Ambystoma gracile*) (nw US, sw Can) crossing a road at an air temperature of 1°C, north of Carson, Skamania County, Washington. High Sierran Yosemite Toads (*Bufo canorus*) (Cal) sometimes "tiptoe" across snow fields to reach their breeding sites, their bodies held well above the snow surface. In stream-bottom hibernators in cold environments, such as the Northern Leopard Frog (*Rana pipiens*) (s Can, cen and n US) in the colder parts of its range, water temperatures at hibernal sites may range from 0.5° to 2.1°C (Cunjak, 1986). Although torpid, the frogs were capable of swimming when disturbed. On the warm side of temperature tolerance, the African Foam-Nest frog (*Chiromantis*) accepts a body temperature of around 40°C in a thermal gradient (Shoemaker et al., 1989).

In experimental studies with ectotherms, useful indicators of temperature tolerance are the "critical thermal maximum" (CTMax) and the "critical thermal minimum" (CTMin), the upper and lower temperature extremes that incapacitate the animal. When an amphibian reaches its upper or lower limit of thermal tolerance, it loses coordination and can no longer right itself; at the CTMax, it ultimately becomes paralyzed and, if exposure is prolonged, it dies in a state of heat rigor. It will usually quickly recover, however, if, following the onset of rigor, it is cooled promptly. However, in determining the onset of the CTMax, the amount of activity that precedes loss of the righting response must be considered, because fatigue can affect such behavior (Burke and Pough, 1976). These critical thermal extremes are, in effect, lethal temperatures should the animal be unable to escape from the adverse temperatures.

The CTMax usually can be determined more precisely than the CTMin, because amphibians are generally less tolerant of high than of low temperatures and their behavior is usually unambiguous when the CTMax is reached. Movements become jerky, muscles twitch, and the mouth often gapes. In many areas where amphibians occur, they probably rarely, if ever, experience CTMax temperatures in their microenvironments, whereas the threat of freezing is more common. Thus the CTMin is of particular ecological interest.

Studies of the CTMax and CTMin have revealed a correlation between these tolerance levels and temperature characteristics of the environment. Amphibians from warm environments tend to be more tolerant of high temperatures and less so of low temperatures than those from cooler areas. In those from cool environments, the reverse is true. These differences may result from long-term thermal selection of individuals best suited for such environments. The capacity for thermal acclimation and acclimatization, discussed below, may also come into play. Observations of Feder (1982) on the effect of acclimation temperature on routine metabolic rate in salamanders are of interest here. Tropical species failed to compensate, whereas all temperate-zone species that have been studied have shown significant acclimation of metabolism. Since tropical species probably have been derived from temperate zone stocks, compensatory capacity may have been lost. That tropical forms have restricted elevational distribution may be of significance (see Feder, 1978).

Differences in a critical thermal mean may correlate with the distributional range of a species, as illustrated by the Green Treefrog (*Hyla cinerea*) (se US). Layne and Romano (1985) found that the mean CTMin was significantly greater in a southern than in a northern population sample of these frogs. In general, northern forms are more cold tolerant than southern ones (Brattstrom, 1968).

Thermal Acclimation

In addition to the day-to-day thermoregulatory adjustments that may occur in a more or less stable thermal environment, amphibians, like other ectotherms, have some ability to develop resistance to thermal extremes that may result from adverse environmental conditions. Amphibians that are subjected to periods of thermal stress—heat or cold—often develop resistance or acclimate to the stressful conditions. As considered here, thermal acclimation is regarded as an adjustment to thermal stress that usually occurs over a period of minutes to days (Brattstrom, 1970). Acclimatization (discussed later) is regarded as involving seasonal adjustments to thermal changes. In laboratory tests, some species commonly acclimated in 1–3 days, and some make such adjustments within hours, displaying a daily rhythm in heat resistance (Mahoney and Hutchison, 1969; Dunlap, 1969; Pough and Wilson, 1970; and Johnson, 1972). In certain salamanders, for example, heat resistance has been observed to increase significantly from morning to afternoon in the field (Pough, 1974).

A mechanism called "temperature hardening" (Maness and Hutchison, 1980), an acute adjustment of thermal tolerance, may require only minutes to a few hours. It is a transitory increase in heat tolerance following exposure to high temperatures that, if prolonged, can be lethal. Temperature hardening has been shown in the Rio Grande Leopard Frog (*Rana berlandieri*) (s US, ne Mex) and the Red-spotted Newt (*Notophthalamus viridescens*) (e US, se Can). Within 1–2 hours of an initial exposure to the CTMax, the CTMax of these species had increased significantly above the initial level. It then decreased to the initial level within 24 hours. Hardening ability is subject to daily and seasonal influences. It provides an acute means of adjustment to extreme fluctuations in diurnal temperatures (Maness and Hutchison, 1980; see also Brattstrom and Regal, 1965).

In experimental studies, a shift in the CTMax has been used as an indicator that acclimation has occurred. In general, the CTMax rises with increasing exposure to high temperatures (Hutchison, 1961; Brattstrom, 1968; Snyder and Weathers, 1975; and Claussen, 1977) and falls with increasing exposure to low temperatures. California Newts (*Taricha torosa*), acclimated to water at 10°, 22°, and 30° for one week, differed in the length of time they could survive in water at their upper lethal temperature. The 30°C group survived the longest, the 10°C group the shortest, and the 22°C group was in between (McFarland, 1955).

The rate and range of acclimatory adjustments, as measured by CTMs, depend on the species, its physiological condition, and the temperature to which individuals are acclimated.

Thus in conducting studies on acclimation capabilities of amphibians, a number of variables that may influence results must be considered. For instance, the CTMax can be altered by body water level (dehydration), fatigue, nutritional status, light changes associated with changing day length, recent thermal exposure including daily environmental temperature changes, and season. With regard to the latter, animals obtained in spring acclimate to CTMax more quickly than those obtained in fall (Rome et al., 1992). See Rome et al. (1992) for a discussion of difficulties in achieving objectivity in application of the term "thermal acclimation."

Except for widely ranging forms such as the Western Toad (*Bufo boreas*) (w N Am) and Pacific Treefrog (*Pseudacris regilla*) (w N Am), there appears to be little geographic variation in the CTMax within a species (Brattstrom, 1968).

What are the physiological mechanisms that participate in temperature acclimation? A study conducted on the European Common Frog (*Rana temporaria*) suggests that the pineal complex may be involved. Kasbohm (1967) found a daily rhythm in oxygen consumption in this species when it was placed on a long photoperiod at a constant temperature. Animals in constant darkness, acclimated to 7°C, had a higher overall oxygen consumption than those acclimated to 23°C. Removal of the eyelike frontal organ (frontalectomy), located on top of the head behind the eyes and presumably sensory to the pineal gland, abolished the daily rhythm in animals acclimated to both temperatures. In addition, similar values in oxygen consumption were recorded from experimental frogs acclimated to 7°C and normal frogs acclimated to 23°C, indicating an inability of frontalectomized animals to adapt to the colder temperatures.

The ability of amphibians to rapidly adjust their CTMs allows them to survive periods of adverse temperatures that might, if behavioral responses failed, be lethal (Brattstrom and Lawrence, 1962). However, since amphibians usually occur in thermally buffered environments (in water or in moist places on land), they probably do not often experience such extremes in nature.

Thermal Acclimatization

Acclimatization, as we apply the word, is a long-term thermal adjustment in temperature tolerances with seasonal changes in temperature. Feder and Pough (1975) found that the Red-backed Salamander (*Plethodon cinereus*) (ne US, se Can) selected higher temperatures in summer and fall than in late spring. This may help the species to maintain activity during warm weather, prolong the period of spermatogenesis, and favor selection of warmer, protected hibernation sites with the onset of winter. Lowering of preferences may occur in winter and suggests the existence of something approaching a true state of "hibernation" that should be distinguished from short-term torpor induced by cold (Brattstrom, 1970). Such seasonal adjustments in temperature selection probably occur in many temperate-zone amphibians and may well have important bearing on many aspects of their biology.

Behaviorally Controlled Fever

Amphibians may "run a fever" by behavioral means. An average increase in the preferred body temperature in thermal gradients has been observed following injections of pathogenic bacteria or other pyrogenic agents (Reynolds and Covert, 1976; Casterlin and Reynolds, 1977; and Kluger, 1977, 1979). Such behaviorally induced fevers have also been found in reptiles and fishes. In the Edible Frog (*Rana esculenta*) (cen Eur), injected with pathogenic bacteria, *Mycobacterium xnopi* or *M. ranae*, the preferred body temperature increased from about 26° to around 31°C (Myhre et al., 1977). The elevated body temperature speeds up the defense mechanisms of the body and aids in coping with pathogens.

The mechanism underlying such fevers may involve release of prostaglandin E1 (induced by substances known as pyrogens released by pathogens), which acts upon neuronal thermoregulatory centers in the anterior hypothalamus (Hutchison and Erskin, 1981).

Coping with Freezing Temperatures

Some amphibians can tolerate varying amounts of freezing of their body fluids for varying lengths of time. They produce their own "antifreeze" by converting liver glycogen to glucose in large amounts in response to ice formation in their tissues. Like glycerol (also found in amphibians), a "cryoprotectant" used in the frozen storage of mammalian spermatozoa, and many other cryoprotectants found especially among insects, glucose acts to inhibit tissue damage caused by freezing.

Resistance to freezing has been found in the Wood Frog (*Rana sylvatica*) (ne N Am), Boreal Chorus Frog (*Pseudacris triseriata maculata*) (N Am) (MacArthur and Dandy, 1982), Gray Treefrog (*Hyla versicolor*) (e US, se Can), and Spring Peeper (*Pseudacris crucifer*) (e US, se Can) (Storey and Storey, 1987; Storey 1990). It probably exists in many other species not yet studied. Such frogs often hibernate at or near the ground surface (Schmid, 1982)—under leaves, rocks, logs, or among tree roots, and their hibernal sites, which may reach −5° to −7°C, are usually covered with snow.

The Wood Frog, under freezing conditions, tolerates freezing of its body fluids until milder weather arrives. When frozen, the body becomes stiff, the eyes opaque, and breathing and heart beat are suspended. Recovery can occur if freezing has not been too prolonged or deep and if ice crystal formation is confined to extracellular fluids. When subzero conditions arise, the frog greatly increases its blood glucose level (to some sixty times normal values) by a massive boost in the breakdown of glycogen stored in the liver.

Cold tolerance of amphibians may persist for a time after emergence from hibernation (Storey and Storey, 1987). This helps protect these animals against occasional bouts of early spring freezes.

Most studies have focused on the tolerance to freezing of anurans. However, there are a number of high altitude and latitude salamanders that also warrant attention. The Blue-spotted Salamander (*Ambystoma laterale*) (se Can, ne US) ranges north to Newfoundland and James Bay. These salamanders frequently migrate across large expanses of snow and ice, moving in great numbers at near-freezing temperatures into 1°–3°C water (Lowcock et al., 1991). Individuals frozen in drop bucket containers with excess moisture after thawing were able to walk away.

Biological Effects of Environmental Temperatures

Environmental temperatures influence many aspects of the biology of amphibians—timing of breeding, duration of the breeding season, rate of development of the eggs and larvae, and rate of growth following transformation. In general, and within limits dictated by genetic factors, cool environments delay breeding and slow development and growth, and warm environments have a reverse effect. Within a species, marked differences in timing of breeding and growth rates may be experienced at different latitudes and elevations, and on a steep mountain slope can occur within a distance of less than a mile. Even adjacent breeding sites may differ in amount of sunshine received, in the temperature of inflowing water, or in other thermal factors with consequent effects on reproductive biology.

Adaptation to local temperatures is often reflected in the thermal tolerances of both adult amphibians and their developmental stages. For example, a variety of anurans from a range of elevations studied by Brattstrom (1968) showed increasing cold tolerance in species from increasingly higher elevations. In general, embryonic temperature tolerances of northern species tend to differ from southern ones in (1) having a lower maximum and minimum temperature for normal development; (2) compensating for low temperatures by more rapid rate of development, most apparent at low temperatures; and (3) having their developmental rate less influenced by differing temperatures. In addition, northern species tend to have larger eggs (more yolk), often smaller egg complements, and their embryos reach the tadpole stage at a later stage than southern ones (Brattstrom, 1970).

In a study of CTMaxs in adult Long-toed Salamanders (*Ambystoma macrodactylum*) (nw US, sw Can) from different elevations (420, 1140, and 2470 m), Howard et al. (1983) found thermal history (as indicated by maximum water temperatures) during developmental stages at sites studied more important than elevation per se. They suggested that the CTMaxs observed in adults, which do not experience the thermal stresses of larvae, represented a holdover of thermal adaptation in the larval stage and echo adaptations to aquatic thermal histories.

In general, early stages of amphibian development are more sensitive to elevated temperature than later ones, and salamander embryos have a considerably more limited range of adaptive temperatures than anurans, suggesting that their limited geographic distribution may be due at least in part to a lack of adaptability of their embryos to high environmental temperatures (Bachmann, 1969). Different geographical races within a single species of amphibian may show significant differences in the tolerance temperatures of their larvae. For further information on the effects of temperature on developmental rates of amphibian embryos and their thermal tolerances, see Moore (1939, 1949a,b), Volpe (1953, 1957a,b), Gosner and Black (1955), Ruibal (1955, 1962a), Ballinger and McKinney (1966), Zweifel (1968, 1977), Licht (1971), Anderson (1972), McLaren and Cooley (1972), Kuramoto (1975), Brown (1967a,b, 1975a,b,c, 1976, 1977b), Hoppe (1978), and Cupp (1980).

The Pineal Complex and
Activity Rhythms

Environmental temperatures may affect physiological and perhaps behavioral aspects of the daily rhythm of activity which is influenced, if not driven, by the pineal complex in amphibians. There is mounting evidence that the pineal mechanism plays an important role in the thermoregulatory biology of both endothermal and ectothermal vertebrates, and the pineal hormone, melatonin, appears to be involved in such thermoregulatory effects. Melatonin levels in the blood increase at night, presumably due to an increase in the activity of enzymes involved in melatonin synthesis from serotonin. The light-dark cycle is thus involved in the rise and fall of melatonin levels. In ectotherms, environmental temperature may affect the light-regulated blood (plasma) melatonin rhythm. Gern et al. (1983) have found such an effect in neotenic Tiger Salamanders (*Ambystoma tigrinum*) (N Am). They observed that high night temperatures depressed plasma melatonin levels. Their findings support the view that light-dark cycles drive the rhythm in plasma melatonin and that, although temperature cannot drive this rhythm, it may modify the amount of melatonin present in the plasma of a salamander at night, and it may do so through the pineal body.

Temperature and Timing
of Reproduction

When consulting information in field guides and other published sources on the seasonal timing of amphibian reproduction, readers must keep temperature effects in mind. Spans of time during which breeding and egg and larval development can be expected to occur may be described. The actual time of these events at a given locality, however, will be influenced by local temperatures, which in turn are dictated by latitude, elevation, and climatic variation. Species differences must be considered in responses to environmental temperatures. Such differences are especially evident in the temperate zones. Different species at a given locality may emerge at different times, the more cold-tolerant ones first, followed by a progression of more heat-tolerant forms.

Some additional publications dealing with temperature characteristics of amphibians are Hutchison (1961); Warburg (1965, 1967); Dole (1967); Lee (1967); Lucas and Reynolds (1967); Licht and Brown (1967); Whittow (1970); Pearson and Bradford (1976); Casterlin and Reynolds (1978); and Feder and Burggren (1992).

12

Body Water Regulation

AMPHIBIAN skin is usually highly permeable to water. When on land, unless the air is saturated with moisture, amphibians usually lose water at a fairly rapid rate, mainly through the skin by evaporation, for they must keep the skin moist for breathing. The rate of dermal water loss in some species can be nearly fifty times that of a lizard of comparable size (Claussen, 1969). In addition, many amphibians lose some water through buccopharyngeal (see chapter 3) and lung respiration. Additional losses occur with excretion and defecation. Water losses can usually be rapidly replaced by dermal absorption from the aquatic environment or moist places on land. Water is also obtained from food. The rate and amount of absorption in a dehydrated amphibian can be dramatic in some species. A desiccated summer-collected adult Ensatina (*Ensatina eschscholtzii*) (w US, sw Can), a completely terrestrial salamander, found desiccated in the field, when placed on a wet surface increased its weight nearly 40% within 20 hours by absorbing water through its skin. Most of the absorption occurred in the first few hours (Stebbins, 1945).

When in water, amphibians face an opposite problem—control of excessive water uptake. Water moves in through the skin by osmosis, moving from a region of low concentration of solute (dissolved salts, etc.) to one of higher concentration. This happens in fresh water. A reverse movement of water can occur in water of high salt content, which explains why nearly all amphibians are intolerant of salt water, although a few have adapted to brackish habitats. In water then, excess water must be eliminated, and it is gotten rid of by the excretory system. In completely aquatic amphibians or those that are aquatic for weeks or months during the breeding season, the skin may be modified, presumably to reduce water uptake, thereby reducing demands placed on the excretory system. For example, in the California Newt (*Taricha torosa*) and probably other *Taricha*, terrestrial for much of their life cycle, skin changes occur with the onset of breeding that are thought to reduce the water permeability of the skin and thus decrease the problem of excess water influx while the animals are in their aquatic breeding sites. The skin modifications are most notable in males, which spend more time in the water than the females. Active sodium uptake by the skin also occurs, compensating for losses imposed by the aquatic environment (Harlow, 1977).

The extensive subcutaneous lymph sac system in anurans with aquatic habits are part of the mechanism for handling absorbed water (Carter, 1979). The pooled or slowly moving water contained in these lymph channels can be drawn upon as needed by the animal's tissues or serve as a water reservoir when the amphibian is on land. Water may also be stored in the bladder (see Ruibal, 1962b).

Most terrestrial plethodontid salamanders, however, have become so specialized for land life that they are unable to cope with dermal water uptake when placed in water or saturated surroundings. Under such circumstances their tissues become bloated.

Hydroregulation

Just as amphibians and many other ectotherms exert control over their body temperature by locomotor movements and positioning their bodies, many amphibians exercise some control over body water levels by moving in and out of water and from dry to moist places on land or, when on land, by reducing or increasing body surfaces exposed to air or wet locations. In some species hydroregulatory movements evidently can be extensive. Marine Toads (*Bufo marinus*) studied in Puerto Rico by Carpenter and Gillingham (1987) periodically, during dry weather, moved from their activity areas 40 meters or more (up to 165 m) to persistent water holes, presumably for rehydration. Return to activity centers sometimes occurred the same or the next night.

The surface-mass ratio of an amphibian has been considered as important in dermal water absorption and loss. Other things being equal, a small amphibian might be expected to gain and lose water faster than a large one, because it has more skin surface in relation to its body mass than a large amphibian. However, review of a study by Cohen (1952), which focused on water absorption and loss only in several California salamander species, revealed no such relationship.

There are differences among species in their tolerance of water gain and loss that relate to habits and/or habitat. Species differences in tolerance to water loss were shown in six anurans studied by Hillman (1980). Couch Spadefoot (*Scaphiopus couchii*) was most resistant to dehydration, and it inhabits the most arid regions; two bufonids, the Western Toad (*Bufo boreas*) and the Great Plains Toad (*B. cognatus*), terrestrial species of semiarid to arid environments, were next; then came two semiterrestrial ranids, the Mountain Yellow-legged Frog (*Rana muscosa*) and the Northern Leopard Frog; and finally, the highly aquatic Clawed Frog (*Xenopus laevis*) (Afr) was least resistant to water loss.

Skin Structure and Water Loss in
Lungless Salamanders

Anatomical characteristics of the skin alone appear not to be a major contributing factor in plethodontid salamanders in resisting desiccation. Physiological factors are evidently of greater importance. Studies of fifteen species from the eastern US revealed little correlation between skin structure and moistness of their habitats (McMahon and Pav, 1982). Thickness of skin layers and numbers and types of glands and numbers of capillaries were measured. Although each species had a characteristic morphology, no correlation was found between wetness of habitat, except for a slight tendency toward larger numbers of capillaries on their dorsal surfaces in the more aquatic species than in the more terrestrial ones. This is to be expected because the oxygen content of water is lower than that of air.

Avoiding Desiccation

In general, amphibians are more often threatened with drying out than with an overdose of water. They resist desiccation in a variety of ways—behavioral, structural, and physiological—depending on the species and its mode of life (see Chew, 1961).

Behavioral responses to drying conditions include (1) reducing exposure of moist surfaces by closing the eyes, tucking in the limbs, curling the body, crouching, and clustering with other individuals; (2) burrowing; (3) nocturnality; and (4) dormancy.

Structural adaptations include (1) the formation when dormant (as a result of drought) of "cocoons" of dead epidermis often consisting of multiple layers of unshed squamous epithelial cells (Lee and Mercer, 1967; McClanahan et al., 1976; and Ruibal and Hillman, 1981; McDiarmid and Foster, 1987; Etheridge, 1990a) or encapsulating hardened mucus (Reno et al., 1972) that slow evaporation; the African Bullfrog (*Pyxicephalus adspersus*) appears wrapped in cellophane when it makes its cocoon; (2) a layer or deposits of mucopolysaccharide ("ground substance") in the skin, which has a spongelike capacity to absorb and bind water and release it as required (Elkan, 1967, 1968, 1976), notably developed in terrestrial anurans and providing some species with a nearly impervious skin; (3) specialized areas of rapid water uptake such as the pelvic or "seat" patch of toads (see Brekke et al. 1991) that acts like a "blotter" (fig. 12.1), and the wrinkles or furrows in the skin of toads and costal and other skin grooves of salamanders which, by capillary action, draw water up onto the skin, if a wet surface can be found (Lillywhite and Licht, 1974; Lopez and Brodie, 1977); and (4) possible effects of skin color on rate of water loss (see below).

Physiological adjustments include (1) a high tolerance in many species for water loss in relation to body weight (greater than most other vertebrates); (2) lowering metabolic rate; (3) resorption of stored bladder water (in some desert forms 50% of body weight may be from such stored water); (4) deriving water from the metabolism of stored fat; (5) increasing the rate of urea production and retention (in blood and other tissues) and sodium concentration, which increases body osmolarity, thereby decreasing the tendency to lose water to the soil and enhancing the capacity for water uptake from the soil (McClanahan, 1972); the capacity for such changes is especially well developed in species of arid and semiarid lands (Warburg, 1965); (6) the action in many species of the antidiuretic neurohypophyseal hormone vasotocin in increasing water uptake by the skin (Bentley and Main, 1972; Bentley, 1974); (7) secretion in some arboreal species of a lipidlike water repellent substance onto the skin; and (8) uricotelic nitrogen excretion (the excretion of urates), as in the leaf-frog *Phyllomedusa sauvagii* (s-cen S Am), foam-nest frogs *Chiromantis xerampelina* (s Afr) and *C. petersii* (e Afr), and perhaps some Australian species—the former storing the urates in the bladder, later to be voided within a mucous envelope as water becomes available (Seymour and Lee, 1974). Some of the above adaptations require further comment.

The "Seat Patch"

Amphibians rarely drink water by mouth. They replace body water shortages chiefly by dermal absorption. The seat patch, or pelvic patch, is an area of thinned vascularized skin on the posterior underside of the body, particularly evident in toads (*Bufo*) (fig. 12.1), which is specialized for water absorption. It is underlaid by an elaborate system of muscle fibers (Winokur and Hillyard, 1992). It is the portion of the body that is broadly in contact with the substratum when an anuran "sits" on land. The pelvic cutaneous musculature may perhaps function in several ways (Winokur and Hillyard, 1992): (1) to reduce abdominal contact when the substratum is dry by elevating the pelvic skin off the substratum and wrinkling it, reducing evaporation; (2) by subtle contractions that enhance contact of the furrowed surface of the skin with the substratum when the animal is absorbing water by capillary action (see Lillywhite and Licht, 1974) from a moist surface; and (3) through compression of pelvic lymph spaces, thereby assisting movement of water through lymph channels and into the venous circulation.

Thirsty Red-spotted Toads (*Bufo punctatus*) (sw US, Mex) are able to "taste" with their skin whether a moist surface contains water suitable for absorption. In experiments, Brekke et al. (1991) and Hoff and Hillyard (1993) were able to demonstrate aversion to water surfaces containing urea or sodium chloride at levels that were unfavorable for water absorption. The water absorption response (WR) consists of pressing the ventral skin, sometimes with a wriggling motion, against the moist surface. Detection of suitable moist surfaces may also involve the skin of the feet. Angiotension 11 was shown to be important in the duration of WR behavior and water weight gain. The reninangiotension system regulates drinking in many vertebrates. Hoff and Hillyard (1991) have now shown angiotension 11 stimulates drink-

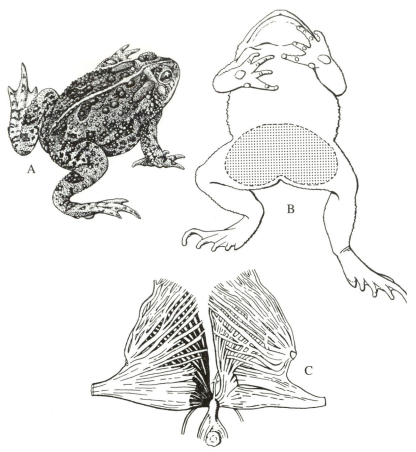

Fig. 12.1. (A) Woodhouse Toad (*Bufo woodhousei*) (N Am), showing (B) location of the "seat patch," a pelvic area of skin that acts like a blotter in absorbing water from the substratum. (C) Elaborate musculature beneath the pelvic patch. Many anurans in arid environments have well developed seat patches. (After Winokur and Hillyard, 1992, redrawn with permission from *Copeia*)

ing in an amphibian, not by mouth but through the skin. Seat patch cutaneous "tasting" may prove to be quite widespread in toads and is probably not confined to these animals.

Burrowing

An amphibian's initial response to desiccation may be an increase in restiveness, as the animal seeks to avoid the drying conditions (Putnam and Hillman, 1977). Species that are able to burrow may then begin to dig in. Although many adult anurans can burrow effectively to escape desiccation and unfavorable temperatures at the surface, juveniles may have difficulty or may be unable to do so. They are often more dependent on natural openings (cracks or other openings in soil, rocks, wood, etc.) and excavations made by other animals (Creusere and Whitford, 1976; Whitford and Meltzer, 1976).

Dormant (Estivating) Amphibians: Cocoons

The sirens (*Siren* and *Pseudobranchus*) (se US), eel-like aquatic salamanders that live in habitats subject to drought, burrow into the mud of pond bottoms and become entombed when the water source dries up. They pass the period of drought, which may last several months, in a cocoon produced by layers of accumulated shed skin (Etheridge, 1990a,b) or skin gland secretions (Lesser Siren, *Siren intermedia*) (Reno et. al, 1972). Respiration is by lungs (the mouth is the only area not covered by the cocoon) and metabolic rate is greatly reduced. McDiarmid and Foster (1987) describe a mummified Mexican Treefrog (*Smilisca baudinii*) (s Tex to Costa Rica) found in the dried silt of a road bed in Costa Rica, surrounded by a cocoon of layers of stratum corneum, each layer separated by a space filled with a mucuslike substance. They note that eleven other species of frogs from six families are known to produce similar cocoons, including the Northern Casque-headed Frog (*Pternohyla fodiens*) (s Ariz, Mex).

Cocoons in some species, the African Bullfrog (*Pyxicephalus adspersus*) and the ceratophryd frog (*Lepidobatrachus llanensis*) (S Am), reduce water loss so effectively that by absorbing bladder water, these animals can survive for several months in dry soil with little change in their internal solutes (Etheridge, 1990a).

Urea Retention

By accumulating urea in their plasma, Western Spadefoot Toads (*Scaphiopus hammondii*) (N Am) can decrease the water potential of their body fluids to such a low point (−15 bars) that they are able to absorb water from any soil with a higher water potential (Ruibal et al., 1969). This capability has been found in a number of arid-land species. Amphibians vary in their resistance to water loss when estivating, depending on the characteristics of the soil with which they are in contact. Clay soils, for example, have small pores and a low water potential even at high moisture content.

Urea retention and production, including an increase in sodium and chloride concentrations in plasma, are involved in the development of tolerance to brackish environments found in some amphibians such as the Crab-eating

Frog (*Rana cancrivora*) (se Asia to Philippines), some slender salamanders (*Batrachoseps*), clawed frogs (*Xenopus*), and others. By elevating the osmotic concentration of their body fluids, these amphibians maintain a small but favorable gradient for the influx of water (Shoemaker et al., 1992).

Skin Color

There are indications that skin color may influence the capability of some amphibians to resist desiccation. The green color phase of mountain-dwelling Striped Chorus Frogs (*Pseudacris triseriata*), Pacific Treefrogs (*P. regilla*), and Cricket Frogs (*Acris gryllus* and *A. crepitans*) (se and e and cen US) is more absorptive of solar radiation than nongreen phases (brown, gray, etc.), which may place them at a disadvantage (through heating effects) when faced with drying. Greens may be favored in the aquatic (breeding) phase of the life cycle, and nongreens (browns, etc.) in the terrestrial and foraging (postbreeding) phase (Tordoff, 1971, and Jameson and Pequegnat, 1971), as evidenced by a shift toward fewer greens in summer. In West Coast populations of Pacific Treefrogs, greens are inversely proportional to aridity (Resnick and Jameson, 1963). However, surface-volume effects and differences among greens in spectral absorption properties complicate the picture. The subject needs further study (see Hoppe, 1979).

Uricotelic Frogs

The method of nitrogenous waste disposal in these frogs represents a major departure from that of most other amphibians, which, after metamorphosis, are primarily urea-excreting or ureotelic. In terrestrial environments, excretion of nitrogenous wastes as urea can result in a considerable loss of body water if replacement water is not readily available. Most amphibians, however, live in wet or moist environments and the loss can be replaced readily by dermal water absorption.

The uricotelic frogs, on the other hand, live in semiarid environments. To conserve water, they excrete their nitrogenous wastes as uric acid, a relatively insoluble, less-toxic compound that is precipitated and discharged while much of the water released in the process is resorbed by the urinary tract. In this respect they resemble birds and reptiles. However, uricotelism would seem to gain an amphibian little if water is freely lost in other ways, as through the skin. It is not surprising, then, that the uricotelic amphibians have evolved mechanisms for greatly retarding dermal evaporative water loss.

In the leaf-frog *Phyllomedusa sauvagii* (S Am), these mechanisms are (1) selection of an appropriate arboreal perch, (2) secretion of a lipid substance (primarily wax esters) onto the skin surface from numerous small integumentary glands, (3) extensive grooming of the skin by a wiping action of the fore and hind limbs, which spreads the lipid secretion and seals the skin against water loss, (4) torpor during periods of diurnal inactivity, (5) and nocturnality. These frogs appear able to sense when the impermeability of the skin surface has been disrupted and they make appropriate secretory and wiping responses. Following grooming movements, the skin assumes a glossy, dry appearance and the rate of water loss drops rapidly. The uricotelic frogs have high rates of water uptake through their ventral surfaces, thus when water becomes available they can quickly replenish their body water levels. *Phyllomedusa sauvagii* not only readily absorbs water in this way, but it may also drink rainwater that wets its head or drips from leaves by pointing its snout upward and engaging in vigorous gular pumping motions (McClanahan and Shoemaker, 1987).

There are other arboreal frogs that display resistance to evaporative water loss but, at the present time, the mechanism involved has not been adequately determined. For example, the waterproofing mechanism is unclear in species of foam-nest tree frogs (*Chiromantis*) and reed frogs (*Hyperolius*) (Afr), in Australian tree frogs (*Litoria*), in hylids such as the Green Treefrog (*Hyla cinerea*), Spring Peeper (*Pseudacris crucifer*), and others (Wygoda, 1984). Arboreal frogs are more exposed to drying air currents and less connected with moist locations on the ground than are nonarboreal species. Some have developed integumentary resistance to water loss that rivals that of reptiles.

In experiments designed to test the capacity of amphibians to resist desiccation, a critical activity point (CAP)—the point at which the animals lose their ability to right themselves (Ray, 1958)—is often recognized.

For further information on amphibian body water regulation, see Boutilier et al. (1992), Shoemaker et al. (1992), and Feder and Burggren (1992), and on estivation and hibernation, see Pinder et al. (1992). For general information on the physiology of amphibians, see Moore, 1964–1976.

13

Protection against Predators

AT FIRST GLANCE amphibians may appear to be rather defenseless animals. Most lack a protective armor of any sort. Many are of small size and move slowly, or are capable of only rather short bursts of activity before tiring (Hutchison and Miller, 1979). Most are without clawlike structures, and their teeth and jaws are generally unsuited for defense against animals larger than they are. The important respiratory function of the skin in most species (see chapter 3) has greatly limited protective thickening or other modifications of the skin that might provide a mechanical barrier against predators. They have, nevertheless, evolved many antipredator adaptations. Here we address some general aspects, particularly as they apply to common vertebrate predators such as snakes, birds (jays, hawks, owls), racoons, skunks, and shrews. Emphasis will be on salamanders and anurans because little appears to be known about defensive mechanisms in caecilians. However, Moodie (1978) found by force-feeding sections of skin and mucus that the secretions of the poison glands of the aquatic caecilian *Typhlonectes compressicauda* (s Am) are lethal to at least one of the predatory fishes, *Holias malabaricus*, with which it coexists at Manaus, Brazil. The mucus causes a burning sensation when placed in the human eye and on cuts. Poison glands occur over the entire body of the animal.

Protective Glands and Their Use
in Defense

All amphibians are supplied with dermal glands that keep the skin moist— important in respiration in most species—and that cause many amphibians to be quite slippery, as anyone who has tried to hold a frog in hand soon discovers. This, in itself, often aids escape. In addition, the glands of many species release a sticky and often toxic secretion that reduces the palatability of many amphibians or sometimes results in their complete rejection by predators (fig. 13.1). More than two hundred toxins have been isolated from only a small percentage of the world's amphibian species (Duellman and Trueb, 1986). The potency of the secretion varies, as does its effect on an attacker and, in some cases, it is the adhesive or other properties of the secretion that seems to be of primary importance in defense. During initial phases of attempts at swallowing

Fig. 13.1 The poison glands of the Marine Toad (*Bufo marinus*) and other toads are concentrated in "warts" on the body and in the large parotoid glands at the back of the head.

an amphibian, some snakes may gape and "yawn" (behavior evidently induced by properties of the skin secretion). This provides opportunity for the prey to escape (see Barthalmus and Zielinski, 1988). The coloration, structure, and behavior of many amphibians is often closely integrated, which makes the most of this important first-line protective mechanism by (1) signaling to predators the possible unpleasant or even dangerous nature of their prospective prey, and (2) delivering the offensive secretions effectively under threat of, or actual, attack.

"Warning" Coloration

Although some amphibians avoid detection by camouflage (figs. 13.2, 13.3), others are conspicuously colored, and some combine both camouflage and bright colors, revealing the latter by posturing. Since there is often a relationship between the presence of bright colors and the potency of skin toxins, it is generally assumed that such colors function as a warning signal to potential predators. However, in many cases, actual experimental evidence demonstrating such a relationship may be lacking. For this reason we have placed the term "warning" in quotes. "Warning" colors are often bright red, orange, or yellow and are frequently associated with black or another dark contrasting color. They are often conspicuous even in dim light. They may be present over the

Fig. 13.2 The color pattern of the California Treefrog (*Pseudacris cadaverina*) resembles that of the rock surfaces of its habitat. Here an individual rests among granitic rocks.

entire body, as in the red eft, which is bright orange red (the eft is the immature terrestrial stage of the Red-spotted Newt), and in the varied dorsal patterns of many of the highly poisonous, gaudy poison-dart frogs (Dendrobatidae) of tropical America. More commonly, however, they are confined to parts usually concealed and displayed by positioning the limbs or other parts of the body. Such markings are often present on the underside of the body, limbs, and feet or back of the thighs, as in some anurans. In these locations they do not interfere with any concealing coloration that may be present. Some markings may resemble eyes, as in the froth-nest frog *Pleurodema brachyops* (n S Am to Panama), which turns on its display by inflating its body and elevating its hindquarters, revealing paired "eyespots," one in each upper groin area and on the back of the thighs (Martins, 1989). Eyespots may cause a fright reaction in some predators.

Often when an amphibian with concealed bright coloration is threatened or attacked, the colors are suddenly revealed. An example of such display is the "unken reflex." The back is arched downward, head thrown back, and, in salamanders such as newts (*Taricha*) (w N Am), the tail is extended over the back, revealing its colorful undersurface. The position of the limbs varies. In fire-

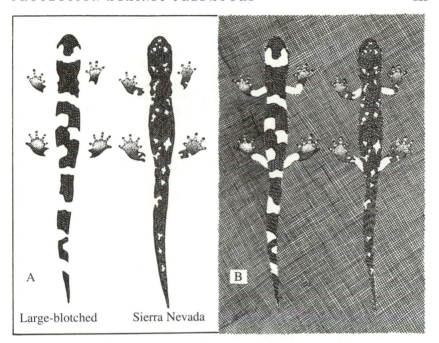

Large-blotched   Sierra Nevada

Fig. 13.3 Versatility in presumed concealing coloration of the Large-blotched Sala-mander (*Ensatina eschscholtzii klauberi*). The pattern of large, black and pale (usually orange) blotches break up the animal's form when seen on either a light (A) or dark (B) background in its semiarid Southern California habitat of scattered patched of leaf litter and soil. Its relative, the Sierra Nevada Salamander (*E. e. platensis*), which lives in a more humid environment on a generally more uniformly dark background, is conspicu-ous on a pale surface (A).

bellied toads (*Bombina*) (Eur to China) the undersides of the limbs are turned upward (fig. 13.4) revealing bright red or yellow markings; in *Taricha* the limbs are usually extended rigidly out to the sides and toe tips are flexed; in eastern newts (*Notophthalmus viridescens*) (e US, se Can), the forelimbs may be drawn inward with toes overlapped or crossed and the animals may rest on their tails and hindlimbs (Petranka, 1987), or the limbs may be "flexed" and they may rest on their foreparts (Neill, 1955). Unken postures sometimes may be held for 2 or 3 minutes.

The potency of the skin poison and degree of palatability of "warningly" colored amphibians varies considerably. The highly toxic Red Eft (land stage of the Red-spotted Newt, *Notophthalmus viridescens*), for example, is avoided by birds both under conditions of captivity and in the field (Brodie, 1968a; Brodie and Brodie, 1980). The Eft is also avoided by the Common Garter Snake (*Thamnophis sirtalis*) (Hurlbert, 1970). Efts have survived without ap-parent ill effect up to 30 minutes in the stomach of toads and snakes and then

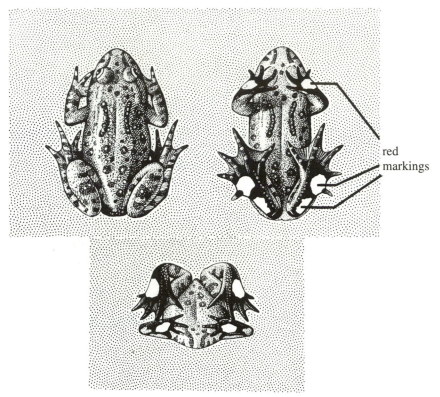

red markings

Fig. 13.4 The "unken reflex" in a Fire-bellied Toad (*Bombina*), with display of "warning" markings on the undersides of its feet.

were regurgitated (Brodie, 1968a). In laboratory tests, however, they were eaten by Bullfrogs (*Rana catesbeiana*) and, after rubbing and/or washing, by Racoons.

The Red Eft is more unpalatable to domestic chickens than the Red Salamander (*Pseudotriton ruber*) (e US) but the latter is intermediate in palatability between Efts and the completely palatable Mountain Dusky Salamander (*Desmognathus ochrophaeus*) (ne US) (Brandon et al., 1979). The Eft is more than ten times as toxic, as are its drab, aquatic adults (Brodie, 1968a). Brown-colored Efts from Illinois, tested by Brandon et al. (1979), have potent skin secretion but are cryptically colored, lacking bright dorsal coloration. However, when attacked they flash their yellow underparts.

The Rough-skinned Newt (*Taricha granulosa*) on Vancouver Island, British Columbia, has low levels of TTX (see chapter 2). Skin extracts from these newts are at least one thousand times less toxic than those obtained from Rough-skinned Newts from the Willamette Valley, Oregon (Brodie and

Brodie, 1991). Studies suggest they have lost most or all of their TTX toxicity. It is of interest that the Common Garter Snake (*Thamnophis sirtalis*), a newt predator that is resistant to newt poison in mainland areas, has either lost or not evolved significant resistance on Vancouver Island, where newt toxicity is low.

Mimicry

Predators learn to associate warning colors with noxious properties of their prey, and they may avoid such animals on sight and to extend their rejection to more palatable species that resemble, or mimic, the distasteful forms. For example, the Red Salamander closely resembles the Red Eft and in experiments with jays and other birds was protected by the resemblance (Howard and Brodie, 1973). Indeed, it has been suggested that it may be a "supermimic" because it is larger than the Eft, has larger black spots, and brighter red coloration (Brodie, 1976). The red morph of the Red-backed Salamander (*Plethodon cinereus*) (ne US, se Can) derived protection from its resemblance to the Red Eft in field and cage trials with bird predators (Brodie and Brodie, 1980; Tilley et al., 1982).

The Jordan Salamander (*P. jordani*) (e US), highly variable in color, may be black above with dark legs, black with red legs, or black with red cheeks. Red-cheeked individuals are found in the Great Smoky Mountains and red-legged individuals in the Nantahala Mountains to the south. In experiments, birds soon learned to avoid the distasteful red-legged and red-cheeked varieties but usually found black individuals more to their taste (Hensel and Brodie, 1976). In the Great Smoky Mountains the Imitator Salamander (*Desmognathus imitator*), considered a palatable species, appears to be a mimic of the red-cheeked Jordan Salamander. Imitator has yellow, orange, or red cheek patches. In the Nantahala Mountains and adjacent Highlands Plateau, some individuals of the Mountain Dusky Salamander (*D. ochrophaeus*) are red legged and red cheeked and may be afforded some protection from their resemblance to the red-legged Jordan Salamander found there.

The small Peaks of Otter Salamander (*P. hubrichti*), found in the Peaks of Otter region of the Blue Ridge Mountains, has noxious skin secretions. It may serve as a model for some individuals of the palatable Mountain Dusky Salamander (Dodd et al., 1974).

In California the orange-brown Yellow-eyed Salamander (*Ensatina eschscholtzii xanthoptica*), considered palatable, may be a mimic of the highly toxic California Newt (*Taricha torosa*). It not only resembles the newt in dorsal coloration but closely matches the newt's yellow eye color and orange venter. The two coexist and are sometimes found together under the same surface objects.

Posturing and Delivery of Noxious Secretions

Posturing is often important in defense (Brodie, 1977; Marchisin and Anderson, 1978; Brodie 1983; Brodie, III, 1989; Ducey and Brodie, 1991). Such behavior may not only position the skin glands for effective use of their noxious secretions but often, as pointed out earlier, reveals warning colors otherwise concealed (fig. 13.4), protects vulnerable parts of the body, and sometimes creates an impression of greater size. The secretion from the poison glands may irritate the eyes, mouth, or nasal passages of predators, gum up the jaws or other structures, cause nausea, and that of some species may occasionally kill. Mason et al. (1982) have offered experimental evidence for the unpalatability of the skin secretion of Tiger Salamanders (*Ambystoma tigrinum*), tested on rats.

The elevated stance of some salamanders with tail arched and writhing (fig. 5.2) and the butting pose of some salamanders and anurans with head tipped downward and eyes closed (fig. 13.5B) help protect the head and eyes and in some species places batteries of poison glands concentrated on the tail and in the parotoid glands in a position for maximal effect. Under stress of attack, the surfaces of these structures become coated with secretion.

In salamanders the tail is frequently the most noxious part of the animal because it is often generously supplied with poison glands and used actively in defense. It is elevated, often wagged or undulated, flipped or turned toward the predator, or sometimes curled over the salamander's head. Sticky, usually whitish, secretion exudes. Attack may be directed toward the tail, often an expendable part that can be regenerated. Tail loss to a predator can contribute greatly to survival (Ducey and Brodie, 1983; Labanick, 1984) (see chapter 5); but for some species there may be costs in impaired reproduction during the period of tail regeneration (chapter 5).

The Fire Salamander (*Salamandra salamandra*) (Eur, sw Asia, nw Afr) and its close relatives the Alpine Salamander (*S. atra*) (Eur) and Mertens Salamander (*Mertensiella luschani*) appear to be unique among amphibians in having skin glands surrounded by skeletal muscle (Brodie and Smatresk, 1990). Contraction of muscles around large turgid poison glands along the back make it possible for the Fire Salamander to squirt its toxic skin secretion in a fine jet for distances ranging from 17.5 to 80 inches (44–200 cm). By tilting the body, the salamander is able to quite accurately aim secretion at its molester. The secretion irritates mucous membranes, affects the central nervous system, and can even cause death by respiratory paralysis in some predators. Controlled spraying of a chemical repellent from selected glands conserves energetically costly secretion and permits the prey to thwart attack before injury occurs.

Specializations for actually "injecting" poison into predators is found in some Old World salamandrids—Ribbed Newt (*Pleurodeles waltl*) (Iberia,

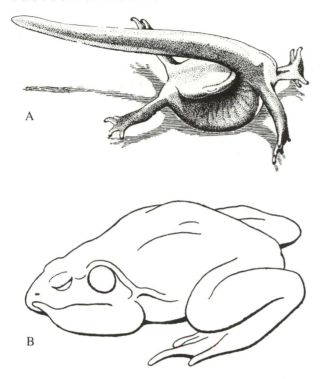

Fig. 13.5 Defensive pose of a salamander, the California Newt
(*Taricha torosa*) (A), and a Bullfrog (*Rana catesbeiana*) (B).

Morocco) and Anderson Salamander (*Echinotriton andersoni*) (w Pacific Is)
and *E. chinhaiensis* (China), which may protrude their sharp-tipped ribs
through their poisonous skins when defending themselves. The poison enters
lacerations made in the skin of the predator by the protruding ribs, causing
increased pain (Nowak and Brodie, 1976, and Brodie et al., 1984). In addition,
E. andersoni has a sharp forwardly curved spine on each quadrate bone. During defense these also may break through the skin. These quadrate spines,
protruding from the sides of the head, would appear essentially to eliminate the
possibility of snake predation on these salamanders.

Some salamandrids, for example the Burmese Newt (*Tylototriton ver-
rucosus*) (se Asia), have large lateral warts filled with batteries of large granular glands. These warts are raised during defensive posturing by erection of the
ribs, thereby increasing the likelihood of a predator contacting them. This species is representative of a stage through which the rib-penetrating species may
have passed in their evolutionary development. The poison of the lateral warts
is potent. In tests it has been shown to be at least as toxic as that of the California (*Taricha torosa*) and Red-bellied (*T. rivularis*) Newts (Cal).

As noted earlier, the adhesive properties of skin secretion in some amphibians may be more important than toxicity. This may be true especially of plethodontid salamanders (Arnold, 1982). The jaws of small garter snakes can be completely immobilized by the sticky skin secretions of the California Slender Salamander (*Batrachoseps attenuatus*) following unsuccessful attacks. In one instance, a young Western Terrestrial Garter Snake (*Thamnophis elegans*) (w US, n Mex, sw Can) was unable to free itself from the adhesive secretion even after 48 hours. Slender salamanders also resist being engulfed by twisting their elongate bodies into a watch-spring-like coil.

Other Antipredator Adaptations

The noxious skin secretions, and the often associated warning coloration and/or behavior, are the primary defense of many amphibians. However, there are other protective mechanisms. Many amphibians when first disturbed or attacked become immobile. Some "play possum" with eyes closed, body sometimes contorted or limp, and limbs clasped. Woodland salamanders (*Plethodon*) may sometimes remain immobile for up to around 3 minutes, after being contacted or disturbed (Dodd, 1989). Such behavior may delay recognition of the prey or reduce the attentiveness of the predator. Hesitancy on the part of the predator may permit the amphibian to escape or it may reduce injury that might be inflicted by the predator prior to the predator's recognition of the noxious properties of its prey. "Flash behavior"—flipping, sudden posturing, warning color display—may precede immobility, creating a predator search image that quickly disappears, thereby startling or confusing the predator, or delaying or misdirecting its attack.

Some amphibians bite in defense, some with a sideways lunge of the head. Biting has been observed in laboratory experiments with the Common Garter Snake (*Thamnophis sirtalis*) and the Mountain Dusky Salamander (*Desmognathus ochrophaeus*) and Black-bellied Salamander (*D. quadramaculatus*) (e US). Biting, often on the head, proved to be highly, but not completely, effective in thwarting the attack of this snake, which commonly feeds on amphibians (Brodie et al., 1989). The snakes used in the trials outweighed the salamanders approximately two to four times. These two salamander species and the Seal Salamander (*D. monticola*) (e US) also responded by biting when attacked by the shrew (*Blarina brevicauda*) (Brodie, 1978). Some amphibians inflate the lungs, increasing girth and making it more difficult for the predator to swallow them (Vestal, 1941). Some vocalize. The explosive bark of the Gray Treefrog (*Hyla versicolor*) (e US) had a repellent effect on *Blarina brevicauda* (Brodie and Formanowicz, 1981). The distress call of some frogs is well described as a scream. Frogs may kick the predator's face with the hind legs when seized by the head.

Variation in Antipredator Responses

The response of a prey animal to a predator varies with the species of each involved, the special circumstances of the attack, the experience of each, the extent to which the behaviors entailed are innate, and other factors. It has been shown that salamanders may vary their antipredator responses depending on the kind of predator and its behavior. Ducey and Brodie (1983) found that terrestrial salamanders (from three families—Salamandridae, Ambystomatidae, and Plethodontidae) responded differently to the flick of the tongue of the Common Garter Snake (*Thamnophis sirtalis*) (US and s Can) than to being contacted by the snake's head or body. Response was thus to a specific cue received from the predator and not simply to the presence of, or contact with, the predator. This snake often attacks moving prey without first protruding its tongue, but it attacks stationary prey usually after first tongue-flicking it. Northern Two-lined Salamanders (*Eurycea bislineata*) (e US) more often survived attacks by the snake when they responded in their usual fashion—running when tongue-flicked or remaining immobile when contacted by the head or body of the snake. Loss of the tail decreased the salamander's chance of survival, because absence of the tail reduced escape speed and forfeited the option of tail loss in thwarting the grasp of the predator until the tail could be regenerated.

In responding to the presence of the snake, distasteful species (*Ambystoma* and *Bolitoglossa*) presented their areas of glandular concentrations by posturing, as they do when attacked by birds or shrews. The newt (*Notophthalmus*), however, walked away with body elevated and tail swinging rather than engaging in the "unken reflex" used during attacks by birds or shrews. Both woodland and brook salamanders (*Plethodon* and *Eurycea*) attempted to escape by flipping the body when tongue-flicked, in contrast to their stationary posture when attacked by birds or shrews.

Hayes (1989) found that young American Toads (*Bufo americanis*) (e US and se Can) responded to the presence of the Common Garter Snake by crouching and remaining immobile. When contacted by the snakes body, they usually remained immobile and were undetected by the snake, but toads contacted by the head of the snake, responded by hopping away and crouching again.

Noxious Properties of Amphibian Eggs
   and Larvae

Some amphibian eggs and larvae are distasteful to predators. Toad (*Bufo*) eggs are often rejected (Licht, 1969a) and the conspicuous dark color of many toad tadpoles has been viewed by some as warning coloration. However, Beiswenger (1981) reports Gray Jays (*Perisoreus canadensis*) in Albany County, Wyoming, making repeated trips to feed on an aggregation of Western Toad (*B. boreas*) tadpoles. Johnson and Schreck (1969) found that Pacific Giant Salamander (*Dicamptodon* species) larvae fed readily on the larvae of the Northwestern Salamander (*Ambystoma gracile*) but not on those of the Rough-skinned Newt (*Taricha granulosa*), presumably because of the latter's strong skin poison.

Brodie et al. (1978) noted that the poisonous constituents of the noxious and toxic skin secretions of toads (*Bufo* spp.), stored in the granular glands, is apparently also deposited in the ova, which may account for ova toxicity and protection from some predators. The toxicity declines with egg development.

Newly hatched and metamorphosing individuals of the American Toad have been found to be unpalatable to both vertebrate (Red-spotted Newt, *Notoph-thalmus viridescens*) and invertebrate (dragonfly naiads, *Anax junius*, and giant water bugs, *Belostoma* sp.) predators, but intermediate tadpole stages are palatable (Brodie, 1987). The chemical defenses of the newly hatched tadpoles may result from a carryover of egg toxicity. The unpalatability at the time of metamorphosis is probably associated with activity of the granular glands of the skin. Palatable intermediate stages tend to be protected somewhat by the noxious properties of the early and late stages (Brodie, 1987). Both early and late stages are less mobile than intermediate ones, thus chemical defenses are of special importance to them.

Kats et al. (1988) studied larvae of fifteen species of North American amphibians from six families, including salamanders and anurans. They found that species that breed in permanent water habitats in which they were associated with predatory fish had developed defenses against these predators. Species that had not been so exposed lacked such defenses. The latter were temporary pool species that breed in fishless habitats. Defenses were chemosensory recognition of the predator, followed by avoidance, and/or distastefulness. The authors concluded that these defenses probably had a genetic basis and were the result of natural selection, and that their absence in temporary-pool species is why the latter cannot successfully coexist with fish in permanent waters.

Toad (*Bufo*) tadpoles and others (see Altig and Christensen, 1981) release an odor or "alarm substance" when injured, causing conspecifics to move away from the source of the chemical. The substance is detected by olfaction. The mechanism is widespread in the family Bufonidae.

For further information on the alarm reaction, see Hews and Blaustein (1985), and on predator-prey relationships, see Feder and Lauder (1986).

14

Home Range and Movements

LIKE MOST vertebrates, amphibians tend to remain within familiar areas or "home ranges" and individuals may be found repeatedly in the same general area and sometimes at the same location. The home range is the area ordinarily traversed by an individual in foraging, mating, and producing and/or caring for its young. During migrations salamanders and frogs may move from one home range to another, as from a land site to a breeding area, and may return with great fidelity to these favored places, even, in some cases, after traveling several kilometers. However, the home range must not be viewed as fixed. For a variety of reasons such as competition, unfavorable environmental changes, and other factors, an individual may shift its home range. Furthermore, use of the home range is seldom uniform. Some parts of it may be used far more than others, and familiarity with the home range is less in peripheral, little used sections, than in more central or more heavily used locations. One or more activity centers may exist where most of the animals' needs are met. Such centers may be located in and around a rich food source, shelter, or favorable breeding location.

In amphibious and aquatic species, a section of shoreline is often such a focal point. It is here that many amphibious species seek land or water for escape, take part in reproductive chorusing and mating, find diversity in food supply, and emerge onto land as transforming individuals. There is considerable evidence that amphibians become familiar with the section of the shoreline where they spend much of their time—their "home" shore—and that their movements are often oriented to it.

Home-range size and shape vary greatly, depending on the species, population density, condition of the habitat, and the individual's sex and age. Small species with weak powers of locomotion, such as slender salamanders (*Batrachoseps*), may have a home range only a few feet in diameter, whereas some of the larger active anurans may have home ranges dozens of yards in width. Male salamanders generally have larger home areas than females, and those of immatures are frequently somewhat unstable or contained within those of adults. Under conditions of crowding, sizes of home ranges are often reduced.

Actual measurements of home ranges and movements are not abundant, and some that have been made may not be entirely reliable. In order to determine the shape and size of an individual's home range, the animal must be recognized and repeatedly relocated. Toe clipping, a common method of marking, possibly may affect the amount of movement and frequency of recapture of the marked animals, and the effects of handling are unknown. These possibilities must be kept in mind in considering the examples to follow. A new method of marking amphibians, with colored fluorescent pigments fired into the dermis with a small air gun, promises to have less effect on behavior (see Nishikawa and Service, 1988). Individuals of some species have distinctive markings that, like fingerprints, can be used in identification. A colored polaroid camera photograph of each individual can be obtained in the field.

Some Measurements of Movements and Home Range in Salamanders and Anurans

Salamanders

Some small terrestrial salamanders probably spend their entire lives in and around a single proven protected site such as a rotting log, rock pile, root tangle, or other shelter, or when shifting to a new location resume their localized movements at the new site. The diameter or length (if a log or stream border) of the home range may be less than 10 ft (3 m). Hendrickson (1954) found the usual cruising radius from favored cover in the lungless California Slender Salamander (*Batrachoseps attenuatus*) in the Berkeley hills, California, to be around 5.5 ft (1.7 m).

The small eastern plethodontid, the Dusky Salamander (*Desmognathus fuscus*) near Fleming, Pennsylvania, was found during summer months to have a mean activity radius of about 3.75 ft (1.14 m) and the mean distance traversed along its stream habitat was about 7.5 ft (2.3 m). These salamanders were found within around 10 ft (3 m) of their original capture sites for 15–87 (average 55.8) days (Barthalmus and Bellis, 1972). An earlier study of movements and home range of this species in Kentucky by Barbour et al. (1969) also recorded limited movements, most less than 2.2 yd (2 m), and home ranges of five individuals, for which considerable data were obtained, averaged 53 yd^2 (28–125 yd^2) (48.4 m^2; range 25.2–114.5 m^2) over a period of 32–59 days.

Mean home range areas of the Red-backed Salamander (*Plethodon cinereus*) (n Mich) measured 4.21 yd^2 (3.85 m^2) for males, 5.27 yd^2 (4.82 m^2) for females, and 3.25 yd^2 (2.97 m^2) for juveniles, and the mean activity radius for each was 14.18 yd (12.97 m) for males, 26.61 yd (24.34 m) for females, and 14.07 yd (12.87 m) for juveniles (Kleeberger and Werner, 1982). Ovaska (1988) reported on the spacing and movements of the Western Red-backed Salamander (*Plethodon vehiculum*), a western counterpart, on Vancouver Island, British Columbia. Mean distance between the two farthest captures was 2.7 yd (2.47 m) for adult males, 1.87 yd (1.71 m) for adult females, and 2.13 yd (1.95 m) for juveniles.

Home ranges in larger plethodons (e US) at Great Smoky Mountains National Park, North Carolina—the Jordan Salamander (*Plethodon jordani*) and the Slimy Salamander (*P. glutinosus*)—have been reported by Merchant (1972). For *P. jordani* the home range was found to be around 123.5 ft^2 (37.6 m^2) for males, 30.3 ft^2 (9.2 m^2) for females, and 18.5 ft^2 (5.6 m^2) for juveniles; and for *P. glutinosus* 154.9 ft^2 (47.2 m^2) for males, 70.2 ft^2 (21.4 m^2) for females, and 81.1 ft^2 (24.7 m^2) for juveniles. For the Jordan Salamander, Madison (1969) reported home ranges of males at around 46 ft^2 (14 m^2), females 6 ft^2 (1.80 m^2), and juveniles 7 ft^2 (2 m^2). In another study, near Highlands, North Carolina, Madison and Shoop (1970) give measurements of home areas for this species at 128.3 and 210.5 ft^2 (39 and 64 m^2) for two males and 13.2–78.9 ft^2 (4–24 m^2) for four females.

In the Southern Appalachian Salamander (*Plethodon teyahalee*) and the Jordan Salamander (*P. jordani*) in the southern Appalachians, studied by Nishikawa (1990), the range of distances between captures was 0–3 m (mean 1.12 m) and 0–8 m (mean .2), respectively. Home ranges of *P. teyahalee* varied from 0.01 to 4.69 m^2 and for *P. jordani* 0.05–6.71m^2, the latter having significantly larger home ranges (both juveniles and adults) from those of *P. teyahalee*. Home ranges of *P. teyahalee*, in addition to averaging smaller than those of *P. jordani*, displayed less overlap (ten of seventeen ranges lacked conspecifics) and were more likely to contain a retreat hole. However, less than 50% of adult *P. jordani* shared their home ranges with an adult of the same sex. During the period of study (May–September, 1983), both species occupied fixed home ranges, and all age classes of both shared, on average, less than 10% of home range area with a conspecific of the same age or sex (Nishikawa, 1990).

Stebbins (1954) found the movements of Ensatina (*Ensatina eschscholtzii*) in the Berkeley hills, California, to be quite localized. Adult females were the most sedentary, and at this locality most of them probably spend their entire lives within an area less than 75 ft (23 m) in greatest dimension. Males were more mobile. One male persistently used an area of 135 ft (41 m) in greatest dimension over a period of 2 years. The home areas of eight adult females ranged in greatest dimension from 20 to 75 ft (6–23 m) (mean 33 ft, 10 m) and those of adult males from 32 to 135 ft (10–41 m) (mean 64 ft, 20 m).

Among species of plethodontid salamanders—including e US *Plethodon* (*jordani*, *glutinosus*, and *cinereus*), *Desmognathus* (*ochrophaeus* and *fuscus*), and *Aneides aeneus*, and w US *Batrachoseps attenuatus* and *Ensatina eschscholtzii*—studied by various authors, maximum distances moved by adults between captures ranged from 7.87 ft (2.4 m) in the Mountain Dusky Salamander (*D. ochrophaeus*) (Huheey and Brandon, 1973) to around 300 ft (91 m) in the rock-dwelling Green Salamander (*A. aeneus*) (Gordon, 1952). Although generally sedentary, where crevices are suitable only for breeding, Green Salamanders may move to outcrops with deeper crevices in the fall. The 300 ft record was for an adult male.

Twitty et al. (1967a), in a marking study of the Red-bellied Newt (*Taricha rivularis*) (nw Cal), found that individuals appeared to confine their migrations principally to the watershed of the stream where breeding occurred. Some moved an airline distance of around 3000 ft (914 m) or more where they were caught in traps along a ridge separating two watersheds. Familiarity with a large area of terrestrial habitat is implied.

Anurans

Male terrestrial home ranges of the Striped Chorus Frog (Ind) ranged from 701 to 6588 yd^2, average 2315 yd^2 (641–6024 m^2, average 2117 m^2), as based upon connecting the outermost capture sites (Kramer, 1973). Postbreeding individuals remained within about 110 yd (100 m) of the breeding ponds. Bellis (1965) found the mean home range of the Wood Frog (*Rana sylvatica*) in Minnesota to be around 77 yd^2 (70 m^2); however, the size of the home range was highly variable.

Martof (1953b) found that adult Green Frogs (*Rana clamitans*) in Michigan had greatly restricted terrestrial home ranges—around 22 to 220 yd^2, average 67 yd^2 (20–200 m^2, average about 60 m^2), which they left for breeding purposes but returned to with great fidelity.

In a study of the tiny tropical frog *Eleutherodactylus johnstonei* (Barbados, W. Indies), Ovaska (1992) found that both sexes were highly sedentary, adult males moving, on average, rarely more than 1.5 m and females seldom more than 2 m. Females, being larger than males, required more food, which may explain their greater mobility. Mean total distance covered per night was 2.8 m for males and 4 m for females. Both adults and juveniles displayed site fidelity. They were usually found within 2 m of original points of capture up to 300 days later. Estimates of movements are conservative because individuals that moved out of the study areas were not included in the calculations. (See also a study of movements of the related Puerto Rican Coqui [*E. coqui*] by Woolbright, 1985.)

The Arroyo Toad (*Bufo microscaphus californicus*) displays marked differences in movements between males and females (Sweet, 1993). The species breeds along low-gradient stream courses in Southern California where there are shallow pools and alluvial deposits from periods of stream overflow. During the breeding season, some males may move over 300 m in intervals of only 7–10 days, both up and down stream, whereas females are highly sedentary, most remaining in the vicinity of a single pool or at best moving less than 100 m to an adjacent pool. Subadults of both sexes, after a sedentary period in March through early June, engage in considerable movement in July and early August, moving up to 1 km, primarily upstream.

Some anurans have been reported to move great distances. Stumpel (1987) reports the Common Treefrog (*Hyla arborea*) (Eur to Caucasus, nw Afr) moving up to around 2.5 miles (4 km) between seasons, and Huesser (1968), the Common Toad (*Bufo bufo*) migrating over a distance of 3 km for breeding. Franz et al. (1988) recaptured a Florida Gopher Frog (*Rana aureolata*) (e US) about 4 months later at 1.2 mi (2 km) from its marking site.

Familiarity with a portion of the habitat contributes greatly to survival because the resident animal becomes aware of places of shelter and food sources, and the location of rivals, predators, and other threats.

15

Territorial Behavior and Fighting

AT ONE TIME amphibians were thought to be largely nonterritorial and unaggressive. There is now much evidence otherwise. Many species of salamanders and frogs are now known to engage in territorial defense. Little is known in this regard about caecilians, although Sanderson (1937) reported that brooding females of *Idiocranium russelli* (Cameroon) defended their clutches by spitting water at him. What follows, therefore, pertains to salamanders and frogs.

Within the home range of an amphibian, one or more areas may be focal points of activity—for breeding, nesting, feeding, or sheltering, and these areas may be defended. Such defended areas qualify as territories. Males of many species are especially antagonistic toward other males, particularly at the time of breeding, and females and juveniles of some species may also engage in territorial behavior.

Although females usually grow larger than males, males are often equal to or larger than females in body size in species that engage in male physical combat. In anurans that fight, spines (on thumb, arms, or chest) and tusks (enlarged teeth) appear to be primarily adaptations to male combat. Combat, large size, and sexually dimorphic weapons appear to be most common in species that are relatively invulnerable to predation while fighting by virtue of large body size or toxic skin secretions (Shine, 1979).

Salamanders

Defense of territory may involve posturing and, ultimately an attack. An attack may involve snapping, lunging, chasing, and sometimes biting, the latter occasionally causing some physical injury, sometimes including loss of the tail.

Thurow (1976) has documented, in laboratory studies, defense of territories, social dominance hierarchies, and feeding competition within and among species of eastern U.S. large and small plethodons. Adults of both sexes and juveniles may engage in such aggressive activities. Spacing of individuals in the field and the stereotyped nature of some of the behavior suggest that it also occurs in the wild. An aggressive individual may bite, or attempt to bite, other individuals or engage in bluff. Attack of eastern large plethodons was sometimes thwarted by appeasment behavior such as wagging the head. Peck orders formed with a tyrant at the top. In the field, male plethodontid salamanders

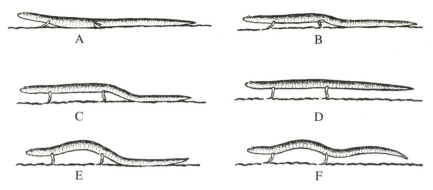

Fig. 15.1 Red-backed Salamander (*Plethodon cinereus*) escalating the intensity (A–F) of its threat display toward an intruder. (After Jaeger and Schwarz, 1991; redrawn with permission from the *Journal of Herpetology*)

have been seen to bite other individuals that entered their shelters, and brooding females have been observed to aggressively guard their eggs against other salamanders. The territory-holding individual is often the victor when confronted by an intruder, as has been observed in the Green Salamander (*Aneides aeneus*) (e US) (Cupp, 1980).

Both male and female (gravid and nongravid) Red-backed Salamanders (*Plethodon cinereus*) (ne US, se Can) defend their territories against intruders in laboratory experiments, and aggressiveness in defense of territory increases with length of territorial ownership (da Silva Nunes and Jaeger, 1989). Defense is by aggressive displays (Jaeger and Schwarz, 1991), biting, and odor marking of areas. Odor marking appears to be achieved by touching the chin and cloacal region against the substratum and may involve deposition of fecal pellets. Touching the nasolabial cirri to fecal pellets seems to be the method for determining the identity of an intruder or rival. This action brings into play the nasolabial groove—chemoreceptive mechanism (see chapter 6). Territories are presumed to be maintained under logs and rocks by both sexes during rainless periods when access to abundant prey in the leaf litter is curtailed. Protection of a food source is evidently an important part of territorial behavior in these animals (Jaeger et al., 1981).

In an aggressive display, a Red-backed Salamander raises its trunk off the substratum and looks toward its opponent (fig. 15.1). A biting lunge may follow, often directed toward the opponent's tail or nasolabial groove area (nasolabial grooves have been damaged by such attacks). A submissive individual lies flat and looks away. Males are usually more aggressive toward other males than females, but females make no such sexual discrimination (Jaeger, 1984). Similar behavior has been observed in the field (Gergits and Jaeger, 1990a).

The focal point of attacks—tail and nasolabial grooves—can reduce the fitness of a rival. The tail may be lost, and thus an important source of fat reserve and/or damage to the nasolabial grooves can impair detection of food, competitors, mates, and perhaps enemies.

Merely the presence of odor markings may cause an intruder to assume a submissive pose (Jaeger et al., 1981). However, sometimes an intruder will impose its own scent markings over those of an absent resident (ibid.). Individuals that have odor marked an area are quick to attack an intruder, usually with little chance of retaliation (ibid.). Laboratory experiments suggest that males in food-poor territories avoid escalated aggressive disputes with males in food-rich territories (da Silva Nunes, 1988b).

Laboratory studies on Red-backed Salamanders are supported by field studies (Mathis, 1989; Gergits and Jaeger, 1990a). Mathis's findings indicated that the species is territorial in natural forest habitats, and that territories are used during both courting and noncourting seasons.

Gergits and Jaeger (1990b) found that 91% of marked individuals recaptured in the field were found within 1 m of their original capture site. The results indicate that after nocturnal wanderings individuals return to specific cover objects (a rock or log), where they presumably guard some scarce resource—a courtship area, nesting site, or prey. Individuals were found to use the same sites across seasons.

Aggressive behavior among salamanders is not confined to plethodontids, the species most studied. Ducey and Ritsema (1988) have observed it in the Spotted Salamander (*Ambystoma maculatum*) (e US, se Can). Adult males in the laboratory actively avoided conspecifics when housed together, and biting on the snout was frequently observed, as were forebody elevations (with head held horizontally or tilted upward) and touching of the snout to the substrate.

The Marbled Salamander (*Ambystoma opacum*) (e US), Long-toed Salamander (*A. macrodactylum*) (nw US, sw Can), and others, tested for aggressive behavior in the laboratory, also showed some forms of intraspecific aggression, some individuals of all of them biting conspecific intruders (Ducey, 1989).

Anurans

Among anurans, spatial separation of males in breeding choruses is frequently observed and their advertisement calls may play a part in such spacing (Fellers, 1979a; Robertson, 1986; Perrill and Shepherd, 1989; Mauger, 1989; Ovaska and Hunte, 1992). Some species give specific calls both during and after the breeding season that are territorial in function. "Encounter calls" may be used in actual territorial defense (Wells, 1978a; Fellers, 1979a; Robertson, 1986) (see chapter 10). In the forest-dwelling Puerto Rican Coqui (*Eleutherodactylus coqui*), aggressive calls increase at dawn when males are returning to their daytime shelters and nest sites, and at dusk when they return to their nocturnal calling territories. Males are highly territorial. Stewart and Rand (1991) found that recaptured males were consistently found within 5 meters of original capture sites. Both sexes defend territories. Males guard their shelters and eggs against cannibalism by conspecifics of both sexes, primarily males. Females can be highly aggressive. Fights may involve lunging and kicking and then seizing the opponent by the head. A female that was occupying a shelter used frequently by another female resisted displacement by holding the intruder's head in her mouth for over 45 minutes. She then dropped her and gave a series of aggressive calls (ibid.).

In anurans, chest to chest wrestling or shoving matches occur (Duellman, 1966; Rosen and Lemon, 1974; Duellman and Savitzky, 1976; Fellers, 1979a; Wells, 1980), as well as jumping upon the back of an opponent (Ovaska and Hunte, 1992), biting, deflating of vocal sacs, pushing an opponent under water or off its perch (Wells, 1981), chasing, splashing, and aggressive vocalizing. Lutz (1960) described dramatic fights between male Blacksmith Treefrogs (*Hyla faber*) (cen S Am) in Brazil at male-constructed mud-pan nest sites, which included pushing the sharp, curved thumb (pollex) rudiment into the opponent.

In the tiny Red-groined Toadlet (*Uperoleia rugosa*) (sw Queensland, Aus), Robertson (1986) observed that males can, on the basis of voice, which is often indicative of size, assess differences in fighting ability between themselves and other individuals, and that territorial fights were usually won by the heavier males. Males of similar weight were more likely to fight, whereas males retreated from opponents that were substantially heavier. Davies and Halliday (1977) note that small male Common Toads (*Bufo bufo*) (Eur to s Siberia, nw Afr) may be displaced in amplexus by larger males. Energy expenditures in calling caused loss of weight and decline in fighting ability, thus some silent "satellite" males (those around the periphery of calling males) who gained weight were eventually able to oust lighter territorial males.

In the small neotropical dendrobatid frog *Colostethus trinitatus* (Trinidad, Venezuela), Wells (1980) noted that both males and females were aggressive. Males turned black when calling and were antagonistic only toward black males (noncalling males were light brown and seemed indistinguishable at a distance from females). The color change occurred within 1–10 minutes after calling began. Females guard feeding and shelter sites along small streams, threatening intruders with pulsating orange-yellow throat, and sometimes jumping on them and wrestling with them (Test, 1954; Wells, 1980).

Male *Eleutherodactylus urichi* (Lesser Antilles) of Trinidad (less than one inch SV) usually vocalized during aggressive encounters, producing a rapid alternation of clicks. Wrestling bouts occurred in which the contestants attempted to push or pull one another from calling perches. The opponents often tumbled to the ground where fighting was resumed. One fight lasted over 2 hours (Wells, 1981). Male *E. johnstonei* (Barbados, W. Indies), observed by

Ovaska and Hunte (1992), in a typical sequence faced their opponents, bumped them with their snouts or extended vocal sacs, then stood on them, both frogs facing in the same direction, and finally dismounted and gave chase. The spacing of calling ranges varied from 0 (all captures at the same location) to 1.34 m² (June) and 0.01 to 1.49 m² (July) with varying degrees of range overlap.

Anurans with established territories, as in salamanders and many other animals, have an advantage over intruding challengers. Stewart and Rand (1991) found that resident Puerto Rico Coquies (*E. coqui*) won 93% of contests when their diurnal retreats were entered by a conspecific. Both sexes give aggressive notes and defend their retreats.

"Dear Enemy" Recognition

Once territorial disputes between neighbors have been resolved, antagonism subsides and a "dear enemy" truce-relationship often develops (Jaeger, 1981). Territorial individuals thus tend to focus their attention on strangers. This saves energy and reduces the risk of frequent combat.

Martof (1953a), who conducted a pioneering study of territoriality in amphibians, found that a group of adult male Green Frogs (*Rana clamitans*) (in Michigan) tended to maintain their spacing, yet remained together, for periods of about two months, in spite of the fact that they made overland movements of more than 110 meters. He recognized that given the long breeding season of Green Frogs, this organization would help conserve energies of the males through reduced antagonism among familiar neighbors.

Territorial behavior functions to maintain a species' population at a sustainable density in relation to the need for shelter, food, and breeding sites. Failure to hold a territory can result in failure to survive or reproduce. Furthermore, territorial and aggressive behavior may play a role in competitive exclusion or forced displacement of one species from an area held by another, as seems to be the case in the Shenandoah Salamander (*Plethodon shenandoah*) (e US) and the Red-backed Salamander (*P. cinereus*) (ne US, se Can) (Jaeger, 1980). For further information on aggressive and territorial behavior, see Martof (1953), Grant (1955), Sexton (1962), Brattstrom and Yarnell (1968), Schroeder (1968), Wiewandt (1969), Emmerson and Kay (1971), Silverstone (1973), Salthe and Mecham (1974), Howard (1978a), Shine (1979), McVey et al. (1981), and Crump (1988).

16

Homing and Migration

How do amphibians find their way within their home ranges and especially during their sometimes lengthy migrations to and from breeding sites? As noted earlier, some species move hundreds of yards and even a mile or more overland during their migrations—an impressive performance for such small earthbound animals. Offhand one might expect that diurnal species would simply become familiar with visual landmarks in their surroundings, but can this alone explain their behavior? May they rely more importantly on other less obvious sensory information? Many amphibians are most active at night and migrations often occur over rough terrain, during or after rains, in darkness, when visibility is poor. How do they find their way?

There are further problems. How does a frog or salamander guide its movements to and from the featureless surface waters off shore and the home shoreline of its breeding site? What guides the similar movements of amphibian larvae and finally directs them shoreward and onto land at the time of metamorphosis? We will consider shoreline orientation first, because the sensory mechanisms that appear to be of primary importance in guiding movements to and from the home shore also may be involved in the homing capabilities of individuals that have been displaced and in the navigation required in migration. This chapter focuses on salamanders and frogs. Nothing appears to be known about homing and possible migration in caecilians.

Shoreline Orientation

An important landmark in the lives of most amphibians, whether completely aquatic or amphibious, is a section of shoreline or the "home" shore. Experiments have shown that they are aware of its location and that, when displaced, they move in relation to it. The orientation movement, whether away from or toward the shore, is often approximately at a right angle to the general trend of the shoreline and, in general, represents the most direct route to deeper water or land. In studies of shoreline orientation, this route of movement is called the Y-axis (Ferguson and Landreth, 1966), whereas the shoreline itself is called the X-axis (fig. 16.1).

Y-axis or shoreline orientation is of importance to amphibians in escaping danger, because it helps to ensure that the threatened animal will move quickly

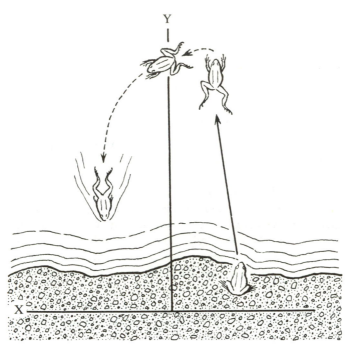

Fig. 16.1 A frog displaying shoreline orientation. When frightened into the water, it turns and swims back to shore. This behavior is expected if the frog is familiar with the area and the water contains predatory fish or other threats. Return to shore tends to be more or less at a right angle (Y-axis) to the general trend (X-axis) of the shoreline with which the frog is familiar.

and directly to places of refuge. Whether, in a given situation, movement is toward or away from shore depends on the species, its physiological state, source of danger, and/or stage of development. For example, shore-dwelling adult cricket frogs (*Acris*) (cen and se US), when thrown or frightened into deep water where fish predators lurk, usually swim promptly back toward shore. On the other hand, a salamander in aquatic breeding condition, when placed on land, usually moves toward water. Amphibian larvae, when frightened, swim to deeper water (Goodyear and Altig, 1971; Tomson and Ferguson, 1972), but when about to transform or emerge on land, they move in the reverse direction toward shore (Dole, 1972b; Tomson and Ferguson, 1972).

   Many experiments have been conducted to obtain information on the nature of shoreline orientation and to determine the sensory structures and information used. A common procedure is to transport the animals to be tested in light-tight containers so they are unable to see their surroundings during transfer to an "arena," a circular solid-walled enclosure, that excludes a view of all familiar landmarks but is open to the sky. The experimental animals, released in water or on land within the center of the arena, move toward its wall and their point of first contact is noted. The arena tests have demonstrated that in most species, recognition of familiar terrestrial or aquatic landmarks—by sight or odor—is not required for Y-axis orientation, although these senses and perhaps others may sometimes help. The appropriate compass direction in relation to the shore can be maintained even when some amphibians are removed great distances from their home shores (exceeding 100 miles). Blinding and severing the olfactory tracts in many cases have not prevented orientation.

Let us clarify further the nature of shoreline orientation and arena tests with a specific, somewhat idealized example. An arena is set up on level terrain on the *west shore* of a pond occupied by male newts (*Taricha*) (w N Am) in breeding condition. The males lurk in the water along sections of the shoreline with which they are familiar, awaiting the arrival of females. If several of these newts are removed from the water and placed on land, they will usually promptly move *eastward* back toward water, even if you point them away from the pond. They will tend to intersect the shoreline at roughly a right angle, thus exhibiting Y-axis orientation. The same behavior occurs when they are placed in the arena where thay can see no terrestrial or aquatic landmarks. Again, they move eastward in the direction of the shoreline, even though they cannot see it.

What happens when the arena is displaced to a new location, say the east side of the pond, and the same animals are retested? They still maintain the same compass direction, heading eastward in the direction which, at their home shore, would have taken them to water, but now their movements are inappropriate. Their route of travel takes them away from rather than toward water.

The direction taken by amphibians in such displacement tests is in the compass direction that at the home site itself would intersect the home shore roughly at a right angle. The animals in an arena that has been moved away from their home shore do not aim toward their actual home shore, but rather move in a compass direction as if they were actually on their home shore. What underlies this kind of behavior?

Senses Used in Shoreline Orientation

If sight and odor are not crucial for Y-axis orientation in many amphibians, how then are they able to orient? What kind of information do they need and how is it acquired? Experiments reveal that in many species three things are required: (1) some kind of light information from the sky (celestial cues) such as provided by the sun, perhaps the moon and/or stars (Milky Way?), and by the polarization of light; (2) familiarity with an area of shore; and (3) a time sense phased to local time.

The particular celestial cues used in shoreline orientation probably depend on the species. Orientation in some species fails under a complete cloud cover and is disrupted or is less precise under a uniformly illuminated sky when the sun is down and the stars are not yet out. It may be impaired at noon when the sun is at its zenith, especially near the summer solstice. It can be perturbed by disturbing the animal's time sense by training it to an artificial light cycle differing from the natural one. When returned to the natural environment, the animal, for a time, "reads" the celestial cues in relation to its entrained new schedule. Although the positions of the constantly moving celestial cues are predictable, such cues are useful for guidance only if the animal "knows" the time of day.

How are celestial cues detected—even in the absence of eyes? They are evidently perceived by photoreceptors located outside the retinas of the eyes—in the pineal body and/or frontal organ (Adler, 1971; Taylor and Auburn, 1978), and perhaps elsewhere, in the upper part of the brain (Landreth and Ferguson, 1967a,b; Taylor and Ferguson, 1970; Taylor, 1972; Adler, 1976; and Demian and Taylor, 1977). Such receptors are referred to as "extraretinal photoreceptors" (outside the retinas), or ERPs for short.

The pineal body lies above the diencephalon, just beneath the skull roof. It contains photoreceptors, so far found in all amphibians. The frontal organ (or stirnorgan) is a small capsule with retinal-like structure, situated beneath an area of translucent or transparent skin on top of the head between the eyes. It is connected to the pineal body by a "frontal nerve" and is photosensory in function.

Tiger Salamanders (*Ambystoma tigrinum*) (N Am) were trained to orient in a particular compass direction under the sun. Their brain was covered from above with a 2×2 cm opaque plastic shield beneath the skin, thus blocking light to the ERPs. As long as the eyes were functional, the animals could orient. However, when this was done to blinded animals, they lost their orientation. Removal of the pineal organ had a similar disorienting effect on the blinded animals. However, the salamanders with either the eyes or pineal intact and unobstructed were able to orient (Taylor and Adler, 1978). In other experiments, blinded animals with ERPs blocked could not be entrained to a new schedule of alternating light and darkness. Both detection of celestial cues and the mechanism for setting the internal clock were apparently disrupted by disturbing the function of the ERPs. It is of interest that the pineal mechanism has been implicated in the control of the daily rhythm of activity and rest (the circadian rhythm) in other vertebrates and in daily color changes in amphibians—blanching of young larvae in darkness (Bagnara and Hadley, 1970) under the melanophore melanin—concentrating influence of the pineal hormone melatonin. It thus appears to be involved, in a fundamental way, with daily timing phenomena.

If the pineal mechanism is indeed involved in registering celestial information, how might it do so? The ERPs do not seem to be arranged for reception of images. However, the frontal organ, in many transformed anurans and tadpoles, in structure and location seems well suited to receive radiant information from above (see Eakin, 1973; Eakin et al., 1963). It is regarded as sensory to the pineal body. However, the pineal body itself (the only pineal structure in salamanders) is deeper and covered by the skull roof and skin. Nevertheless, these tissues do allow some light to penetrate to the brain.

It appears that in those species that use the sun in orientation, a direct view of the sun is not necessary. In the Tiger Salmander, ERPs perhaps respond to linearly polarized light (Adler and Taylor, 1973; Taylor and Adler, 1973). Bullfrog (*Rana catesbeiana*) tadpoles (US) have been shown to orient on plane-polarized light (Auburn and Adler, 1976; Taylor and Auburn, 1978). Polarization patterns that can be used to locate the position of the sun exist under water and in different parts of the sky. Sky polarization is maximal during twilight when the sun cannot be seen, a time when many amphibians are abroad. Yet, as noted earlier, some amphibians seem to be less able to orient at this time.

Although photoreceptive detection of celestial cues so far appears to be the most common mechanism involved in Y-axis orientation in amphibians, use of other senses may also play a role. They may provide backup information and, in some species may even predominate. Hershey and Forester (1980) found that in arena tests, eyeless eastern Red-spotted Newts (*Notophthalmus viridescens*) (e US, se Can) with pineal area covered failed to orient on their home pond, although they did exhibit directional movements. However, newts with their olfactory tracts severed (anosmic newts) displayed random movements. Olfaction seemed to be the sensory mechanism most essential to home pond orientation in these animals. Photoreception apparently acted in conjunction with olfaction to refine directional accuracy. Possible use of the earth's magnetic field must also be considered (Phillips and Adler, 1978; Phillips, 1986).

Shoreline orientation is probably widespread among amphibians and may be a basic and an ancient mechanism that goes back to very early stages in amphibian evolution. It is present in the primitive Tailed Frog (*Ascaphus truei*) (nw US). It can also be quite flexible. Cricket Frogs (*Acris crepitans*) (cen and e US) can learn a new home shore within a few hours to a few days when on a regular light cycle.

For further information on shoreline orientation and related topics, see papers by Ferguson (1963, 1971); Ferguson et al. (1965, 1967, 1968); Landreth and Ferguson (1967a,b,c, 1968); Jordan et al. (1968); Taylor and Ferguson (1969); Landreth and Christensen (1971); Adler (1969, 1970, 1971, 1976); Dole (1972a); Adler and Taylor (1973); Underwood (1979); and Hershey and Forester (1980).

Homing Behavior during Migrations

Many frogs, toads, newts, and other salamanders migrate to and from regularly used aquatic breeding sites and familiar haunts on land. They thus engage in true migration. In studies thus far, homing on breeding sites has been best documented. It is so strong in some species that individuals have been observed to return for several years even after a familiar pond has been destroyed, as by land fills (Heusser, 1960).

Some homing movements are extensive, several hundred meters to several miles in extent in displaced Red-bellied Newts (*Taricha rivularis*) (Twitty et al., 1967b), and return to breeding sites, even after such long-distance shifts, as in the newt, may be accurate sometimes to within a few yards. Entry into and exit from a given breeding habitat was found to be at essentially the same site in the Spotted Salamander (*Ambystoma maculatum*), Marbled Salamander (*A. opacum*), and the Jefferson Salamander (*A. jeffersonianum*) (e N Am) (Douglas and Monroe, 1981).

In a study conducted by Phillips and Sexton (1989) in east-central Missouri in 1985–86, 24% and 45%, respectively, of individually marked Spotted Salamanders exited their breeding site within 5 m of their entry points. In 1986, 35% entered within 5 meters of their 1985 entry point. No differences in orientation ability could be detected between the sexes.

Site fidelity is known in the Pacific Treefrog (*Pseudacris regilla*). In a study in Oregon, Jameson (1957) found that 83.1% of 173 recoveries of marked individuals in one pond were made (in 1953) in the same portion of the pond where the frogs were originally captured. Of thirty-eight males captured in 1954, 71.1% were found in the same portion of the pond where they were marked in 1953.

There have been few studies of the actual route followed by migrating amphibians. An observer's presence risks influencing their movements. However, present indications are that at least in some species approximately straight-line cross-country travel occurs for much, if not all, of the homing route. Douglas and Monroe (1981) found that Spotted Salamanders in Kentucky moved an average of around 500 feet (150 m) from the pond and that the route of migration was linear and unaffected either by presence or absence of vegetation or by topography. Semlitsch (1981), in a study in South Carolina, found that adult Mole Salamanders (*Ambystoma talpoideum*) (se US) moved at night 266–856 feet (81–261 m) from their aquatic breeding sites to summer home ranges—underground burrow systems characterized by several focal points of activity. Densely vegetated corridors were preferred during overland travel. The study was of insufficient duration to determine if individuals returned repeatedly to established terrestrial sites.

Other studies have demonstrated homing on terrestrial sites following breeding. It occurs in the Green Frog (*Rana clamitans*) (e US, se Can) (Martof, 1953b) and evidently also in the Wood Frog (*R. sylvatica*) (ne US, Can) (Bellis, 1965). Individuals of the Eastern Spadefoot (*Scaphiopus holbrookii*) (e and se US), marked in Florida in 1951, were still found in the same terrestrial home ranges in 1956, after an elapse of nearly 5 years. These animals may return to the same burrow after breeding (Pearson, 1955, 1957). The Canadian Toad (*Bufo hemiophrys*) (s cen Can, n cen US) is known to return to established terrestrial hibernation sites (Kelleher and Tester, 1969).

Homing ability has been demonstrated in such relatively sedentary terrestrial amphibians as the Jordan Salamander (*Plethodon jordani*), the Red-backed Salamander (*P. cinereus*), and Dusky Salamanders (*Desmognathus*) (e US), all lungless salamanders of the family Plethodontidae (Barthalmus and Bellis, 1969, 1972; Madison, 1969; Madison and Shoop, 1970; Huheey and Brandon, 1973; Barthalmus and Savidge, 1974). In *P. jordani*, individuals homed on familiar living areas at night under a forest canopy and were able to do so even when blinded (Madison, 1969). They were able to return after up to 195 feet (60 m) displacements (Madison and Shoop, 1970). Course headings 3.2 feet (1 m) from release were random, but those at 6.5 feet (2 m) were more home-oriented. Once initiated, homing was direct and rapid.

In the Red-backed Salamander in Michigan, displacements up to around 100 feet (30 m) from the center of home ranges resulted in an average 90% return rate, and for around 300 feet (90 m) averaged 25% returns. Two individuals homed successfully from 300 feet (90 m) displacements after remaining for 10 days to 2 weeks at the displacement site. After some initial seemingly random movements, routes of return were generally direct and occurred within 24 hours (Kleeberger and Werner, 1982). Dusky Salamanders were also able to home under a heavy forest canopy when displaced 100 feet (30 m) upstream, downstream, and 100 feet (30 m) from the stream. More individuals displaced downstream returned than those from upstream (Barthalmus and Bellis, 1969). Displaced Southern Dusky Salamander (*Desmograthus auriculatus*) (se US) females displayed ability to home on nest sites, their success depending on distance of displacement. Females displaced at right angles to the stream did less well than those displaced along the stream (Rose, 1966).

Role of Olfaction in Homing

Although celestial cues loom large in the orientation and navigation required in the homing of some amphibians, olfaction and other kinds of sensory input may be used and may, in some cases, supplement or even supplant in importance the photoreceptive information (Oldham, 1967; Endler, 1970; Grubb, 1975, 1976). The sense of smell has been shown to be important in homing in newts (*Taricha*) (w N Am) and some anurans, and it perhaps contributes to the homing navigation of many other species of amphibians. In the *P. jordani* study mentioned above, displaced individuals displayed an increased frequency of climbing into vegetation where the animals could presumably more effectively sniff the air. The Red-backed Salamander can detect differences between their own substrate markings and those of other individuals, evidently by the sense of smell (Tristram, 1977). Female Mountain Dusky Salamanders (*Desmognathus ochrophaeus*) (ne US) tend to return to breed along the same segments of stream during successive years (Forester, 1977). The sense of smell is probably important in such orientation. Barthalmus and Bellis (1972) found that individuals of the Dusky Salamander (*D. fuscus*) (e US, se Can) became disoriented when the olfactory sense was destroyed, whereas even blinded animals with sense of smell intact returned to home sites. In laboratory trials conducted in South Carolina with the Spotted Salamander (*Ambystoma maculatum*) (e US, se Can), individuals prefered a substrate of mud and water from their home pond area to that from a foreign pond (McGregor and Teska, 1989). Earlier, Shoop (1968) had found that many individuals when displaced to foreign ponds chose to migrate back to their home pond rather than remaining at the new pond. Perhaps odors at the new pond sites were unacceptable.

Studies involving blockage of the olfactory sense have shown that some toad (*Bufo*) species use olfaction in homing and that olfaction is perhaps more important to those species that move long distances to breeding sites, such as the Western Toad (*Bufo boreas*) (w NAm) and the Common Toad (*B. bufo*) (Eur), than it is to species that live near their breeding sites (see Sinsch, 1987). Wind blowing from the breeding site improved orientation of Common Toads (ibid.).

How Does Homing Ability Become Established?

At aquatic sites, it is thought that, like salmon, many amphibians return to breed at or near the place where they developed as larvae, recognizing the area by familiar odors imprinted on them during natal life. They perhaps return by using Y-axis information and site familiarity acquired during transformation and early life on land and during the time of dispersal from the natal pond (Ferguson and Landreth, 1966).

There is great diversity in the plant, animal, and mineral sources of odor in any given habitat, and the mosaic of potential sources of olfactory information along a given migratory route must indeed be great and unique. In addition, habitual use of a route may mark it with the species' pheromones. The senior author has seen droplets of fluid exuding from the vents of California Newts (*Taricha torosa*) as they make their way along their migratory routes. Other sensory information employed in navigation might include visual recognition of landmarks—topographic features, such as bushes, trees, rocks, and a body position or kinesthetic sense—that would help the migrating animal keep on course.

Endler (1970) obtained some information on a possible role of the kinesthetic sense in orientation in the California Newt. He suggests that once the animal has obtained its initial orientation from celestial and perhaps other cues, use of a body position sense corrects for deviations from the desired direction of travel required to avoid obstacles or predators. Newts that were whirled about in light-tight chambers and allowed time to recover from dizziness became disoriented.

In conclusion, it is probable that the migrating, homing amphibian uses a variety of sensory information in maintaining its course and that the most important sense (or senses) varies with the species and perhaps the environmental conditions encountered.

Homing and spatial localization within animal populations has decided advantages. As has been pointed out by Twitty (1959), such behavior makes possible return to familiar, reliable living and breeding areas and thus makes individuals less vulnerable to predation and other dangers, helping to guard against wasted reproductive effort. It tends to stabilize and equalize distribution of members of the population, thus probably reducing competition. It reduces the effective size of breeding populations, hence minimizing swamping of mutant genes that may arise and thereby facilitating genetic differentiation and speciation. It allows individuals to venture beyond an established home range to extend or shift the range in response to predation pressure, decreased food supply or available cover and to return if a more favorable location is not found (Kleeberger and Werner, 1982). A strong homing instinct, however, also carries a penalty, for accidental displacement may be equivalent to reproductive death if the homing animal is unable to relocate the home area, and loss of a habitually used breeding site also can temporarily, at least, reduce reproductive success (Twitty, 1959).

See Sinsch (1992) for a review of amphibian homing mechanisms.

17

Reproduction

Breeding Patterns and Their Control

In the temperate zones, except for some opportunistic breeders in areas of uncertain rainfall, breeding of amphibians is cyclic or seasonal, usually occurring in spring or early summer. In the tropics, however, although some species are cyclic, many breed continuously or at times when rainfall is plentiful, a portion of a given population nearly always in breeding readiness. For example, Houck (1977) found males of a number of neotropical plethodontid salamander species with viable sperm and physiologically prepared to court at any time of year. Factors regulating the reproductive cycles of amphibians are poorly understood, but timing of breeding is geared to ensure that the young are produced at a time most suitable for their survival.

In temperate latitudes amphibians initiate breeding activities in response to rainfall, rising temperatures, and changes in day length, the response to these factors varying with the species. Internal (endogenous) controls also contribute (van Oordt, 1960; Weathers and Snyder, 1977; Rastogi, 1980; Jørgensen, 1988). Even secretive species that live in thermally buffered environments and are exposed only to the weak, indirect light penetrating beneath objects may respond to temperature and light (photoperiodic) changes. Werner (1969) in Michigan accelerated the normal spermatogenic cycle of the Red-backed Salamander (*Plethodon cinereus*) (ne US, se Can) nearly 2 months by maintaining his animals on a 16 hour light—8 hour dark cycle at 68°F (20°C). Temperature appears to play a major role in the regulation of amphibian reproductive cycles, but the triggering effect of rainfall on reproductively ready individuals often is also important. It may help to synchronize breeding.

The interaction of endogenous factors and temperature in the regulation of the testicular cycles in frogs is shown by the work of Rastogi (1980), who studied testicular activity in the Common European Frog (*Rana temporaria*) and in the Old World Edible Frog (*R. esculenta*). *Rana temporaria*, an inhabitant of the temperate zone, has a seasonal spermatogenic cycle, and testicular recrudescence and regression seem to depend on an endogenous trigger. However, it appears that temperature plays a permissive role, especially in modifying the onset of testicular activity and its subsequent rate. *Rana esculenta*, on the other hand, has a potentially continuous type of spermatogenic cycle. In this species, day length evidently acts in a permissive way to facilitate the temperature response of the testes. Under constant temperature conditions and a fixed photoperiod of 12 hours of light and 12 hours of darkness (a seasonless environment) in the laboratory, evidence was obtained for an internally controlled (endogenous) chain of testicular events. The fact that testicular synchrony is achieved in the natural environment points to the existence of a "Zeitgeber," or "time giver." The Zeitgeber seems to be temperature.

Among frogs and other anurans, vocalizations may also contribute to breeding synchrony in both males and females. As a breeding chorus forms, the vocalizations of the more reproductively active males stimulate the endocrine activity of the testicular interstitial cells of the males that are still at a low endocrine level, thereby bringing them into full reproductive condition (Obert, 1977). There is also evidence that in some species male vocalizations stimulate ovulation in females (Oldham, 1975). For information on physiological mechanisms involved in amphibian reproduction, see Lofts (1974).

In many salamanders and frogs, breeding is preceded by migratory movements. Males often begin their migrations to breeding sites in advance of females, and they usually arrive first and stay longer. In species in which the males spend long periods at the breeding site, early arrival of the males gives time for resolution of territorial disputes prior to the appearance of the females.

Secondary sexual characteristics, those other than the primary sex organs—the gonads (ovaries and testes)—are frequently referred to in the accounts to follow. Some of them are shown in fig. 17.1.

Reproductive Activities

Caecilians

Fertilization is internal, by copulation. The cloaca of the male is extruded during mating and serves as the intromittent organ ("phallodeum"). Murphy et al. (1977) observed mating in the aquatic caecilian *Typhonectes compressicauda* from the Amazon drainage of northeastern South America. Coitus continued for at least 3 hours after copulation was first noted. Barrio (1969) reported on copulation in *Chthonerpeton indistinctum* (e-cen S Am) and noted that the diameter of the vent was greater in the male than in the female, a difference also noted in *T. compressicauda* by Murphy. The cloacal opening in caecilians is located at the extreme end of the body.

Males have paired Müllerian glands that release into the cloaca a secretion resembling that of the mammalian prostate. The glands are derived from embryonic Müllerian ducts, which are vestigial or absent in males of other vertebrates. In females, they become the ovarian ducts. Wake (1981) has suggested that the caecilian Müllerian gland may represent a primitive state in the evolution of the prostrate and the secretion of material for transport and maintenance of sperm in terrestrial situations.

Little is known about sex recognition and courtship in these animals.

See Wake (1980a) for a comprehensive study of reproduction and other aspects of the biology of a caecilian.

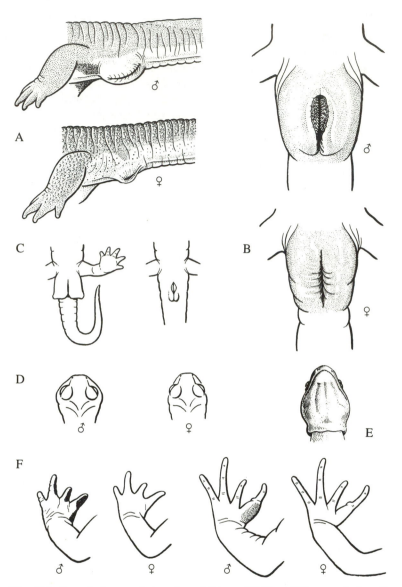

Fig. 17.1 Sexual characteristics of amphibians. (A) Vent differences in breeding Rough-skinned Newts (*Taricha granulosa*) (w N Am). (B) Differences in the lining of the vents of plethodontid salamanders. Males have papillae or villosities from which cloacal gland secretion is discharged in producing the gelatinous base of the spermatophore (see text). Females have smooth folds. (C) Some male salamanders have vent lobes from which a chemical sex attractant is released. (D) Sex differences in head shape in Web-toed Salamanders (*Hydromantes*) (Cal). (E) Mental gland (see text) on the chin of a male Arboreal Salamander (*Aneides lugubris*) (Cal); (F) Nuptial pads on the front toes of breeding male anurans, *Bufo* on the left, *Rana* on the right.

Salamanders

FERTILIZATION

In most salamanders (about 90% of all species), fertilization is internal. In most, the male deposits sperm packets (spermatophores) on the substratum, which the female takes into her vent (fig. 17.2B,C). The spermatozoa swim to the spermatheca (fig. 17.2A), a chamber or group of chambers in the roof of her cloaca, there to be stored until the time of egg laying (see Trauth, 1983, 1984; Sever, 1987; and Brizzi et al., 1989, for discussions of spermathecal anatomy). A typical spermatophore is around 10 mm or less in height, has a gelatinous, often cone-shaped base secreted by the male's cloacal glands, and a packet of sperm (the sperm capsule) on top. Details of structure of spermatophores of some plethodontid salamanders have been described by Organ and Lowenthal (1963) and Sever and Houck (1985). Spermatophore descriptions have also been supplied by Zalisko et al. (1984) for five species of *Ambystoma*, including the Tiger Salamander (*A. tigrinum*) (N Am), several salamandrids, and the Jordan Salamander (*Plethodon jordani*), a plethodontid (e US). Cloacal anatomy in male salamanders, involved in spermatophore formation, is discussed by Sever (1978).

The spermatophore is deposited in water, on land, or both, depending upon the species. Then, using a sometimes elaborate courtship, the male induces the female to pick up the sperm capsule, which she plucks with her vent from its gelatinous base. As the eggs pass down the oviducts, they are fertilized by sperm from the spermatheca.

In some species spermatozoa can remain alive in the spermatheca for long periods. In the Fire Salamander (*Salamandra salamandra*) (Eur), storage for a year (Zeller, 1891) to more than two years (Boisseau and Joly, 1975) has been reported. Female Red-bellied Newts (*Notophthalmus viridescens*) (e US, se Can) are able to fertilize eggs from sperm carried over winter and apparently nurtured by the tubule epithelium of the spermatheca (Benson, 1968). In this species storage can occur over a period of at least 10 months (Massey, 1990). In the European Spectacled Salamander (*Salamandrina terdigitata*) (Italy), the period of spermathecal sperm storage occurs from autumn to spring (Brizzi et al., 1989).

Female Mountain Dusky Salmanders (*Desmognathus ochrophaeus*) (ne US) store sperm from fall and spring inseminations until late spring or summer when the ova are fertilized just before egg laying. Furthermore, evidently viable, unused sperm may persist in the spermatheca after oviposition (Houck and Schwenk, 1984). Such sperm retention has been reported for the Northern Two-lined Salamander (*Eurycea bislineata*) (e US, se Can) (Sever, 1988a) and for a period of 8 months by the Dwarf Salamander (*E. quadridigitata*) (se US) (Pool and Hoage, 1973).

In the Dusky Salamander (*Desmognathus fuscus*) (e US), viable sperm were

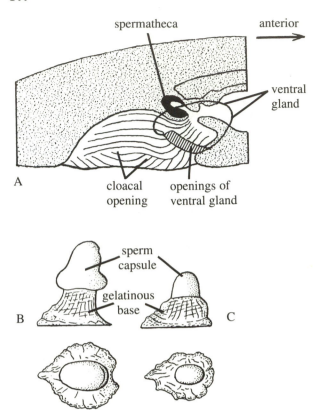

Fig. 17.2 (A) Longitudinal section through the cloacal region of a female Northern Two-lined Salamander (*Eurycea bislineata*), showing the position of the ventral gland (circled area) and its openings. The spermatheca, where sperm is stored, is shown in black. (After Sever, 1988a) (B) Spermatophore of Jordan Salamander (*Plethodon jordani*), and (C) Northern Two-lined Salamander; top views as bottom. (After Organ and Lowenthal, 1963; illustrations redrawn with permission from *Copeia*)

found throughout the year in 79% of individuals examined. Since the breeding season occurs 3 months prior to egg laying, spermatozoa survived in the reproductive tract of the females for at least 3 months, and probably longer (Marynick, 1971). In such a breeding system, mixed paternity can occur, as has been demonstrated in the Mountain Dusky Salamander (Tilley and Hausman, 1976; Houck et al., 1985).

The few salamanders that do not deposit spermatophores are members of primitive families that practice external fertilization in water—Asiatic land salamanders (Hynobiidae) and giant salamanders (Cryptobranchidae, e US and e Asia). In these salamanders males release sperm onto the egg mass.

COURTSHIP AND MATING

In salamanders with internal fertilization, depending upon the species, the female may find the spermatophore on her own or the male may place it directly into her vent, or he may control or guide her in picking it up. Direct transfer and guidance require physical restraint (holding the female or blocking her forward progress) and/or "persuasion." Persuasion is aided in some species by visual displays; secretions from "courtship glands," including, in some plethodontid salamanders, "vaccination" of the female, presumably with courtship gland secretions (fig. 17.3 D–F); release of scent; and tactile cues that may precede the more intimate stages of pairing.

SEX RECOGNITION

Odor Cues

In contrast to anurans, salamanders are essentially nonvocal and in many species the sexes look much alike. In such species, visual cues in sex recognition may be subordinate to olfactory and tactile cues. In many salamanders, males contact the female's skin with their snouts prior to spermatophore deposition (Arnold, 1977). In the Red-bellied Newt (*Taricha rivularis*) (nw Cal) and Old World Smooth Newt, males prefer to court the larger, more fecund females, using either odor and/or appearance in assessing the size and thus the fecundity of their potential mates (Verrell, 1985, 1986).

In an experiment with three species of Old World newts, the Italian (*Triturus italicus*) (Italy) and Alpine (*T. alpestris*) (Eur) newts and *T. carnifex* (Eur), Belvedere et al. (1988) found that each species preferred water flowing from a tank holding a concealed conspecific courting pair over that with a sexually inactive pair. The response was most pronounced in the species with less sexual dimorphism, which supports the viewpoint that olfaction tends to dominate when visual cues are weak.

The yolk precursor, vitellogenin, produced in the liver and then transferred to the ovary in the blood, might be the chemical released by female newts (perhaps through their highly vascular and permeable skins) that provides the olfactory cue to the males as to female fecundity levels. The amount of vitellogenin produced is probably related to the number of eggs to be yolked. Male odors also stimulate the females. Sexually active female *Triturus carnifex* respond to progesterone, one of the products of the male's abdominal gland, secreted into the water during courtships (Belvedere et al., 1988).

Moore (1978) has been able to enhance the sexual attractivity of female Rough-skinned Newts (*Taricha granulosa*) (nw N Am) with injections of progesterone, and Deviche and Moore (1988) have connected male sexual behavior in this species with testosterone.

In the Red-bellied Newt, a species that breeds in streams in northern coastal California, Twitty (1955) found that males located females evidently by their odor. This was indicated by the strong positive response of males to sponges anchored upstream after saturating them in water in which female newts had previously been stored.

Pheromones, chemical signals, clearly play an important role in salamander sex recognition, but their source is often not clear. Releases from the skin and cloaca have been implicated. Secretions from the ventral gland, located within the cloaca of some salamanders, including both sexes, may also be involved (see Sever, 1988a) (fig. 17.2A). Many spermatophore-producing salamanders (various male salamandrids, ambystomatids, and plethodontids) release mating substances (hedonic) from the cloaca during courtship, yet the ventral gland has not been implicated in these species. The cloacal glands of these salamanders are primarily involved in spermatophore production, but there are perhaps elements, representing parts of the ancestral ventral gland, that have retained a hedonic function.

The dorsal (= abdominal) gland of the Warty Newt (*Triturus cristatus*) (Eur to cen Russia) may represent such a derivative. Courtship pheromones are released by this gland in a related species, the Smooth Newt (*T. vulgaris*) (Eur to w Asia) (Sever et al., 1990). During the breeding season the anterior portion of the gland enlarges and may account for 10% of total body weight!

Some male salamanders have posterior-projecting lobes at the rear of the vent (fig. 17.1C). In torrent salamanders (*Rhyacotriton* species) (nw US), they are occupied by glandular tissue that secretes externally onto the skin and may function to attract the female during courtship (Sever, 1988b.) See Sever (1991) for a comprehensive survey of the comparative anatomy and evolution of cloacal structure in salamanders.

Visual Signals

In sexually dimorphic salamanders, such as Old World Newts (*Triturus*) (Eur to Ural Mts), the males have colorful markings, a variously enlarged dorsal fin and broad tail, and they display in front of the female, wafting vent secretions toward her with rapid movements of the tail. There is no amplexus. Males may also respond to the colors of females. Himstedt (1979) has shown with models that the red underside of female Alpine Newts (*T. alpestris*) (Eur) is the sign stimulus that releases the initial reactions of male courtship behavior, and Verrell (1986) found evidence that Smooth Newt (*T. vulgaris*) males (s England) preferred the larger, more fecund females as mates. There are also indications that male size may be important to female Smooth Newts. In experiments, smaller females remained closer to smaller males and larger females closer to larger males. Such associations may aid insemination of females. During spermatophore pickup, the male blocks the forward progress of the female equivalent to about his body length (SV) beyond the spermatophore. At this point, if she equals the male in size, her vent would be in the vicinity of the spermatophore (see Verrell, 1991).

Visual cues are also thought to be important in some plethodontid salamanders.

OBTAINING FEMALE COOPERATION IN MATING

After pairing occurs, a variety of methods are used to induce female receptivity and control. Male courtship glands often play an important role. Such glands commonly occur on the chin (mental gland) (fig. 17.1E) (see Sever, 1976), but also on the side of the head (genial or cheek gland), upper base of the tail (Sever, 1989), or elsewhere. A mental gland is present in most male plethodontid salamanders. It consists of a cluster of glands that form a slightly raised, often rounded or heart-shaped pad. In seasonal breeders the gland becomes more prominent during the breeding season under the influence of testosterone produced by the testes.

In salamanders with internal fertilization, the female may find the spermatophore on her own, the male may place it directly into her vent, or he may control or guide her in picking it up. Direct transfer and guidance require physical restraint (holding the female or blocking her forward progress) and/or "persuasion." Persuasion is aided in some species by visual displays, secretions from "courtship glands" including, in some plethodontid salamanders, "vaccination" of the female, presumably with courtship gland secretion (fig. 17.3 D–F), release of scent, and tactile cues that may precede the more intimate stages of pairing.

Persuasion by "vaccination" typically involves the male applying mental gland secretion to the body of the female, then puncturing her skin with projecting premaxillary teeth, thereby introducing the secretion into her blood stream. The secretion is thought to "prime" the female for breeding (Arnold, 1977) and to perhaps act as an aphrodisiac. Species whose males have projecting premaxillary teeth and that bite or slap their mates during courtship with their chins are likely to be using vaccination in enticing females to mate. Often such males jerk backward following mental gland contact. This action presumably brings into play the scratching action of the premaxillary teeth.

MATING PATTERNS

Salthe (1967) and Arnold (1977) have described salamander mating patterns. Many of the following remarks are based on their studies. Some other contributors have been Organ (1958, 1960, 1968), Organ and Lowenthal (1963), Organ and Organ (1968), and Joly (1966).

SALAMANDRIDAE

Several patterns may be recognized, and most involve the male clasping the female in a sexual embrace known as "amplexus." In the European mountain newts (*Euproctus*), the male captures the female with his tail and embraces her, transferring the spermatophore directly to her vent with his hind feet, the only salamanders known to do so. In Old World *Salamandra* and the monotypic

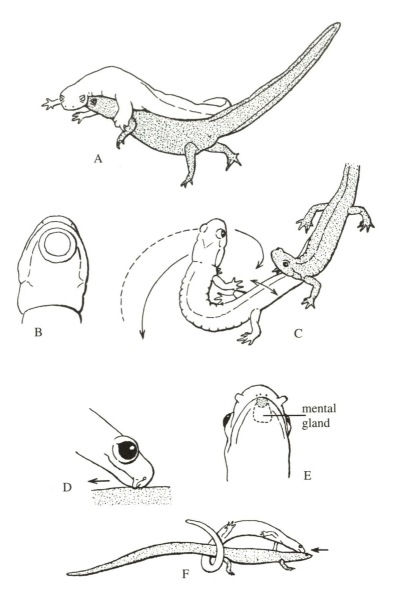

Fig. 17.3 Mating patterns in salamanders, females shown in gray. (A) Red-spotted Newt (*Notophthalmus viridescens*), showing cephalic amplexus. (B) Mental gland of Jordan Salamander (*Plethodon jordani*). (C) During the tail-straddling walk the male slaps his mental gland on the female's nostrils. (D–F) Delivery of mental gland secretions in the Northern Two-lined Salamander (*Eurycea bislineata*) (e US). (D) Male scratching skin surface of female with his projecting upper-jaw teeth, while at the same time presumably introducing mental gland secretion into her blood stream. (E) Position of the mental gland. (F) Male in the act of "vaccinating" the female. (After Arnold, 1977, redrawn, with permission from the author and D. H. Taylor and S. I. Guttman, from *The Reproductive Biology of Amphibians*, Plenum Press, New York, 1977)

Golden-striped Salamander (*Chioglossa lusitanica*) (n Portugal and nw Spain) (Arnold, 1977), females are also restrained, but spermatophore transfer is indirect. The male crawls under the female and entwines his forelimbs around hers, holding her in a piggyback position (she on top), a process called "ventral capture." After depositing the spermatophore, he swings to one side, maintaining his grip, and she lowers her hindquarters to remove the sperm capsule. In Pacific newts (*Taricha*) (w N Am) and others, the male uses "dorsal capture," amplexing the female from above (fig. 17.4). In *Taricha*, amplexus is thought to be required to achieve insemination, and courtship glands on the male's throat are pressed against her nose and he titillates her vent with his toes. This induces a quiescent or "obedient" state in the female. Amplexus permits the male to monopolize the female and to transport her away from rival males. In the Red-spotted Newt (*Notophthalmus viridescens*) (e US, se Can), amplexus is optional. The male may clasp the female's head with his hind limbs, especially if she is refractory, and genial gland secretion is rubbed against her nostrils. Such steps may be omitted with a receptive female (Arnold, 1977). The male may display in front of the female, undulating his body and tail from side to side. Spermatophore deposition occurs if the female nudges his tail (Verrell, 1990). In Old World newts (*Triturus*) (Eur e to Ural Mts and Caspian Sea), the male displays in front of the female, waving his tail. A receptive female is led to a position over the spermatophore (Hedlund, 1990).

Following spermatophore deposition, males of many salamandrids swing the body in an arc laterally, often pivoting on one forelimb. In *Taricha*, the animal's sacrum may be swung through an arc of 90°. Such maneuvers may aid the female to find the sperm capsule, since her path is blocked at a distance of about one body length in front of the spermatophore (Arnold, 1977; Hardy and Dent, 1988). In Old World *Pleurodeles* (Iberia and nw Afr) the pair interlock forelimbs while facing each other. After the male deposits the spermatophore, they rotate some 180°, pivoting about their forelimbs, a movement that brings the female's vent over the spermatophore.

A *Taricha*-like courtship pattern occurs in the Ambystomatidae and Plethodontidae, perhaps having evolved independently but in parallel in these two families (Salthe, 1967).

Ambystomatidae

In the Spotted Salamander (*Ambystoma maculatum*) (e US, se Can), the sexes engage in a "Liebespiel" (love play), milling about and probing one another with their snouts. Females find the spermatophores without amplexus and unguided by the males. In the Tiger Salamander (*A. tigrinum*) (N Am) and Axolotl (*A. mexicanum*) (Mex), there is likewise no amplexus. However, the male leads the female over the spermatophore as she places her nose near his vent in the "tail-nudging walk." Scent released from his exposed cloacal papillae

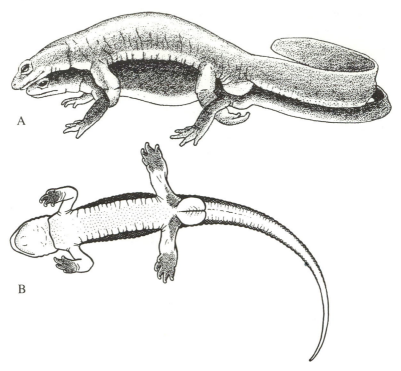

Fig. 17.4 (A) Amplexus in California Newts (*Taricha torosa*) (Cal), male above female. (B) Ventral surface of a breeding male newt (*Taricha*), showing bulbous vent and nuptial pads (darkened roughened area on feet and hind-limb bases) that aid the male in clinging to the female.

apparently attracts her and may be wafted toward her by undulations of his tail. A somewhat comparable tail-nudging walk has also been observed in some lungless salamanders (Plethodontidae). In other ambystomatids, the North-western Salamander (*Ambystoma gracile*) and Long-toed Salamander (*A. macrodactylum*) (nw N Am), amplexus occurs much as in the newts, and the sexes disengage for spermatophore deposition and pickup.

Plethodontidae

The male often strokes the female with his head, chin, and body or projecting upper jaw teeth, engages in a "tailstraddling" walk with her head applied to his sacral region or upper tail base, and leads her over the spermatophore (fig. 17.5). At the time of spermatophore pickup, the male of some species strokes the back of the female with his tail. Hedonic glands on the upper base of the tail in some brook salamanders (*Eurycea*) (cen and e US, se Can) may help keep the female in place during the tail walk, through nasolabial groove trans-

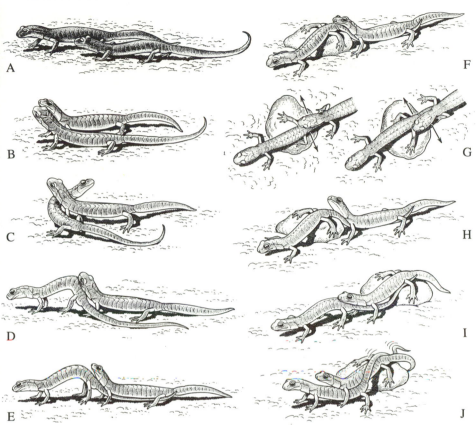

Fig. 17.5 Courtship and mating sequence in Ensatina (*Ensatina eschscholtzii*) (w N Am). (A) Male cautiously approaches female; (B) rubs her throat with his head; (C–E) crawls under her elevated head and brings his arched back under her chin; (F) leads her forward in the "tail-straddling" walk; (G) deposits spermatophore as the pair mutually stroke each other (arrows show direction of movements); (H) the female lifts her chin; (I) the "tail-straddling walk" is resumed until (J) the female's vent is over the spermatophore; the male then lunges backward and thrashes her with his writhing tail as she picks up the spermatophore with her vent.

port of hedonic secretion as she contacts the male's tail base with her snout (see Sever, 1989).

Gergits and Jaeger (1990a) report courtship of Red-backed Salamanders (*Plethodon cinereus*) (e US, ne Can) observed at night, under short-wave illumination, in the field. Males, upon encountering a female's trail, followed the trail precisely, "nose-tapping" enroute. Upon encountering the female, the male approached with body held low, in submissive posture, and sometimes nose-tapped the female, then assumed a position in front of her with tail arched and wriggled from side to side. If the female remained, he rubbed her back with his mental gland, eventually reaching her snout, whereupon she assumed a submissive posture. He then moved forward, aligned with her body, and again tail-wagged, and she placed her chin on his back just anterior to his vent. They then engaged in the "tail straddling" walk followed by spermatophore pickup.

DYNAMICS OF SPERMATOPHORE INSEMINATION

Female salamanders are thought to feel the spermatophore with their ventral surface as they crawl over it. In the Red-spotted Newt (*Notophthalmus viridescens*) (e US, se Can), Hardy and Dent (1988) observed that after the male had assumed his blocking position in front of the female, she crawled toward him so that the sperm cap brushed against her midventral skin in a continuous path from her chin to her cloaca. As the sperm cap neared her vent she arched her body upward until her vent reached its height. Touch appeared to aid her in precisely positioning her vent to detach the sperm cap with the lips of her cloaca. Such tactile stimuli may account for the rather high success in obtaining the sperm capsule in some species. In others, however, Arnold (1977) suggested that success rate may be as low as 50%.

There is great variation in the number of spermatophores produced by male salamanders during a courtship episode with a single female, ranging from one or two per night in plethodontids to over eighty in the Spotted Salamander (*Ambystoma maculatum*) (e US, se Can). Torrent salamanders have been reported to produce one to three, the Tiger Salamander (*A. tigrinum*) (N Am) eight to thirty-seven, and Old World newts (*Triturus*) one to four (Arnold, 1977). The number relates to a variety of factors—species differences in capacity for spermatophae production (Verrell, 1988), the extent of rivalry among males for females, extent of male control over females, and perhaps differences in female receptivity, length of the breeding season, and other factors. In the polyandrous Spotted Salamander, many males (ten to fifty) may vie for a single female. Amplexus does not occur and males do not lead females to their spermatophores. Males evidently maximize their chances of inseminating a female by depositing many scattered spermatophores and by covering spermatophores encountered, even their own, with a new spermatophore. Such inactivation of the spermatophores of rivals is a general phenomenon in *Ambystoma*. Such behavior promotes the success of the male by increasing his spermatophore count while simultaneously eliminating a rival's spermatophores (Arnold, 1976).

In the Tiger Salamander, males monopolize females and reduce sexual interference by rival males by transporting the female away, just before sperm transfer (Arnold, 1976). The male thus has more control over the female than the Spotted Salamander. Fewer spermatophores are deposited and females are led to them with the "tail-nudging walk." Control, however, is somewhat lax.

A rival male sometimes interposes himself between a pair engaged in the "tail-nudging walk" and covers the courting male's spermatophore with his own. The female, now following the rival, picks up his spermatophore instead. Males of the Pacific newts (*Taricha*) (w N Am) strongly monopolize females through amplexus and can sometimes avoid rivals by swimming away with the female. Amplexus may last for hours and few spermatophores are deposited. Plethodontids are the most conservative and invest much energy per spermatophore. They spend much time in courtship and some tend to achieve monopoly of females by their territoriality and by aggressively driving off rivals by chasing and biting them. The long courtship helps to ensure that the female will find the spermatophore and be inseminated. Even so, some rival male interference occurs. Male Ensatinas (*Ensatina eschscholtzii*) (w US, sw Can) have been seen to behave like a "following" female and to "dupe" the leading male into unprofitable spermatophore deposition.

The breeding season in ambystomatids is short, whereas in plethodontids it may last for 6–7 months (many temperature zone species) or throughout the year (some neotropical species). In species with a short breeding season, a premium is placed on males expending all their spermatophores on the first few females encountered, whereas in those with a long breeding season conservation of spermatophores ensures their availability for females encountered late in the season. Differences in female receptivity might also be involved, since high receptivity would be advantageous when the breeding season is short and less so when it is long. Indeed, low receptivity in the latter case would allow time for females to screen males and exercise sexual selection (Arnold, 1976).

EVOLUTION OF SALAMANDER BREEDING BEHAVIOR

Salthe (1967) has speculated on ecological factors in the evolution of salamander breeding behavior. He hypothesizes that the courtship of *Euproctus* (Eur) and the salamandrids that use ventral capture evolved in mountain streams. Dorsal capture is considered to be related to mating in still waters, and such salamanders are presumed to have spread from upland areas into the quiet waters of the lowlands. Plethodontid courtship shows modifications probably evolved for mating on land, and these animals are thought to have reinvaded upland regions. The spermatophore perhaps originally was an adaptation for mating in running water in ancestral salamanders that lived in montane regions.

Verrell (1989) has reviewed aspects of the reproductive biology of newts and salamanders that may shed light on the evolution of sexual patterns in natural populations. These aspects included the dynamics of breeding populations (including the average ratio of fertilized females to sexually active males at any given time, the operating sex ratio or OSR), competition between males

for females, mate choice, parental care, and physiological constraints on reproductive performance. The review focused primarily on the Plethodontidae,
Salamandridae, and Ambystomatidae. The duration of the mating period
emerged as an important determinant of the sexual pattern of a population,
exerting its major influence through OSR. When breeding periods are short,
males aggregate and scramble for matings by interfering with one another's
attempts to inseminate females. With prolonged breeding periods, males are
more likely to be territorial and to defend areas to which females are attracted
for mating. Females are more likely to exercise choice in the selection of
mates. A similar pattern occurs in anurans. In most salamanders that exercise
parental care, it is the female that does so. Male parental care seems to be
favored when fertilization is external and the oviposition site is flowing waters,
as in the hellbenders (*Cryptobranchus*). Physiological constraints include
available energy levels of sexually active males engaged in display, temperature and moisture conditions in terrestrial settings (plethodontid salamanders)
that may limit sexual activity, spermatophore supply, and the length of time
over which responsive females are available.

LIFE HISTORY MODES AMONG SALAMANDERS

Chiefly on the basis of egg size and number, Salthe (1969) recognizes three life
history modes among salamanders: Mode I—small eggs deposited in unpro-
tected quiet pond (lentic) waters (*Ambystoma*, *Taricha*); Mode II—fewer
larger eggs in hidden nest sites in flowing (lotic) waters and often guarded or
attended by the parents (usually the female) (Pacific Giant Salamanders,
Dicamptodon species; eastern and southern hemidactylines; and most dusky
salamanders, *Desmognathus*); Mode III—still fewer but larger eggs in well-
hidden terrestrial sites (larval stage completed within the egg), almost always
attended, usually by the female (plethodontines and bolitoglossines).

Anurans

MATING AND FERTILIZATION

With few exceptions (the Tailed Frog [*Ascaphus truei*] [nw US, sw Can], some
eleutherodactyline frogs, nectophrynoid toads, and perhaps others) anurans
engage in external fertilization, the males releasing sperm onto the egg mass.
Sperm is usually expelled into water surrounding the eggs, but in stream-
dwelling hylid frogs and some terrestrial species it is released directly onto the
eggs as they are extruded or after they have been deposited on land (neotropical poison-dart frogs). With few exceptions (some dendrobatid frogs, for example), male anurans clasp the female at the time of egg laying and thereby

Fig. 17.6 Red-legged Frogs (*Rana aurora*) (w N Am) in pectoral amplexus.

ensure nearly direct transfer of sperm to the eggs. As in salamanders, the sexual clasp is called amplexus. An amplexing male typically assumes a piggyback position, with his forelimbs encircling the female's body. Roughened nuptial pads that appear on his inner fingers during the breeding season help to ensure a tight grip.

Amplexus may be *pectoral* or *axillary*, the male's forelimbs encircling the female's chest just behind her forelimbs (fig. 17.6); *pelvic* or *inguinal*, with his forelimbs around her waist, just in front of her hindlimbs; or *cephalic*, as in the Neotropical dendrobatid frog *Epipedobates tricolor* (sw Ecuador). In the latter, the male, in piggyback position, places his forelimbs around the female's neck and presses the upper surface of his hands against her chin (Myers et al., 1978). The pectoral clasp is most common and considered "more advanced" than the pelvic clasp, which almost always occurs in water. The latter occurs in the Tailed Frog, spadefoot toads (*Scaphiopus* [N Am] and *Pelobates* [Eur, w Asia, nw Afr]), and several species of bufonids (Graybeal and Queiroz, 1992).

In amplexing anurans, elevation of the female's cloaca by a downward arching of her back is often the signal to the male that oviposition is to occur, and he brings his cloaca next to hers. Ejaculation occurs upon extrusion of the eggs.

Fertilization efficiency in water is helped by close approximation of the cloacae of the mating pair and in some (perhaps many) species by the male restraining and gathering the eggs with his hind limbs. In the Great Plains Toad

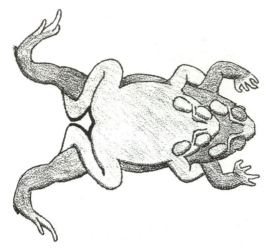

Fig. 17.7 "Basket" formation in a pair of Great Plains
Toads (*Bufo cognatus*) (cen US, Mex). The male (on
top) gathers the eggs as they are extruded into the
thickly outlined space between his limbs where
they are held for fertilization.

(*Bufo cognatus*) (cen US, sw Can, n Mex), studied by Krupa (1988), large
males positioned themselves more posteriorly than males paired with females
of similar length. Restraining of the eggs was accomplished by creating a
"basket," a triangular space formed between the male's legs and the legs and
body of his mate (fig. 17.7). As the eggs were extruded, the male used his legs
and feet to gather them into the basket, where they were held for approximately
3 minutes. "Basket" formation has been observed in other species and may be
widespread among anurans.

In an unusual form of fertilization, Neotropical male and female Granular
Poison-Arrow Frogs (*Dendrobates granuliferus*) (Costa Rica) place their
vents together while facing away from each other, and presumably eggs and
sperm are released simultaneously (Wells, 1977b). Males of the Flaming Poison-Arrow Frog (*D. pumilio*) (cen Am) in captivity were observed to moisten
dry leaves with seminal fluid before oviposition. Although males were seen to
briefly amplex females with their forelimbs around the female's neck, the final
mating position was with vents close together and each sex facing in a different
direction. Usually the male left before all eggs were laid (Weygoldt, 1980).
Vent apposition also occurs in the Mountain Viviparous Toad (*Nectophrynoides occidentalis*) (w Afr), which practices internal fertilization.

The Tailed Frog (*Ascaphus truei*) (nw US, sw Can) is the only anuran
known to engage in copulation (fig. 17.8). The frog lives in cold, often turbulent streams of the Pacific Northwest. Copulation ensures fertilization in fast-
moving water.

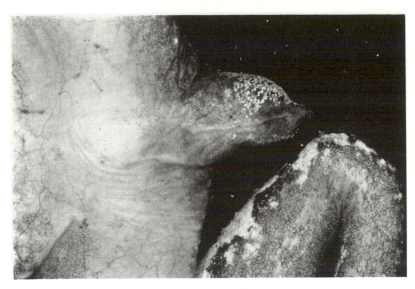

A

B

Fig. 17.8 (A) Copulatory organ of the male Tailed Frog (*Ascaphus truei*) (nw US, sw Can), an extension of the cloaca. (B) Overview of an adult male.

COURTSHIP

Most male anurans "court" females by means of their advertisement calls or modifications thereof. The call is the chief form of display in most species. The vocalizations of the male indicate his sex, since females usually have weak voices or are mute.

Males of several small Neotropical dendrobatid frogs, however, are exceptional in their use of visual displays. Male *Colostethus trinitatis* (s Colombia, n Ecuador) and *C. palmatus* (Colombia) turn black and engage in attention-getting movements, the former jumping up and down on their calling perches (Wells, 1980), and the latter performing elaborate postural changes when females approach. Display by the inch-long Venezuelan *C. collaris* has been described as a courtship dance (Dole, 1974). First the male turns toward the female, increasing the rate and vigor of his call; he then may crouch, crawl backward while swinging to one side, and leap upward, poised momentarily in a vertical position, balanced on his hind feet. The action is often repeated. A refractory female ignores the performing male and, facing him, with her head held high (she is usually larger than he is) and her bright sulphur-yellow throat slowly pulsing, drives him off. An attentive female, however, may repeatedly shift position to watch the performing male. An "audience" of up to eighteen females has been seen facing a dancing male, the females shifting their positions in unison to follow his actions. After one performance a male was seen to move off slowly, stopping frequently, a female following. He was perhaps leading her to the spawning site. Males guard the eggs and carry the tadpoles on their backs.

In another dendrobatid, the Green Poison-Arrow Frog (*Dendrobates auratus*) (cen Am to Colombia), the female actively courts the male. She seeks out a calling male, touches his snout with hers, places her forefeet on his body, drums her hind feet on his body, and may rub her head on his chin. He may reciprocate, but with less intensity. This behavior occurs as the male leads the female to the oviposition site. There is no amplexus. Males tend the eggs and transport the tadpoles to water, carrying one to three of them on their backs at a time. Males have been observed to fight over females, and there is also some evidence that females may fight in the presence of a calling male (Wells, 1978b).

In the Wood Frog (*Rana sylvatica*) (se US, Can), the Northern Leopard Frog (*Rana pipiens*) (n and w US, s Can), and certain other anurans, female qualities that cause the male to maintain amplexus are silence, wide girth, firmness (body distended with eggs), and receptiveness to the male's clasp (Noble and Farris, 1929; Noble and Aronson, 1942; Aronson, 1943). These characteristics may apply quite widely among anurans. After the female has laid her eggs she may reject the male by producing "release" calls, vibrating her body (*Bufo*, etc.), arching her back downwards, rolling, stretching with hind legs extended, kicking, or lunging. The particular procedure depends upon the species. Voiceless or nearly voiceless toads (*Bufo*) of both sexes rely primarily on body vibrations to thwart unwanted amplexus. Female Red-legged Frogs (*Rana aurora*) (w US, sw Can), which sometimes arrive at breeding sites before they are receptive, vibrate the abdomen and vocalize, but usually also must employ major body movements—extending the hind legs, rolling to one side, and remaining stiff and outstretched (Licht, 1969b) to break free from the male. The Spotted Frog (*Rana pretiosa*) (nw US, w Can) uses a release call and abdominal vibrations to escape clasping males. In addition to these active efforts to gain release, the female's reduced girth and soft abdomen following laying also evidently tend to "turn off" the male. The clasping response may be very strong but at times not very discriminating and at the height of breeding sometimes involves inanimate objects, including dead frogs. Storm (1960) reported a male Red-legged Frog in amplexus with a floating apple in which pits had been formed by the frog's hands, and Brown (1977a) observed male Western Toads (*Bufo boreas*) (w N Am) clasping the floral portions of floating cattails (*Typha*).

PATTERNS OF ANURAN REPRODUCTION

Wells (1977b) recognized two temporal patterns in anuran reproduction—*explosive* breeding and *prolonged* breeding, with intermediate stages. Explosive breeders are often species that use temporary pools (occasionally permanent waters) and breed whenever conditions are suitable. Females tend to arrive more or less together (synchronously) and they are available for only a short time. Rapid acquisition of mates is crucial for male success. Males are favored that actively seek out females. As a result, males engage in *scramble competition* for females and sometimes fight violently for them. They often greatly outnumber females, which come and go at the breeding site. When a male secures a female, amplexus is usually tenacious and prolonged. The male's legs may be extended and used to kick intruders away. In this breeding system females have little opportunity to select a mate. Many explosive breeders tend to call in unison and a chorus may be a din of voices—a "communal call" that transmits the species advertisement call as far and as continuously as possible. Spadefoot Toads (*Scaphiopus*) (N Am) are an example. Others that use the same reliable sites year after year may have weak voices, such as the Western Toad and Sonoran Desert Toad (*Bufo alvarius*) (sw US, nw Mex).

Prolonged breeders, on the other hand, typically use more reliable breeding sites and breeding extends over a long period (sometimes for several months). Females arrive irregularly (asynchronously) and males outnumber females at the breeding sites. The irregular arrival of females favors males that attract females from stationary calling sites. The calling males space themselves and guard territories, oviposition sites, and/or courtship areas against rivals, although physical contacts between males may be uncommon. Vocalizations may play a role in reducing fighting. For example, the "encounter call" of male Pacific Treefrogs is a trill which seems to inhibit the calling of a nearby male if he is too close, causing him to withdraw. If he fails to do so a fight may ensue. Males with high-quality territories are more attractive to females and may obtain several mates a season, for the females are attracted to calling males and are the agent of mate selection. The breeding structure resembles the "lek" situation in other vertebrates, the males displaying in small areas and the females moving among them in making their selections. There is some evidence that Bullfrogs (*Rana catesbeiana*) (US) change from a territorial to lek system, with increasing population density. It should be noted that aggressive behavior among prolonged breeders is not always around fixed sites because males may shift their positions.

Calls of prolonged breeders often alternate with one another (are antiphonal). It has been suggested that this minimizes sound interference, resulting from call overlap, thereby increasing the females' chances of finding and choosing among males. The possible adaptive significance of antiphonal calling, however, is not fully resolved. Sullivan (1985) found that in the Woodhouse Toad (*Bufo woodhousei*) (US, n Mex), call rate was *slowed* in response to playback of the species' advertisement call, played both at fast and slow rates. Slowing of the calls is presumed to help avoid acoustic overlap with neighbors. Slowing occurred even though females appeared to prefer fast-calling males. Slowing was most pronounced to high-rate recordings. However, in Sullivan's study the Desert (Red-spotted) Toad (*Bufo punctatus*) (sw US, Mex) did not reduce its call rate in response to playback. Instead, it usually initiated a call during each call broadcasted, resulting in extensive overlap of calls. Such behavior is often noted in choruses of these toads in the field.

The suggestion that antiphonal vocalizations may aid females in locating calling males has been discounted at least in one species, the Painted Reed Frog (*Hyperolius marmoratus*) (e Afr) studied by Passmore and Telford (1981). Females located speakers broadcasting calls simultaneously as readily as when calls were played back asynchronously. These authors suggest that in this species call alternation may be important in the spatial distribution of males rather than in the ability of females to locate males.

It is important to recognize that not all species or their populations can be expected to fit precisely into the "explosive" breeding and "prolonged" breeding categories. For example, the Gulf Coast Toad (*Bufo valliceps*) (s cen US, ne Mex), generally regarded as an explosive breeder, studied by Wagner and Sullivan (1992), in south-central Texas displayed traits of both explosive and prolonged breeders.

SATELLITE BEHAVIOR

In both explosive and prolonged breeders, silent "satellite" (sometimes called "parasitic") males may be present near calling individuals, sometimes nearly in contact but more often inches or a few feet away, awaiting opportunity to intercept females or take over vacated territories (see Forester and Czarnowsky, 1985; Roble, 1985; Mauger, 1988; Ovaska and Hunte, 1992). Satellite males usually crouch and maintain a low profile. Some individuals have been observed to alternate between satellite and calling behavior. In the Pacific Treefrog (*Pseudacris regilla*) (w N Am) and Northern Cricket Frog (*Acris crepitans*) (e US) the satellite tactic is adopted by males of all sizes and they may switch back and forth from calling to the satellite role (Forester and Lykens, 1986; Perrill and Magier, 1988).

In the Bullfrog (*Rana catesbeiana*) (in Illinois), Mauger (1988) observed that smaller sexually mature males engaged in parasitic (satellite) behavior and did not vocalize. However, medium-sized males, which sometimes vocalized, were opportunists. They occupied the fringes of territories held by large males and remained there until challenged by the resident or until the territory was vacated. When a territory-holding male was engaged in amplexus, other males infiltrated the dominant's territory and vocalized. Mauger notes that such infiltration behavior emphasizes the importance of territorial quality and that it may serve to increase a male's probability of mating.

In *Eleutherodactylus johnstonei*, Ovaska and Hunte (1992) (Barbados, W. Indies) noted that interfering males called in unison, facing the female at close range. Such simultaneous calling would likely interfere with reception by the female of the male's voice she had targeted and improve the mating opportunities of such male neighbors.

Satellites of the African Leaf-folding Frog (*Afrixalus delicatus*) have been observed to chase amplexing pairs and to grapple with the amplexed male, but without success (Backwell and Passmore, 1991).

Satellite behavior is by no means confined to subordinate males. Because of the energetic costs of vocalizing, which may, as has been pointed out earlier, result in weight loss in intense vocalizers, it appears to be advantageous for even larger males among prolonged breeders occasionally to take time off from calling, particularly at high population densities.

Satellite behavior is probably widespread among anurans, having been observed in many species—the Bullfrog (*Rana catesbeiana*), Striped Chorus Frog (*Pseudacris triseriata*), Northern Cricket Frog (*Acris crepitans*), Pacific Treefrog (*Pseudacris regilla*), Spring Peeper (*P. crucifer*) (Forester and Lykens, 1986), and others. In the Bullfrog and Spring Peeper, satellites are smaller than calling males, but in the Striped Chorus Frog and Northern Cricket Frog, size differences have not been found. Satellite behavior appears to have some advantages—reduced energy expenditure and reduced threat of predation (Perrill and Magier, 1988). Predators such as snakes that hunt by sight, and predatory large frogs and others that use sound and/or sight to find prey, may miss the quiet satellites. Although satellites often are observed over the short term to have a low level of mating success, because of their less energy-expensive lives and risk behavior they may perhaps live longer than callers and over many breeding seasons be as successful as callers (see Backwell and Passmore, 1991).

For further information on amphibian courtship, reproductive patterns, and biology, see Rabb (1973), Salthe and Mecham (1973), Vial (1973), and Taylor and Guttman (1977).

Eggs

Gelatinous Capsules

Amphibian ova are typically surrounded by one to several translucent or transparent gelatinous envelopes (containing acidic, neutral, or sometimes sulphated mucopolysaccharides and mucoproteins) secreted by the oviducts (fig. 17.9). Water, oxygen, carbon dioxide, and ammonia pass quite freely through the capsules. In most anurans the ovum is rigidly held by the high viscosity of the innermost gelatinous layer. After fertilization, a fluid appears between the ovum and its vitelline membrane, freeing it to rotate and orient with the animal pole uppermost. Later, as the embryo grows, the liquefied zone enlarges, aided partly by softening of the mucoid capsules. In salamanders the innermost mucoid layer or capsule liquefies shortly after the eggs are laid, whether fertilized or not, and the developing embryo rotates, more slowly, within its investing vitelline membrane (Salthe, 1963). Hatching occurs when secretions from hatching glands on the head of the embryo and a general softening of the capsules cause a rupture of their walls.

The gelatinous envelopes provide support, help protect the eggs against mechanical damage, desiccation, some kinds of predation (Ward and Sexton, 1981; Semlitsch, 1988), and penetration by pathogens and other damaging agents. In illuminated surroundings they may help protect against ultraviolet radiation (Higgins and Sheard, 1926; Urbach, 1969). When the eggs are first laid, the gelatinous capsules are inconspicuous but they quickly absorb water and swell to much greater size.

The eggs of some salamanders and anurans contain green algae. Examples are the eggs of the Spotted Salamander (*Ambystoma maculatum*), Jefferson Salamander (*A. jeffersonianum*), Tiger Salamander (*A. tigrinum*), Northwestern Salamander (*A. gracile*), Red-legged Frog (*Rana aurora*), and Wood Frog (*R. sylvatica*). Gilbert (1942, 1944) observed that in the Spotted and Jefferson Salamanders the alga was a unicellular species (*Oophila* = *Chlamydomonas*

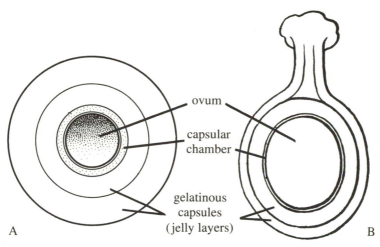

ovum

capsular
chamber

gelatinous
capsules
(jelly layers)

A   B

Fig. 17.9 Structure of amphibian eggs. Eggs are surrounded by one or more
gelatinous, often transparent, capsules. (A) The ovum of eggs laid in illuminated surroundings has melanic pigment over its upper surface that protects
it against overdoses of ultraviolet light, whereas that of eggs on the right (B),
laid in dark locations, is unpigmented. Some salamanders suspend their eggs
by gelatinous strands.

amblystomatis). It occurred throughout the jelly envelopes of the eggs but, in
the Spotted Salamander, in later development, was most abundant in the inner
envelope. It was determined that the alga penetrated the eggs after they were
laid. This has been confirmed by Gatz (1973). There was some experimental
evidence that it reduced mortality and sped embryonic growth and time of
hatching.

Using an oxygen-sensitive microelectrode probe in Spotted Salamander
eggs, Bachmann et al. (1986) determined that when exposed to light the
chlamydomonad alga produced photosynthetic oxygen in excess of that required by the respiration of both the developing embryos and the alga itself,
and the oxygen-rich environment of the eggs persisted even when the surrounding aquatic environment was almost without oxygen. These results raise
questions concerning the conclusions of Hutchison and Hammen, 1958; Hammen and Hutchison, 1962), who reported that any benefit to the embryos was
not due to increased availability of oxygen produced by the alga, nor to an
energy source derived from photosynthesis (Hammen and Hutchison, 1962).
Salthe and Mecham (1973) speculated that perhaps some growth-promoting
substance was produced by the alga or the alga was simply an indicator of
good health of the embryos. Anderson (1971) also reported no beneficial effects from the egg-alga relationship in field studies on the Tiger Salamander
and, in fact, found a consistent correlation of algae with higher mortality.

It is important to do further careful measurements with microelectrodes and to determine the kind and location of algae found in each species studied. Controlled experiments should be performed charting embryonic rates of development and mortality in eggs with and without algae.

The Ovum

VARIATION IN SIZE AND ENERGY CONTENT

Ovum size variation in amphibians occurs among species, among populations, within populations, and within the egg complement of individual females. There is a general tendency for the larger females to produce the larger ova, as has been observed, for example, in the Northwestern Salamander (*Ambystoma gracile*) (nw Cal, sw Can) (Eagleson, 1976) and the Wood Frog (*Rana sylvatica*) (ne US, s Can) (Berven, 1988), and for ova size to increase with increasing latitude and elevation.

Ova size can also be influenced by nutritional levels (Fraser, 1980) and the length of the growing period between metamorphosis and the time of ova maturation. In a study of Wood Frogs in Maryland, Berven (1988) found that females that matured the same summer in which they metamorphosed develop small eggs, whereas those that matured the following year, or bred for the second time, develop larger eggs. The former, actively engaged in body growth, had less time and energy to devote to egg maturation. Furthermore, fewer eggs are "recruited" for development in 2- or 3-year-old frogs. This evidently makes it possible for them to make their eggs larger.

Because of such variation in ova size and associated energy content, some rather large differences may exist in the energetic potential offered the developing embryo even within a single species. Thus some female Tiger Salamanders (*Ambystoma tigrinum*) (N Am) produce eggs with as many as 29 calories per ovum, whereas others in the same population, at the same time, produce eggs with as few as 16.5 calories. Caloric level has been found to increase directly with ovum size in this and several other species of *Ambystoma* (Kaplan, 1980a). The offspring of the latter would begin life with only 57% of the energy reserves of the former.

These maternal effects on survival success via the ovum can ramify throughout development and even extend to metamorphosis and beyond. Ova size and energy content can affect timing of developmental events, hatching time, size at hatching and subsequent growth and maturation rates, and the size at which larval foraging begins, size at metamorphosis, and ultimately even adult mating success. In so doing they can affect larval competition for food and space between species and within individuals in a species population. In a study reported by Kaplan (1985) on the California Newt (*Taricha torosa*), it was found that when food was abundant, larvae from large eggs metamorphosed in less time and at a larger size than those from small eggs. However, when food was limited, although they still metamorphosed at larger size, they took longer to do so.

In his study of ambystomid salamanders, Kaplan (1980a) found that hatching size tends to vary directly with ovum size—the larger the ovum, the larger the hatchling. Furthermore, after feeding began, the size differences became amplified with time. Since a continuum of ovum sizes may exist even within one population, such variation may provide flexibility in coping with environmental conditions. For example, larger eggs, which produce larger larvae, may be superior to smaller ones in a competitive environment with numerous predators. However, such larger eggs may be produced at a cost of smaller numbers if the body size and shape of females is constraining. Smaller eggs, on the other hand, which can be produced in larger numbers, would enable females to be equally successful if environmental conditions do not place a premium on size of embryos or larvae.

The increase in ovum size with latitude and elevation requires further comment. In his study of ambystomid salamanders, Kaplan (1980b) found greater efficiency in development to the feeding stage in embryos that develop from larger ova. "Efficiency" was measured by determining (1) how much initial energy contained in the egg was still present at the beginning of larval feeding; (2) the amount of larval length produced on a given amount of energy; (3) the increase in length between the hatching and feeding periods; and (4) the energy contained per unit length of larvae at the beginning of feeding. Since variability in overall efficiency of development is positively correlated with temperature (as temperature rises efficiency increases), an increase in egg size could compensate for the decrease in energetic efficiency of development in cold waters. This can explain the association of large eggs with cold environments that occurs both within and between species.

The problem of low temperatures for development in cold environments is often eased by the tendency for females at high latitudes and elevation to lay their eggs in well-illuminated shallow sites where rather high water temperatures may be reached, often even higher than at sites selected at lower latitudes and elevations.

PIGMENTATION

Most amphibian ova have melanic pigment distributed over the animal hemisphere. Such eggs are laid in illuminated surroundings. Some, however, are unpigmented and are laid underground, in tree hollows, deep in the recesses of springs and caves, beneath stones in streams, and in other dark locations. Examples are the unpigmented ova of caecilians, most plethodontid salamanders, eleutherodactyline frogs, the Tailed Frog (*Ascaphus truei*) (nw US, sw Can), and others.

Ovum pigment protects against ultraviolet radiation and it has heat-concentrating properties. An early experiment by Sergeev and Smirnov (1939), using the eggs of an ambystomid salamander, supported the concept of the protective role of egg pigmentation against ultraviolet light. The nuclei of clawed frog (*Xenopus*) (Afr) eggs can be completely inactivated by small doses of ultraviolet light (Gurdon, 1960), showing the vulnerability of these crucial structures to such radiation under experimental conditions. The dark pigment of the animal pole readily absorbs solar radiation and radiates heat (black-body radiation), and the jelly surrounding the eggs acts as an insulator. In retaining heat, it acts much like the glass of a greenhouse in trapping long-wave radiation. An elevation of the temperature of the eggs and egg masses above the surrounding water may occur.

The effect is notable in globular egg clusters laid at or near the surface, and is enhanced by aggregation or clumping of clusters, as has been shown in the Wood Frog (*Rana sylvatica*) (ne US, s Can) (Waldman and Ryan, 1983). Globular clusters have less surface in relation to mass than eggs in strings or "rafts" (spread out floating layers) and they gain and lose heat more slowly. Hassinger (1970) found an average increase of 1.60°C within Wood Frog clusters and 0.63°C within Northern Leopard Frog (*Rana pipiens*) (N Am) masses. Savage (1961) reported an average deviation of 0.63°C in Common Frog (*Rana temporaria*) (Eur) egg clusters in the field, and Licht (1971) a high of 3.6°C in those of the Red-legged Frog (*Rana aurora*) (w N Am).

Waldman and Ryan (1983) have demonstrated the thermal advantage of egg-cluster clumping. They obtained temperatures as high as 4°–6°C above water temperatures in a large clump of 110 clusters of the Wood Frog. Temperature elevation was directly proportional to the number of clusters in a clump. Elevation of temperature occurred on both sunny and overcast days.

The temperature effects described accelerate development and sometimes can mean the difference between life and death in cold waters.

Clumping of clusters in the Wood Frog, and perhaps other communal layers, may also contribute to survival during pond recession between periods of rainfall. Forester and Lykens (1988) found that some eggs of this frog survived exposure for as long as 2 weeks.

Location and Shape of Egg Clusters (the "Spawn")

We discuss here general aspects. Some of the many and diverse methods, particularly in anurans, for special handling of spawn, from foam-nest building to stomach brooding, are discussed in chapter 18. Most amphibians lay their eggs in fresh water (figs. 17.10A, 11A). Many, however, deposit them in moist places on land (figs. 17.10B, 11B), as do caecilians, most plethodontid salamanders, and evidently all eleutherodactyline frogs. Eggs laid in water may be deposited separately or in small groups of two or three, or they may be deposited in grapelike clusters (figs. 17.12A,B), spheres, and in some anurans in

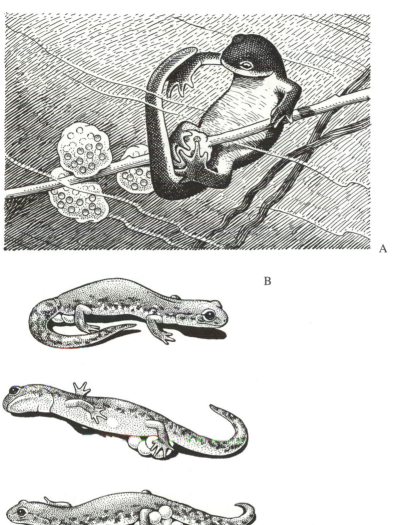

Fig. 17.10 (A) An amphibious amphibian, the California Newt (*Taricha torosa*) laying its eggs in water. The rubbery egg clusters are attached to roots, stems and other objects. (B) A terrestrial amphibian (*Ensatina eschscholtzii*) (w N Am) laying its eggs on land. Three stages are shown.

A

B

Fig. 17.11 (A) California Newt (*Taricha torosa*) eggs at an advanced stage of development. (B) The terrestrial egg cluster of the Arboreal Salamander (*Aneides lugubris*) (Cal), suspended from the roof of the nesting cavity.

A

B

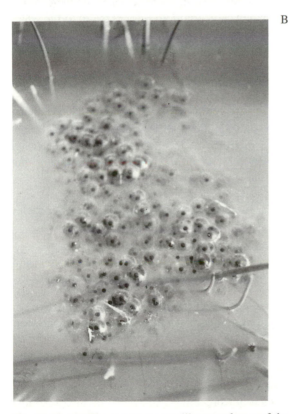

Fig. 17.12 (A) The compact grapelike egg cluster of the Foothill Yellow-legged Frog (*Rana boylii*) (w US). Eggs are usually laid in riffly waters, often on the downstream side of stones. (B) Floating loose egg cluster of the Red-legged Frog (*Rana aurora*) (w N Am).

floating "rafts," and in beadlike or cylindrical strings (many bufonids). Eggs may be free or attached to objects in the water. Terrestrial plethodontid salamanders lay their eggs in grapelike clusters, some with the eggs variously connected with slender strands of jelly in a rosarylike string (the strands sometimes broken) or attached to surfaces by individual pediceled bases. In some species, the eggs are suspended by jelly strands from the ceiling of the nest cavity (fig. 17.11B). In the Sticky Caecilian (*Ichthyophis glutinosus*) (Sri Lanka), a terrestrial species, two or three dozen eggs are laid in a grapelike cluster in moist soil near a spring, pond, or stream (Breckenridge and Jayasinghe, 1979). The eggs are attached by slender stalks. Nipplelike structures at the free end of some of the eggs may represent broken stalks, suggesting that the eggs emerge in a rosarylike string.

Factors that can influence the placement of eggs and the shape of the egg cluster are detectability by predators, rate of water flow, risk of flooding, and temperature. For example, eggs in strings or attached singly are probably less likely to be swept away by water currents than those deposited in masses; and those attached in small groups or singly, less likely to be detected by predators. Those grouped in strings or floating rafts are more fully exposed to the water than those in globular masses and may have an advantage in warmer waters where oxygen tension is low; eggs in globular masses, on the other hand, are better insulated and less likely to freeze (Zweifel, 1968).

With respect to choice of egg-laying sites, Resetarits and Wilbur (1989) found, in the treefrog (*Hyla chrysoscelis*) (e US and se Can) tested in experimental outdoor pools (Durham County, North Carolina), that females tended to avoid pond sites where there were significant threats of predation and intraspecific larval competition. Likewise, the Streamside Salamander (*Ambystoma barbouri*) (e US) has been shown to select egg-laying sites along streams that reduced exposure of its young larvae to predatory fish (Kats and Sih, 1992), and larger male Bullfrogs (*Rana catesbeiana*) may control egg-laying sites that have significantly lower larval mortality than the sites of smaller males (Howard, 1978b).

Frequency of Laying and Number of Eggs Laid

The frequency of laying, the number of eggs laid during the reproductive period, and the sizes and nutrient-packaging of the eggs deposited are variables that reflect the species' mode of life and the environmental conditions under which the eggs must develop. Probably most species in the temperate zones are determinant layers—most individuals in a population depositing all or most of their mature ova in one or several egg-laying sessions lasting hours, days, or perhaps weeks and then not breeding again until the next breeding period, a year or more hence. Multiple clutches (two or three) in a single season have been documented for a number of temperate-zone anurans (see Perrill and Daniel, 1983). There are other species, however, that are known to oviposit repeatedly over many months or throughout the year. Although much more study is needed to determine the laying behavior of individuals, population behavior suggests that some of these species may approach a continuum in production of mature ova and, as individuals, may oviposit at intervals more or less continuously throughout the year. The equitable conditions for amphibian breeding in the tropics favors such indeterminant maturation of ova, although it is well known that many species there are "seasonal" in their reproductive patterns and are evidently determinant breeders.

Amphibians living in arid environments are also candidates for the indeterminant pattern, for such environments favor opportunism in breeding to take advantage of occasional and unpredictable rainfall. Long (1989) found that in the Southern Spadefoot Toad (*Spea multiplicata*) in Texas, an arid land species (sw US, Mex), about half the number of ovarian follicles present the first night of mating were ovulated and the remainder were retained throughout dormancy and enlarged to ovulatory size. A backup was thus available should the first laying meet with poor success. In such studies, individual reproductive behavior must be clearly separated from population behavior.

There is great variation in the egg complement (the total number of eggs available for deposition at any given time) among species and some variation within species. Complement size ranges from the single egg of the tiny Cuban Tree Toad (*Eleutherodactylus limbatus*), to many thousands in the larger toads (*Bufo*) and frogs (*Rana*). Among seasonal temperate-zone species, many plethodontid salamanders have a complement of usually less than a few dozen eggs, laid over a period of hours or days. Caecilians also fall into the few dozen eggs or less category. At the other extreme are some of the ranid frogs, in which, over a similar time span, their full complement of many thousands of eggs is expelled. The size of the egg complement produced by a species has a genetic basis.

A correlation exists between the size of the egg complement and presence or absence of parental care of the eggs and sometimes of the larvae. Some poison-dart frogs (Dendrobatidae) lay only one or two eggs in terrestrial sites that are tended, and the larvae are transported on the back of the parent to water. Many plethodontid salamanders and caecilians also tend their eggs. On the other hand, many ranid frogs, highly fecund species, depart the egg site and make no direct effort to protect the eggs. A female Bullfrog (*Rana catesbeiana*) (US) or Marine Toad (*Bufo marinus*) may deposit up to around 25,000 eggs.

In addition to genetic factors, the egg complement can be influenced by the nutritional condition of the female, temperature and length of the growing season, delays in reproduction, amount of repetitive breedings, and population densities. In the Wood Frog (*Rana sylvatica*) (ne US, s Can), Berven (1988) found that females that delayed reproduction or those that bred a second time produce proportionally smaller clutches for their body size than those individuals that reproduced at a younger age. High population density was correlated with juvenilization of the gonads and failure of oviposition in California Slender Salamanders (*Batrachoseps attenuatus*) on islands in San Francisco Bay (Anderson, 1960).

In general, within a given mode of reproduction (for example, terrestrial or aquatic breeding), as species body size (volume) increases so does clutch size, and within a given population or species, larger females (except ageing ones) will generally produce larger clutches than smaller ones. Such relationships have yet to be shown, however, in caecilians and appears not to be the case in Guatemalan *Dermophis*. There is no correlation of clutch size and female body size in this viviparous form (Wake, 1980a).

Some species lay one or more times every year, some every other year or even less frequently. Some anurans in arid environments may go several years without breeding. An extreme case of a slow reproductive rate is that of the Alpine Salamander, which gives birth usually to two young every 3–5 years.

See Jørgensen (1992) for a comprehensive review of reproductive modes and patterns among amphibians.

Larvae

Caecilians

Terrestrial caecilians lay their eggs in moist places on land, often near a spring, pond, or stream. The eggs of some species undergo direct development, but those of others give rise to free-living aquatic larvae. Breckenridge et al. (1987) have provided an excellent account of the biology and development of the Sticky Caecilian (*Ichthyophis glutinosus*) (Sri Lanka), a species that has a free-living larval stage. Larvae, eel-like in form, hatch with three pairs of red feathery gills, a blunt head, eyes with a lens and optic cup, a lateral line system, and a short, finned tail. They soon make their way to water and lose their gills within 2 days. They swim with eel-like movements and appear to be mainly active at night. Metamorphosis is gradual, the head becomes more pointed, the eyes degenerate, the lateral line system disappears, and the skin thickens and develops annuli and imbedded scales; sensory tentacles appear and the tail fin and tail are lost, at an age of about 10–12 months following hatching. Soon after entering water, sorties to land begin. Within a year, the young animals are firmly established in soil, where they construct burrows. Their heads may sometimes be seen at the burrow openings. Throughout metamorphosis, length increases steadily but weight greatly accelerates after about 60–70 weeks.

The embryos of viviparous caecilians, probably the majority of species, un-

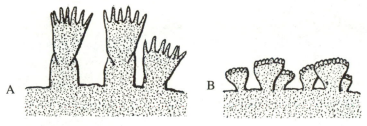

Fig. 17.13 Dentition of fetal viviparous caecilians, specialized for scrap-ing the walls of the maternal oviducts to stimulate the release of nutrients which they ingest. Lower jaw teeth of (A) a 57 mm *Gymnopis multipli-cata* (Honduras to Panama), and (B) a 75 mm *Typhlonectes compressi-cauda* (S AM). Diagrammatic drawings made from modified Schlieren photography. (After Wake, 1976, with permission from John Wiley & Sons, Inc.)

dergo full development within the oviducts of the mother. They are elongate, have gills (in typhlonectids, paired and saclike), eyes that develop normally for a time but later regress, and have specialized scraping dentition (fig. 17.13) with which they stimulate the secretion of nutrients (lipids and mucoproteins) from the wall of the oviducts, which they ingest and depend upon as their yolk sac food supply declines. Some oviducal wall tissue may also, at times, be ingested. A female *Typhonectes compressicauda* (S Am) may bear as many as nine young (Wake, 1977a) and they may increase their length six times the length reached before yolk absorption. Each may be 40% of the female's total length at birth! Even larger percentages have been reported for this and other species (Wake, 1977b). The energetic demands on the mother are great. Meta-morphosis involves loss of the gills, thickening of the skin, development of the tentacles, and resorption of the fetal teeth which are replaced by the adult dentition shortly after birth.

Salamanders and Anurans

Larvae may hatch with eyes and mouth not fully formed, without or with only rudiments of limbs, and with only rudiments of gills. The young amphibian continues to live on its yolk as further development takes place (fig. 17.14). Terrestrial larvae undergo development within the egg. For example, eleuth-erodactylid frogs and most lungless salamanders (Plethodontidae) lay their large-yolked unpigmented eggs in damp places on land, and development is completed within the egg, the young emerging fully formed (fig. 17.15). In the plethodontids and others, gills, which serve in respiration while in the egg, are resorbed at hatching; eleutherodactylids, however, have only fleeting develop-ment of gills or lack them entirely. Hatching glands on the snout of embryos

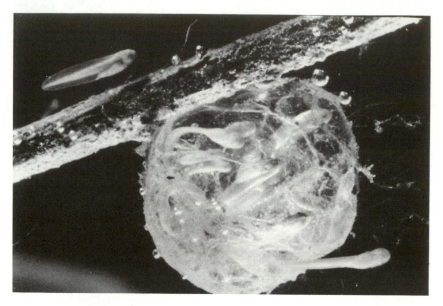

Fig. 17.14 Hatching of Pacific Treefrog (*Pseudacris regilla*) eggs. For a time the young tadpoles live on their yolk until their mouth parts more fully develop.

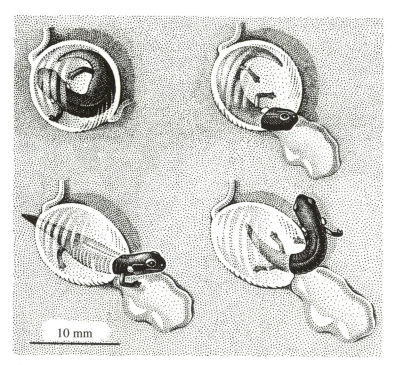

10 mm

Fig. 17.15 Hatching of a terrestrial salamander, the Oregon Slender Salamander (*Batrachoseps wrighti*). Young emerge fully formed. The white patches on the neck are the stubs of resorbed gills.

secrete enzymes that liquefy the egg capsule and aid escape from the egg. Eleutherodactylid frogs, however, slit the egg membrane with an egg tooth.

The larval period commonly varies from one to three months, but there are much shorter periods associated with ephemeral ponds, especially in arid regions, and far longer periods in permanent waters of low temperature; in cold areas larvae may overwinter one or more times.

Salamander Larvae

The eggs of many salamanders hatch into a larva typically with three pairs of external gills, lidless eyes, and a long body and a tail somewhat flattened from side to side with dorsal and ventral fins. Forelimbs may be present as buds or developed to the stage of toe formation. True teeth form in both jaws, but a true tongue is lacking. Salamander larvae are carnivorous, although there is some evidence for occasional feeding on algae and other plants.

On the basis of their ecology and manner of development they may be classified as quiet water ("pond"), moving water ("stream" or "mountain brook"), and terrestrial types (discussed above) (fig. 17.16). However, there is not always a strict ecological separation of aquatic larval types in nature. Pond-type larvae, exemplified by *Ambystoma* (N Am), typically have broad tail fins, and the dorsal fin extends forward to the shoulder region. They have a balancer (fig. 17.16D), a slender projecting rodlike structure on each side of the head during early stages; long gill filaments (fimbriae); well-developed gill rakers; and a biconvex gular fold. The rakers, typically erect, conical, pointed structures, are on the inner faces of the gill arches (rami), and the rakers of adjacent arches tend to interfinger, forming a sieve to prevent clogging of the gills. Balancers perhaps function to prop the young larva off the substratum, preventing fouling of the gills with bottom muck. They may also help the young larvae maintain balance before the forelimbs assume this function. The hind limbs are rudimentary at hatching. Stream-type larvae, as exemplified by *Dicamptodon* (nw US), typically have a more depressed body and narrow fins, and the dorsal fin usually extends only to the lower back or sacral region; the gill filaments are short, the gill rakers are reduced, and the gular fold is less biconvex. They lack balancers and the hind limbs are functional at hatching.

Valentine and Dennis (1964) consider it desirable to distinguish between "stream" and highly specialized "mountain brook" dwellers. The latter, as exemplified by torrent salamanders (*Rhyacotriton*) (nw US), differ from stream and pond dwellers in their modified and reduced gill rami, short fimbriae, the loss of the second row of gill fimbriae, heavy, broadly concave gular fold, and restriction of the tail fins to posterior to the vent.

In some species (notably in *Ambystoma* and in the Pacific Giant Salamanders, *Dicamptodon* species) larvae may be of three types: (1) those that regu-

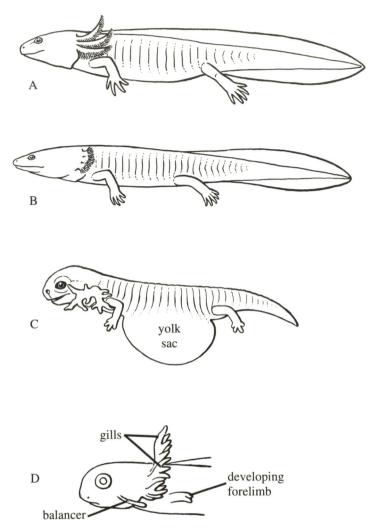

Fig. 17.16 Salamander larvae. (A) Pond type with well-developed tail fins and large feathery gills. (B) Stream type with reduced tail fins and short gills. (C) Terrestrial type that undergoes full development within the egg, nourished by its yolk supply. (D) Recently hatched pond-type larva with balancer.

larly transform, (2) those in which transformation is facultative, (occurring or not), depending upon genetics and environmental factors, and (3) obligate larvae, which persist as larvae and do not transform. Larvae of types (2) and (3) may breed (see below). The number of these metamorphic types and their proportions vary with the species and among species populations. For example, larvae of the California Tiger Salamander (*Ambystoma californiense*) appear to be only of type (1)—all transform, whereas populations of the related Tiger Salamander (*Ambystoma tigrinum*) and the Northwestern Salamander (*A. gracile*) include all three, and the proportions of the three types vary depending upon local conditions and probably genetics. All three types (and a cannibal morph) are found in some populations of the Barred Tiger Salamander (*Ambystoma tigrinum mavortium*) of the Great Plains, and many populations of this salamander have larvae of types (1) and (2), whereas some populations of the Gray Tiger Salamander (*A. t. diaboli*), far to the north, and of the Northwestern Salamander (*A. gracile*) (nw US, sw Can), are predominantly of type (3). In some populations of the Tiger, Northwestern, and Pacific Giant Salamanders, nontransforming larvae (type 3) appear to be absent or rare.

NEOTENY

Prolongation of larval life (with or without breeding) beyond the usual time of transformation is a particular kind of paedomorphosis (neoteny), a retention of youthful features (see below). It is associated with a reduction in rate of growth, the causes of which may not always be clear. Neotenic larvae are usually found in semipermanent or permanent waters, for there is often insufficient time in transient waters for such delay in transformation without high mortality.

Perhaps the most important environmental factor promoting retardation of larval growth is low temperature. Neotenics are often found in the cool waters of lakes and ponds at high elevation or latitude (Sexton and Bizer, 1978). Low temperature not only slows growth but it either inhibits the release of thyroxin by the thyroid, essential to metamorphosis, or it inhibits the ability of the body tissues to respond to thyroxin. Food shortages (as on the shores of ponds in arid lands or mountain lakes and in caves), missing or scant trace substances (iodine), severe temperature fluctuations, aridity, lack of cover on land, competition, and genetic factors probably also contribute (Sprules, 1974a,b). The influence of genetics is seen in the existence of obligate and facultative metamorphics and obligate breeding larvae in single populations of the Northwestern Salamander in southwestern British Columbia (Sprules, 1974b), and in breeding larval strains of the Tiger salamander that are genetically isolated from the segments of the population that regularly transform (Glass, 1951; Knopf, 1962).

Larval breeding provides the species with flexibility in adjusting to environmental conditions. It permits a population to persist when conditions on land are inhospitable to survival of transformed individuals. In species in which neotenic breeding is not genetically obligatory among all members of the larval population, individuals can give rise to larvae that transform, keeping open the option of dispersal to new breeding sites and avoiding predation and competition (neotenic populations often do not compete well with fish) that might develop in permanent waters. The colonists in turn may resort to the neotenic mode should conditions at new sites so dictate. Furthermore, some breeding or nonbreeding larvae can grow to large size before metamorphosis, thereby shortening the hazardous growing period on land. Such a flexible system has been found in populations of the Tiger Salamander in the Gunnison Basin, at around 9000–11,000 feet (2800–3400 m), in west-central Colorado (Sexton and Bizer, 1978).

PAEDOMORPHOSIS

Obligate (genetically fixed) larval breeding represents a form of paedomorphosis ("shaped like a child or larva"). Paedomorphosis, in a variety of manifestations, has been important in animal evolution (see Gould, 1977; Alberch et al., 1979; and Alberch, 1980), and numerous examples of it are to be found among salamanders (see Shaffer, 1984). It involves incorporation of larval or youthful characteristics of ancestral stock into later stages of development, often including the adult morphology of the descendants. Changes in a few developmental processes can greatly increase variation in later, including adult, stages without the necessity of major genetic reorganization, and can provide natural selection with much new variation with which to work. For example, the spatulate feet of some bolitoglossine salamanders (Fig. 4.2C) represent a carryover into the adult of some features of embryonic foot pad structure, common to many developing salamanders. The evolution of permanently larval forms such as the gilled brook salamanders (*Eurycea*) (e and se US) and the blind and gilled cave salamanders, the Texas Blind Salamander (*Typhlomolge rathbuni*), and the Georgia Blind Salamander (*Haideotriton wallacei*) (se US) of the family Plethodontidae and the completely aquatic gilled salamanders ("perennibranchs") of the families Sirenidae (sirens) and Proteidae (mudpuppies) (e US) have also involved the paedomorphic process.

KIN RECOGNITION

Kin or neighbor recognition has been documented in tadpoles, but there has been little study of this phenomenon in larval salamanders. Larval Marbled Salamanders (*Ambystoma opacum*) are known to be aggressive and cannibalistic but they are less aggressive and more submissive to siblings than to nonsiblings. However, this seems not to be a matter of neighbor recognition (Walls and Roudebush, 1991).

METAMORPHOSIS

In salamanders larval transformation to the terrestrial stage requires less reorganization of structure than in anurans. A major dietary shift with its accompanying extensive anatomical and physiological changes is not required. At transformation, tail fins are reduced or lost, gills are resorbed, gill slits close, and the skin changes to adult form with a stratified epithelium. Modifications may occur in the head region—eyelids develop, there are often changes in dentition, and a fleshy tongue forms, often of elaborate structure.

As with transforming anurans, as larval tail fins are reduced or lost and other changes occur, swimming speed, especially burst speed, declines and the animal becomes more vulnerable to predation (see Shaffer et al., 1991).

Anuran Larvae (Tadpoles)

STRUCTURE AND CHANGES WITH GROWTH (FIG. 17.17)

At hatching a typical pond-type tadpole (Type IV, p. 191) usually has three pairs of external gill rudiments (one pair is indistinct), lateral line organs, and an adhesive organ or organs (sucker or cement organs) on the underside of the head by means of which the rather helpless young larva (fig. 17.14) can attach itself to objects in the water. The adhesive organs produce a sticky mucus. They usually disappear by the time the larva has acquired coordinated swimming movements. Later the opercular folds overgrow the gill region, completely enclosing it except for the spiracular opening, and form an opercular chamber. The spiracle is single and opens on the left side of the body. Internal gills develop, eyes and mouth become functional, the former without lids, and horny mandibles appear. The head and body assume a compact mass. The tail broadens into a sculling organ with dorsal and ventral fins, and hind-limb buds form. The limbs develop at more or less the same rate, the anterior pair inside the opercular chamber.

In most tadpoles, the mouth contains upper and lower horny jaws (beaks) and rows of tiny replaceable horny labial teeth or denticles, often with curved, comblike tips (see Altig and Johnston, 1989). True teeth are lacking. The jaws may be coarsely or finely serrate and the upper jaw may have a short to long slender posterolateral extension, often nonserrate, and extending varying distances beyond the lower jaw. At the sides of the mouth, and sometimes nearly encircling it, are oral fringes with sensory papillae. The sides of the oral disk may or may not be indented.

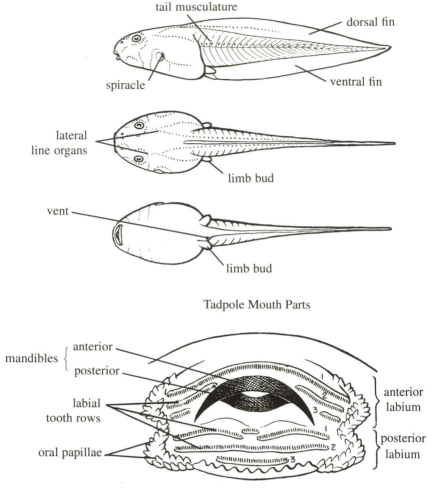

tail musculature

dorsal fin

spiracle

ventral fin

lateral
line organs

limb bud

vent

limb bud

Tadpole Mouth Parts

mandibles { anterior
posterior

labial
tooth rows

oral papillae

anterior
labium

posterior
labium

Fig. 17.17 Structure of a representative tadpole, a pond type with large tail fins.

TADPOLE DESCRIPTIONS

Mouthparts of tadpoles are particularly useful in species identification. The number and position of rows of labial teeth can be arranged as a fraction—the numerator indicating the number of rows on the anterior (A) labium, and the denominator the number of rows on the posterior (P) labium (fig. 17.17). The rows are numbered in sequence from anterior to posterior on each labium: A1, A2, and P1, P2, etc. The fraction is usually written in a line (see below), with rows that have a median gap indicated in parentheses. A range in number of rows is hyphenated, and variability in the presence of a median gap within a given tooth row is indicated by placing the row number in which the gap occurs in brackets. For example, the formula 2(2)/3–4[1] indicates a tadpole with two rows of labial teeth on the anterior labium, the second with a median gap, and three or four rows on the posterior labium, the first with or without a median gap.

Tail height is the greatest distance between the edges of the dorsal and ventral fins, measured at a right angle to the longitudinal axis of the body across the tail; and the height of the tail musculature is measured at its widest point. Tail length is measured from the midpoint of the tail musculature, where it contacts the body, to the tip of the tail.

When viewed from above, eyes may be indicated as lateral (situated on or near the outline of the head) or dorsal (located well in from the outline of the head). The anal opening may be dextral (toward the right of the edge of the ventral fin or medial (lined up with the fin). The position of the spiracle(s) may also be noted.

Descriptions of larvae should indicate the developmental stage. There have been species-specific staging tables developed for a number of anuran and salamander species to aid comparisons in developmental studies, both within and between species (Dodd and Dodd, 1976). Different stages in the developmental sequence, often beginning with the fertilized egg and extending to hatching or metamorphosis, are designated sequentially by number. For example, in Gosner's (1960) guide for anurans, developmental stage 25 is the time of closure of the larval operculum and 40 is just before eruption of the front legs. A sequence from egg to hatching has been set forth by Harrison (1969) for normal development of a salamander.

Pond, stream, and terrestrial larval types occur, as in salamanders. Most tadpoles are of the pond type, rather deep bodied and with prominent dorsal and ventral fins, as in the Bullfrog (*Rana catesbeiana*) (fig. 17.17), Wood Frog (*Rana sylvatica*) (se US, Can), and Striped Chorus Frog (*Pseudacris triseriata*) (US and Can). Pond-type tadpoles are not confined to ponds and sometimes occur even in rather fast streams in the quieter side pools. Stream-type larvae have reduced fins, thick tail musculature, a flattened streamlined body, and often a large suctorial mouth as in the Tailed Frog (*Ascaphus truei*) (nw US, sw Can) (fig. 17.18B) and the Torrent Tree Frog (*Litoria nannotis*) (ne Aus) (Tyler, 1989), or a suctorial disk behind the mouth, as in Asiatic *Amolops*, and others, for clinging to objects in fast waters. Terrestrial larvae usually undergo full development in the egg and have no aquatic stage.

FEEDING HABITS

Most tadpoles have sievelike filter organs in the pharynx—branchial food traps interposed between the mouth cavity and gills. These organs trap bacteria, protozoans, free-floating algae, pollen grains, and other small particles suspended in the water passing from the pharynx over the gills. A pumping action of the floor of the mouth cavity maintains the flow. The finer material

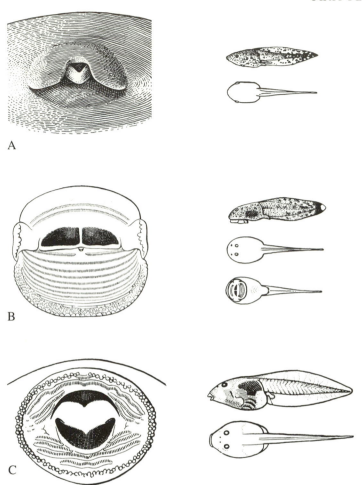

Fig. 17.18 Variation in structure and habits of tadpoles. (A) A surface film filter feeder, the tadpole of the narrow-mouthed toads (*Gastrophryne*). (B) A fast-water stream dweller, the tadpole of the Tailed Frog (*Ascaphus truei*) with large suctorial, scraping mouth, thick tail musculature, and reduced tail fins. (C) A carnivorous quiet-water dweller, the tadpole of the Plains Spadefoot Toad (*Spea bombifrons*). The "cannibal" form of this tadpole has a beak on the upper jaw and a notch in the lower.

accumulates on mucous threads and webs secreted by the filter organs and is transported in mucous cords via a ciliary groove to the esophagus (Wassersug, 1972). Coarser materials may be shunted directly to the esophagus. The particulate food source is obtained from filtering the surrounding water, from skimming off the surface film, or from larger food masses through the biting, chopping, and scraping action of the jaws, the scraping action of the labial teeth, and, to a lesser extent, the labial papillae.

Microphagy

Tadpoles that feed on such small particles are referred to as microphagous. They typically have large branchial food traps, well supplied with columnar mucous-secreting cells and secretory ridges and dense gill filters. They often include the "typical" tadpole bottom feeders of quiet ponds, with a single spiracle on the left side that clears bottom muck, and with mouth directed downward facilitating feeding on algal crusts and mats, detritis, and leaves of submerged plants.

Extremes in microphagy are reached in the "filter feeding" tadpoles (Types I and II). African clawed frog (*Xenopus*) (fig. 17.19A) and most microhylid frog tadpoles (fig. 17.18A) are examples. *Xenopus* tadpoles, beautifully translucent creatures, hang head down and move slowly thorough the water, propelled by the rapidly beating tip of their tail. They are capable of removing suspended particles down to 0.13μ in diameter, equaling in efficiency the best mechanical sieves designed by humans. In a confined space, they can virtually sterilize the water. They have soft mouth parts and lack beaks and labial teeth. Such suspension feeders have a spiracle on each side or a single midventral spiracle, thus exiting spiracular water flow is not destabilizing and there is little disturbance of food items in the water column (Starrett, 1973).

The Pe-ret' Toad (*Otophryne robusta*) (family Microhylidae), a leaf-mimic inhabitant of forests (S Am), has a bizarre tadpole that buries itself in sand of clear shallow streams where, judging from its stomach contents of bacteria and other microorganisms, it forages as a microphagous suspension feeder (fig. 17.19C). It has minute daggerlike denticles on both upper and lower jaws that apparently keep sand grains out of its mouth as water enters, then exits through a remarkably long spiracular tube that extends above the sand surface (Wassersug and Pyburn, 1987).

Macrophagy

Macrophagous tadpoles, including carnivorous forms, are adapted to scrape, bite, and pulverize food materials and to feed on much larger objects than the microphagous tadpoles. They have a reduction in pharyngeal structures associated with phytoplanktonic entrapment, and regularly lack secretory ridges and sometimes completely lack columnar mucous-secreting cells. Stream-bottom forms can generate a coarse suspension of food particles from algal filaments

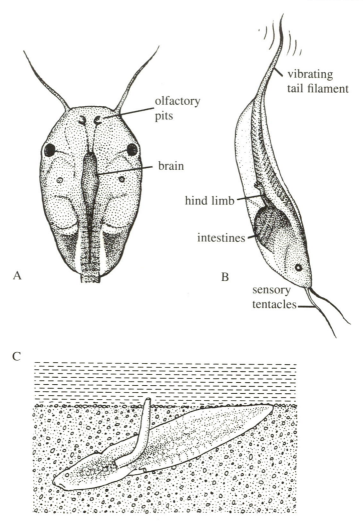

Fig. 17.19 Variation in structure and habits of tadpoles. (A) Filter-feeding tadpole of the African Clawed Frog (*Xenopus leavis*). On the left, head-body region from above showing the brain, nasal pits, and other structures seen through the translucent body wall; (B) on the right, a tadpole in foraging position. (C) Tadpole of the Pe-ret' Toad (*Otophryne robusta*), with snorkel-like spiracular tube, in presumed foraging position beneath sand of a shallow stream bottom. (After Wassersug and Pyburn, 1987, redrawn with permission from Academic Press Ltd., London)

and leaf fragments with their keratinized mouth parts and they have many closely set buccal papillae for straining such coarse particles. However, they have highly porous gill filters not well suited for entrapment of very small plankton (Wassersug and Rosenberg, 1979; Wassersug, 1980).

Carnivorous macrophagous tadpoles are diverse. They include the pipoid dwarf clawed frogs *Hymenochirus* (equatorial Afr) that ingest small invertebrates by suction; the Neotropical hylid, the Spine-headed Tree Frog (*Anotheca spinosa*) (cen Am) that swallows anuran eggs whole; and spadefoot toads (*Scaphiopus*) (N Am), which chop up their prey (fig. 17.18C). However, the presently known extreme among them is the tadpole of *Lepidobatrachus laevis*, a leptodactylid from the Paraguayan Chaco, which swallows large living prey whole. It has a large flattened head with a wide mouth and can ingest tadpoles that are nearly equal to itself in size (Ruibal and Thomas, 1988).

Carnivorous spadefoot toad tadpoles resemble the typical microphagous bottom feeders but have a large mouth, well-developed beak on the upper mandible (fig. 17.18C), strong jaw musculature, no filter mechanism, and relatively short gut. They feed on relatively large animal prey, including other tadpoles; some are at times cannibalistic.

Other structural modifications and habits associated with tadpole feeding are found in certain microhylid surface-film feeders of tropical forest pools that have their lips expanded into a funnel-like structure with which they glean fallen insects, perhaps pollen grains, and other organic matter that falls on the water surface. Neotropical arboreal tadpoles (including *Anotheca*) of water pockets in bromeliads and tree cavities are slim bodied and of carnivorous habits, feeding on mosquito larvae and some, like *Anotheca*, on the eggs of anurans.

Tadpoles of the Flaming (*Dendrobates pumilio*) (cen Am) and Granular (*D. granuliferus*) (Costa Rica) Poison-Arrow Frogs and relatives of the Neotropics, and the hylid frog *Osteopilus brunneus* (Jamaica) (Lannoo et al., 1987), are fed unfertilized eggs by conspecific females. Females of *D. pumilio*, observed in captivity, carried their tadpoles on their backs to water-filled bromeliad leaf axils and regularly fed them by depositing unfertilized eggs. The resident tadpoles changed their swimming behavior upon the approach of the attendant frog. This was the first frog known to feed its free-living larvae (Weygoldt, 1980). Subsequently, additional species have been found that do so (see van Wijngaarden and Bolaños, 1992). For more information on this remarkable habit, see chapter 18.

SCHOOLING AND GROUP BEHAVIOR OF TADPOLES

Tadpoles often form aggregations, especially in shallows. These clusters, usually composed of individuals of the same species, may have a number of beneficial effects. They may (1) help stir up food; (2) form pits which retain water when a pool threatens to dry up; (3) elevate temperature through en masse bodily absorption of sunlight, thereby accelerating growth and metamorphosis; and (4) sometimes help protect against predation. As noted by Brodie and Formanowicz (1987), the latter benefit may result from (a) increased ability to detect and avoid predators through alarm behavior or release of "alarm substances"; (b) enhancement of effectiveness of chemical defenses through more rapidly acquired avoidance learning by predators (Waldman, 1982); (c) predator "confusion" resulting from attempts to single out prey from a mobile aggregation; and (d) lower probability of attack as a result of a dilution or masking effect or satiation of the predator.

Black (1970) observed that cannibalistic tadpoles of the Plains Spadefoot Toad (*Spea bombifrons*) (cen US, sw Can, n Mex) and predaceous water beetles attacked tadpoles at the periphery of tadpole aggregations but did not penetrate them. The cannibals fed on herbivorous members of their own kind. Aggregations were not seen in pools where cannibals and water beetle larvae were absent, suggesting that schooling was a protective response to predation. Tadpoles of the Neotropical hylid, *Hyla geographica* (S Am, Trinidad), which may form schools of two to three thousand individuals, have been observed to continually swim toward the middle of the school, presumably where threat from predators is lower. Test and McCann (1976) reported a large aggregation of American Toad (*Bufo americanus*) (e US, se Can) tadpoles that evidently formed to feed on a rich suspension of protozoans and other microorganisms.

In some species the formation of aggregations apparently has a strong social component and is not based solely on mass exploitation of food or other nonsocial factors. Individuals may be attracted to one another through visual presence alone, as has been shown in African Clawed Frog (*Xenopus laevis*) tadpoles by Wassersug and Hessler (1971), but a combination of vision and lateral line sense (chapter 9) may often also be involved in some species (Wassersug et al., 1981). Lateral line organs respond to water currents.

Tadpole "schools" resemble fish schools in that neighboring individuals tend to be of similar size and oriented in the same direction and parallel to nearest neighbors (avoiding positions directly in front of or behind neighbors) (Wassersug et al., 1981; Breden et al., 1982). However, they differ in being less evenly spaced and less strongly oriented, perhaps related to the less mobile nature of tadpole aggregations.

The similar size of tadpoles in a conspecific school suggest that they may be siblings (hatched from the same clutch of eggs), but other factors may be involved. Studies on the Cascades Frog (*Rana cascadae*) (nw US) indicate that sibling tadpoles in this species are somehow able to recognize members of their group (by chemoreception?) and when given a choice associate with them rather than with unrelated tadpoles (Blaustein and O'Hara, 1987). The response occurs in tadpoles reared from eggs separated from the clutch even at an early embryonic stage (Blaustein and O'Hara, 1982; O'Hara and Blaustein, 1981).

In experiments, Blaustein and O'Hara (1982) found that Cascade Frog tadpoles preferred to associate with full siblings over half siblings and half siblings over nonsiblings when reared with siblings or as isolates. Half siblings may be of two kinds: maternal half sibs having the same mother but a different father and paternal half sibs having a different mother. Cascade Frog tadpoles thus can use cues of either maternal or paternal origin in distinguishing sibs from nonsibs, but maternal cues are preferred over paternal ones. Evidently a hierarchy of cue importance exists. The stronger maternal effects may relate to chemical influences of egg or egg jelly constituents during development. All members of the egg clusters of the mother would be subject to such effects. Paternal effects could be expected to be far less because sperm heads contain little more than genetic information. Cascade Frog tadpoles may therefore hatch with an innate, genetically based system of kin recognition (probably based primarily on chemoreception) or they may quickly learn to recognize one another, or both innate and learned components may exist. It should be noted that in a study of American Toad (*Bufo americanus*) tadpoles (Waldman, 1981), half sibs showed no preference for full sibs over maternal half sibs, but they showed a preference for full sibs over paternal half sibs (see also Waldman, 1985). Blaustein and O'Hara (1982) conclude that kin recognition may facilitate preferential treatment of kin, such as cooperation in food finding or in warning against predators, and therefore those individuals behaving "altruistically" in kin groups increase their inclusive fitness.

Sibling recognition has also been observed in the Red-legged Frog (*Rana aurora*) (w N Am) (Blaustein and O'Hara, 1986) and Wood Frog (*R. sylvatica*) (ne US, Can) (Fishwild et al., 1990), and, in the latter, has been shown to extend to the recently transformed froglets (Cornell et al., 1989).

Siblings may respond to habitat cues at the oviposition site (Pfennig, 1990). Often the members of a clutch tend to remain in the area where they hatched, thus their association, in some cases, may result from their attraction to their natal site, rather than to each other. The tendency to associate with oviposition sites usually diminishes with time. There is evidence that adults of some species assess the environmental quality of breeding sites. Thus natal sites may contain fewer predators (Howard, 1978b, 1980), more suitable temperatures (Seale, 1982), and/or pH levels (Gascon and Planas, 1986) than other sites in the same pond. Survival would be enhanced at such sites.

Another factor in size sorting may be the tendency for younger (smaller) tadpoles to actively avoid larger, older ones (Alford and Crump, 1982), as has been inferred from study of the schooling of tadpoles of the Southern Leopard Frog (*Rana utricularia*) (se US). Although hatchling tadpoles of the neotropical frog (*Hyla geographica*) stayed with their respective schools even when the schools were transferred to a new pond site, it was unknown whether this was due to size sorting or sibling recognition (Caldwell, 1989). Tadpole sibling recognition contributes to the maintenance of schooling behavior and the benefits of clustering described above.

It is evident that the subject of sibling (or kin) recognition in tadpoles has not been fully resolved. Siblings, during development at oviposition sites, are subjected to parental influences and cues emanating from both their physical surroundings and each other. The relative importance of these cues and the possible role of genetic factors in recognition are, at present, unclear.

Effects of Crowding

Under conditions of crowding, investigated chiefly in the laboratory, the growth of tadpoles may be inhibited (Woodward, 1987) or more variable than occurs under less crowded conditions. Larger tadpoles may grow faster than smaller ones because they obtain a larger share of the available food and their exploitation of the food source (often tadpole feces) retards the growth of smaller tadpoles. When the food supply is low, there is less opportunity for them to engage in such exploitation. Under these conditions, the production of chemical inhibitors to growth may be favored—the release by tadpoles of a chemical substance that inhibits growth. If those individuals that interfere obtain a disproportionate share of the food, then interference would be of value despite its energetic costs (Steinwascher, 1978). As a result of growth inhibition, metamorphosis may be delayed and there may be some reduction in average transformation size (Brockelman, 1969; Wilbur, 1977). Such effects can influence subsequent survival rates (see below).

Density-dependent effects on growth and size at metamorphosis have also been observed in salamanders. Petranka (1989a) found that by reducing the density of Marbled Salamander (*Ambystoma opacum*) (cen and e US) larvae in natural ponds, body size was increased (except at an early stage of larval growth) and less crowded larvae transformed at larger size.

John and Fenster (1975) have reviewed literature on growth inhibition and have reported on their experimental work with Northern Leopard Frog (*Rana pipiens*) (N Am) tadpoles. They observed that growth retardation in this species was in proportion to the density of the population. "Psychological stress" appeared to be the major cause of inhibition and resulted from the frequency of physical encounters between tadpoles. Both volume and shape of the available space were found to be important, but visual responses and chemical factors appeared not to be. The presence of alga-like cells found in the feces of crowded tadpoles, regarded as a factor in retardation (Richards, 1958, 1962), was considered by them to be a special case, a consequence of crowding perhaps, but not the primary cause of retardation. Under natural conditons, normal growth of retarded tadpoles may be resumed when large numbers of more advanced individuals metamorphose and leave a crowded pond. Thus, as pointed out by Licht (1967), the inhibition of growth of smaller tadpoles by larger ones can have the beneficial effect of spreading the foraging of the population over both aquatic and terrestrial food resources as the larger tadpoles transform and leave the water. Mass mortality due to predation or unfavorable environmental conditions on land at the time of metamorphosis is also less likely (Hodge, 1976).

How common is density-related growth retardation in tadpoles living in natural ponds? Petranka (1989b) found that water collected early in the larval period from tadpole aggregation sites of the Southern Leopard Frog (*Rana utricularia*) (cen and e US) strongly inhibited hatchling growth in laboratory tests. Such early-season tadpoles, when crowded in the laboratory, also produced growth inhibitors, but inhibition disappeared as tadpole density declined seasonally. To check on the prevalence of chemical growth interference in natural tadpole communities, Petranka assayed water for growth-inhibiting properties on thirteen occasions from eleven breeding sites in North Carolina, most of which had high densities of tadpoles. Water collected from the ponds inhibited growth of tadpoles in only two of thirteen instances, and then much less than typically seen in crowded laboratory stock. Some natural habitats may have physiochemical conditions adequate for the production and transmission of growth inhibitors, but how common it is in natural ponds remains an open question.

LARVAL GROWTH RATES AND METAMORPHIC AND ADULT SUCCESS

The differences that may occur in larval growth and development among individuals of the same species at a given site may be an important factor in determining metamorphic success. Individuals with higher growth rates will have shorter larval periods, less exposure to predators, and an advantage in competition with their rivals (Travis, 1980). Some predators may no longer be a threat when increase in size of their prey places the prey beyond their interest or reach. In such cases, rapid larval growth reduces exposure time to predation (see Brodie and Formanowicz, 1983).

In ephemeral ponds, larval growth rate may relate to the rapidity with which available food sources are depleted and space is restricted by drying conditions. Crump (1989) found accelerated development of larvae with consequent reduction in body size at metamorphosis under simulated drying conditions in the treefrog *Hyla pseudopuma* in Costa Rica. This species breeds in ponds and puddles that form after heavy rains, and frequently the sites dry before the tadpoles can metamorphose. A similar situation occurs with spadefoot toads (*Scaphiopus*) (N Am). In the Couch Spadefoot (*Scaphiopus couchii*) (in w Tex), Newman (1988a,b) found flexibility in development rates in sibling tadpoles that contributed to survival in ponds of greatly varied duration. In ponds of short duration, rapid developers were favored and the slowest developing tadpoles suffered the highest mortality. However, in more lasting ponds, the slowest developers (with more time for growth) transformed at the largest average size, thus gaining the advantages of large size as discussed below. Larvae in ponds with abundant food transformed sooner than those in ponds with scarce food and low larval density (Newman, 1989). Ponds of short duration yielded metamorphs more rapidly and of smaller size, compared to ponds of longer duration. Both genetic factors and phenotypic plasticity have been important in the response to pond drying of this species.

Large size at transformation can influence juvenile survival and/or size at reproduction, as observed in the Wood Frog (*Rana sylvatica*) (ne US, Can) (Berven and Gill, 1983), Western Chorus Frog (*Pseudacris t. triseriata*) (cen and ne US), and Mole Salamander (*Ambystoma talpoideum*) (se US) (Semlitsch, 1988). John-Alder and Morin (1990) note that such large metamorphs can jump farther per hop and can hop for longer periods of time than small ones, thus they can be expected to disperse more rapidly from hazardous pond margins and more readily escape predation and find suitable microenvironments than the smaller metamorphs.

Larval growth and developmental differences may also have important consequences for subsequent success of adults, not only in anurans, but probably in amphibians generally. Collins (1979) noted that the increase in body size at metamorphosis in Bullfrog (*Rana catesbeiana*) (N Am) tadpoles, resulting from larval growth while overwintering, influences body size at first reproduction. In males, this increased size has a significant effect on mating success and in females on fecundity. In paedomorphic Mole Salamanders (*Ambystoma talpoideum*), Semlitsch (1988) found that environmental conditions (pond-drying regime, population density, and food availability) could strongly affect the fecundity of adults at first reproduction. Early larval growth was positively correlated with adult body size and large body size with the number of ova females contained. Larvae grew fastest, reached largest body size, and contained the most ova in constant water, high food, and low-density ponds. Selection of egg-laying sites by parents can thus be expected to affect the ultimate reproductive fitness of the next generation.

KINDS OF TADPOLES

Orton (1953) recognized four kinds of anuran larvae and Starrett (1973) provided names for Orton's larval types. These types are characterized as follows:

Type I (xenoanura). Pipidae (Clawed Frogs, *Xenopus*, and others) and Rhinophrynidae (Mexican Burrowing Toad, see chapter 8). No horny beaks or denticles; two separate branchial (gill) chambers with two separate external openings (spiracles); forelimbs develop posterior to the branchial chambers and lateral to the spiracular openings. Such larvae live chiefly in quiet water and feed on ciliate protozoa and other suspended organisms by filtering water.

Type II (scoptanura). Most Microhylidae (Narrow-mouthed Toads, *Gastrophryne*, and others). Also lack beaks and denticles; two separate branchial chambers each with a separate opening, but they open into a common tube that continues posteriorly, opening to the exterior in a single midventral spiracule near the base of the tail; forelimb development and feeding habits as in Type I; a mechanism for projecting the lower jaw facilitates feeding on ciliates (protozoans).

Type III (lemnanura). Ascaphidae (Tailed Frog) and Discoglossidae (Fire-bellied Toads and others). Beaks and denticles present; two separate branchial chambers joined at midline by two very short opercular tubes that open as a single ventral spiracle at the posterior level of the branchial chambers near the midpoint of the body; forelimbs develop close to but outside the branchial chambers, possibly breaking through the chambers at metamorphosis.

Type IV (acosmanura). (All other anuran families—the common tadpoles or polliwogs). Beaks and denticles present; branchial chambers joined internally by a communicating chamber ventral to the heart; usually a single spiracle on the left side; forelimbs usually develop within the branchial chambers. Many are adapted for bottom feeding (lateral spiracle, thus unobstructed); lateral tail movements stir up food particles on the bottom; oral papillae and denticles used in scraping, beaks in biting.

Types III and IV tadpoles have a long coiled gut related to feeding on algae and other plant material and a flexible scraping and biting mouth. The branchial area is reduced. The single spiracle increases filtering and respiratory efficiency.

Studies subsequent to Orton's classification have more fully characterized morphological futures present in her four tadpole types. Further, it appears that Types I and II, which have been regarded as "primitive," may have been derived through truncation, or shortening, of developmental processes involved in the development of "advanced" Types III and IV. See Sokol (1975), Wassersug (1984), Wassersug and Duellman (1984), Duellman and Trueb (1986), and Altig and Johnson (1989) for further information on tadpole variation and types.

There has been a great increase in larvae available for study since Orton's classification. This has added greatly to information on the diversity of tadpole morphology and habits. Among arboreal tadpoles, for example, this has led to recognition of five distinct types (Lannoo et al., 1987): (1) elongate tadpoles with denticle rows less than $2/3$ (usually $1/1$ or less), little or no pigment, associated mainly with water pockets in bromeliads and leaf axils, and oophagous (egg eating) at least part of their lives; (2) stout tadpoles with denticle rows less than $2/3$ (usually $2/2$ or less), mainly bromeliad dwelling, carnivorous, and macrophagous, with frog eggs a major part of their diet; (3) elongate tadpoles with denticle rows more than $^2/_3$ and oral features resembling those associated with microphagous feeding of pond larvae; (4) stout tadpoles with denticle rows greater than $^2/_3$, oral features largely associated with microphagy, and darkly pigmented; (5) the bufonid *Mertensophryne micranotis* (Kenya, Tanzania), most similar to group (1) but with a specialized head crown that may help keep the nostrils at or near the water surface, perhaps allowing for surface-film respiration.

ECOLOGICAL ROLE OF TADPOLES

Wassersug (1975) comments on the ecological role of tadpoles. The anuran tadpole stage appears to be primarily an adaptation to exploit environments characterized by seasonal rainfall and the formation of temporary or semipermanent bodies of water. Tadpoles, with their ability to filter suspended material in the water, are able to feed on the microorganisms—bacteria, unicellular algae, protozoans, and other organic material—that quickly grow or accumulate in such waters. They evidently do so opportunistically and indiscriminately. They are also able to use large organisms for food, for with their horny mandibles and keratinized labial denticles they can bite and scrape through plant and animal tissues and break up organic debris that accumulates on the bottom or on objects in the water. Their filtering mechanism is employed here also as they pulverize these large food masses. Since their larval habitat is often transient, growth must be rapid to permit escape to the terrestrial stage of the frog. Their relatively small size and their structural organization, basically as a feeding machine, are important in achieving this rapid transition. They have apparently sacrificed or delayed development of certain body parts and reproductive structures in favor of tissues related to feeding, digestion, and food storage, hence, in contrast to salamanders, no breeding neotenic anuran larvae are known. In a sense, no tadpole has "abandoned" its frog (Wassersug, 1975).

In reflecting on the ecological implications of the tadpole way of life, Wassersug (1975) further notes that the amphibious life cycle of anurans (and we would add that of amphibious salamanders) constitutes a living mechanism for transporting nutrients out of bodies of water back into terrestrial ecoystems, for many transformed amphibians die on land and their substance, in part derived during aquatic life, returns to the terrestrial ecosystem.

At some sites the impact of tadpoles on the standing crop of phytoplankton (small floating plants), protozoans, and filamentous algae may be quite massive. Numbers of grazers may reach high levels. Seale (1980) noted in a pond near St. Louis, Missouri, that natural variations in *Rana* tadpole numbers (biomass) were accompanied by shifts in patterns of nutrient cycling (nitrogen) and in the standing crop of suspended particles, including phytoplankton, the tadpoles' major food source. The tadpoles appear to regulate primary production by both reducing the standing crop and altering specific growth rates of algae. When the tadpoles transformed and left the pond, rates of primary production increased dramatically.

Because of their herbivorous habits, tadpoles are probably often a major lower consumer in the food chain, and they provide food for a number of invertebrate and vertebrate predators. Turnipseed and Altig (1975) estimated a peak population of 26,000 hylid tadpoles, mostly Cricket Frogs (*Acris*) (660 g dry weight), in a small pond about 4000 m^2 in surface area in Mississippi. A study by Dickman (1968) suggests that grazing by tadpoles may be a major cause of the massive spring reduction in the standing crop of filamentous green algae in some lakes.

Polls Pelaz and Rougier (1990) have determined larval buccal pump volumes in the Marsh Frog (*Rana ridibunda*) (Eur to China) and the Agile Frog (*R. dalmatina*) (cen Eur), larvae that normally graze and pump water at the sediment-water interface. When these tadpoles are 35–40 mm in total length they pumped an estimated one liter of water each day. The grazing impact of a large population of tadpoles in the confined space of a pond can be great.

METAMORPHOSIS

In contrast with salamander metamorphosis, much greater changes occur in tadpoles when they transform into a frog. Typically limb growth accelerates, the hind limbs enlarge, the forelimbs, if ensconced, break through the operculum enclosing the gills, larval mouth parts disappear and are replaced by true jaws, teeth, and usually a tongue; movable eyelids form, lungs become more fully developed, the tail is resorbed, skin glands and a stratified epithelium develop, the gut assumes adult form, including a true stomach, and the vertebral column and limb bones ossify. The long, coiled intestine in herbivorous tadpoles changes to the shortened gut of the carnivorous terrestrial froglet. Thyroid hormones are importantly involved in promoting and accelerating the process of metamorphosis in all amphibians, including anurans.

Metamorphosis is usually a time of increased hazard from predation (see Huey, 1980) because locomotion in water is slowed by the presence of limbs and on land by the resorbing tail. At this time, there may even be risk of attack from conspecific tadpoles. Crump (1986) observed attacks of Cuban Treefrog (*Osteopilus septentrionalis*) (West Indies) tadpoles on transforming individuals. The former, at the two-legged stage, bit the tail and legs of the smaller emerging individuals and pulled them into the water and ate them.

The developing poison glands at transformation help to protect some species by making them unpalatable to both aquatic and terrestrial predators. Formanowicz and Brodie (1982) determined, for example, that larvae of the predaceous diving beetle (*Dytiscus verticalis*) readily ate premetamorphic stages of several species of amphibians, including the Wood Frog (*Rana sylvatica*), but rejected metamorphic stages.

Fortunately the transformation period is brief.

For further information on amphibian metamorphosis, including the important role of hormones, see Etkin (1964), Dent (1968), Etkin and Gilbert (1968), Dodd and Dodd (1976), and Gibert and Frieden (1981). There is vast literature on amphibian metamorphosis, a subject that has been extensively investigated over a period of over three quarters of a century.

18

Parental Care

ALTHOUGH most amphibians depart their egg sites following egg laying, and provide no care for their eggs or young, many display varying degrees of parental care. We include here the entire range of care from guarding and transport of eggs and larvae, to retention of developing eggs to various levels of development, including full metamorphosis, on or within the body of the female. Indeed, the variety in amphibian methods of nurturing appears to exceed that of all other classes of vertebrates. Their presumed ancestral, and presently widespread, amphibious mode of life—adults on land and untended eggs and larvae in water—appears to have set the stage for the evolution of this diversity. As amphibians have expanded in numbers of species and into many different habitats, they have evolved varying degrees of terrestrialism, and some shifts from the amphibious pattern have been profound. Here we describe some reproductive modes, touching only briefly on a subject of great evolutionary interest and significance. In our survey we proceed roughly in sequence from modest deviations from the "ancestral" life-style to complete abandonment of aquatic reproduction. The pervasiveness of parental care is notable among anurans, in which it appears in some form in most of the major families. (For a review, see McDiarmid, 1978.)

Guarding of Eggs and Nest Sites

Many amphibians remain with, or tend, their eggs and some species care for their larvae. Egg tending has evolved independently in caecilians, salamanders, and anurans. Some examples among salamanders are the Hellbender (*Cryptobranchus alleganiensis*) (e US) (completely aquatic), Marbled Salamander (*Ambystoma opacum*) (cen and e US) (eggs on land and larvae washed into aquatic sites by flooding), the sirens, Pacific Giant Salamanders (*Dicamptodon* species) (nw US), and many lungless salamanders; and among anurans, the African Bullfrog (*Pyxicephalus adspersus*) and many leptodactylid frogs. Among the poison-dart frogs are species that tend both their eggs and larvae, transporting the latter from terrestrial eggs sites to water.

The attending parent may contribute to survival of the eggs (and sometimes the larvae) in several ways: (1) by guarding against predation and disturbance by conspecifics (fig. 18.1A); (2) by reducing the threat of desiccation at terres-

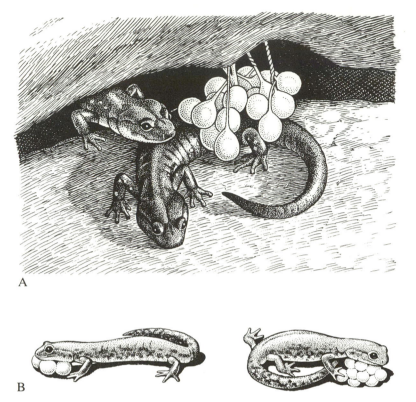

A

B

Fig. 18.1 (A) Arboreal Salamanders *(Aneides lugubris)* (Cal) attending their eggs (sketched from life following removal of a stump in the senior author's backyard in Berkeley, California). (B) Ensatinas *(Ensatina eschscholtzii)* brooding their eggs.

trial sites by contacting the eggs, or coiling around them and sometimes moving them in a loop of the body to a damper location (some lungless salamanders), by urinating on them (Flaming Poison-Arrow Frog, *Dendrobates pumilio*) (cen Am) (Weygoldt, 1980), and, at shallow aquatic sites, by aiding larvae to reach deeper water; (3) by applying protective skin secretions that appear to retard the growth of pathogenic molds and bacteria or eating moldy eggs or those that fail to develop (Tilley, 1972; and (4) in a few species by feeding larvae unfertilized eggs deposited by the attending female.

Brooding Ensatinas *(Ensatina eschscholtzii)* (w US, sw Can) often coil around, or lie against, their egg clusters and frequently rest their pulsating gular region on individual eggs, thereby, in effect, massaging the eggs with skin secretion (fig. 18.1B).

The male African Bullfrog, which may reach 6–8 inches (2.4–3.2 cm) SV attacks cranes, other bullfrogs, and even lions and people who wade into the frog's territory and nesting area. Both eggs and tadpoles are guarded. The frog has sharp teeth in the upper jaw and two horny spikes at the tip of the lower jaw. The animal may repeatedly strike an intruder with a butting, biting action. Kok et al. (1989) obtained evidence that attending males dig escape channels between isolated puddles containing tadpoles and the main body of water when the puddles are threatened with drying.

Small fossorial frogs of the family Hemisotidae, chiefly found in east Africa, lay their eggs in pits close to water. When the tadpoles hatch, the attending female digs them a tunnel to water (Goin et al., 1978).

Foam Nests

Foam nests are constructed by anurans from at least five families (Leptodactylidae, Myobatrichidae, Rhacophoridae, Hyperoliidae, and Hylidae). The nests are made by beating extruded mucus into foam with the fore- or hind-limbs. The nests reduce the threat of desiccation of eggs laid in terrestrial, semiterrestrial, or shallow aquatic locations and possibly, in some strongly illuminated locations (Haddad et al., 1990), protect against intensive sunlight through the reflective properties of the foam's whiteness. Foam-nest building may have evolved independently in the families mentioned. Many anurans are able to secrete mucus from their skin and reproductive tract and are thus preadapted for foam-nest construction (Heyer, 1969). In several leptodactylid species, a parent remains with the nonfeeding tadpoles in an aquatic or terrestrial nest (Wells and Bard, 1988).

The Leaf-folding Frog (*Afrixalus delicatus*), an African species around one inch or less in length, constructs an over-water leaf nest for its eggs during oviposition. The amplexing pair use their hind limbs to draw the margins of a leaf together to create a basket for the eggs as they are deposited. Oviducal secretion is used to glue the leaf margins together. After the tadpoles develop, the nest breaks down and they fall into the water below. The nest protects the eggs from exposure and predation (see Backwell and Passmore, 1990a).

Tadpole Herding

Herding of tadpoles to more favorable waters appears to occur in the Neotropical *Leptodactylus bolivianus* (S Am), a shallow-water, foam-nest species (Wells and Bard, 1988). The attending female uses a pumping action of her hindquarters, usually while facing away from the tadpoles, creating water currents (or possibly sending a chemical signal), which results in the tadpoles following her. They are strongly attracted to her body, sometimes completely surrounding her.

Transport of Eggs and Larvae

Such transporting behavior may have evolved in response to high-risk aquatic environments where dangers to early developmental stages are greater in the water than on land. There may also be advantages to delaying the free-living larval stage until a larger size is achieved, less vulnerable to aquatic predators. Transported larvae usually develop from large eggs with abundant yolk.

In the Midwife Toads (*Alytes obstetricans*, *A. cisternasii*, and *A. muletensis*) (w Eur), amplexus occurs on land, and as the eggs are laid the male thrusts his hind legs through the egg mass (usually of some twenty to sixty eggs laid in rosarylike strings) and carries the eggs wrapped around his thighs and waist until the tadpoles are ready to hatch. He then transports them to water, where they complete their development.

Neotropical dendrobatid frogs, and some hylid and ranid frogs (see below), carry their larvae attached to the back of the attending frog. Depending on the species, the number of tadpoles may vary from one in the Green (*Dendrobates auratus*) (cen Am to Colombia), Granular (*D. granuliferus*) (Costa Rica), and some other Poison-Arrow Frogs to around two dozen in *Colostethus subpunctatus* (n Colombia). In the former, the tadpole is transported to water-filled hollows in vegetation.

Colostethus subpunctatus lays its eggs under stones and other objects, and the "nurse" frog guards the egg cluster (fig. 18.2). A tiny male nurse, slightly under one inch in length, stood its ground when the senior author uncovered a nesting site on the hills above Bogota, Colombia. Study of the tadpole-carrying habit of frogs from this area revealed that the tadpoles were attached by an adhesive sticky mucus, presumably secreted by the nurse. The tadpoles remained firmly in place until the frog entered water and remained there long enough for the mucous attachment to soften. In laboratory test, release of tadpoles occurred over a period of around 10–30 minutes. Brief exposures to wet vegetation and shallow waters would not likely result in tadpole release (Stebbins and Hendrickson, 1959).

The males of two species of diminutive Bornean ranid frogs, *Rana finchi* and *R. palavanensis*, guard their eggs, which may be attached to the underside of leaves on the forest floor, and transport their tadpoles on their backs to water (Inger et al., 1986; Inger and Voris, 1988).

Frogs That Feed Their Young

Brust (1993) has obtained confirmation in the field (in Panama) of the tadpole-feeding behavior described in chapter 17 of this book, based on observations made on captive animals. Females of the Flaming Poison-Arrow Frog (*Den-*

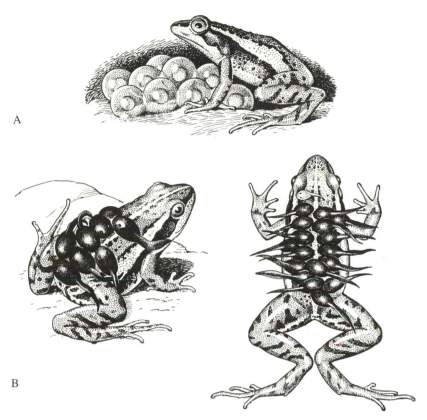

Fig. 18.2 The dendrobatid frog, *Colostethus subpunctatus*, guarding its eggs (A), and transporting its tadpoles to water (B). The tadpoles are attached to the back of the nurse frog by a sticky mucus.

drobates pumilio) of the Neotropics transported their tadpoles, up to four at a time, from nest sites on the forest floor to separate water-filled hollows in vegetation (often leaf axils of bromeliads and other plants), where during morning hours they fed their offspring ova released from their own reproductive tracts. At intervals of several days, the tending females went to the natal sites, lowered their hindquarters to the water surface, and usually released one to five jelly-coated eggs. Young tadpoles bit through the jelly coat and sucked out the yolk, whereas older tadpoles were able to break down and engulf the entire egg. Tadpoles responded to the arrival of the female by stiffening their bodies and vibrating. Through experiments, Brust showed that the tadpoles, at the sites studied, required ova in order to survive. Van Wijngaarden and Bolaños (1992) obtained evidence that female Granular Poison-Arrow Frogs (*Dendrobates granuliferus*) also carry their tadpoles to small water pockets in vegetation where they nurture them with unfertilized eggs. Although tadpole oophagy seems to be quite widespread among arboreal anurans, sources of the eggs consumed have not been clear and no tadpoles had been shown to rely for nutrients solely on ova provided by the mother.

Pouch Brooding

We include here species in which development of the eggs occurs outside the reproductive tract but within recesses or chambers upon or within the body of the nurse frog.

The eggs of the Surinam Toad (*Pipa pipa*) (S Am) (fig. 18.3B), an aquatic species, undergo complete development to fully formed toadlets in individual pockets in the skin on the back of the female. During amplexus the pair executes a somersault at the peak of which, when upside down, the male catches the eggs on his belly, and the female, using her hind limbs, propels them onto her back, where they adhere and are overgrown by skin. The looping action of the pair is repeated many times.

Among egg-brooding Neotropical hylid frogs of the subfamily Hemiphractinae (the back brooders), the eggs may be (1) exposed and adherent to the back of the female, (2) in a shallow basin on her back, or (3) in a dorsal pouch (Duellman and Maness, 1980). Those species having pouches, *Flectonotus* (Venezuela, Tobago, and Trinidad) and *Gastrotheca* (Panama, S Am), are the "true" marsupial frogs. Openings, size, and shape of the pouch varies among species, and the male frog, during amplexus, may insert his toes, sometimes his entire foot, into a pouch in directing the eggs into position within. The eggs are fertilized by sperm deposited on the female's lower back. Embryonic development is slow. The embryos draw on nutrients from a large supply of egg yolk. Their large, highly vascular, often bell-shaped gills and the vascular tissues of the female's pouch come into intimate association, separated only by an extremely thin egg jelly capsule. Thus there is provision for exchanges of gases, fluids, and wastes in a manner resembling the placental arrangement in mammals. Evolutionary pressures that may have led to back brooding may have been high levels of competition for aquatic sites among a great array of anuran species, and predation risks in streams and ponds (del Pino, 1989).

The number of developing embryos in species examined by del Pino (1980) varied from 6 to 138, the latter in the Marsupial Frog (*Gastrotheca marsupiata*) (S Am). In some species of back-brooding tree frogs, the eggs hatch directly into froglets, but in others into advanced, nonfeeding tadpoles that complete their development in water pockets in bromeliads or tree hollows, or into free-living feeding tadpoles that undergo a lengthy period of development in

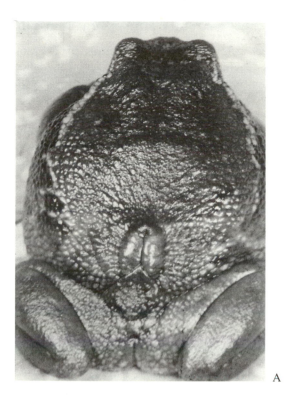

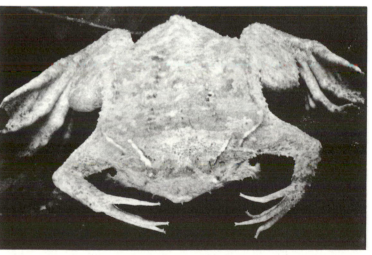

Fig. 18.3 (A) A female Marsupial Frog (*Gastrotheca*), showing the opening to the brood pouch beneath the skin of her back. (B) The Surinam Toad (*Pipa pipa*) (S Am), a flattened, highly aquatic species, rears its developing young in individual pockets in the skin of the back of the female. The young emerge fully formed. The slender forefingers are tactile in function, sensing the presence of prey. They are also used to cram food into the mouth.

ponds. The large genus *Gastrotheca* (fig. 18.3A), with a diverse assemblage of species, most of which produce froglets, contains some species of the latter type. Studies of albumin evolution suggest that the tadpole-producing species of *Gastrotheca* may have evolved from lineages having direct development (Duellman et al., 1988).

The Australian Pouched Frog (*Assa darlingtoni*) (around 30 mm SV), of rain forests of the McPherson Ranges and adjacent mountainous areas in southeast Queensland and northeast New South Wales, carries its developing embryos in brood pouches of the male, one on each side, that open on the frog's upper sides in front of the hind limbs. Complete development occurs within the pouches. The pouches, when distended with froglets, extend throughout the space formed by the ventrolateral and abdominal subdermal lymph sacs. Hatching embryos wriggle their way through the loose mucoid material of the egg mass, deposited on land, onto the moistened body of the attending frog and thence into the pouches. They have a slender tail, undeveloped eyes and olfactory structure, and a large yolk sac. During development in the pouches, they live off their yolk and evidently respire by diffusion of respiratory gases between the lining of the male's pouch and the body wall of the embryo. The habitat is one of high rainfall with quick-flowing and short-lived drainage systems. Perhaps uncertainties associated with egg and larval development in such waters has contributed to the evolution of this remarkable reproductive pattern. (See Straughan and Main, 1966; Tyler, 1972; Ingram et al., 1975.)

Vocal Sac Brooding

The diminutive (just over one inch SV) Darwin Frog (*Rhinoderma darwinii*) (fig. 18.4) of southern Chile and adjacent Argentina is a vocal sac brooder. Eggs, laid on land, after fertilization and some 10–20 days of development on moist ground, are engulfed by one or more attending males and carried in greatly enlarged vocal sacs, until the young, which may number five to fifteen, metamorphose at about one-half inch in length (Cochran, 1961). The beginning of muscular activity of the developing embryos is apparently the stimulus that causes the frogs to pick up the eggs, one by one, and introduce them into the vocal sac. A viscous bubbly fluid develops around the larvae and may be the source of some nourishment, as suggested by the use of tracers. Up to embryonic stage 10 the tracers were taken in through the skin and rear part of the digestive tract. At later stages the intestines were the main route of entry (Goicoechea et al., 1986). In their development, the larvae pass through a quite typical tadpole stage. However, the mouth parts do not cornify. *R. rufum*, a close relative, is the only other member of the family Rhinodermatidae.

Fig. 18.4 (A) Darwin Frog (*Rhinoderma darwinii*) (w S Am). (B) Ventral view showing conspicuous pattern of dark and light markings. (C) Dissected vocal pouch of male with advanced tadpoles. (After Noble, 1931)

Stomach Brooding

The discovery, and rapid demise, of the gastric or stomach-brooding frogs of eastern Australia has been, at once, one of the most surprising and depressing stories to emerge in the annals of amphibian field biology. The Gastric Brooding Frog (*Rheobatrachus silus*) (to around 2 in; 54 mm) was found in the Conondale Range of southeastern Queensland in 1973, and a second species (*R. vitellinus*) (to around 3 in; 78 mm) in Eungella National Park in central coastal Queensland in 1974 (Corben et al., 1974; Tyler, 1976; Tyler and Davies, 1985). Both species may now be extinct! A study by M. N. Hutchison and

Maxson (1987) indicated that these frogs, of ancient lineage, are related to the leptodactylids (myobatrachids). Both species inhabited boulder-strewn cool, usually clear, fast-flowing creeks in rain forests.

The female swallows the fertilized eggs, which develop in her stomach. A tadpole stage with finned tail and spiracle occurs, but the forelimbs develop outside the body (based on observations made on *R. silus*). The babies, fully transformed, are born by mouth and sit on the tongue of the parent before stepping out through widely open jaws (Tyler, 1989).

In *R. vitellinus* the developing young are protected from the stomach's digestive juices by the jelly surrounding the eggs which contains prostaglandin E_2 (PGE_2), a substance known to switch off the production of hydrochloric acid in the stomach. Later, the developing larvae release mucoid threads from the gill arches, which are thought also to contain PGE_2 and which maintain the stomach in a nonfunctional state. The stomach becomes greatly distended and membranous, the lungs collapse, and the frog respires through its skin. In one birth, a clutch of twenty-one froglets, varying in size from 11.9 to 12.9 mm (Tyler, 1989), emerged from the parent's mouth. In *R. silus*, the glands that secrete hydrochloric acid disappear and the stomach shuts down the production of gastric juice.

Viviparous Amphibians

These are species that give birth to fully formed young that are nurtured, not by a placental connection between the developing embryos and the mother, as in mammals, but by larval feeding by mouth on secretions from the walls of the maternal oviducts. Viviparous amphibians include a number of caecilians, the Alpine Salamander (*Salamandra atra*) (Eur), and two species of nectophrynoid toads (Afr) (see chapter 1).

For an overview and discussion of the modes of reproduction in amphibians and their evolutionary derivation, with particular focus on the evolution of viviparity, see Wake (1982).

19

Contributions of Amphibians to Human Welfare

IN ADDITION to the important role amphibians play in the functioning of the Earth's living systems, discussed in the introduction to this book, they "serve" mankind in many other ways.

Food

In many parts of the world, frogs are an important part of subsistence and gourmet diets of humans. In some impoverished societies they are (or have been) among the most important sources of animal protein.

Affluent countries import amphibian products in large amounts—1,389,734 pounds of frog legs by the United States (January to May 1988) (Beltz, 1988), and 46,579 tons by France (1973 to 1987, inclusive), equivalent to one to two billion frog legs in fifteen years (Beltz, 1989). France's imports amount to around 3.4 million tons a year, mostly from Indonesia and Bangladesh. The value of U.S. imports of amphibians as specimens or products in 1989 was estimated by Scott and Seigel (1992) to be in excess of $25 million. The U.S. imports between 1000 and 2000 tons of frog legs annually (ibid.). Bangladesh has joined India and China in controlling the harvest because of a flareup in insects (mosquitoes, etc.).

Teaching and Research

Millions of high school and college students have learned basic facts of vertebrate anatomy and physiology from study of "the frog." According to Gibbs et al. (1971), U.S. suppliers shipped approximately 9 million frogs (around 360 tons) annually for education and research purposes alone. Amphibian studies have greatly advanced the sciences of embryology, endocrinology, and physiology. Journals in these fields are replete with articles on amphibians. The translucent (often transparent) jelly coats of the eggs of many species are a window to embryonic growth (fig. 19.1), and the exposed egg and the ease with which it can be manipulated morphologically and genetically is a boon to experimental biologists. Metamorphosis is a phase in the life cycle ideal for the study of problems in genetics, developmental biology, and tissue transplanta-

Fig. 19.1 Eggs of a Red-legged Frog (*Rana aurora*) (w N Am), showing the translucency of many amphibian egg capsules.

tion. Amphibians have tissues that function over a wide range of temperature. Thus, in experiments, temperature can be used as a valid variable for many physiological processes. Meaningful experiments can be performed at low temperatures (where preparations die more slowly), which is especially useful to physiologists and biochemists (Gibbs et al., 1971; and see Nace, 1970). Two Nobel Prize winners made their discoveries through the use of amphibians. Hans Spemann developed the concept of the organizer role of the dorsal lip of the blastopore through study of embryonic development of amphibian eggs, both salamander and frog. Using frog hearts, Otto Loewi found that acetylcholine is the transmitter of the vagus nerve in slowing the heart—the first demonstration of a neurotransmitter.

Because many amphibians are tolerant of human presence and manipulation in the field (some frogs continue to vocalize even when abruptly illuminated), they appeal to the investigating field naturalist. During breeding and migration they can be directly and sometimes easily observed, in contrast to many other vertebrates.

Amphibians have contributed enormously to studies of animal behavior and evolution. Many of the articles listed in this book pertain to these subjects. Evolutionary studies focus on the process of species formation. Because most amphibians are vulnerable to desiccation and high temperatures, they are, among terrestrial vertebrates, particularly prone to population fragmentation during periods of drought and high temperatures. Such fragmentation, if sufficiently prolonged, leads to genetic divergence and sometimes speciation. Many important discoveries of significance to speciation theory have resulted from the study of amphibians, in recent years aided by the use of biochemical and molecular techniques.

Studies of terrestrial salamanders, in particular, have made important contributions to community ecology. Longevity, restricted movements, abundance, and ease in observation have made some salamanders particularly useful in studying effects of competition, predation, and other factors that play a part in species composition, abundance, and change in natural communities (see Hairston, 1987).

Other fields that have benefited from amphibian investigations include brain circuitry and function (aided by the simplicity of amphibian brains), basic studies of vision (see chapter 7), and regeneration of lost parts (salamanders are capable of regenerating entire limbs, including the digits).

Toxicology

Amphibian eggs and larvae have been extensively used in toxicological studies in assaying the biotic effects of a great variety of substances, many of them synthetic, that are of significance to environmental and human health (see Harfenist et al., 1989).

Medicine

Fever Therapy

Basic research undertaken without human-welfare goals in mind often is more productive in achieving such goals than a human-centered approach. Studies of "behaviorally controlled" fever in amphibians are an example (see chapter 11). Amphibians, injected with pathogenic bacteria, when not allowed to voluntarily raise their body temperature by moving to a warm location, succumb to infection in greater numbers than those allowed to do so. Similar results have been obtained with other ectotherms—fish and reptiles. These findings have contributed to a reevaluation of the traditional treatment of fevers in humans: unless a fever is excessively high, in most cases it should be allowed to run its course.

A Pharmacopeia of Skin Secretions

Because of the respiratory and osmoregulatory roles of amphibian skin, the skin's outer protective layer, the epidermis and its stratum corneum, usually must be thin to allow gaseous exchange and hydroregulation. The outer skin is also perforated by the many openings of the skin glands that keep the skin moist and protect against predators. The skin, particularly the stratum corneum, is thus considerably limited as a mechanical barrier to biotic and physical impacts. This circumstance has contributed to the formation of a vast array of chemically diverse secretions produced by amphibian skin. Some of these have potent antimicrobial properties, protecting amphibians against molds, bacteria, and other pathogens present in the water, air, soil, and duff with which their skin comes into contact (Zasloff, 1987; Bevins and Zasloff, 1990; Stone et al., 1992). Caerin 1.1, a novel hypotensive peptide isolated from the parotoid glands of three closely related Australian tree frogs—the Green Tree Frog (*Litoria caerulea*) (Aus, New Guinea, New Zealand), *L. splendida* (nw Aus), and the Centralian Tree Frog (*L. gilleni*) (cen Aus)—shows promising antibiotic and even antiviral activity (Stone et al., 1992). Caerin from *L. caerulea* has been shown to vary (Stone et al., 1993). Frogs collected at different sites show subtle but reproducible differences. Other secretions protect against predators by repellent taste and/or odor, adhesive properties that interfere with ingestion, and poisoning, causing nausea, loss of coordination, and sometimes death. This variety of host defense peptides is usually located in the granular glands (see chapter 2).

Study of amphibian skin secretions promises important advances in physiology and medicine. The curare-like painkilling properties of the skin secretion of the Neotropical poison-arrow frogs have been known for some time. Now another painkiller has been found in the secretion of the Phantasmal Poison-Arrow Frog (*Epipedobates tricolor*) (Ecuador), appropriately called "epibatidine." In tests on mice, one of its constituents was found to be two hundred times as effective as morphine in blocking pain. Efforts are underway to synthesize the chemical as a possible first step toward producing a long-sought drug: a powerful, nonsedating painkiller (Bradley, 1993). Some secretions have psychedelic effects. The latter may prove to be of value in brain research and the treatment of mental disturbances.

Study of the skin secretion of the large Bicolored Tree Frog (*Phyllomedusa bicolor*) (S Am) (fig 19.2) has resulted in the discovery of a peptide that interacts with a message-reading receptor system common to the surface of all cells—the adenosine system (Daly et al., 1992). This system is involved in communication between cells of many different types. In the brain it has been linked to a variety of brain malfunctions, including Alzheimer's disease and depression. The polypeptide was discovered by John Daly and associates at the National Institutes of Health in Bethesda, Maryland. It is the first substance known to interact with the adenosine receptor system and this discovery in itself, regardless of possible health benefits, is opening up new avenues of research in brain function. The discovery stems from observations made by Katherine Milton (a University of California at Berkeley anthropologist) on the Mayoruna Indians of Brazil, who create "hunting magic" by using the

Fig. 19.2 The large neotropical Bicolored Tree Frog (*Phyllomedusa bicolor*). (From a photograph by K. Milton)

frog's secretion, rubbed into self-inflicted burned areas of skin. She notes that, upon awakening from a comalike sleep, the Indians said they could hunt all day without getting hungry or tired, and their arrows never miss the mark. "Taking frog" is like getting high in reverse: "First you vomit, then you get a hangover, then you feel terrific" (Slack, 1993).

Some amphibians produce a thick, gluelike mucus that is difficult to remove even with soap and water. Michael Tyler has been exploring its use in repairing damaged soft organs, such as the spleen and liver, which cannot be effectively stitched.

The Australian Stomach-brooding Frogs and Gastric Ulcers

As reported above, two species have been described, but both may now be extinct. Fortunately, before their apparent loss, some information was obtained on how the developing offspring were protected from the mother's gastric juice. The key substance is prostaglandin E_2, which is known to switch off the stomach's production of hydrochloric acid. This discovery may lead to a new treatment for gastric ulcers.

20

Declining Amphibians

AT THE FIRST World Congress of Herpetology held at Canterbury, England, in 1989, participants discovered a recurring theme: amphibians, particularly frogs and toads, from many widely separated parts of the world appeared to be declining. The widespread nature of the reports and the magnitude and rapidity of many of the declines (some having resulted in extinctions) suggested some far-reaching, damaging environmental cause or causes, rather than simply natural fluctuations in population densities. Since then, a comprehensive effort has been undertaken under the guidance of the International Union for the Conservation of Nature's, Declining Amphibian Populations Task Force and other agencies, to standardize methods of study of amphibian population changes and the environmental factors that may be affecting amphibian reproductive success and survival. A comprehensive coverage of such methods for measuring and monitoring amphibian populations has now been set forth (Heyer et al., 1994).

Regrettably, little is known about natural fluctuations in amphibian populations—their magnitude, frequency, degree of regularity, and causes (see Blaustein et al., 1994; Pechmann and Wilbur, 1994). Given the pervasiveness of growing human environmental impacts, chances of getting such information, except in special circumstances, are now declining. Yet it is crucial that long-term monitoring be expanded, such as that reported here by Pechmann et al. (1991), Kagarise Sherman and Morton (1993), and others, otherwise much uncertainty will plague our efforts to understand the dynamics of amphibian population behavior.

It has long been known to naturalists that amphibian populations, particularly those in marginal habitats, are prone to wide fluctuations from time to time with occasional extinctions (see Tyler, 1991). Thus to track long-term trends will probably require decades of monitoring.

During the fluctuating climate of the ice ages there were die-offs, including extinctions, declines with recolonization, and expansions of amphibian species and populations along with other members of the biota. In the present (presumed) interglacial period, to what extent are amphibian declines related to natural climatic events as opposed to human-caused (anthropogenic) factors? In most cases we do not have adequate information to answer this question. Caution is called for in reaching conclusions concerning amphibian declines (see Pechmann et al., 1991, and Wake, 1991).

Examples of Declines with Comments on Possible Causes: Selections from Western North, Central, and South America and Australia

The first question to be addressed is this: Can any declines be convincingly documented? We believe the following examples demonstrate that many of them can. Most of the North American examples concern species with which we have had long experience in the field, which has helped in evaluating the information we have gathered. See Vial and Saylor (1993) for a comprehensive discussion of declines.

Western North America

WESTERN TOAD (*Bufo boreas*) (w N Am) (FIG. 20.1)

California: Sierra Nevada

In 1980 T. Papenfuss (Museum of Vertebrate Zoology, U.C. Berkeley) surveyed thirty-two (one-mile long, 100 m wide) transects for amphibians and reptiles in the foothills of the Sierra Nevada, from Nevada to Mariposa Counties. The transects ranged in elevation from 900 to 3900 feet. (Papenfuss, 1980). Each transect was covered twice—February to April and May to July. Presence of the Western Toad was classed as highly probable on twenty-three of the transects and probable on four, but toads were found only on five. In their resurvey of six sites of occurrence of Western Toads reported by Grinnell and Storer (1924), Drost and Fellers (1993), in 1992 found toads and eggs and larvae only at one site (Yosemite Valley), and the numbers were low. They concluded that a serious decline had occurred.

Martin (1992) reported on an extensive standardized amphibian survey conducted in 1992 of randomly selected townships in the Sierra National Forests (El Dorado, Stanislaus, Sierra, and Sequoia). He found only 11 Western Toad larvae in Stanislaus and 203 larvae and 667 postmetamorphic individuals in Sequoia. There was no evidence of presence in El Dorado or Sierra National Forests. However, in El Dorado National Forest many hybrids with the Yosemite toad (*Bufo canorus*) were found. In a similar survey in 1993, Martin (pers. comm.) reported postmetamorphics and larvae, respectively, as 11 and 497 in El Dorado, 202 and 11,050 in Stanislaus, 0 and 20,920 in Sierra, and 5024 and 3803 in Sequoia. 1993 was a wetter year than 1992.

Colorado

Cynthia Carey (1993 and pers. comm.) abandoned field studies on Western Toads begun in 1971 in the West Elk Mountains, Gunnison County, because

Fig. 20.1 Western Toad (*Bufo boreas*).

of severe population declines. Her study populations were gone by 1979. Between 1971 and 1982, eleven populations had vanished.

From 1986 to 1988, a survey of fifty-nine historic localities in the central Rocky Mountains (Front and Park Ranges in northern Colorado and Medicine Bow Mountains of Colorado and Wyoming) yielded toads at only ten sites (17%) (Corn et al., 1989). Acid precipitation, a well-known problem for amphibians, especially in heavily industrialized parts of the world, had been suspected as a major cause of declines in the Rockies but recent studies have not borne this out (Corn et al., 1989; Vertucci and Corn, 1993). However, effects of sublethal pH on adult survival and on growth and development of tadpoles there have not yet been investigated.

In 1982 Theo Colborn (pers. comm.) recorded snowmelt pH levels in the lower Gunnison Mountains west of the Continental Divide, at a level toxic for amphibians. This is the general area where C. Carey lost her study populations.

New Mexico: San Juan Mountains (Charles Painter,
    pers. comm., New Mexico Department of Game
    and Fish, and Stuart and Painter, 1994.)

The last evidence for the presence of Western Toads was around 1987. Prior to that, the species was known from three lake areas-Lagunitas, Canjilon, and Trout. Repeated efforts to find the toads, most recently in 1993, have failed. However, four toads, presumably of this species, were seen in late July in meadows along Elk Creek (around 3000 m elevation) in Conejos County, Colorado, some 17 miles north of the New Mexico border.

Oregon

Blaustein et al. (1994b) reported that a circumglobal fungus, *Saprolegnia ferax*, had contributed to high mortality of Western Toad eggs in the Cascade Mountains. These were losses of 50%, 60%, and 95%, respectively, of eggs laid at Three Creeks, Lost, and Todd Lakes. Unusual egg mortality had been found in the population at Lost Lake every year since 1989, yet from 1980 to 1989 natural mortality of eggs had never been more than 5%. The fungus is a common pathogen of fishes and may have been introduced by fish stocking. The dispersal and migration of amphibians may contribute to its spread. The fungal infection is perhaps secondary, reflecting other environmental factors that may be stressing the toads.

Elevated levels of UV radiation have also been implicated in the decline of hatching success in the Cascade Mountains (see p. 242). This is evidently the first documented case of a significant biological impact presumably resulting from thinning of stratospheric ozone, reported for the north temperate zone.

Utah: Wasatch and Uinta Mountains

(David Ross, pers. comm., Utah Department of Wildlife)

Western toads were quite common up to around the 1960s. The species now appears to be absent or in severe decline throughout the state. The only presently known (1993) breeding population is in southwestern Kane County near Kanab, a new locality for the species. Stocking with predatory fish, water developments, road construction, increased recreational activities in the vicinity of breeding sites, and drought may have contributed to declines of this species in Utah.

Wyoming

Declines have apparently occurred in Yellowstone and Grand Teton National Parks. Peterson et al. (1992) in 1991 found the species at only three of the eight sites investigated in the parks. Only ten adults were observed, and at one site only a single juvenile was found. Carpenter (1953) had reported the species as the most widespread amphibian in the Jackson Hole region.

In Targhee National Forest, adjacent to the parks to the west, Western Toads were found at only nine of ninety-eight sites surveyed in 1992, including historical localities (Clark et al., 1993).

YOSEMITE TOAD (*Bufo canorus*) (FIG. 20.2)

The Yosemite Toad is confined to high elevations in the California Sierra Nevada. A significant decline has occurred in this species. Kagarise Sherman and Morton (1993) report the following (Tioga Pass area). Breeding aggregations were surveyed yearly from 1971 to 1982 (less systematically in 1983 to

Fig. 20.2 Yosemite Toad (*Bufo canorus*), showing
pattern difference between male (above) and female.

1991). From 1974 to 1982 a ninefold decrease was observed in the total number of marked males entering the largest pools at Tioga Pass. The average
number on daily searches dropped over the 20-year study. Similar declines
also occurred at smaller breeding sites. In 1990 reproduction occurred at all but
one study site but it was minimal. Death of adults from disease (apparently
redleg) occurred at Tioga Pass, and predation also contributed to losses.
Drought may also have been a factor. Snow depths from 1976 to 1977 and
1987 to 1991 were below a 62-year average. There may have also been some
deleterious effects from toe-clipping and handling of the animals. However, a
nearby population that was not under study had disappeared by about 1975.

    In 1990 David Martin (1991) checked seventy-five historic localities over
the entire species range and found 47% lacked any sign of the toads or their
tadpoles or eggs. In 1992–93 about 50% of sixty-four sites, *randomly selected*,
also lacked any evidence of species presence. In 1992, Martin (1992), using
standardized methods (see Western Toad account, this chapter) surveyed
Sierran National Forests (El Dorado to Sequoia). He found only 2 larvae and
57 postmetamorphic individuals—in Sierra National Forest. No effort was

made to find eggs. In 1993, in a similar survey, he (pers. comm.) reported 184 postmetamorphics and 47 larvae in Sierra National Forest. No postmetamorphs or larvae were found in El Dorado, Stanislaus, or Sequoia National Forests.

Drost and Fellers (1993) obtained similar results in their resurvey of the Grinnell and Storer (1924) sites in the Yosemite region in 1992. They found the species at only about half of the historic sites and generally in low numbers. Most records were of tadpoles. In the summer of 1993, Fellers found the species in many areas but rarely in large numbers. The Yosemite Toad is classified as a category 2 species by the U.S. Fish and Wildlife Service (potential candidate for listing but more information needed).

WYOMING TOAD (*Bufo hemiophrys baxteri*) (FIG. 20.3)

This is a relict subspecies of the Canadian Toad (*Bufo hemiophrys*). The only known locality is the Laramie Basin, Wyoming. Contributors: Lewis et al. (1985); Baxter et al. (1982); William Gern, Ron Beiswenger, and Stephen Corn, pers. comm.

The following history of population decline, and its possible causes, was contributed chiefly by S. Corn. The Wyoming Toad was abundant prior to a population crash in the mid-1970s. It was rare from 1976 to 1978 and none was found in 1979. In 1980, a population of around twenty-five individuals was located 10 miles west of Laramie, but in 1981, only one male and one female were found. In 1983, during an intensive search from May to August, two juveniles were observed, the first evidence of reproduction since 1975. In 1984, approximately thirty males were discovered, but in 1985–86, no toads were found. In 1987, a single, seemingly healthy, population was located in the Mortenson Lake area, now a U.S. Fish and Wildlife Service Refuge, raising hopes for recovery. In 1988, eight or nine egg masses and many yearlings were observed, but the following summer (after a severe winter) only a few young were found. In 1990, around 120 two-year-olds and older individuals were discovered. In 1991, about 400 individuals (some twenty adults from 1990 and an influx of two-year-olds) were observed; but in 1992 no reproduction occurred although about 150 toads were present (around one-third were two-year-olds and older, the rest yearlings). The foregoing trends in mortality and lack of reproduction led to a captive breeding program, currently underway. Surveys in August 1993 yielded only two adult females.

Like the California Condor, the Wyoming Toad now appears to depend for its survival on the uncertainties of direct human intervention. The animal was listed as endangered in February 1984.

Spraying for mosquitoes with Baytex (Fenthion) from aircraft had begun when the reduction in the toads (and Northern Leopard Frogs) in the Laramie

Fig. 20.3 Wyoming Toad (*Bufo hemiophrys baxteri*). (Photo courtesy of Lu Ray
Parker, Wyoming Department of Game and Fish)

Basin was first noted. The site where the toads were found in 1980 was adjacent to a ranch where spraying for mosquitoes did not occur. Herbicides (2–4-
D, Tordon, and Benvel) have also been used in the Basin. Test results with
Baytex revealed no outright lethal effects but the possibility of sublethal impacts has yet to be ruled out. Baytex was taken off the market and Malathion
replaced it for mosquito control. The Environmental Protection Agency has
proposed restricting the use of some forty-three pesticides within part of the
Laramie Basin, but at present the situation surrounding this proposal is fluid
and may change (per W. Gern). Drought and cold weather may have also
played a part in the decline. Gulls, cormorants, white pelicans, raccoons, foxes,
and skunks are plentiful in the Basin and most have increased in numbers
during the past 50 years, but there are no observations directly tying any of
them to the toad decline. Toads at Mortenson Lake had redleg disease but this
might have been a symptom of deeper problems underlying the population
collapse.

   According to W. Gern, the demise of the Wyoming Toad has been accompanied by a drastic decline in the Northern Leopard Frog (*Rana pipiens*) within
the Laramie Basin (which, although still in trouble in the lowlands, is now
coming back in the mountains) and the Western Toad (*Bufo boreas*) in the
mountains of Albany County. However, the Plains Spadefoot Toad (*Spea
bombifrons*) has increased and the Striped Chorus Frog (*Pseudacris triseriata*)
and the Wood Frog (*Rana sylvatica*) appear to be holding their own.

CANADIAN TOAD (*Bufo hemiophrys hemiophrys*) (cen Canada, n cen US)

This subspecies is also apparently in trouble. Wayne Roberts, University of Alberta, Museum of Zoology (pers. comm.), reports that in the Red Deer River drainage in central and southeastern Alberta, where the toad was formerly abundant and widespread, a decline was first noticed in the late 1980s and has been in progress into the 1990s. Many populations have completely disappeared. However, it appeared that the species was still doing well (until 1993) in the badlands of the river, an enormous tract of undeveloped land. In 1993 the toad was rarely heard. The Wood Frog and Striped Chorus Frog throughout Alberta and, not far to the northwest, the Western Toad appear to be doing well. The first two species are freeze-tolerant (the Canadian Toad is not) and the Western Toad overwinters in habitats with a milder microclimate. The Canadian Toad is thus more likely to experience greater cold stress than the others. Roberts has been a resident naturalist in the area since the 1950s.

ARROYO TOAD (*Bufo microscaphus californicus*) (s Cal, n Baja Cal) (FIG. 20.4)

Southwestern California

This toad is a habitat specialist closely restricted to broad, low-gradient stream courses with sandy banks. Distribution is spotty. The following information is from Sweet (1992) and S. Sweet and M. Jennings (pers. comm.). Intensive field work was conducted from 1989 to 1993 by Sweet and Jennings. The species is currently estimated by them to be extinct over 75% of its former range. Sweet comments that about half of the range reduction has been caused by dams that have inundated habitat and which, during flow regulation, cause scouring of stream channels during water releases and drying during shutdowns. Remaining damage has been caused by a host of local effects—recreational use along drainages where eggs, young, and adults are trampled or run over. Off-road vehicles sometimes enter the water, destroying breeding habitat and egg clusters. Wading fishermen trample the eggs. Swimmers, waders, and off-road vehicles stir up silt that smothers eggs and larvae, and coats algal and other food sources. Road maintenance and suction dredging for gold cause extensive down-stream silting. Introduction of Bullfrogs (fig. 20.11) and predatory fish have also caused damage. Steps are underway to remedy some of these problems.

In the Los Padres National Forest, only an estimated 340–350 adults (an aging population) remained in 1991. Increased rainfall and remedial measures resulted in some recovery. Adults were estimated at around 530 in 1992 and projected to reach around 750 in 1993.

Fig. 20.4 Arroyo Toad (*Bufo microscaphus californicus*).

Only one population is currently known in the Angeles National Forest, one in the San Bernardino National Forest, and five in the Cleveland National Forest (Jennings, pers. comm.). The Arroyo Toad has been proposed for listing as endangered by the U.S. Fish and Wildlife Service (August 3, 1993).

NORTHERN LEOPARD FROG (*Rana pipiens*) (N Am) (FIG. 20.5)

Canada: Alberta

The following information is from Wayne Roberts, University of Alberta Museum of Zoology. In the spring of 1978, in the wetlands of central Alberta, this species was still abundant (Roberts has been a resident naturalist in the area since the 1950s). A decline in Northern Leopard Frogs began in eastern North America in the 1960s and spread westward, reaching Manitoba in the mid-1970s and Alberta in 1978–79. In the meantime, some recoveries occurred in the east. In Alberta the loss along the Red Deer River (from the foothills area to the vicinity of Drumheller), where Roberts made repeated surveys since the 1950s to 1994, has apparently been total. It has included an area of numerous pristine springs on the lower Clearwater River, a tributary of the North Saskatchewan, in west-central Alberta. The frogs were last heard there in 1978, and have not been found since. Two lakes in northeastern Alberta have small localized populations (1993), and a prairie population in the Cypress Hill area

Fig. 20.5 Northern Leopard Frog (*Rana pipiens*).

of southeastern Alberta yielded a count of about 300 frogs along a 50 meter swath in 1990. They still seem to be doing well. A number of isolated populations along the South Saskatchewan River, lower Red Deer River, and the Milk River are still extant.

Redleg disease has been associated with the decline, but it may not be the proximate cause.

According to Roberts (pers. comm.), fish predation appears also to be inadequate in explaining the declines. Northern Leopard Frogs overwinter in water inhabited variously by northern pike, walleye, and burbot. They sometimes reproduce in the same waters. Western Toads and Wood Frogs continue to reproduce well in formerly fishless lakes where brook and rainbow trout and yellow perch have been introduced. Roberts suspects that in special cases predation by fish may be significant but in many others it is not.

United States (this species has declined in the central prairies
    at least partly as a result of drainage of wetlands)

ARIZONA. Clarkson and Rorabaugh (1989) reported on twenty-five localities surveyed from 1983 to 1987; thirteen lacked frogs. One previously unreported population was discovered.

CALIFORNIA. It appears to be absent from its historic range except for perhaps a few small populations in the extreme northeastern part.

COLORADO: LARAMIE COUNTY.   The following information is from Corn and Fogleman (1984). Between 1973 and 1982 nine populations in the Red Feather Lakes region disappeared. One site was recolonized in 1980, but no frogs were found at any of the sites in 1981 or 1982. Drying of ponds is thought to have caused the loss of six of the populations. Habitat is marginal for this species in this area and extinctions may be common. In a survey (1986–88) of thirty-three historically known localities in Colorado, Leopard Frogs were only found at four (12%) (Corn et al., 1989).

IDAHO.   No Leopard Frogs were found in the Targhee National Forest of western Wyoming and adjacent Idaho in a survey (1992) of ninety-eight sites. There are historical records for the area (Clark et al., 1993).

OREGON.   A careful survey in the mid-1970s of sections of the Columbia River, where Leopard Frogs previously occurred, failed to turn up this species (Storm, 1986). St. John (1985b) failed to find the frog on his Owyhee River drainage survey of 1984–85 in eastern Oregon, where the species formerly occurred.

WASHINGTON.   All historic sites were checked by Sandy Andelman in 1993: the Pend Oreille River area, Pend Oreille County; the lower Snake River Basin, southeastern Washington; Diamond Lake, Spokane County; Alderdale, Klickitat County; Spectacle Lake, Okanagan County (frogs possibly introduced); and Potholes Reservoir, Grant County. The species was found only at the latter site (S. Andelman and W. Leonard, pers. comm.).

Bullfrogs were introduced for recreational hunting into the Columbia National Wildlife Refuge along the lower Snake River in 1980. Before that, the Northern Leopard Frog was ubiquitous. By 1986 it had disappeared. The Diamond Lake area also has Bullfrogs and they are present along the Pend Oreille River. Some historic frog sites have been drained for agriculture and sites along the lower Snake River are now under water. Many Pothole localities now have carp. Pesticides to control mosquitoes may also be implicated in the Leopard Frog losses.

WYOMING.   See account of the Wyoming Toad.

Extensive use of this species and its relatives for education and research is contributing to scarcities in populations in Canada, the United States, and Mexico (see Gibbs et al., 1971). The animals are obtained by a network of collectors working for large supply companies. However, the severe declines and apparent extinctions of populations of this frog cannot be explained by overcollecting alone.

CHIRICAHUA LEOPARD FROG (*Rana chiricahuensis*) (sw New Mex, Ariz, Mex)

Arizona

This species was found at only two of thirty-six localities where it was present in the 1960s and 1970s; two new localities were discovered (Clarkson and Rorabaugh, 1989).

LOWLAND LEOPARD FROG (*Rana yavapaiensis*) (sw US, nw Mex)

Arizona and Southeastern California

There have been no sightings of this frog in the Imperial Valley since the early 1960s. Along the lower Colorado River it was rare by the 1960s, and gone by 1974. Bullfrogs and exotic predatory fish are now present. However, populations in upland Arizona are relatively intact. The Rio Grande Leopard Frog (*Rana berlandieri*) has replaced this species along the Colorado and Gila Rivers, Arizona, and has spread to the Coachella Valley, California (M. Jennings, pers. comm.).

PLAINS LEOPARD FROG (*Rana blairi*) (cen US)

Arizona

This frog is found in the Sulphur Springs Valley area and Ashurst Lake, southeast of Flagstaff. Ground-water pumping, agricultural development, and introduction of the Bullfrog and predatory fish threaten the species. Acid precipitation, including resultant heavy-metal leaching, might be involved in some of the declines. Leopard frogs are sensitive to acid precipitation (Clarkson and Rorabaugh, 1989).

SPOTTED FROG (*Rana pretiosa*) (w N Am) (FIG. 20.6)

California

The Spotted Frog has been recorded from three localities in extreme northeastern California. It was last reported from the area in 1911.

Oregon

This species was abundant throughout the state until the mid-1970s. It is now considered extinct in the lowlands west of the crest of the Cascade Mountains. This amounts to a loss of about one third of its Oregon range.

Marc Hayes has undertaken an extensive study of Spotted Frogs in western Oregon. Little current information appears to be available concerning the

Fig. 20.6 Spotted Frog (*Rana pretiosa*).

status of the species elsewhere in the state, where it may prove to be a different taxon (or variety). Formerly, it was widely distributed and abundant. Hayes's studies have focused on the species distribution, primarily west of the Cascade crest. The frog's historic range in this area is considered to have been the Willamette and Klamath hydrographic basins (Hayes, 1994a). In the Willamette Basin, historic records indicate that the species was broadly distributed over roughly the western two-thirds of the lowland valley, at least into the 1930s, and it ranged north to the Portland area. The last verifiable record in the valley occurred in 1966 (Sweet Home). The frog apparently disappeared during the 1950s and 1960s. Dam-building on tributaries of the upper Willamette River, which reduced flooding and warm-water marsh habitat favored by the frog, and the introduction of Bullfrogs, crayfish, and a variety of warm-water fishes, has contributed to the loss of this species in the basin.

The status of the frog is unclear on the western slope of the Cascade Mountains adjacent to the Willamette Valley. It has been found at two historic localities and one new locality, all above 4000 feet (1219 m) elevation. These are localities where hydrographical modification and exotic predators are having less impact than in the lowlands. Regrettably, the populations at two of these localities are experiencing high adult mortality and poor recruitment of young. Historically, the frog appears to have been common in the lower Klamath Basin. Present status there is unknown but similar changes have occurred to those in the Willamette Valley.

A survey of all historic localities in western Oregon indicates, conservatively, that the Spotted Frog has disappeared from 90% of its former range in this region (Hayes, 1994b).

At a study site at Mill Creek, Umatilla County, east of the Cascade Mountains, mortality in these frogs, reported by Kirk (1988), appeared to be related to spraying with DDT (June and July 1974) to control the Douglas Fir Tussuck Moth. The dead frogs contained DDT residues, but how much above "background" levels was unknown. All species of fish, birds, and mammals, for which prespray residue information was collected, showed prespray background levels of DDT in their tissues. Unfortunately, amphibians were not included in the prespray studies. Spraying involved 172,695 hectares of forest in Oregon, Washington, and Idaho. To what extent has chemical treatment of forest lands impacted this and other species of amphibians (see account of Mountain Yellow-legged Frog, this chapter)? See Cooper (1991) for effects of pesticides on wildlife.

Utah

The Spotted Frog is still present at fifty-four sites in the western desert area and Wasatch Front Range (David Ross, Utah Department of Wildlife, pers. comm.).

Washington: West of Cascade Mountains

This species was formerly widespread but spotty in distribution in the lowlands in western Washington east of the Olympic Mountains and Coast Range to the foothills of the Cascade Range, an area known as the Puget Trough (McAllister and Leonard, 1991). Herpetologists have long known that the species was in decline in this area. Surveys had yielded only one individual since 1968, found in 1990, in Thurston County. On May 17, 1994, Kelly McAllister found two juvenile Spotted Frogs at the Thurston County site, and the next day William Leonard and K. McAllister found 17 more juveniles. At least one population remains in western Washington (W. Leonard, pers. comm.). The introduction of Bullfrogs and centrarchid fishes and widespread habitat alterations appear to be primarily responsible for the loss of this frog throughout much of its range in western Washington (McAllister et al., 1993). The frog is now a candidate for federal listing in this area.

Washington: Cascade Mountains

A distributional study of amphibians was conducted in the national forests of this area in 1993 (McAllister and Leonard, 1993). The Spotted Frog was found at the crest of the North Cascades (Rainy Pass vicinity), Swauk Creek headwaters, near the North Fork Teanaway River, and in the Fish Creek drainage at Rimrock Lake. East of the Cascade crest, populations appear to increase from south to north.

Wyoming

Charles Peterson (Idaho State University) (pers. comm.) and Stephan Corn have resurveyed sites studied by Turner (1958, 1960) in Yellowstone National Park. Turner worked in the area from 1953 to 1956. In the Lake Lodge area, a focal point of Turner's study, Peterson and Corn estimated a total of 245 frogs (adults and immatures) in 1991. In 1953–55 Turner had estimated a population of around 1000–1600 frogs at this locality. An 80% decline is considered to have occurred in this population (Patla and Peterson, 1993). Road construction and drought may have contributed to the decline. Following a visit to his former study sites, Turner remarked that no thesis like his would now be possible (pers. comm.).

In their survey (1991) of the Yellowstone and Grand Teton National Parks, Peterson et al. (1992) reported that this species was "present, abundant, and reproducing at all eight sites" investigated. However, they note that population trends are unknown. The frog was also found to be abundant in Targhee National Forest, adjacent to the parks on the west. It was found at forty-one of ninety-eight survey sites (Clark et al., 1993).

CASCADES FROG (*Rana cascadae*) (Cascade Mts, Cal, Ore, Wash) (FIG. 20.7)

California: Lassen Volcanic National Park and Vicinity

Fellers and Drost (1993) conducted a survey in 1991. Fifty localities were visited, sixteen of them historic, but only one yielded frogs (two). In 1993 Fellers found the species still rare. Remarkably, he discovered the same two frogs at the locality visited in 1991. They were recognized by their distinctive color patterns. A population was found south of Lassen Park along a tributary of Butte Creek, Tehama County.

A precipitous decline appears to have occurred in this species in fifteen years. Introduction of non-native predatory fish, loss of breeding habitat to a 5-year drought, and loss of open meadows and associated aquatic habitats as a result of fire suppression and elimination of grazing, appear to be implicated in the decline.

Fig. 20.7 Cascades Frog (*Rana cascadae*). (Photo courtesy of William Leonard)

Oregon: Central Cascade Mountains

The following information is from Andrew Blaustein (pers. comm.). From 1990 to 1993, eighty populations were extensively monitored at historic sites; 22% lacked frogs. The species appears to be suffering from an increase in UV light penetration that appears to be impacting hatching success. Formerly hundreds could be present in areas of less than one hectare (2.2 acres) (Nussbaum et al., 1983). Whether such numbers still exist anywhere is unknown.

Washington

During surveys from 1991 to 1993, the frog was found to be locally abundant throughout the Cascade Mountains from Skagit to Skamania Counties (William Leonard, pers. comm.; see also McAllister and Leonard, 1993). However, historic population densities are unknown.

The Cascades Frog is classified as a category 2 species by the U.S. Fish and Wildlife Service (potential candidate for listing but more information needed).

MOUNTAIN YELLOW-LEGGED FROG (*Rana muscosa*) (Cal, w Nev) (FIG. 20.8)

California: Sierra Nevada

Lawrence Cory (Saint Mary's College, Moraga, California) began field work on this species in the high Sierra in the late 1950s and 1960s. He worked the

Fig. 20.8 Mountain Yellow-legged Frog (*Rana muscosa*).

length of the Sierra. The species was abundant. It was still present in good numbers in 1970. He returned in 1988 and 1989 and found no Yellow-legged Frogs anywhere in the northern Sierra; a few were found to the south. However, his survey did not cover all historic sites.

Bradford et al. (1994c) report surveys of two study areas in the Sierra comprising the headwaters of seven creek systems in Sequoia and Kings Canyon National Parks. The surveys were conducted in 1978–79, and again in 1989. In 1978–79, Mountain Yellow-legged Frogs were found at twenty-seven sites greater than 200 m apart, but at only one site in 1989, and that population had disappeared by 1991. In 1989–90, a survey of twenty-one historical (1955–79) and recent (1989–90) localities scattered throughout the parks yielded frogs at only eleven sites. The authors conclude that the Mountain Yellow-legged Frog has disappeared from about half of the historical localities in these parks during the last three decades and has been extirpated in some drainages. The magnitude of the decline appears to be even greater outside the parks.

Mark Jennings surveyed the entire Sierra Nevada from 1988 to 1992, checking known localities. He found 50% lacked frogs (Jennings et al., 1992). The species was absent south of Kings Canyon and in the north, including the Feather River Canyon area. Coon Hollow, where sympatry occurred among the Cascades (*Rana cascadae*), Mountain (*R. muscosa*), and Foothill Yellow-legged (*R. boylii*) Frogs, lacked frogs.

In their resurvey (1992) of the Grinnell and Storer (1924) historic sites in the

Yosemite region, Drost and Fellers (1993) found only one tadpole and one adult. In the summer of 1993, Fellers and his crew checked about 250 sites in Yosemite and found the species present in a variety of places but absent in many others. At Sequoia and Kings Canyon National Parks, the frog has entirely disappeared from large contiguous portions of its former range. In Sequoia none was found in the Kaweah River drainage (Fellers, 1994). Fellers's crew checked 651 sites within the species range and found frogs at a total of 138 localities. Grinnell and Storer (1924) reported it as one of the commonest amphibians in their Yosemite survey.

Martin, in his survey (1992) of Sierran National Forests (El Dorado to Sequoia) (see Western Toad account for details), reported 4 postmetamorphic individuals and 223 larvae for Stanislaus and 2 postmetamorphs for Sierra National Forests. No evidence of presence was found in El Dorado and Sequoia National Forests. In 1993 (pers. comm.), in a similar survey, he reported postmetamorphs and larvae, respectively, as 13 and 18 in El Dorado, 6 and 48 in Sierra, and 14 and 22 in Stanislaus National Forests. No evidence of presence was found in Sequoia National Forest.

Southern California (south of the Santa Clara River)

Where it was formerly widespread and abundant, the frog is now known at only six sites in the San Gabriel, San Bernardino, and San Jacinto Mountains, with a total of fewer than one hundred adults observed during surveys form 1988 through 1993 (M. Jennings, pers. comm.). Only three populations are known from the San Gabriels, and all are estimated to contain fewer than fifteen individuals (M. Jennings in Fellers, 1994). These are wilderness areas with habitats that look intact.

A contributing cause to declines in the Sierra has been the introduction of fish (trout and brook charr) that prey upon the frogs and their tadpoles. Prior to these introductions, the high mountain lake habitat occupied by the frogs lacked fish (see Bradford, 1989). However, this may not be the main cause of the declines because frogs and fish coexist at some sites (L. Cory and M. Jennings, pers. comm.) and apparently complete losses have occurred at others where fish are absent (Cory, pers. comm., and Drost and Fellers, 1993). The frog remained the most numerous frog species at Westfall Meadows in Yosemite National Park as late as 1977, long after fish were introduced (Yoon, 1977). It has since disappeared. Furthermore, fish introductions began long before the decline began in the late 1970s, and after introductions peaked in the late 1930s and 1940s, populations have steadily declined since 1951 (Drost and Fellers, 1993).

Fish introductions fragment frog habitat by excluding populations and severing dispersal links between breeding sites, making recolonization of vacated sites difficult, if not impossible. Such introductions have been particularly damaging in the fragmented high mountain lake and meadow habitat of the frogs. They have increased chances of extinction through the isolation of small populations.

Lawrence Cory found DDT and its principal metabolite, DDE, in the fat-bodies of frogs from all parts of the Sierra, even to elevations up to 12,000 ft (Cory et al., 1970). The presence of DDT is attributable to windborne residues from cropdusting in the adjacent Central Valley of California. There are also Forest Service records of massive applications of DDT directly to areas within the Sierra (Cory et al., 1970), as well as some use of malathion to control lodgepole needle miner (Drost and Fellers, 1993). Despite this, Cory does not consider DDT to have been responsible for the declines in frog populations. During the 1950s and 1960s, when DDT use was at its height, the frog populations were thriving. As far as can be determined, the major declines in their populations began in the 1980s, more than ten years after the use of DDT ceased in 1970.

Other chemicals have replaced DDT for control of agricultural and forest pests. These should be identified and their effects on amphibian populations determined, particularly with respect to possible impacts on sexual and functional development (see p. 243) (L. Cory, pers. comm.).

Contaminants that are fat-soluble (such as DDT) accumulate on the water surface film and presumably in bottom muck. The frogs are sun baskers and are in and out of water, frequently passing through the film. They possibly absorb contaminants through their skin as well as from their food.

The possible role of acid precipitation in the decline of the Mountain Yellow-legged Frog is presently unclear (Bradford and Gordon, 1992). Low pond pH levels are known to impair amphibian hatching success (Gascon and Planas, 1986). Experimentally, sublethal effects at pH 5.0 and 5.25, leading to reduced body size in embryos (Bradford et al., 1992), suggest that acid surges into the breeding sites during snowmelt could be a factor. However, pH below 5.4 has not been measured in ponds or lakes during snowmelt except in rare circumstances associated with iron pyrite deposits (Melack et al., 1993; Bradford et al., 1993, 1994a,b). Although adults may enter such waters, tadpoles have not been found.

From 1987 to 1993, California experienced a severe drought which may well have caused some population declines, but California has a history of droughts and its biota is adapted to withstand drought conditions. This is reflected in the fragmented ranges of many California amphibian species.

Big floods (estimated as once-in-500-years events) in 1968 and 1969 took out many frog populations in Southern California. These populations also have been subjected to airborne contaminants.

The Mountain Yellow-legged Frog has been classified as a category 2 species by the U.S. Fish and Wildlife Service (potential candidate for listing but more information needed).

Fig. 20.9 Foothill Yellow-legged Frog (*Rana boylii*).

FOOTHILL YELLOW-LEGGED FROG (*Rana boylii*)
(w Ore, Cal, n Baja Cal) (FIG. 20.9)

California

Sam Sweet (U.C. Santa Barbara) reports a major decline throughout most of the state. The Foothill Yellow-legged Frog is now extinct in many areas in Southern California (Sweet, 1983). Isolated populations in the San Gabriel Mountains (Camp Rincon) and Elizabeth Lake Canyon are gone. It has apparently disappeared from the San Pedro Martír Mountains in Baja California. In the San Gabriel Mountains it was presumed extinct by 1977. Populations in Ventura, Santa Barbara, and coastal San Luis Obispo Counties are now apparently extinct (gone by 1969–71) except for a population in extreme northwestern San Luis Obispo County. In the 1960s it was a common frog in central Ventura County. None has been reported since 1971 in the Sespe Creek drainage (per S. Sweet). A small population exists on San Benito Mountain in the Inner Coast Range, south of Pinnacles National Monument. Along the Big Sur coast, Monterey County, it is still present but nowhere common.

A marked decline has occurred along the west slope of the Sierra, where it was formerly common. David Martin (1992) reports postmetamorphs and larvae, respectively, from national forest lands as follows: *Sequoia* and *Sierra*, none found; *Stanislaus*, 4 and 233; *El Dorado*, 4 and 150. In 1993 Martin (pers. comm.) found only one postmetamorph in El Dorado National Forest and 8 postmetamorphs and 3 larvae in Stanislaus National Forest. Results were negative in Sierra and Sequoia National Forests. In Stanislaus County, he noted stream channel damage from overgrazing and a recent burn; a small population at Rose Creek was threatened by silting from gold-mining activities.

Drost and Fellers (1993) failed to find this species in 1992 in rechecking historic sites recorded by Grinnell and Storer (1924), and they were unable to find it anywhere in the southern Sierra. Field work in 1993 (Fellers, 1994) yielded only on subadult frog south of Calavaras County. The survey covered 310 sites in the southern Sierran foothills within the frog's known range.

The species has been hard hit in the Los Padres National Forest and San Gabriel Mountains. Severe winter flooding occurred in Southern California during the winter of 1968–69. However, G. Fellers (summer 1993) found this species common along the north coast of California.

Fellers (1994) reports healthy, reproducing populations in essentially all perennial streams of the Diablo Range with suitable habitat in Alameda, western Stanislaus, Santa Clara, San Benito, and western Fresno Counties. The species, however, was not found in Pinnacles National Monument.

Oregon

Little appears to be known about the present status of this species in Oregon. St. John found the frog in the Umpqua River drainage in 1985 and it was widespread along streams in Jackson and Josephine counties in 1984. It was common along streams in Curry County in 1982 (see St. John, 1982–86).

This species is classified as a category 2 species by the U.S. Fish and Wildlife Service (potential candidate for listing but more information needed).

TARAHUMARA FROG (*Rana tarahumarae*) (s Ariz, Mex)

Arizona (Clarkson and Rorabaugh 1989)

This frog apparently has been eliminated recently from the U.S. at certain headwater springs and streams of the Rio Altar and Santa Cruz drainages and from some localities in northern Sonora, Mexico. Pollution from copper mining may have been a factor in the U.S. The frogs have shown signs of heavy-metal poisoning, but other impacts have also probably contributed to its disappearance.

RED-LEGGED FROG (*Rana aurora*) (BC to n Baja Cal)

California Red-legged Frog (R. a. draytonii) (Fig. 20.10)

This frog has disappeared from sizable portions of its historic range (discussed by Hayes and Jennings, 1988), including all historic sites on the floor of the Great Valley. It appears to have been nearly eliminated from the Sierran foot-

Fig. 20.10 California Red-legged Frog (*Rana aurora draytonii*).

hills from El Dorado National Forest to Sequoia National Park (Martin, 1992, and pers. comm.). No eggs, larvae, or adults were found by Martin during a standardized survey of the national forest lands in 1992 and 1993 (see Western Toad account for details). The surveys included all historic sites (twelve). Scattered populations still exist north of El Dorado National Forest in Tahoe and Plumas National Forest.

Drost and Fellers (1993) failed to find the species in 1992 at the two sites reported by Grinnell and Storer (1924) in their survey of the Yosemite region, but found the species at an artificial pond along Cunes Creek near Coulterville. However, no tadpoles or transformed frogs have been found in subsequent searches.

Populations still exist in eastern Contra Costa and Alameda Counties and at Pinnacles National Monument (Fellers, 1994). In the Coast Range, north of Ventura County, scattered populations still exist in small coastal streams and tributaries where there are no Bullfrogs (S. Sweet, pers. comm.).

The frog appears to be extinct in most of Southern California, south of the Santa Clara River. A small population exists on the Santa Rosa Plateau of southwestern Riverside County, protected by a Nature Conservancy preserve. In the 1960s, it was considered the most common true frog in San Diego County (Sloan, 1964); now it appears to be extinct.

A survey (summer, 1993) by G. Fellers revealed the species to be still quite abundant in appropriate habitat along the coast from Crescent City to Point Reyes National Seashore. The California Red-legged Frog was exploited as a food source during the 1800s and early 1900s. Introduction of predatory fish

Fig. 20.11 Bullfrog (*Rana catesbeiana*).

and the Bullfrog (fig. 20.11) and habitat destruction (agriculture, cattle grazing, urbanization, and dam building) have contributed to its decline.

The California Red-legged Frog has been recommended for listing by the
U.S. Fish and Wildlife Service.

Northern Red-legged Frog (R.a. aurora)

OREGON. Andrew Blaustein (pers. comm.) reports that this frog is now apparently gone from the Willamette Valley, having not been reported there
since at least 1978. It was formerly "extremely abundant" there (Blaustein and
Wake, 1990). However, there are breeding populations along the coast.

CALIFORNIA TIGER SALAMANDER (*Ambystoma californiense*) (Fig. 20.12)
    (Confined to California)

In a study (unpublished) conducted by the senior author in 1989, this salamander was found to be absent from many historic sites and unreported for many
years from many others. There have been many local extinctions. Of forty-
three sites for which the last year of observation was known, 52% represented
observations made before 1975 and 24% antedated 1970. The species is extinct at a number of these localities, but additional field work is needed to
determine the status of the animal at many of the others.

In a survey (1990–92), Shaffer et al. (1994) documented, in most cases,
from 50% to 100% loss of historical localities. These localities were a combi-

Fig. 20.12 California Tiger Salamander (*Ambystoma californiense*).

nation of sites that no longer exist and sites where ponds still exist but the animals are absent. Among 324 ponds surveyed, which included nonhistoric sites that were considered to be suitable habitat, only 92 (28.4%) yielded sala-manders. They estimated ("conservatively") that at least 75% of the original grassland habitat of the species had been irrevocably lost. Genetic studies identified at least seven genetically distinct units within the species, and sug-gested low levels of migration between breeding complexes. Thus recoloniza-tion following extirpations can be expected to be difficult if not impossible. This places the species at high risk.

Urban and suburban developments, conversion of grazing lands to crop ag-riculture, construction of reservoirs, Mosquito Fish and other predatory fish introductions, presence of the Bullfrog, road kills, poisoning campaigns to destroy rodents (particularly the California Ground Squirrel), and environ-mental pollution (biocides, acid precipitation, etc.) are likely implicated in the decline of this species. Habitat loss and fragmentation are regarded by Shaffer et al. (1994) as the primary causes of the decline.

TIGER SALAMANDER (*Ambystoma tigrinum*)

Colorado Rockies

Harte and Hoffman (1989) studied this species at the Mexican Cut Nature Conservancy preserve west of the crest. The salamanders (many of them paedogenic; see chapter 17) breed in pools that form primarily from snowmelt.

A decline of 65% in the adult population (classed as greater-than-one-year-olds) occurred over a 7-year period from 1982 to 1988, and larval recruitment declined steadily overall except the last year (1988), when a resurgence occurred in larval numbers. The study site is in an acid-sensitive watershed. The acid comes primarily from airborne pollution sources to the southwest and falls with rain and snow. During the course of the study, pulses of acidity that accompanied snowmelt in spring may have accounted for the declines. Pulses are transient ("episodic") surges of acidity resulting from temporary lowering of surface-water pH and alkalinity and a simultaneous increase in sulfates and nitrate levels following snowmelt (Harte and Hoffman, 1989). Such surges have been observed in the Sierra Nevada of California (Melack et al., 1987) and in the Colorado Rockies (Blanchard et al., 1987). Field tests revealed that the rate of embryonic development and survivorship of the salamander eggs was markedly impaired at pH levels between 6.1 and 5.7. These are levels that have been recorded in the field. Some of the lowest recordings have been from shoreline areas where the salamander's eggs are laid. The resurgence in larval numbers that occurred in 1988 perhaps can be explained by an early snowmelt and a spring snow pack that was less acidic than average. This resulted in pond pH values of 6.0 or above during egg development.

From 1988 to 1991, Wissinger and Whiteman (1992) found no evidence that survival of either embryos or larvae was affected by pH. During that period pulses of snowmelt acidification were either benign or occurred earlier than egg deposition. The largest source of mortality at that time was pond drying. Their study occurred during a period of drought when there was not much snow. Much snow is needed to get an acid pulse (J. Harte, pers. comm.).

Corn and Vertucci (1992) reported no evidence of either chronic or episodic acidification as the cause of observed amphibian declines in the mountains of northern Colorado and Wyoming. However, two of the areas in which they worked were in Wyoming, east of the Continental Divide.

The western slope of the Rockies receives more acid precipitation (oxides of sulfur and nitrogen) than the eastern because of air flow from the southwest. Important contributors to acidity have been the Navajo and Four-Corners coal-fired electric generating plants and the Douglas, Arizona, copper smelter (Harte, pers. comm.). There probably have also been contributions from urban areas. The coal-fired plants have reduced emissions and the Douglas smelter closed in the late 1980s. Air quality has improved. In 1982, T. Colborn (pers. comm.) recorded low snowmelt pH in the lower Gunnison Mountains before these changes occurred. This was the beginning of the decline in the population of Tiger Salamanders studied by Harte and Hoffman (1989).

For a discussion of the many factors involved in acid tolerance and exposure, see Pierce (1985) and Dunson et al. (1992).

Fig. 20.13. Golden Toad (*Bufo periglenes*). (Photo courtesy of Martha Crump)

Central and South America

GOLDEN TOAD (*Bufo periglenes*) (Fig. 20.13)

Costa Rica Monteverde Cloud Forest Reserve

The following information is from Crump et al. (1992) and pers. comm. This toad is an explosive breeder in ephemeral rain and forest condensation pools. Since the early 1970s toads had been emerging every year. In 1987 over 1500 adults were seen but only a few tadpoles. From 1988 to 1990, frequent surveys were conducted for toads during the breeding period. In 1988 only one adult male was found at one site and seven adult males and two adult females at another; no eggs or tadpoles were found. In 1989, one adult male was found at the first site (above). There was an unconfirmed report of forty males and four females from a site at least 5 km away from the main area of study. From 1990 to 1993, no toads were found, thus 6 years transpired without any observed reproduction. David Wake (pers. comm.) reports no breeding in 1994.

  In 1987 many pools with eggs and larvae had dried out. Late formation of pools may have limited toad activity. Increase in ultraviolet light seemed an unlikely cause of the declines and pH measured did not seem low enough. However, rainfall was lower and water temperature higher than usual in 1987–90. In the late 1970s and early 1980s, the Harlequin Frog (*Atelopus varius*) and many species of *Eleutherodactylus* were present, and hylids, ranids, and centrolenids were common. By the late 1980s, most were infrequently encountered. Is the decline of the Golden Toad and the others a result of climatic factors (El Niño drought effects more frequent?) or some other cause (contaminants from burning of tropical rain forest, biocides, etc.)?

Pounds and Crump (1994) suggest that while desiccation or direct temperature effects may have been factors in the declines, moisture and temperature conditions may have interacted with some other, unidentified agent. They offer two hypotheses: (1) climatic factors may cause microparasites to reach epidemic proportions, or (2) atmospheric contaminants, scavenged by mist and cloud water in montane areas, may reach critical concentrations when conditions are abnormally warm and dry.

HIGHLAND FROGS OF ECUADOR AND VENEZUELA
(William Duellman, pers. comm.)

High Andes, Ecuador: Volcán Cotopaxi Area

In the early 1980s *Atelopus ignescens* (Ecuador, s Colombia) was very abundant. Some were seen in 1984 but few in 1988–89 by Duellman's student Luis Coloma. Algal growth has increased in streams, perhaps related to reduced foraging by *A. ignescens* tadpoles. The study site has no significant direct impact from humans.

Cordillera de Merída, Venezuela

The following information is from La Marca and Reinthaler (1991). Five *Atelopus* species historically were among the most prominent and ubiquitous frogs in their respective environments. In 1972, one hundred *A. carbonerensis* (Venezuela) could be collected in less than an hour. During thirty-four field trips in 1990, only three *Atelopus* individuals were found. Deforestation for cattle farming and crops, scouring of stream courses by rapid rainfall runoff, road kills, pollution from biocides, and other factors may be responsible for the declines.

STREAM FROGS OF THE ATLANTIC MOUNTAINS OF BRAZIL

Weygoldt (1989) made observations during a period of fifteen years. Of thirteen frog species present in the Reserva Atlântica (Santa Teresa area) until 1981, eight species were missing or reduced in numbers in 1987 and 1988. *Cycloramphus fuliginosus* (Brazil) has disappeared. The loud birdlike voices of the diurnal hylodine frogs are silent. The most likely causes for extinctions are believed to have been some extremely dry winters. However, similar extinctions from the states of Rio de Janeiro and São Paulo suggest that there might be an unknown common cause. Pollution including acid rain, starting in the heavily industrialized south and slowly spreading north, may be a possible cause. The acidity of stream water is elevated.

Australia

The following information is from Tyler (1991). Endemic tropical rain forest frogs, stream-dwelling species mainly at high altitude, are declining. These include the Mount Glorious Forest Frog (*Taudactylus diurnus*), last seen in 1979, and the two species of stomach brooders (see chapter 18). The demise of the stomach-brooding frog (*Rheobatrachus silus*), originally so abundant that a good observer might find one hundred per night, occurred in about 1980 (Tyler, 1991). The loss has so far not been explained; gold panning, logging, drought, and overcollecting appear not to be responsible.

Tyler (1991) listed twenty-two species of Australian frogs as exhibiting declines—seven of them as serious and two as perhaps extinct. Some other species in Australia, particularly the introduced Marine (Cane) Toad (*Bufo marinus*), however, are expanding their ranges. In fact, the Australian state and federal governments have committed several million dollars to finding a means of controlling the toad and halting its advance across northern Australia (Tyler, pers. comm.).

So ends our survey of selected examples of declines. Declines have been reported in many other parts of the world, including Europe, Africa, and Asia. Major declines in frogs have occurred in India, China, and Bangladesh. However, many species do not appear to be declining, and at some localities declines are occurring in some species and apparently not in others. Some species are expanding their ranges (e.g., the non-native Marine Toad in eastern Australia). Studies by C. Carey (pers. comm.) suggest that this amphibian has an immune system that is resistant to stress.

In concluding this section on case histories, some cautionary comments are in order. Given the effects of local weather conditions on activity, difference in field survey techniques of different observers, and the difficulties in identifying historic sites, it is clear that results from brief field surveys must be interpreted with caution. Many studies, however, have been long term and comprehensive, and at many sites individuals were once abundant and conspicuous and now *none* can be found. Furthermore, in the absence of long-term, precise information on population changes, it is impossible to say that a seemingly abundant species has not undergone a decline. Declines may be occurring in some areas where amphibian diversity is great and population densities are high, yet not readily detected because environments are favorable and opportunities for dispersal and recolonization are great. Decline rates may be slower in such areas. In marginal, fragmented habitats, chances of detecting declines are much more likely. There are some indications that declines are greater in populations living at high elevations than in those at lower elevation (see Wake, 1991). Some support was found for this in a study of the Pacific Treefrog in the California Sierra Nevada (see Drost and Fellers, 1993).

We are convinced that declines in the species on which we have reported are real and that many of the declines have been catastrophic. We are impressed by their apparent synchrony and feel there is, in many cases, some widespread cause that goes beyond drought effects and obvious local anthropogenic factors. The period between the mid-1970s and the early 1980s seems to have been a time of accelerated, and, in some cases, abrupt declines for a number of our western North American anurans—the Western Toad, Yosemite Toad, Wyoming Toad, Northern Leopard Frog (western Oregon), Cascades Frog (southern part of its range), Mountain Yellow-legged Frog, and Willamette Valley (Oregon) populations of the Northern Red-legged Frog. This time frame seems also to fit some of our neotropical examples and the Australian Mount Glorious Frog, last seen in 1979.

The seeming synchrony and pervasiveness of these declines suggest a contributing atmospheric effect. Airborne chemical contamination seems a likely culprit. This is discussed later in this chapter.

Amphibians as "Bio-indicators"

Are amphibian declines any greater, or faster, than those in other major animal groups? Human activity is driving great numbers of plant and animal species to extinction. Are amphibians any worse off than many of the others (see Wilson and Peter, 1988; McVey et al., 1992)? For example, the American Fisheries Society notes that 364 fish species in North America are now listed as endangered, threatened, or of special concern, and birds are in precipitous decline in many parts of the world as well (Youth, 1994a). There are some 9,600 species of birds of which approximately 6,600 (around 69%) are in decline. Among these the populations of an estimated 1000 species have dropped to the point where they are now threatened with extinction. An estimated 3000 species are stable or increasing (Youth, 1994b).

Hall and Henry (1992) have considered the problem of assessing the effects of pesticides on amphibians and reptiles. The great phylogenetic diversity in these groups makes them difficult to use in testing pesticides for registration purposes. Some anurans tested were remarkably resistant to some cholinesterase inhibitors, the class of pesticides in greatest use, apparently far more so than other vertebrates. Yet this may not apply to all amphibian species and all chemicals. Safety standards for other kinds of vertebrates thus cannot be assumed to apply to amphibians.

Harfenist et al. (1989), after compiling more than 250 references on the effects of toxicants on amphibians, have stated that "Amphibians are particularly sensitive to metals and acidification. They are considered to be useful indicator species for measuring the effects of local changes in environmental studies" (see also Vitt et al., 1990).

Characteristics of amphibians which, taken together, might make them more sensitive to environmental changes, including the effects of contaminants, than the other major groups of vertebrates are the following.

1. *The amphibious life cycle.* Most amphibians live both on land and in fresh waters. This complex life pattern requires that conditions be favorable for their survival in the water where they breed (where their eggs and larvae develop), in their "home" areas on land, and also along their migratory pathways.

2. *Absorptive surfaces.* All amphibians depend, in varying degrees, on skin respiration and dermal absorption of water when faced with water deficits on land. Their surfaces, permeable to gases and liquids, including those of their eggs and larvae, are potential avenues for entry of chemical contaminants and pathogens coming form air, water, and terrestrial substrates. When greatly dehydrated, large amounts of water are taken up rapidly (see chapter 12). Their gut is also permeable.

3. *Exposure to ultraviolet light.* Melanic pigment on the upper surfaces of the eggs and larvae of amphibians that develop in areas exposed to sunlight protects against ultraviolet light damage at sensitive developmental stages. In clear, shallow waters, especially at high elevations, such protection is particularly important. Postmetamorphic individuals living at high elevations and latitudes are often heliothermic (sun baskers), exposing themselves to direct sunlight to elevate their body temperatures. These characteristics may make many amphibians vulnerable to increased ultraviolet light levels as a result of thinning of the atmospheric ozone layer.

4. *Food habits.* Most tadpoles forage extensively on particles of plant and animal matter in the water, at the surface film, and in bottom muck. As their lungs develop, they rise to the surface to breathe. They also shred algae and other plant materials. Some persistent chlorinated chemicals "stick" to such particulate matter and accumulate at the water surface and in bottom sediments. Being fat soluble, they accumulate in fat deposits, and some residues may persist for the life of the animal. Amphibian larvae may be susceptible to the deleterious effects of such agents through ingestion and their permeable gills and skin. After transformation from the larval stage, all amphibians feed entirely, or almost entirely on animals, particularly invertebrates, and are thus especially subject to the biomagnification effects of persistent chemical contaminants in the food web (see p. 242).

5. *Susceptibility to cold and drought.* As moisture-dependent ectotherms, amphibians are vulnerable to extremes of cold and dryness. Cold weather and/ or drought can prevent reproduction, sometimes for a number of years. The

fact that some species live as adults for one or more decades may, in some cases, relate to such climatic factors. A long life increases opportunities for successful breeding in uncertain environments.

6. *Fragmented Distributions.* Dependent on moist, usually cool environments, amphibian species commonly show natural fragmentation of ranges, even when widely ranging. Species with fragmented distributions, especially those with restricted ranges, are particularly susceptible to population losses. In many areas (isolated canyon drainages, moist refugia in arid lands), recolonization of places lost to extinction may be *rare or impossible.* Low vagility, site fidelity, and physiological constraints limit the capacity of many amphibians to recolonize areas from which they have been expirtated (Blaustein et al., 1994).

7. *Sequestered Tissue Contaminants and the Amphibious Life.* Metamorphosis is a time of great vulnerability for amphibians, especially anurans, because of the profound reorganization of structure and physiology that occurs as the tadpole transforms into a frog. Feeding and locomotion are impaired (see chapter 17) and rapid anatomical, hormonal, and other physiological changes occur. Might there be a surge in the release of chemical contaminants (pesticides or other toxicants), particularly those sequestered in lipid sources, at this critical time in the life of the animal? Are salamanders better off than anurans because they undergo far less bodily reorganization at transformation?

Metamorphosis, driven by hormones, may make amphibians especially vulnerable to hormone mimics (see chapter 17), intruding chemicals that interfere with hormone signals.

During postmetamorphic growth, fat reserves are drawn upon during estivation and/or hibernation of young amphibians prior to reaching sexual maturity. In an experiment which measured metabolism of fat in burrowed Southern Spadefoot Toads (*Spea multiplicata*) (sw US, Mex) (from New Mexico), Whitford and Meltzer (1976) found that the animals used 40% of their fat reserve over a period of about 6 months (October to May 1972–73). During that time they also lost 16% of their initial body water. Assuming continued similar rates of water loss and fat depletion, it was estimated that some individuals could have survived another 6 months. Clearly such sequestered animals emerge from their retreats physiologically stressed, depleted in energy and water reserves. They thus might be particularly susceptible to the impact of internally released chemical contaminants.

8. *Breeding Cycle.* Amphibious species, particularly in the temperate zones and in some species also in the tropics (Golden Toad and others), as adults, undergo great swings in energy demands, from low levels during hibernation and/or estivation to extremely high ones during reproduction. Vocalization by male anurans draws heavily on energy reserves (see chapter 10) at a time when feeding activities are often reduced or may stop altogether. As in metamorpho-

sis, we theorize that as fatty tissues are metabolized, any fat-soluble chemical contaminants present could be released. Release can be expected to be rapid in some species as metabolism accelerates upon emergence from hibernation and reproductive activities get under way. Effects might be particularly damaging if the emerging animal's immune system has been stressed by low temperatures, desiccation, or other factors. Some species, in environments subject to drought and/or low temperatures (deserts, high mountain habitats), may forgo reproduction for one or more years.

Females draw upon their fat reserves in vitellogenesis (establishing the yolk supply of their eggs). With the breakdown of fat, contaminants are carried in the blood. Might some ultimately be off-loaded into the developing eggs during the yolking process, resulting in a contaminated fuel supply for developing embryos? Such off-loading has been observed in other animals (see p. 243). In this respect, females would be better off than males, which would not have such an off-loading mechanism. However, females of many species, when faced with serious energy deficits, may resorb their eggs, and at that time, along with draw-down of other fat sources, might experience a surge in release of toxicants.

Known and Possible Causes of Amphibian Declines

In surveying the evidence for amphibian declines, often direct local impacts seem largely, though often not entirely, responsible. There are also many losses with less obvious explanations—declines in seemingly pristine habitats. They suggest the existence of more widespread effects.

A Diversity of Local Impacts

Human-caused local effects are many: direct chemical assaults by the biocides or pesticides (insecticides, nematocides, herbicides, and fungicides), heavy metals (lead, mercury, cadmium, etc.), radioactivity, and the mostly unknown effects of the thousands of other chemicals released in the industrial age (see Carson, 1962; Tyler, 1989; Hayes and Laws, 1991; Amato, 1993); habitat losses to crop agriculture, overgrazing, silviculture, landfills, residential, commercial, and recreational developments; on- and off-road vehicle kills and habitat destruction; deforestation; wetlands drainage; water diversions; pollution effects and water demands of mining and treated and untreated sewage; introduction of competitors and predators, especially fish; gathering for food (see chapter 19), classroom and scientific use, the pet trade, and medicine (Asian apothecary use).

Many of these impacts now occur worldwide, and some are increasing exponentially, along with exponential human population growth and accompanying resource demands.

Global Impacts

There are also possible widespread atmospheric and climatic effects resulting from increasing pollution that may be affecting amphibians: thinning of the ozone layer, from the impact of chlorofluorocarbons, which allows an increase in the penetration of ultraviolet light; dispersal of biocides and other chemicals far from their sources (see p. 245); and acid precipitation and global warming resulting from increased atmospheric CO_2 and other gases, chiefly the result of deforestation and the burning of fossil fuels.

Blaustein et al. (1994a) have presented evidence that current levels of UV radiation in a temperate zone area (Oregon) can contribute to amphibian population declines and that some species are more susceptible to damage than others. They focused on species differences in the ability of amphibian eggs to repair UV radiation damage to DNA and differences in hatching success of embryos exposed to solar radiation at natural egg-laying sites. They compared ten amphibian species from the Cascade and Coastal Mountains of Oregon as to photolyase activity, a UV-damage-specific repair enzyme. They found that while levels were characteristic for a given species, activity varied more than eightyfold among species. The highest activity was shown by the Pacific Treefrog (*Pseudacris regilla*), whose populations are not known to be in decline. The Western Toad (*Bufo boreas*) and the Cascades Frog (*Rana cascadae*), whose populations have severely declined, displayed, respectively, one-sixth and one-third lower photolyase levels. In the field, hatching success of embryos of the Pacific Treefrog was significantly greater than in the Western Toad and Cascades Frog and was greater in embryos of the latter two species when they were shielded from UV radiation.

The Role of Biomagnification

Some of the aforementioned chemicals persist in the environment and are subject to "biomagnification" as their concentration increases through movement up a food web. Consider what can happen to persistent chlorinated molecules, such as PCBs, in an aquatic system (the U.S. Great Lakes, for example) (see Colborn, 1991). PCBs (polychlorinated biphenyls) derive from fire retardants used in electrical equipment, plastics, preservatives, varnishes, certain waxes, etc. They were also used as an insecticide dispersant. Molecules of PCBs attach to microscopic plants (algae) and suspended particles in the water that are engulfed in large numbers by small animals (zooplankton). Many of the molecules are retained in their fatty tissues. Other, larger animals eat the zooplankton, also in large amounts. The concentration of the chemical reaches still higher levels. In this way, such substances can increase by orders of magnitude as they move up through the food web. By the time a PCB molecule reaches a Lake Ontario Herring Gull (*Larus argentatus*) egg, it may have "biomagnified" 25 million times (Colborn, 1991). Lake fish that are at the top of the food web, Coho Salmon (*Oncorhynchus kisutch*) and others, also reach high levels of contamination, not only with PCBs but with other toxic chemicals that biomagnify: DDT and others. This explains why the Bald Eagle (*Haliaeetus leucocephalus*) has disappeared from much of the Great Lakes area—it feeds on fish and birds. Abandoned eagle eggs, collected in 1986 from the Lake Michigan area, held 30.2 parts per million (ppm) DDE (DDT's break-down product) and those from Lake Huron, 41.1 ppm. A loss of reproductive capability occurs at around 15 ppm DDE. The eggs of these birds have received their toxicants during the yolking process, lipophilic contaminants having been off-loaded from the female onto her developing eggs. Many other animals have also suffered population declines in the Great Lakes—fish, cormorants, terns, mink, and the snapping turtle (Colborn, 1991). Maternal transfer of contaminants to the eggs has also been reported in the Double-crested Cormorant (Tillitt et al., 1992) and in the Snapping Turtle (Bryan et al., 1987).

Many impacts may be acting synergistically or additively, perhaps each one, in itself, not damaging or life-threatening, but together causing a cascade of damage that finally overwhelms the immune system, resulting in an AIDS-like collapse. The target animal then succumbs to infections or stress. Redleg disease, caused by a ubiquitous bacterium found in fresh water, *Aeromonas hydrophila*, seen in stressed populations of frogs, may reflect such immune system deficiency (see Carey, 1993).

The Endocrine Connection

This section is based in part on the "Consensus Statement" from the work session on "Chemically Induced Alterations in Sexual Development: The Wildlife/Human Connection," reported in Colborn and Clement (1992), and in a follow-up session, in 1993, concerning "Environmentally Induced Alterations in Development: A Focus on Wildlife," held at the Wingspread Conference Center, in Racine, Wisconsin, on December 9–11, 1993.

A diverse array of man-made chemicals (synthetic xenobiotics)[1] interact

---

[1] Estrogenic xenobiotics may also be natural constituents of the environment such as estrogenic substances produced by certain plants, including fungi. However, information from animal experiments and human epidemiology suggests that many phytoestrogens have a protective effect and actually lower the risk of cancer (see Hileman, 1994).

with cell receptors including many that interact with receptors that respond to the hormone estrogen. They not only bond to receptors for which known ligands (binding chemicals) exist, but some also are known to bind with so-called orphan receptors whose endogenous ligands are unknown (McLachlan et al., 1992). An example is dioxin. Thus the potential for a great breadth in response to certain synthetic chemicals exists.

Many of these chemical compounds are known to intrude into developmental processes blocking intercellular communication, inducing the production of enzymes that break down hormones, and mimicking or interfering with the action of naturally occurring hormones (see Colborn, 1991). They thus participate in the vital dynamics of cell growth and differentiation.[2] The consequences of such disruption can be far-reaching because of the crucial role that hormones play in controlling development.

Although amphibians appear to have been little used in studies of endocrine effects of this nature, the evidence for damage in birds, mammals, reptiles, and fish is well documented, including effects on humans (see Colborn and Clement, 1992).

With regard to humans the therapeutic drug diethylstilbestrol (DES) is a case in point. It is a synthetic compound that like many of those mentioned earlier (biocides, etc.) is estrogenic. DES was used to prevent premature births until its insidious endocrine-disruptive effects were discovered, resulting in malformations at birth, infertility, and even cancers and other disorders in offspring late in life. Since 1940 sperm counts have fallen about 50%, semen volume has declined, the incidence of testicular cancer has more than tripled in some countries (Denmark, for example) and that of prostate cancer has doubled; the incidence of female breast cancer has risen in the United States and Western Europe. These effects may have a common cause and may be the consequence of fetal events tied in, in part at least, with the introduction into the environment of synthetic chemicals that mimic or interfere with the action of the natural hormone estrogen at critcal times during development (see Carlsen et al., 1992; Sharpe and Skakkeback, 1993; also see Hileman, 1994, and Raloff, 1994, for semipopular reports).

Impacts of endocrine intruders include thyroid dysfunction, decreased fertility, birth deformities, metabolic abnormalities, effects on degree of masculinization and feminization, and damage to the nervous and immune sys-

---

[2] Chemicals known to disrupt the endocrine system include DDT and its degradation products, DEHP (di(2-ethylhexyl)phthalate), dicofol, HCB (hexachlorobenzene), kelthane, kepone, lindane and other hexachlorocyclohexane congeners, methoxychlor, octachlorostyrene, synthetic pyrethroids, triazine herbicides, EBDC fungicides, certain PCB congeners, 2, 3, 7, 8-TCDD and other dioxins, 2, 3, 7, 8-TCDF and other furans, cadmium, lead, mercury, tributyltin and other organo-tin compounds, alkyl phenols (non-biodegradable detergents and anti-oxidants present in modified polystyrene and PVCs), styrene dimers and trimers, soy products, and laboratory animal and pet food products. (From "Work Session" Consensus Statement in Colborn and Clement, 1992.)

tems. Effects vary, depending on the species, the compound, and timing of impact on development, but are most likely to be manifest in offspring. Levels of tolerance and possible synergistic and additive effects are little understood.

Work session participants concluded that "unless the environmental load of synthetic hormone disrupters is abated and controlled, large-scale dysfunction at the population level is possible." Despite the mounting evidence of threats to wildlife and people (see Colborn and Clement, 1992), application of pesticides and the use of industrial chemicals capable of disrupting endocrine and immune systems continue on a large scale. Over 2.5 billion pounds of pesticide-active ingredients were applied in the United States in 1991 (Colborn, pers. comm.). Use of DDT, one of the most important culprits, is only restricted (not outlawed) in the United States, and DDT is exported to other parts of the world, including the biologically rich tropics.

Assessment of potential exposure and risk to biocides is limited due to the inaccessibility of production data resulting from the desire to keep "confidential business information" secure for marketing purposes (Bason and Colborn, 1992). See Hall and Henry (1992) for information on assessing the effects of pesticides on amphibians and reptiles.

Many of these chemicals, at varying concentrations, now exist essentially worldwide, move great distances by air and water currents, migrating and dispersing animals, and commerce. It is estimated that a large part of the DDT entering the Great Lakes today comes from Central America and Mexico by atmospheric transport (Rapaport, 1985). Many of these chemicals are not only within the food web, but also occur as residues in food and water (including ground water). Some herbicides are highly volatile and have been detected in large amounts in the atmosphere. They may occur in rainwater and fog (Clement and Colborn, 1992). Perhaps no place in the biosphere is now completely free from exposure. There are no longer any truly "pristine" areas (see Bason and Colborn, 1992; Barrie et al., 1992).

Some xenobiotics have the potential for causing damage at extremely low levels in the environment.[3] Thus, what has traditionally been regarded as a low level of a contaminant at any particular place gives no assurance that biological risks do not exist: (1) Although a xenobiotic may be one hundred to one thousand times weaker than a naturally occurring free hormone, it may intrude at a very high concentration relative to that of the natural hormone and outcompete the latter for receptor sites. Sensitivity may be especially high at a

---

[3] Olson et al. (1987) report that aldicarb (a carbonate insecticide and nematode poison), used worldwide on a variety of crops including citrus, potatoes, cotton, peanuts, beans, soybeans, and others, is capable of altering immune parameters in mice. Aldicarb presently occurs in ground water in many parts of the U.S., and thus it occurs in drinking water in some areas. The chemical was found to cause some immune suppression in mice at concentrations as low as one part per billion (1 ppb) in their drinking water.

critical period of development. Estrogenic and other endocrine "activity" is usually currently defined in terms of assay results using adult organisms. Activity in developing organisms, including embryonic and larval amphibians, may be much greater. There is evidence for this from studies of mammals (Bern, 1992). (2) Biomagnification can raise the concentration of persistent contaminants in the environment to very high levels (see p. 242). (3) Little is known about possible synergistic effects of contaminants, which may cause an innocuous chemical to become dangerous when it interacts with another chemical compound. (4) There is also evidence that endocrinally active contaminants at concentrations that are individually too low to cause developmental or functional effects can together (additively or cumulatively) trigger cell growth.

There is far more of concern here than threshold levels that cause acute toxicity, outright mortality, abrupt mutagencity, or cancers in postnatal experimental animals. Developmental effects and transgeneration exposure via the mother, must also be considered (see Clement and Colborn, 1992). In addition, the lag time (in some slowly reproducing species measured in decades, as in humans) necessary for widespread population debility to be expressed must be taken into account. Just because a population appears healthy—represented by breeding adults and *seemingly* viable offspring—there is no cause for complacency because delayed effects can be expected. In particular, it is important to focus on the health of offspring throughout their life history. Populations of short-lived species whose adults breed for only one or two seasons are particularly susceptible to extinction because they can be eliminated by only a few years of reproductive failure.

The possibility that the "endocrine connection" may be involved in the declining amphibians syndrome needs investigation. Reduced fertility and compromised immune systems are among the notable effects. By misdirecting embryonic development, endocrine disrupters can set the stage not only for reduced survival of offspring, but also for reduced survival and reproductive success of adults. Many pesticides and industrial chemicals affect the developing immune system. For example, the thymus, an organ involved in immune response, may not develop or it atrophies in vertebrates that have been studied. Amphibians have a thymus gland. Whether this happens to them as well must be investigated.

The widespread environmental contamination by chemicals of the industrial age, in particular the vast numbers of biocides, now airborne, perhaps comes closest to being a "single cause" behind widespread amphibian declines. Widespread chemical pollution will not be the only cause in most cases, but it appears to be the most pervasive one and may be a contributing factor in many declines. It may explain some of the declines in so-called pristine areas, where no obvious local impacts can be identified. It may also contribute to the disabilities that make the animals vulnerable to a variety of other kinds of damage.

If developmental disrupters and other health-damaging synthetic xenobiotics are, indeed, behind not only many amphibian declines but also those found in many other animals, until they are removed they will compromise our best efforts to rehabilitate declining populations.

Amphibians as Subjects for Study of the Effects of Chemical Contaminants at the Hormonal and Developmental Levels

In studies of toxicity of biocides and other synthetic chemicals at the endocrine and developmental levels, many amphibians have characteristics that make them excellent subjects. Embryonic development can be directly observed through their transparent egg capsules, so stages at which morphological disturbances occur can be readily identified. The energetic demands and the cascade of anatomical and physiological changes that occur at metamorphosis are likely to highlight developmental problems. Their fecundity (some species lay hundreds to thousands of eggs) would aid statistical analyses. The rapidity of development from fertilized egg to metamorphosis of some species (around two weeks in Spadefoot toads, *Scaphiopus*) offers quick results. Spadefoot toads, African Clawed Frogs (*Xenopus*), and others are opportunistic breeders, thus eggs for study can be obtained over a prolonged period and fertilized artificially as necessary. As a result of the popularity of amphibians in developmental and biomedical research, much is already known about their developmental biology and the laboratory techniques for experimentation, rearing, and care.

The American Society for Testing and Materials (ASTM) (1916 Race Street, Philadelphia, PA 19103) has a guide for obtaining laboratory data concerning the developmental toxicity of test materials on an anuran. Request the Standard guide for Conducting the Frog Embryo Teratogenesis Assay-Xenopus (Fetax), 1991.

Some Topics Needing Study in Relation to the Possible Role of Synthetic Chemicals in Amphibian Declines

1. What are environmental levels and the locations of chemical contaminants (particularly estrogen mimics) in the physical environment and in food webs? How do they relate to species biology? (See note 2 for substances of special concern).

2. What are levels of contaminants in the fat bodies, carcass fat, and liver in species in the field?

3. Are there surges in release of contaminants at metamorphosis, emergence from hibernation and/or estivation, and with resorption of eggs?

4. Are there sex differences in physiological responses to contaminants? To what extent do females off-load them to their developing ova? Are males more vulnerable because of longer periods in the water at breeding sites and the high-level energy demands of their vocalization, territorial and mating behavior, combined with feeding deprivation during the mating period?

5. To what extent are immune responses compromised by periods of dormancy, low temperatures, drought, or other kinds of stress? How might this relate to physiological responses to contaminants?

6. To what extent can DDT, PCBs, etc., be absorbed through amphibian skin and egg capsules?[4]

7. At what stages in development (fertilized egg to transformation) are contaminants most likely to cause problems, and what form do they take?

8. In what ways do contaminants affect adults, in particular their sexual development, including secondary sexual characteristics, egg and sperm formation, and viability?

9. What is the age and sex structure of populations in relation to exposure to chemical contamination?

10. Are there species differences in physiological responses to contaminants.

Lipophylic contaminants may be widespread in the tissues of animals throughout a food web, yet may be absent or at very low levels in the environment. At Lake Apopka in Florida, male American Alligators (*Alligator mississippiensis*) have undergone marked reproductive impairment apparently caused by the feminizing effect of DDT contamination of their aquatic habitat. The pesticide and its metabolities modify the endocrine environment of the developing embryo so as to produce a hormonal milieu that is predominately estrogenic. The lake waters are now largely free of the pesticide but it persists in the lake's biota and can be expected to do so for many years (see Guillette et al., 1994).

Possible Impacts of Amphibian Declines

In many terrestrial ecosystems amphibians constitute a large part of the vertebrate biomass (see chapter 1). In some, they constitute the largest part. They are thus an important constituent in ecosystems. One effect of their decline would be a shift in patterns of predation. In their absence, populations of certain insects and other invertebrates would likely be greatly expanded. An in-

---

[4] Since environmental estrogen mimics such as PCBs can be absorbed through reptilian eggshells and influence sex determination in species with temperature-sensitive sex determination (Crews et al., 1994), it seems probable that they can penetrate amphibian eggs. In amphibian sex-reversal experiments, sex hormones (testosterone propionate and estradiol benzoate) may be administered by releasing the hormone to be tested into aquaria water, where it is absorbed by developing larvae. Might estrogenic xenobiotics also be readily absorbed?

crease in mosquitoes and other insects in the Orient has been linked to heavy cropping of frogs for food. With loss of predators (at or near the top of food chains), explosive increases in opportunistic species may follow—symptomatic of stressed ecosystems (Regier and Baskerville, 1986).

Predators (such as some invertebrates and birds, mammals, and reptiles) that feed extensively on amphibians would be affected. For example, amphibians are a primary food for the Western Terrestrial Garter Snake (*Thamnophis elegans*) in the California Sierra Nevada. Two of its important food species are now undergoing major declines—the Mountain Yellow-legged Frog (*Rana muscosa*) and the Yosemite Toad (*Bufo canorus*). Fortunately, the Pacific Treefrog (*Pseudacris regilla*) is still present in good numbers. Should this species collapse, however, the snake might be in serious trouble (see Jennings et al., 1992). Decline in the Garter Snake, in turn, might affect raptorial birds and other predators that feed on the snake.

In many freshwater habitats, the foraging of herbivorous tadpoles inhibits growth of algae and other plants. In some small ponds they are probably the most important animal regulators of such growth. In their absence, algal overgrowth could lead to eutrophication and, through decomposition, depletion of aquatic oxygen supplies. This could lead to unpredictable changes in the biota of such ecosystems. They also forage extensively on detritus, organic fragments that accumulate on the bottoms of streams and ponds. They are an important source of nutrient flow (through their transformation and death) from freshwater habitats to land (see chapter 17), interruption of which would have unknown but probably significant ecological repercussions.

What of the Future?

There is growing concern over the rapid, worldwide decline in biodiversity. Amphibians are a part of this trend. As with humanity's many other gambles (atmospheric tampering and nuclear energy with its nagging problems of waste disposal), the biocide game is high risk. Considering the large quantities of chemicals in use, the many possible exposure pathways and events, the remarkable lack of knowledge as to their biological effects, and the global atmospheric and aquatic distribution of many of them (including ones restricted in some countries but exported), it is clear that widespread exposure exists and will likely continue, unless regulatory agencies develop new approaches to eliminate release of substances of this nature into the environment (Bason and Colborn, 1992).

The burden of proof as to the harmlessness of a substance must now rest with those who propose release of a new chemical compound—not with society—and there must be an open-book policy with respect to its constituents and application (Colborn and Clement, 1992).

The problem of chemical contamination of the environment must be addressed through an interdisciplinary approach. There must be information exchange and collaboration among naturalists, wildlife biologists, toxicologists, and laboratory animal and human health investigators to determine the scope and intensity of the threat to humans. Such studies should receive high priority in funding from both governmental and private sources, and the problem of environmental toxicants should receive important media and educational attention.

But there is a still larger issue—the rapid growth and demands of the human population. There can be no lasting solution to the "declining amphibians" problem and most other environmental and, indeed, social issues facing humanity until this problem is solved. From our perspective, the primary goal of conservation and humanitarian efforts should be to achieve pupulation stabilization and, ultimately, a humane reduction in human numbers. But this action must be combined with a deep concern for the well-being of others and for the living fabric of this planet upon which our lives depend. Rampant selfishness, often driven by the power of wealth and influence, will bring ruin to all. There must be a shift from the currently widespread self-centered, human-centered worldview to a less egocentric, more nature-centered one. Changing this mindset is, in our opinion, education's greatest challenge.

If we fail to achieve these goals, we shall likely lose most of the irreplaceable living beings with which we share this planet, and we will condemn humanity to the horrors of nature's population-regulating processes—famine, increasing strife, and disease. This inexorable process is already under way and will, in the absence of population decline and changing attitudes toward nature, we believe, defy all our scientific and technological efforts to change nature's course. The aim should be to achieve a steady state of population and resource use, at a level that is sustainable over the long haul and *capable of withstanding climatic variation*. To do so, human population and resource demands will need to be at a far lower level than now exists. The measure of economic health should not be the "growth" of the GNP but rather a GNP "steady state." In the meantime, concerned people must continue to fight the many local battles to save what is possible of our natural heritage for the day when human pressures are lessened and the natural process of restoration can be accelerated.

The time is long overdue for rapid local and global action on the population/resource issue. Recent expressions of the scientific community and some religious leaders make clear that there can be no solution to humanity's manifold problems of environmental and human degradation unless human population growth is controlled (see Meadows et al., 1992, and pronouncements by the U.S. National Academy of Sciences, the British Royal Society, the Union of Concerned Scientists, and the statement of religious leaders at the Summit on

Environment; Beck, 1992–93). Will humanity, at last, be able to set aside self-interests and ingrained ways of thinking to face its greatest common peril? The alternative to not doing so is disastrous.

If we continue to devote our chief energies to . . . further extending our commerce and our wealth, the evils which necessarily accompany these, when too eagerly pursued, may increase to such gigantic dimensions as to be beyond our power to alleviate.

Alfred Russel Wallace
[In *The Malay Archipelago*, 1869, 1st ed.]

Literature Cited

Adler, K., 1969. Extraoptic phase shifting of circadian locomotor rhythm in salamanders. *Science*, 164: 1290–1292.

Adler, K., 1970. The role of extraoptic photoreceptors in amphibian rhythms and orientation: A review. *Jour. Herp.*, 4: 99–112.

Adler, K., 1971. Pineal end organ: Role in extraoptic entrainment of circadian locomotor rhythm in frogs. In M. Menaken, ed., *Biochronometry*. Proc. of a symposium at Friday Harbor, September 1969. Publ. U.S. Natl. Acad. Sci., Washington, D.C.

Adler, K., 1976. Extraocular photoreception in amphibians. *Photochem. and Photobiol.*, 23: 275–298.

Adler, K., and D. H. Taylor, 1973. Extraocular perception of polarized light by orienting salamanders. *J. Comp. Physiol.*, 87: 203–212.

Alberch, P., 1980. Ontogenesis and morphological diversification. *Amer. Zool.*, 20: 653–667.

Alberch, P., S. J. Gould, G. F. Oster, and D. B. Wake, 1979. Size and shape in ontogeny and phylogeny. *Paleobiology*, 5: 296–317.

Albuquerque, E. X., J. W. Daly, and B. Witkop, 1971. Batrachotoxin: Chemistry and pharmacology. *Science*, 172: 995–1002.

Alexander, T. R., 1964. Observations on the feeding behavior of *Bufo marinus* (Linne). *Herpetologica*, 20: 255–259.

Alford, R. A., and M. L. Crump, 1982. Habitat partitioning among size classes of larval southern leopard frogs, *Rana utricularia*. *Copeia*, 1982: 367–373.

Allan, D. M., 1973. Some relationships of vocalization to behavior in the Pacific treefrog, *Hyla regilla*. *Herpetologica*, 29: 336–371.

Altig, R., and M. T. Christensen, 1981. Behavioral characteristics of the tadpoles of *Rana hecksheri*. *Jour. Herp.*, 15: 151–154.

Altig, R., and G. F. Johnston, 1989. Guilds of anuran larvae: Relationships among developmental modes, morphologies, and habits. *Herp. Monogr.*, 3: 81–109.

Amato, I., 1993. The crusade against chlorine. *Science*, 261: 152–154.

Anderson, J. D., 1971. The egg-alga relationship in *Ambystoma t. tigrinum. Herp. Rev.*, 3: 76.

Anderson, J. D., 1972. Embryonic temperature tolerance and rate of development in some slamanders of the genus *Ambystoma*. *Herpetologica*, 28: 126–130.

Anderson, P. K., 1960. Ecology and evolution in island populations of salamanders in the San Francisco Bay region. *Ecol. Monogr.*, 30: 359–385.

Arnold, S. J., 1976. Sexual behavior, sexual interference and sexual defense in the salamanders *Ambystoma maculatum*, *Ambystoma tigrinum* and *Plethodon jordani*. *Z. Tierpsychol.*, 42: 247–300.

Arnold, S. J., 1977. The evolution of courtship behavior in new world salamanders with some comments on old world salamandrids. In D. H. Taylor and S. I. Guttman, eds., *The Reproductive Biology of Amphibians*. Plenum Press, New York.

Arnold, S. J., 1982. A quantitative approach to antipredator performance: Salamander defense against snake attack. *Copeia*, 1982: 247–253.

Aronson, L. R., 1943. The "release" mechanism and sex recognition in *Hyla andersonii*. *Copeia*, 1943: 246–249.

Asquith, A., and R. Altig, 1990. Male call frequency as a criterion for female choice in *Hyla cinerea*. *Jour. Herp.*, 24: 198–201.

Auburn, J. S., and D. H. Adler, 1976. Orientation by means of polarized light in bullfrog tadpoles, *Rana catesbeiana*. *Herp. Rev.*, 7: 74.

Bachmann, K., 1969. Temperature adaptation of amphibian embryos. *Amer. Nat.*, 103: 115–130.

Bachmann, M. D., R. G. Carlton, J. M. Burkholder, and R. G. Wetzel, 1986. Symbiosis between salamander eggs and green algae: Microelectrode measurements inside eggs demonstrate effect of photosynthesis on oxygen concentration. *Can. J. Zool.*, 64: 1586–1588.

Backwell, P.R.Y., 1988. Functional partitioning in the two-part call of the leaf-folding frog, *Afrixalus brachycnemis*. *Herpetologica*, 44: 1–7.

Backwell, P.R.Y., and N. I. Passmore, 1990. Suitable approach perches affect female phonotaxis in an arboreal frog. *Herpetologica*, 46: 11–14.

Backwell, P.R.Y., and N. I. Passmore, 1990a. Polyandry in the leaf-folding frog, *Afrixalis delicatus*. *Herpetologica*, 46: 7–10.

Backwell, P.R.Y., and N. I. Passmore, 1991. Satellite behavior in the leaf-folding frog, *Afrixalis delicatus*. *Jour. Herp.*, 25: 497–498.

Bagnara, J. T., 1976. Color change. In B. Lofts, ed., *Physiology of the Amphibia*, vol. 3. Academic Press, New York and London.

Bagnara, J. T., and M. E. Hadley, 1969. The control of bright colored pigment cells of amphibians and fishes. *Amer. Zool.*, 9: 465–478.

Bagnara, J. T., and M. E. Hadley, 1970. Endocrinology of the amphibian pineal. *Amer. Zool.*, 10: 201–216.

Bagnara, J. T., J. D. Taylor, and M. E. Hadley, 1968. The dermal chromatophore unit. *J. Cell Biol.*, 38: 67–79.

Ball, R. W., and D. L. Jameson, 1966. Premating isolating mechanisms in sympatric and allopatric *Hyla regilla* and *Hyla californiae*. *Evolution*, 20: 533–551.

Ballinger, R. E., and C. O. McKinney, 1966. Developmental temperature tolerance of certain anuran species. *J. Exper. Zool.*, 161: 21–28.

Barbour, J. W., R. W. Hardin, J. P. Schafer, and M. J. Harvey, 1969. Home range, movements and activity of the dusky salamander, *Desmognathus fuscus*. *Copeia*, 1969: 293–297.

Barrie, L. A., D. Gregor, B. Hargrave, R. Lake, D. Muir, R. Shearer, B. Tracey, and T. Bidleman, 1992. Arctic contaminants: Sources, occurrence and pathways. *Society of the Total Environment* (Elsevier Publishers) 122: 1–74.

Barrio, A., 1969. Observaciones sobre *Chthonerpeton indestinctum* (Gymnophiona, caecilidae) y su reproduccion. *Physis*, 28: 499–503.

Barthalmus, G. T., and E. D. Bellis, 1969. Homing in the northern dusky salamander, *Desmognathus fuscus fuscus*. *Copeia*, 1969: 148–153.

Barthalmus, G. T., and E.D. Bellis, 1972. Home range, homing and the homing mechanism of the salamander, *Desmognatus fuscus*. *Copeia*, 1972: 632–642.

Barthalmus, G. T., and E. R. Savidge, 1974. Time: An index of distance as a barrier to salamander homing. *Jour. Herp.*, 8: 251–254.

Barthalmus, G. T., and W. J. Zielinski, 1988. Xenopus skin mucus induces oral dyskinesias that promote escape from snakes. *Pharmacol. Biochem. Behav.*, 30: 957–959.

Bason, C. W., and T. Colborn, 1992. US application and distribution of pesticides and industrial chemicals capable of disrupting endocrine and immune systems. In T. Colborn and C. Clement, eds., *Chemically-Induced Alterations in Sexual and Functional Development: The Wildlife/Human Connection.* Princeton Scientific Publishing Co., Princeton, N.J.

Baxter, G. T., M. R. Stromberg, and C. K. Dodd, Jr., 1982. The status of the Wyoming toad (*Bufo hemiophrys baxteri*). *Environ. Conserv.*, 9: 348 and 388.

Beachy, C. K., and R. C. Bruce, 1992. Lunglessness in plethodontid salamanders is consistent with the hypothesis of a mountain stream origin: A response to Ruben and Boucot. *Amer. Nat.*, 139: 839–847.

Beck, A., and J. P. Ewert, 1979. Prey selection by toads (*Bufo bufo* L.) in response to configurational stimuli moved in the visual field z,y-coordinates. *J. Comp. Physiol. (A)*, 129: 207–209.

Beck, R., 1992–93. Religions and the environment: Commitment high until U.S. population issues raised. *Social Contract*, 3: 76–79.

Beiswenger, R. E., 1978. Responses of *Bufo* tadpoles (Amphibia, Anura, Bufonidae) to laboratory gradients of temperature. *Jour. Herp.*, 12: 449–504.

Beiswenger, R. E., 1981. Predation by gray jays on aggregating tadpoles of the boreal toad (*Bufo boreas*). *Copeia*, 1981: 459–460.

Bellis, E. D., 1965. Home range and movements of the wood frog in a northern bog. *Ecology*, 46: 90–98.

Beltz, E., 1988. HerPET-POURRI. *Bull. Chi. Herp. Soc.*, 23: 167.

Beltz, E., 1989. HerPET-POURRI. *Bull. Chi. Herp. Soc.*, 24: 57.

Belvedere, P., C. Giacoma, G. Malacarne, and G. E. Andreoletti, 1988. Comparative ehtological and biochemical aspects of courtship pheromones in European newts. *Monit. Zool. Ital.*, 22: 397–404.

Bemis, W. E., K. Schwenk, and M. H. Wake, 1983. Morphology and function of the feeding apparatus of *Dermophis mexicanus* (Amphibia: Gymnophiona). *Zool. J. Linnean Soc.*, 77: 75–96.

Beneski, J. T., Jr., 1989. Adaptive significance of tail autotomy in the salamander, *Ensatina. Jour. Herp.*, 23: 322–324.

Benson, D. G., Jr., 1968. Reproduction in urodeles, II. Observations on the spermatheca. *Experientia*, 24: 853–854.

Bentley, P. J., 1974. Actions of neurohypophysial peptides in amphibians, reptiles, and birds. In E. Knobil and W. H. Sawyer, eds., *Handbook of Physiology*, Section 7: *Endocrinology*, vol. 4, Amer. Physiol. Soc., Washington, D.C.

Bentley, P. J., and A. R. Main, 1972. Effect of vasotocin on cutaneous water uptake by an Australian frog, *Crinia georgiana. Copeia*, 1972: 885–886.

Bern, H. A., 1992. The fragile fetus. In T. Colborn and C. Clement, eds., *Chemically-induced Alterations in Sexual and Functional Development.* Princeton Scientific Publishing Co., Princeton, N.J.

Berven, K. A., 1988. Factors affecting variation in reproductive traits within a population of wood frogs (*Rana sylvatica*). *Copeia*, 1988: 605–615.

Berven, K. A., and D. E. Gill, 1983. Interpreting geographic variation in life-history traits. *Amer. Zool.*, 23: 85–97.

Bevins, C. L., and M. Zasloff, 1990. Peptides from frog skin. *Ann. Rev. Biochem.*, 59: 395–400.

Billo, R., and M. Wake, 1987. Tentacle development in *Dermophis mexicanus* (Amphibia, Gymnophiona with an hypothesis of tentacle origin). *Jour. Morph.*, 192: 101–111.

Birukow, G. and M. Meng, 1955. Eine neue Methode zur Prüfung des Gesichtssinnes bei Amphibien. *Naturwissenschaften*, 42: 652–653.

Black, J. H., 1970. A possible stimulus for the formation of some aggregations in tadpoles of *Scaphiopus bombifrons*. *Proc. Okla. Acad. Sci.*, 49: 13–14.

Blair, W. F., 1955. Mating call and stage of speciation in the *Microhyla olivacea–M. carolinensis* complex. *Evolution*, 9: 469–480.

Blair, W. F., 1974. Character displacement in frogs. *Amer. Zool.*, 14: 1119–1125.

Blanchard, C., H. Michaels, A. Bradman, and J. Harte, 1987. Episodic acidification of a low-alkalinity pond in Colorado. ERG Publ. 88–1, 15 pp. Energy and Resources Group, University of California, Berkeley.

Blaustein, A. R., 1994. Chicken Little or Nero's fiddle? A perspective on declining amphibian populations. *Herpetologica*, 50: 85–97.

Blaustein, A. R., P. D. Hoffman, D. G. Hokit, J. M. Kiesecker, S. C. Walls, and J. B. Hays, 1994a. UV repair and resistance to solar UV-B in amphibian eggs: A link to population declines? *Proc. Natl. Acad. Sci.*, 91: 1791–1795.

Blaustein, A. R., D. G. Hokit, R. K. O'Hara, and R. A. Holt, 1994b. Pathogenic fungus contributes to amphibian losses in the Pacific northwest. *Biol. Conserv.*, 67: 251–254.

Blaustein, A. R., and R. K. O'Hara, 1986. An investigation of kin recognition in the red-legged frog (*Rana aurora*) tadpoles. *J. Zool., London (A)*, 209: 347–353.

Blaustein, A. R., and R. K. O'Hara, 1987. Aggregation behavior in *Rana cascadae* tadpoles: Association preferences among wild aggregations and responses to non-kin. *Anim. Behav.*, 35: 1549–1555.

Blaustein, A. R., and D. B. Wake, 1990. Declining amphibian populations. A global phenomenon? *Trends Ecol. Evol.*, 5: 203–204.

Blaustein, A. R., D. B. Wake, and W. P. Sousa, 1994. Amphibian declines: Judging stability, persistence and susceptibility of populations to local and global extinction. *Conserv. Biol.*, 8: 60–71.

Boice, R., and R. C. Williams, 1971. Competitive feeding behavior of *Rana pipiens* and *Rana clamitans*. *Anim. Behav.*, 19: 548–551.

Boice, R., and D. W. Witter, 1969. Hierarchical feeding behavior in the leopard frog (*Rana pipiens*). *Anim. Behav.*, 17: 474–479.

Boisseau, C., and J. Joly, 1975. Transport and survival of spermatozoa in female Amphibia, in *The Biology of Spermatozoa*, 94–104. Inserm. Int. Symp., Nouzilly, 1973, Karger, Basel.

Borchers, H. W., H. Burghagen, and J. P. Ewert, 1978. Key stimuli of prey for toads (*Bufo bufo* L.): Configuration and movement patterns. *J. Comp. Physiol. (A)*, 128: 189–192.

Boutilier, R. G., D. F. Stiffler, and D. P. Toews, 1992. Exchange of respiratory gases, ions, and water in amphibious and aquatic amphibians. In M. E. Feder and W. W. Burggren, eds., *Environmental Physiology of Amphibians*. University of Chicago Press, Chicago and London.

Bradford, D. F., 1984. Temperature modulation in a high elevation amphibian, *Rana muscosa. Copeia*, 1984: 966–976.

Bradford, D. F., 1989. Allotopic distribution of native frogs and introduced fishes in high Sierra Nevada lakes of California: Implication of the negative effect of fish introductions. *Copeia*, 1989: 775–778.

Bradford, D. F., S. D. Cooper, A. D. Brown, T. M. Jenkins, K. Kratz, and O. Sarnelle, 1994a. Distribution of aquatic animals relative to naturally acidic waters in the Sierra Nevada. Final report to California Air Resources Board, Sacramento.

Bradford, D. F., and M. S. Gordon, 1992. Aquatic amphibians in the Sierra Nevada: Current status and potential effects of acidic deposition on populations. California Air Resources Board, Sacramento.

Bradford, D. F., M. S. Gordon, D. F. Johnson, R. D. Andrews, and W. B. Jennings, 1994b. Acidic deposition as an unlikely cause for amphibian population declines in the Sierra Nevada, California. *Biol. Conserv.*, 69: 155–161.

Bradford, D. F., D. M. Graber, and F. Tabatabai, 1994c. Population declines of the native frog, *Rana muscosa*, in Sequoia and Kings Canyon National Parks, California. *Southwestern Naturalist*, 39: 323-327.

Bradford, D. F., C. Swanson, and M. S. Gordon, 1992. Effects of low pH and aluminum on two declining species of amphibians in the Sierra Nevada, California. *Jour. Herp.*, 26: 369–377.

Bradley, D., 1993. Frog venom cocktail yields a one-handed painkiller. *Science*, 261: 1117.

Bradley, S. G., and L. J. Klika, 1981. A fatal poisoning from the Oregon rough-skinned newt (*Taricha granulosa*). *J. Amer. Med. Assoc.*, 246: 247.

Brandon, R. A., G. M. Labanick, and J. E. Huheey, 1979. Relative palatability, defensive behavior, and mimetic relationships of red salamanders (*Pseudotriton ruber*), mud salamanders (*Pseudotriton montanus*), and red efts (*Notophthalmus viridescens*). *Herpetologica*, 35: 289–303.

Brattstrom, B. H., 1963. A preliminary review of the thermal requirements of amphibians. *Ecology*, 44: 238–255.

Brattstrom, B. H., 1968. Thermal acclimation in anuran amphibians as a function of latitude and altitude. *Comp. Biochem. Physiol.*, 24: 93–111.

Brattstrom, B. H., 1970. Amphibia. In G. C. Whittow, ed., *Comparative Physiology of thermoregulation*, vol. I. Academic Press, New York.

Brattstrom, B. H., 1979. Amphibian temperature regulation studies in the field and laboratory. *Amer. Zool.*, 19: 345–356.

Brattstrom, B. H., and P. Lawrence, 1962. The rate of thermal acclimation in anuran amphibians. *Physiol. Zool.*, 35: 148–156.

Brattstrom, B. H., and P. Regal, 1965. Rate of thermal acclimation in the Mexican salamander *Chiropterotriton. Copeia*, 1965: 514–515.

Brattstrom, B. H., and R. M. Yarnell, 1968. Aggressive behavior in two species of leptodactylid frogs. *Herpetologica*, 24: 222–228.

Breckenridge, W. R., and S. Jayasinghe, 1979. Observations on the eggs and larvae of *Ichthyophis glutinosus. Ceylon J. Sci. (Bio. Sci.)*, 13: 187–202.

Breckenridge, W. R., N. Shirani, and L. Pereira, 1987. Some aspects of the biology and development of *Ichthyophis glutinosus* (Amphibia: Gymnophiona). *J. Zool., London*, 211: 437–449.

Breden, F., A. Lum, and R. Wassersug, 1982. Body size and orientation in aggregates of toad tadpoles *Bufo woodhousei*. *Copeia*, 1982: 672–680.

Brekke, D. R., S. D. Hillyard, and R. M. Winokur, 1991. Behavior associated with water absorption response by the toad, *Bufo punctatus*. *Copeia*, 1991: 393–401.

Brenowitz, E. A., W. Wilczynski, and H. H. Zakon, 1984. Acoustic communication in spring peepers. *J. Comp. Physiol. (A)*, 155: 585–592.

Brizzi, R., G. Delfino, and C. Calloni., 1989. Female cloacal anatomy in the spectacled salamander, *Salamandrina terdigitata* (Amphibia: Salamandridae). *Herpetologica*, 45: 310–322.

Brockelman, W. Y., 1969. An analysis of density effects and predation in *Bufo americanus* tadpoles. *Ecology*, 50: 632–644.

Brodie, E. D., Jr., 1968a. Investigation on the skin toxin of the red-spotted newt, *Notophthalmus viridescens viridescens*. *Amer. Midland Natur.*, 80: 276–280.

Brodie, E. D., Jr., 1968b. Investigations on the skin toxin of the adult rough-skinned newt, *Taricha granulosa*. *Copeia*, 1968: 307–313.

Brodie, E. D., Jr., 1976. Additional observations on the Batesian mimicry of *Notophthalmus viridescens* efts by *Pseudotriton ruber*. *Herpetologica*, 32: 68–70.

Brodie, E. D., Jr., 1977. Salamander antipredator postures. *Copeia*, 1977: 523–535.

Brodie, E. D., Jr., 1978. Biting and vocalization as antipredator mechanisms in terrestrial salamanders. *Copeia*, 1978: 127–129.

Brodie, E. D., Jr., 1983. Antipredator adaptations of salamanders: Evolution and convergence among terrestrial species. In N. S. Margaris and R. J. Reiter, eds., *Adaptations to Terrestrial Environment*. Plenum Press, New York.

Brodie, E. D., Jr., 1987. Antipredator mechanism of larval anurans: Protection of palatable individuals. *Herpetologica*, 43: 369–373.

Brodie, E. D., Jr., and E. D. Brodie, III. 1980. Differential avoidance of mimetic salamanders by free-ranging birds. *Science*, 208: 181–182.

Brodie, E. D., Jr., T. G. Dowdey, and C. D. Anthony, 1989. Salamander antipredator strategies against snake attack: Biting by *Desmognathus*. *Herpetologica*, 45: 167–171.

Brodie, E. D., Jr., and D. R. Formanowicz, Jr., 1981. Palatability and antipredator behavior of the treefrog *Hyla versicolor* to the shrew *Blarina brevicauda*. *Jour. Herp.*, 15: 235–236.

Brodie, E. D., Jr., and D. R. Formanowicz, Jr., 1983. Prey size preference of predators: Differential vulnerability of larval anurans. *Herpetologica*, 39: 67–75.

Brodie, E. D., Jr., and D. R. Formanowicz, Jr., 1987. Antipredator mechanisms of larval anurans: Protection of palatable individuals. *Herpetologica*, 43: 369–373.

Brodie, E. D., Jr., D. R. Formanowicz, Jr., and E. D. Brodie, III, 1978. The development of noxiousness of *Bufo americanus* tadpoles to aquatic insect predators. *Herpetologica*, 34: 302–306.

Brodie, E. D., Jr., J. L. Hensel, Jr., and J. A. Johnson, 1974. Toxicity of the urodele amphibians *Taricha*, *Notophthalmus*, *Cynops* and *Paramesotriton* (Salamandridae). *Copeia*, 1974: 506–511.

Brodie, E. D. Jr., R. A. Nussbaum, and M. DiGiovanni, 1984. Antipredator adaptations of Asian salamanders (Salamandridae). *Herpetologica*, 40: 56–68.

Brodie, E. D., Jr., and N. J. Smatresk, 1990. The antipredator arsenal of fire salamanders: Spraying of secretions from highly pressurized dorsal skin glands. *Herpeto-logica*, 46: 1–7.

Brodie, E. D., Jr., and M. S. Tumbarello, 1978. The antipredator functions of *Dendrobates auratus* (Amphibia, Anura, Dendrobatidae) skin secretion in regard to a snake predator (Thamnophis). *Jour. Herp.*, 12: 264–265.

Brodie, E. D., III, 1989. Individual variation in antipredator response of *Ambystoma jeffersonianum* to snake predators. *Jour. Herp.*, 23: 307–309.

Brodie, E. D., III, and E. D. Brodie, Jr., 1991. Evolutionary response of predators to dangerous prey: Reduction of toxicity of newts and resistance of garter snakes in island populations. *Evolution*, 45: 221–224.

Brown, C. W., 1968. Additional observations on the function of the nasolabial grooves of plethodontid salamanders. *Copeia*, 1968: 728–731.

Brown, H. A., 1967a. Embryonic temperature adaptations and genetic compatibility in two allopatric populations of the spadefoot toad, *Scaphiopus hammondii*. *Evolution*, 21: 742–761.

Brown, H. A., 1967b. High temperature tolerance of the eggs of a desert anuran, *Scaphiopus hammondii*. *Copeia*, 1967: 365–370.

Brown, H. A., 1975a. Temperature and development of the tailed frog, *Ascaphus truei*. *Comp. Biochem. Physiol.*, 50A: 397–405.

Brown, H. A., 1975b. Reproduction and development of the red-legged frog, *Rana aurora*, in northwestern Washington. *Northwest Sci.*, 49: 241–252.

Brown, H. A., 1975c. Embryonic temperature adaptations of the Pacific treefrog, *Hyla regilla*. *Comp. Biochem. Physiol.*, 51A: 863–873.

Brown, H. A., 1976. The time-temperature relation of embryonic development in the northwestern salamander, *Ambystoma gracile*. *Can. J. Zool.*, 54: 552–558.

Brown, H. A., 1977a. A case of interbreeding between *Rana aurora* and *Bufo boreas* (Amphibia, Anura). *Jour. Herp.*, 2: 92–94.

Brown, H. A., 1977b. Oxygen consumption of a large cold-adapted frog egg *Ascaphus truei* (Amphibia: Ascaphidae). *Can. J. Zool.*, 55: 343–348.

Brown, L. E., and M. J. Littlejohn, 1972. Male release calls in *Bufo americanus* group. In W. F. Blair, ed., Evolution in the genus *Bufo*. University of Texas Press, Austin.

Bruce, K. J., and J. L. Christiansen, 1976. The food and food habits of Blanchard's cricket frog, *Acris crepitans blanchardi* (Amphibia, Anura, Hylidae), in Iowa. *Jour. Herp.*, 10: 63–74.

Brust, D. G., 1993. Maternal brood care by *Dendrobates pumilio*: A frog that feeds its young. *Jour. Herp.*, 27: 96–98.

Bryan, A. M., W. B. Stone, and P. G. Olafsson, 1987. Disposition of toxic PCB congeners in snapping turtle eggs: Expressed as toxic equivalents of TCDD. *Bull. Environ. Contam. Toxicol.*, 39: 791–796.

Buchanan, B. W., 1992. Bimordal nocturnal activity patten of *Hyla squirella*. *Jour. Herp.*, 26: 521–522.

Bucher, T. L., M. J. Ryan, and G. A. Bartholomew, 1980. The cost of croaking in a frog, *Physalaemus pustulosus* (Leptoactylidae). *Amer. Zool.*, 20: 909 (abstr.).

Burggren, W. W., 1988. Role of the central circulation in regulation of cutaneous gas exchange in amphibians. *Amer. Zool.*, 28: 985–998.

Burke, E. M., and F. H. Pough, 1976. The role of fatigue in temperature resistance of salamanders. *J. Thermal Biol.*, 1: 163–167.

Burton, T. M., 1976. An analysis of the feeding ecology of the salamanders (Amphibia, Urodela) of the Hubbard Brook Experimental Forest, New Hampshire. *Jour. Herp.*, 10: 187–204.

Burton, T. M., and G. E. Likens, 1975a. Salamander populations and biomass in the Hubbard Brook Experimental Forest, New Hampshire. *Copeia*, 1975: 541–546.

Burton, T. M., and G. E. Likens, 1975b. Energy flow and nutrient cycling in salamander populations in the Hubbard Brook Experimental Forest, New Hampshire. *Ecology*, 56: 1068–1080.

Caldwell, J. P., 1989. Structure and behavior of *Hyla geographica* tadpole schools, with comments on classification of group behavior in tadpoles. *Copeia*, 1989: 938–950.

Capranica, R. R., 1977. Auditory processing of vocal signals in anurans. In D. H. Taylor and S. I. Guttman, eds., *The Reproductive Biology of Amphibians*. Plenum Press, New York.

Capranica, R. R., L. S. Frishkopf, and V. Nevo, 1973. Encoding of geographic dialects in the auditory system of the cricket frog. *Science*, 182: 1272–1275.

Capranica, R. R., and A.J.M. Moffat, 1975. Selectivity of the peripheral auditory system of spadefoot toads (*Scaphiopus couchi*) for sounds of biological significance. *J. Comp. Physiol.*, 100: 231–249.

Carey, C., 1993. Hypotheses concerning the causes of the disappearance of boreal toads from the mountains of Colorado. *Conserv. Biol.*, 7: 355–362.

Carlsen, E., A. Giwercman, N. Keiding, and N. E. Skakkebaek, 1992. Evidence for decreasing quality of semen during the past 50 year. *Brit. Med. Jour.*, 305: 609–613.

Carpenter, C. C., 1953. An ecological survey of the herpetofauna of the Grand Teton–Jackson Hole area of Wyoming. *Copeia*, 1953: 170–174.

Carpenter, C. C., and J. C. Gillingham, 1987. Water hole fidelity in the marine toad, *Bufo marinus*. *Jour. Herp.*, 21: 158–161.

Carroll, R. L., and P. J. Currie, 1975. Microsaurs as possible apodan ancestors. *J. Linn. Soc. (Zool.)*, 57: 229–247.

Carson, R., 1962. *Silent Spring*. Houghton Mifflin, Boston.

Carter, D. B., 1979. Structure and function of the subcutaneous lymph sacs in the Anura (Amphibia). *Jour. Herp.*, 13: 321–327.

Casterlin, M. E., and W. W. Reynolds, 1977. Behavioral fever in anuran amphibian larvae. *Life Sciences*, 20: 593–596.

Casterlin, M. E., and W. W. Reynolds, 1978. Behavioural thermoregulation in *Rana pipiens* tadpoles. *J. Thermal Biol.*, 3:143–146.

Chew, R. M., 1961. Water metabolism of desert-inhabiting vertebrates. *Biol. Rev.*, 36: 1–31.

Christman, S., 1959. Sound production in newts. *Herpetologica*, 15: 13.

Clark, R. J., C. R. Peterson, and P. E. Bartelt, 1993. The distribution, relative abundance, and habitat associations of amphibians on the Targhee National Forest. Final report to Targhee National Forest.

Clarkson, R. W., and J. C. Rorabaugh, 1989. Status of leopard frogs (*Rana pipiens* complex: Ranidae) in Arizona and southeastern California. *Southwest. Nat.*, 34: 531–538.

Claussen, D. L., 1969. Studies on water loss and rehydration in anurans. *Physiol. Zool.*, 42: 1–14.

Claussen, D. L., 1977. Thermal acclimation in ambystomatid salamanders. *Comp. Biochem. Physiol.* 58A: 333–340.

Clement, C. R., and T. Colborn, 1992. Herbicides and fungicides: A perspective on potential human exposure. In T. Colborn and C. Clement, eds., *Chemically-induced Alterations in Sexual and Functional Development: The Wildlife/Human Connection*. Princeton Scientific Publishing Co., Princeton, N.J.

Cochran, D. M., 1961. *Living Amphibians of the World*. Doubleday, Garden City, N.Y.

Cohen, N. W., 1952. Comparative rates of dehydration and hydration in some California salamanders. *Ecology*, 33: 462–479.

Colborn, T., 1991. Global implications of the Great Lakes wildlife research. *Internatl. Environ. Affairs*, 3: 3–24.

Colborn, T., and C. Clement, eds., 1992. *Chemically-induced Alterations in Sexual and Functional Development: The Wildlife/Human Connection*. Princeton Scientific Publishing Co., Princeton, N.J.

Collins, J. P., 1979. Intrapopulation variation in the body size at metamorphosis and timing of metamorphosis in the bullfrog, *Rana catesbeiana*. *Ecology*, 60: 738–479.

Conant, R., and J. T. Collins, 1991. *A Field Guide to Reptiles and Amphibians: Eastern and Central North America*. 3d ed. The Peterson Field Guide Series. Houghton Mifflin, Boston.

Cooper, K., 1991. Effects of pesticides on wildlife. In W. J. Hayes, Jr., and E. R. Laws, eds., *Handbook of Pesticide Toxicology*, vols. 1–3. Academic Press, San Diego.

Corben, C. J., G. J. Ingram, and M. J. Tyler, 1974. Gastric brooding: Unique form of parental care in an Australian frog. *Science*, 186: 946–947.

Corn, P. S., and J. C. Fogleman, 1984. Extinction of montane populations of the northern leopard frog (*Rana pipiens*) in Colorado. *Jour. Herp.*, 18: 147–152.

Corn, P. S., W. Stolzenburg, and R. B. Bury, 1989. Acid precipitation studies in Colorado and Wyoming: Interim report of surveys of montane amphibians and water chemistry. U.S. Fish and Wildlife Service, Research and Development, Biological Report 80 (40.26), Report No. 26.

Corn, P. S., and F. A. Vertucci, 1992. Descriptive risk assessment of the effects of acidic deposition on Rocky Mountain amphibians. *Jour. Herp.* 26: 361–369.

Cornell, T. J., K. A. Berven, and G. J. Gamboa, 1989. Kin recognition by tadpoles and froglets of the wood frog *Rana sylvatica*. *Oecologia*, 78: 312–316.

Cory, L., P. Fjeld, and W. Serat, 1970. Distribution patterns of DDT residues in the Sierra Nevada Mountains. *Pesticide Monitoring Jour.*, 4: 204–211.

Creusere, F. M., and W. G. Whitford, 1976. Ecological relationships in a desert anuran community. *Herpetologica*, 32: 7–18.

Crews, D., J. M. Bergeron, J. J. Bull, D. Flores, A.Tousignanat, G. K. Skipper, and T. Wibbels, 1994. Temperature dependent sex determination in reptiles: Proximate mechanisms, ultimate outcomes, and practical applications. *Developm. Gen.*, 15: 297–312.

Crump, M. L., 1986. Cannibalism by younger tadpoles: Another hazard of metamorphosis. *Copeia*, 1986: 1007–1009.

Crump, M. L., 1988. Aggression in harlequin frogs: Male-male competition and possible conflict of interest between the sexes. *Animal Behav.*, 36: 1064–1077.

Crump, M. L., 1989. Effect of habitat drying on development time and size at metamorphosis in *Hyla pseudopuma*. *Copeia*, 1989: 794–797.

Crump, M. L., F. R. Hensley, and K. L. Clark, 1992. Apparent decline of the golden toad: Underground or extinct? *Copeia*, 1992: 413–420.

Crump, M. L. and D. S. Townsend, 1990. Random mating by size in a neotropical treefrog, *Hyla pseudopuma*. *Herpetologica*, 46: 383–386.

Cunjak, R. A., 1986. Winter habitat of the northern leopard frogs, *Rana pipiens*, in a southern Ontario stream. *Can. J. Zool.*, 64: 255–257.

Cupp. P. V., Jr., 1980. Thermal tolerance of five salientian amphibians during development and metamorphosis. *Herpetologica*, 36: 234–244.

Czopek, J., 1962. Vascularization of respiratory surfaces in some Caudata. *Copeia*, 1962: 576–587.

Daly, J. W., G. B. Brown, M. Mensah-Dwumah, and C. W. Myers, 1978. Classification of skin alkaloids from neotropical poison-dart frogs (Dendrobatidae). *Toxicon*, 16: 163–188.

Daly, J. W., J. Caceres, R. W. Moni, F. Gusovsky, M. Moos, Jr., K. B. Seamon, K. Milton, and C. W. Myers, 1992. Frog secretions and hunting magic in the upper Amazon: Identification of a peptide that interacts with an adenosine receptor. *Proc. Natl. Acad. Sci.*, 89: 10960–10963.

Daly, J. W., H. M. Garraffo, and T. F. Spande, 1993. Amphibian alkaloids. In G. Cordell, ed., *The Alkaloids*, vol. 43. Academic Press, New York.

Daly, J. W., H. M. Garraffo, T. F. Spande, C. Jaramillo, and A. S. Rand, 1994. Dietary source for skin alkaloids of poison frogs (Dendrobatidae)? *J. Chem. Ecol.*, 20: 943–955.

Daly, J. W., F. Gusovsky, C. W. Myers, M. Yotsu-Yamashita, and T. Yasumoto, 1994. First occurrence of tetrodotoxin in a dendrobatid frog (*Colostethus inguinalis*), with further reports for the bufonid genus *Atelopus*. *Toxicon*, 32: 279–285

Daly, J. W., C. W. Myers, and N. Whittaker, 1987. Further classification of skin alkaloids from neotropical poison frogs (Dendrobatidae), with a general survey of toxic/noxious substances in amphibia. *Toxicon*, 25: 1021–1095.

da Silva-Helio, R., M. C. de Britto-Pereira, and U. Caramaschi, 1989. Frugivory and seed dispersal by *Hyla truncata*, a neotropical treefrog. *Copeia*, 1989: 781–783.

da Silva Nunes, V., 1988a. Vocalizations of treefrogs (*Smilisca sila*) in response to bat predation. *Herpetologica*, 44: 8–10.

da Silva Nunes, V., 1988b. Feeding asymmetry affects territorial disputes between males of *Plethodon cinereus*. *Herpetologica*, 44: 386–391.

da Silva Nunes, V., and R. G. Jaeger, 1989. Salamander aggressiveness increases with length of territorial ownership. *Copeia*, 1989: 712–718.

David, R. S., and R. G. Jaeger, 1981. Prey location through chemical cues by a terrestrial salamander. *Copeia*, 1981: 435–440.

Davies, N. B., and T. R. Halliday, 1977. Optimal mate selection in the toad *Bufo bufo*. *Nature*, 269: 56–58.

Davis, J. R., and B. H. Brattstrom, 1975. Sounds produced by the California newt, *Taricha torosa*. *Herpetologica*, 31: 409–412.

Davis, M. S., 1987. Acoustically mediated neighbor recognition in the North American bullfrog, *Rana catesbeiana*. *Behav. Ecol. Sociobiol.*, 21: 185–190.

Dawley, E. M., 1986. Behavioral isolating mechanisms in sympatric terrestrial salamanders. *Herpetologica*, 42: 156–164.

Dawley, E. M., 1987a. Salamander vomeronasal systems: Why plethodontids smell well. *Amer. Zool.*, 27: 166A (abstr.).

Dawley, E. M., 1987b. Species discrimination between hybridizing and non-hybridizing terrestrial salamanders. *Copeia*, 1987: 924–931.

Dawley, E. M., 1992. Sexual dimorphism in a chemosensory system: The role of the vomeronasal organs in salamander reproductive behavior. *Copeia*, 1992: 113–120.

Dawley, E. M., and A. H. Bass, 1989. Chemical access to the vomeronasal organs of a plethodontid salamander. *Jour. Morph.*, 200: 163–174.

de Jongh, H. J., and C. Gans, 1969. On the mechanism of respiration in the bullfrog, *Rana catesbeiana*: A reassessment. *Jour. Morph.*, 127: 259–290.

del Pino, E. M., 1980. Morphology of the pouch and incubatory integument in marsupial frogs (*Hylidae*). *Copeia*, 1980: 10–17.

del Pino, E. M., 1989. Marsupial frogs. *Sci. Amer.*, 260 (May): 110–118.

Demian, J. J., and D. H. Taylor, 1977. Photoreception and locomotor rhythm entrainment by the pineal body of the newt, *Notophthalmus viridescens* (Amphibia, Urodela, Salamanderidae). *Jour. Herp.*, 11: 131–139.

Dent, J. N., 1968. Survey of amphibian metamorphosis. In W. Etkin, and L. I. Gilbert, eds., *Metamorphosis, a Problem in Developmental Biology*. Appleton-Century-Crofts, New York.

Dent, J. N., 1988. Hormonal interaction in amphibian metamorphosis. *Amer. Zool.*, 28: 297–308.

Deviche, P., and F. L. Moore, 1988. Steroidal control of sexual behavior in the rough-skinned newt (*Taricha granulosa*): Effects of testosterone, estradiol, and dihydrotestosterone. *Horm. Behav.*, 22: 26–34.

Dickman, M. 1968. The effect of grazing by tadpoles on the structure of a periphyton community. *Ecology*, 49: 1188–1190.

Dimmitt, M. A., and R. Ruibal, 1980. Environmental correlates of emergence in spadefoot toads (*Scaphiopus*). *Jour. Herp.*, 14: 21–29.

Dodd, C. K., Jr., 1989. Duration of immobility in salamanders, genus *Plethodon* (Caudata: Plethodontidae). *Herpetologica*, 45: 467–473.

Dodd, C. K., Jr., J. A. Johnson, and E. D. Brodie, Jr. 1974. Noxious skin secretions of an eastern small *Plethodon*, *P. nettingi hubrichti*. *Jour. Herp.*, 8: 89–92.

Dodd, M.H.I., and J. M. Dodd, 1976. The biology of metamorphosis. In B. Lofts, ed., *Physiology of the Amphibia*, vol. 3, Academic Press, New York.

Dole, J. W., 1972a. The role of olfaction and audition in the orientation of leopard frogs, *Rana pipiens*. *Herpetologica*, 28: 258–260.

Dole, J. W., 1972b. Evidence of celestial orientation in newly-metamorphosed *Rana pipiens*. *Herpetologica*, 28: 273–276.

Dole, J. W., 1974. Home range in the canyon tree frog (*Hyla cadaverina*). *Southwest. Nat.*, 19: 105–107.

Dole, J. W., B. B. Rose, and K. H. Tachiki, 1981. Western toads (*Bufo boreas*) learn odor of prey insects. *Herpetologica*, 37: 63–68.

Donnelly, M. A., 1991. Feeding patterns of the strawberry poison frog, *Dendrobates pumilio* (Anura: Dendrobatidae). *Copeia*, 1991: 723–730.

Douglas, M. E., and B. L. Monroe, Jr., 1981. A comparative study of topographical orientation in *Ambystoma* (Amphibia: Caudata). *Copeia*, 1981: 460–463.

Douglas, R. H., T. S. Collett, and H. J. Wagner, 1986. Accommodation in anuran Amphibia and its role in depth vision. *J. Comp. Physiol. (A)*, 158: 133–143.

Drost, C. A., and G. M. Fellers, 1993. Decline of frog species in the Yosemite section of the Sierra Nevada. Report to Yosemite National Park and the Yosemite Association.

Ducey, P. K., 1989. Agonistic behavior and biting during intraspecific encounters in *Ambystoma* salamanders. *Herpetologica*, 45: 155–160.

Ducey, P. K., and E. D. Brodie, Jr., 1983. Salamanders respond selectively to contacts with snakes: Survival advantages of alternative antipredator strategies. *Copeia*, 1983: 1036–1041.

Ducey, P. K., and E. D. Brodie, Jr., 1991. Evolution of antipredator behavior: Individual and populational variation in a neotropical salamander. *Herpetologica*, 47: 89–95.

Ducey, P. K., and P. Ritsema, 1988. Intraspecific aggression and responses to marked substrates in *Ambystoma maculatum* (Caudata: Ambystomatidae). *Copeia*, 1988: 1008–1013.

Duellman, W. E., 1966. Aggressive behavior in dendrobatid frogs. *Herpetologica*, 22: 217–221.

Duellman, W. E., 1988. Patterns of species diversity in anuran amphibians in the American Tropics. *Ann. Missouri Bot. Gard.*, 75: 79–104.

Duellman, W. E., and S. J. Maness, 1980. The reproductive behavior of some hylid marsupial frogs. *Jour. Herp.*, 14: 213–222.

Duellman, W. E., L. R. Maxson, and C. A. Jesiolowski, 1988. Evolution of marsupial frogs (Hylidae: Hemiphractinae): Immunological evidence. *Copeia*, 1988: 537–543.

Duellman, W. E., and R. A. Pyles, 1983. Acoustic resource partitioning in anuran communities. *Copeia*, 1983: 639–649.

Duellman, W. E., and A. H. Savitzky, 1976. Aggressive behavior in a centrolenid frog with comments on territoriality in anurans. *Herpetologica*, 32: 401–404.

Duellman, W. E., and L. Trueb, 1986. *Biology of Amphibians*. McGraw-Hill, New York.

Dunlap, D. G., 1969. Evidence for a daily rhythm of heat resistance in the cricket frog, *Acris crepitans*. *Copeia*, 1969: 852–854.

Dunson, W. A., R. L. Wyman, and E. S. Corbett, 1992. A symposium on amphibian declines and habitat acidification. *Jour. Herp.*, 26: 349–442.

Dyson, M. L., N. I. Passmore, P. J. Bishop, and S. P. Henzi, 1992. Male behavior and correlates of mating success in a natural population of African painted reed frogs (*Hyperolius marmoratus*). *Herpetologica*, 48: 236–246.

Eagleson, G. W., 1976. A comparison of the life histories and growth patterns of populations of the salamander *Ambystoma gracile* (Baird) from permanent low-altitude and montane lakes. *Can. J. Zool.* 54: 2098–2111.

Eakin, R. M., 1973. *The Third Eye*. University of California Press, Berkeley.

Eakin, R. M., W. B. Quay, and J. A. Westfall, 1963. Cytological and cytochemical studies on the frontal and pineal organs of the treefrog, *Hyla regilla*. *Z. Zellforsch.*, 59: 663–683.

Eatock, R. A., D. P. Corey, and A. J. Hudspeth, 1987. Adaptation of mechanoelectrical transduction in hair cells of the bullfrog's sacculus. *Jour. Neurosci.*, 7: 2821–2836.

Elepfandt, A., 1986. Wave frequency recognition and absolute pitch for water waves in the clawed frog. *Xenopus laevis. J. Comp. Physiol. (A)*, 158: 235–238.

Elkan, E., 1967. The defence system of the anura against desiccation. *Brit. J. Herp.*, 3: 311–312.

Elkan, E., 1968. Mucopolysaccharides in the anuran defense against desiccation. *J. Zool., London*, 155: 19–53.

Elkan, E., 1976. Ground substance: An anuran defense against desiccation. In B. Lofts, ed., *Physiology of the Amphibia*, vol. 3. Academic Press, New York and London.

Emerson, S. B., 1988. Convergence and morphological constraint in frogs: Variation in postcranial morphology. *Fieldiana*, 43: 1–19.

Emerson, S. B., 1992. Courtship and nest-building behavior of a Bornean frog, *Rana blythi. Copeia*, 1992: 1123–1127.

Emerson, S. B., and D. Berrigan, 1993. Systematics of southeast Asian ranids: Multiple origins of voicelessness in the subgenus *Limnonectes* (Fitzinger). *Herpetologica*, 49: 22–31.

Emerson, S. B., and D. Diehl, 1980. Toe pad morphology and adhesive mechanisms in frogs. *Biol. J. Linn. Soc.*, 13: 199–216.

Emerson, S. B. and M.A.R. Koehl, 1990. The interaction of behavior and morphological change in the evolution of a novel locomotor type: "Flying" frogs. *Evolution*, 44: 1931–1946.

Emerson, S. B., and R. F. Inger, 1992. The comparative ecology of voiced and voiceless Bornean frogs. *Jour. Herp.*, 26: 482–49.

Emmerson, F. H., and F. R. Kay, 1971. Agonistic behavior in some captive frogs (*Rana*) from Nevada. *Herp. Rev.*, 3: 39.

Endler, J. A., 1970. Kinesthetic orientation in the California newt (*Taricha torosa*). *Behavior*, 37: 15–22.

Etges, W. J., 1987. Call site choice in male anurans. *Copeia*, 1987: 910–923.

Etheridge, K., 1990a. Water balance in estivating sirenid salamanders (*Siren lacertina*). *Herpetologica*, 46: 400–406.

Etheridge, K., 1990b. The energetics of estivating sirenid salamanders (*Siren lacertina* and *Pseudobranchus striatus*). *Herpetologica*, 46: 407–414.

Etkin, W., 1964. Metamorphosis. In J. A. Moore, ed., *Physiology of the Amphibia*. Academic Press, New York and London.

Etkin, W., and L. I. Gilbert, eds., 1968. *Metamorphosis, a Problem in Developmental Biology*. Appleton-Century-Crofts, New York.

Ewert, J.- P., 1976. The visual system of the toad: Behavioral and physiological studies on a pattern recognition system. In K. V. Fite, ed., *The Amphibian Visual System: A Multidisciplinary Approach*. Academic Press, New York.

Ewert, J.- P., B. Arend, V. Becker, and H. W. Borchers, 1979. Invariants in configurational visual prey selection by the toad *Bufo bufo* (L.). *Brain, Behav. Evol.*, 16: 38–51.

Ewert, J.- P., N. W. Borchers, and A. V. Wietersheim, 1978. Question of prey feature detectors in the toad's *Bufo bufo* (L.) visual system: A correlation analysis. *J. Comp. Physiol. (A)*, 126: 43–47.

Fairchild, L., and J. Kandel. 1980. Discrimination between conspecifics by Fowler's toads. *Amer. Zool.*, 20: 724 (abstr.).

Feder, M. E., 1978. Environmental variability and thermal acclimation in neotropical and temperate zone salamanders. *Physiol. Zool.*, 51: 7–16.

Feder, M. E., 1982. Thermal ecology of neotropical lungless salamanders (Amphibia: Plethodontidae): Environmental temperatures and behavioral responses. *Ecology*, 63: 1665–1674.

Feder, M. E., and W. W. Burggren, 1985. Cutaneous gas exchange in vertebrates: Design, patterns, control and implications. *Biol. Rev.*, 60: 1–45.

Feder, M. E., and W. W. Burggren, 1992. *Environmental Physiology of Amphibians*. University of Chicago Press, Chicago.

Feder, M. E., and G. V. Lauder, eds., 1986. *Predator-Prey Relationships: Perspectives and Approaches from the Study of Lower Vertebrates*. University of Chicago Press, Chicago and London.

Feder, M. E., and F. H. Pough, 1975. Temperature selection by the red-backed salamander, *Plethodon cinereus* (Green) (Caudata: Plethodontidae). *Comp. Biochem. Physiol.*, 50A: 91–98.

Fellers, G. M., 1979a. Aggression, territoriality, and mating behaviour in North American treefrogs. *Anim. Behav.*, 27: 107–119.

Fellers, G. M., 1979b. Mate selection in the gray treefrog, *Hyla versicolor*. *Copeia*, 1979: 286–290.

Fellers, G. M., ed., 1994. California/Nevada declining amphibian working group. Newsletter 1, May 1, 1994. 10 pp.

Fellers, G. M., and C. A. Drost, 1993. Disappearance of the Cascades frog *Rana cascadae* at the southern end of its range, California, USA. *Biol. Conserv.*, 65: 177–181.

Ferguson, D. E., 1963. *Ambystoma macrodactylum* (Baird). Long-toed salamander. *Cat. Amer. Amphib. Rept.*, 4.1–4.2.

Ferguson, D. E., 1971. The sensory basis of orientation in amphibians. *Ann. N.Y. Acad. Sci.*, 188: 30–36.

Ferguson, D. E., and H. F. Landreth, 1966. Celestial orientation of Fowler's toad *Bufo fowleri*. *Behavior*, 26: 107–123.

Ferguson, D. E., H. F. Landreth, and J. P. McKeown, 1967. Sun compass orientation of the northern cricket frog, *Acris crepitans*. *Anim. Behav.*, 15: 45–53.

Ferguson, D. E., H. F. Landreth, and M. R. Turnipseed, 1965. Astronomical orientation of the southern cricket frog, *Acris gryllus*. *Copeia*, 1965: 58–66.

Ferguson, D. E., J. P. McKeown, O. S. Bosarge, and H. F. Landreth, 1968. Sun-compass orientation of bullfrogs. *Copeia*, 1968: 230–235.

Fishwild, T. G., R. A. Schmidt, K. M. Jankens, K. A. Berven, G. J. Gamboa, and C. M. Richards, 1990. Sibling recognition by larval frogs (*Rana pipiens*, *R. sylvatica*, and *Pseudacris crucifer*). *Jour. Herp.*, 24: 40–44.

Fite, K. V., ed., 1976. *The Amphibian Visual System. A Multidisciplinary Approach*. Academic Press, New York.

Fitzpatrick, L. C., 1976. Life history patterns of storage and utilization of lipids for energy in amphibians. *Amer. Zool.*, 16: 725–732.

Forester, D. C., 1977. Comments on the female reproductive cycle and philopatry by *Desmognathus ochrophaeus* (Amphibia, Urodela, Plethodontidae). *Jour. Herp.*, 11: 311–316.

Forester, D. C., 1979. Homing to the nest by female mountain dusky salamanders (*Demognathus ochrophaeus*) with comments on the sensory modalities essential to clutch recognition. *Herpetologica*, 35: 330–335.

Forester, D. C., and R. Czarnowsky, 1985. Sexual selection in the spring peeper, *Hyla crucifer* (Amphibia, Anura): Role of the advertizement call. *Behaviour*, 92: 112–128.

Forester, D. C., K. Harrison, and L. McCall, 1983. The effects of isolation, the duration of brooding, and non-egg olfactory cues on clutch recognition by the salamander, *Desmognathus ochophaseus. Jour. Herp.*, 17: 308–314.

Forester, D. C., and D. V. Lykens, 1986. Significance of satellite males in a population of spring peepers (*Hyla crucifer*). *Copeia*, 1986: 719–724.

Forester, D. C., and D. V. Lykens, 1988. The ability of wood frog eggs to withstand prolonged terrestrial stranding: An empirical study. *Can. J. Zool.*, 66: 1733–1735.

Formanowicz, D. R., Jr., and E. D. Brodie, Jr., 1982. Relative palatabilities of members of a larval amphibian community. *Copeia*, 1982: 91–97.

Fouquette, M. J., Jr., 1975. Speciation in chorus frogs. I. Reproductive character displacement in the *Pseudacris nigrita* complex. *Syst. Zool.*, 24: 16–23.

Fox, H., 1986. Early development of caecilian skin with special reference to the epidermis. *Jour. Herp.*, 20: 154–167.

Foxon, G.E.H., 1964. Blood and respiration. In J. A. Moore, ed., *Physiology of the Amphibia*. Academic Press, New York and London.

Franz, R., C. K. Dodd, Jr., and C. Jones, 1988. *Rana areolata aesopus* movement. *Herp. Rev.*, 19: 33.

Fraser, D. F., 1976. Coexistence of salamanders in the genus *Plethodon*: a variation of the Santa Rosalia theme. *Ecology*, 57: 238–251.

Fraser, D. F., 1980. On the environmental control of oocyte maturation in a plethodontid salamander. *Oecologia*, 46: 302–307.

Freed, A. N., 1980. An adaptive advantage of basking behavior in an anuran amphibian. *Physiol. Zool.* 53: 433–444.

Freed, A. N., 1982. A treefrog's menu: Selection for an evening's meal. *Oecologia*, 53: 20–26.

Fritzsch, B., and M. H. Wake, 1986. The distribution of the ampullary organs in gymnophiona. *Jour. Herp.*, 20: 90–93.

Fritzsch, B., and M. H. Wake, 1988. The inner ear of gymnophione amphibians and its nerve supply: A comparative study of regressive events in a complex sensory system (Amphibia, Gymnophiona). *Zoomorphology*, 108: 201–217.

Frost, D. R., ed., 1985. *Amphibian Species of the World: A Taxonomic and Geographical Reference*. Allen Press, Inc., and the Association of Systematic Collections (ASC), Lawrence, Kansas.

Fuhrman, F. A., 1967. Tetrodotoxin. *Sci. Amer.*, 216: 60–71.

Fuhrman, F. A., 1986. Tetrodotoxin, tarichatoxin, and chiriquitoxin: Historical perspectives. In C. Y. Kao and S. R. Levinson, eds., *Tetrodotoxin, Saxitoxin, and the Molecular Biology of the Sodium Channel. Ann. N.Y. Acad. Sci.*, 479: 1–14.

Gans, C., 1970. Strategy and sequence in the evolution of the external gas exchanges of ectothermal vertebrates. *Forma Functio*, 1970: 61–104.

Gans, C., 1973. Sound production in the Salientia: Mechanism and evolution of the emitter. *Amer. Zool.*, 13: 1179–1194.

Gans, C., H. J. de Jongh, and J. Farber, 1969. Bullfrog (*Rana catesbeiana*) ventilation: How does the frog breathe? *Science*, 163: 1223–1225.

Gans, C., and G. C. Gorniak, 1982a. Functional morphology of lingual protrusion in marine toads (*Bufo marinus*). *Amer. J. Anat.*, 163: 195–222.

Gans, C., and G. C. Gorniak, 1982b. How does the toad flip its tongue? Test of two hypotheses. *Science*, 216: 1335–1337.

Gascon, C., and D. Planas, 1986. Spring pond water chemistry and the reproduction of the wood frog, *Rana sylvatica. Can. J. Zool.*, 64: 543–550.

Gasser, F. and J.M.J. Joly, 1972. Existence d'un cycle sexuel biennal chez la femelle de *Salamandra salamandra fastuosa* Schreiber (Urodèle, Salamandridae) a différentes altitudes dans les Pyrénées Centrales: Influence des facteurs génétiques et climatiques. *Ann. Sci. Nat. Zool.*, 14: 427–444.

Gatz, A. J., Jr., 1973. Algal entry into the eggs of *Ambystoma maculatum. Jour. Herp.*, 7: 137–138.

Gatz, R. N., E. C. Crawford, Jr., and J. Piiper, 1974. Respiratory properties of the blood of a lungless and gill-less salamander, *Desmognathus fuscus. Respiration Physiol.*, 20: 33–41.

Gaymer, R., 1971. New method of locomotion in limbless vertebrates. *Nature*, 234: 150–151.

Gehlbach, F. R. and S. E. Kennedy, 1978. Population ecology of a highly productive aquatic alamander (*Siren intermedia*). *Southwest. Nat.*, 23: 423–430.

Gehlbach, F. R., and B. Walker, 1970. Acoustic behavior of the aquatic salamander, *Siren intermedia. BioSci.*, 20: 1107–1108.

Gergits, W. F., and R. G. Jaeger, 1990a. Field observations of the behavior of the red-backed salamander (*Plethodon cinereus*): Courtship and agonistic interactions. *Jour. Herp.*, 24: 93–95.

Gergits, W. F., and R. G. Jaeger, 1990b. Site attachment by the red-backed salamander, *Plethodon cinereus. Jour. Herp.*, 24: 91–93.

Gerhardt, H. C., 1975. Sound pressure levels and radiation patterns of the vocalizations of some North American frogs and toads. *J. Comp. Physiol. (A)*, 102: 1–12.

Gerhardt, H. C., and G. M. Klump, 1988. Phonotactic responses and selectivity of barking treefrogs (*Hyla gratiosa*) to chorus sounds. *J. Comp. Physiol. (A)*, 163: 795–802.

Gern, W. A., D. O. Norris, and D. Duvall, 1983. The effect of light and temperature on plasma melatonin in neotenic tiger salamanders (*Ambystoma tigrinum*). *Jour. Herp.*, 17: 228–234.

Gibbs, E. L., G. W. Nace, and M. B. Emmons, 1971. The live frog is almost dead. *BioSci.*, 21: 1027–1034.

Gilbert, L. I., and E. Frieden, eds., 1981. *Metamorphosis, a Problem in Developmental Biology.* 2d ed. Plenum Press, New York.

Gilbert, P. W., 1942. Observations on the eggs of *Ambystoma maculatum* with special reference to the green algae found within the egg envelopes. *Ecology*, 23: 215–227.

Gilbert, P. W., 1944. The alga-egg relationship in *Ambystoma maculatum*, a case of symbiosis. *Ecology*, 25: 366–369.

Given, M. F., 1987. Vocalizations and acoustic interactions of the carpenter frog, *Rana virgatipes. Herpetologica*, 43: 467–481.

Given, M. F., 1990. Variation in the citrate synthase activity in calling muscles of carpenter frogs, *Rana virgatipes. Copeia*, 1990: 863–867.

Glass, B. P., 1951. Age at maturity of neotenic *Ambystoma tigrinum mavortium* Baird. *Amer. Midland Nat.*, 46: 391–294.

Goicoechea, O., O. Garrido, and B. Jorquera, 1986. Evidence for a trophic paternal-larval relationship in the frog *Rhinoderma darwinii. Jour. Herp.*, 20: 168–178.

Goin, C. J., 1949. The peep order in peepers: A swamp water serenade. *Quart. J. Florida Acad. Sci.*, 11: 59–61.

Goin, C. J., O. B. Goin, and G. R. Zug., 1978. *Introduction to Herpetology.* W. H. Freeman, San Francisco.

Goode, R. P., 1967. The regeneration of limbs in adult anurans. *J. Embryol. Exp. Morph.*, 18: 259–267.

Goodyear, C. P., and R. Altig, 1971. Orientation of bullfrogs (*Rana catesbeiana*) during metamorphosis. *Copeia*, 1971: 362–364.

Gordon, R. E., 1952. A contribution to the life history and ecology of the plethodontid salamander *Aneides aeneus* (Cope and Packard). *Amer. Midland Nat.*, 47: 666–701.

Gosner, K. L., 1960. A simplified table for staging anuran embryos and larvae with notes on identification. *Herpetologica*, 16: 183–190.

Gosner, K. L., and Black, I. H., 1955. The effect of temperature and moisture on the reproductive cycle of *Scapiopus h. holbrooki. Amer. Midland Nat.*, 54: 192–203.

Gould, S. J., 1977. *Ontogeny and Phylogeny.* Cambridge University Press, Cambridge, U.K.

Grant, W. C. Jr., 1955. Territorialism in two species of salamanders. *Science*, 121: 137–138.

Graybeal, A., and K. de Queiroz, 1992. Inguinal amplexus in *Bufo fastidiosus* with comments on the systematics of bulfonid frogs. *Jour. Herp.*, 26: 84–87.

Green, D. M., 1979. Treefrog toe pads: Comparative surface morphology using scanning electron microscopy. *Can. J. Zool.*, 57: 2033–2046.

Green, D. M., 1981. Adhesion and the toe-pads of treefrogs. *Copeia*, 1981: 790–796.

Greene, H. W., 1994. Systematics and natural history, foundations for understanding and conserving biodiversity. *Amer. Zool.*, 34: 48–56.

Grinnell, J., and T. I. Storer, 1924. *Animal Life in the Yosemite.* University of California Press, Berkeley.

Grubb, J. C., 1975. Olfactory orientation in southern leopard frogs, *Rana utricularia. Herpetologica*, 31: 219–221.

Grubb, J. C., 1976. Maze orientation by Mexican toads, *Bufo valliceps* (Amphibia, Anura, Bufonidae), using olfactory and configurational cues. *Jour. Herp.*, 10: 97–104.

Grüsser-Cornehls, U., and W. Himstedt, 1976. The urodele visual system. In K. V. Fite, ed., *The Amphibian Visual System: A Multidisciplinary Approach.* Academic Press, New York.

Guillette, L. J., T. S. Gross, G. R. Masson, J. M. Matter, and others, 1994. Developmental abnormalities of the gonad and abnormal sex hormone concentrations in juvenile alligators from contaminated and control lakes in Florida. *Env. Health Persp.*, 102: 680–688.

Gurdon, J. B., 1960. The effects of ultraviolet irradiation on uncleaved eggs of *Xenopus laevis. Quart. J. Micr. Sci.*, 101: 299–311.

Haas, J. D., 1976. Individual differences in the vocalizations of the bullfrog (*Rana catesbeiana). Herp. Rev.*, 7: 86.

Habermehl, G., 1971. Toxicology, pharmacology, chemistry and biochemistry of salamander venom. In W. Bücherl and E. E. Buckley, eds., *Venomous Animals and Their Venoms*, vol. 2, *Venomous Vertebrates.* Academic Press, New York.

Haddad, C.F.B., J. P. Pombal, Jr., and M. Gordo, 1990. Foam nesting in a hylid frog (Amphibia, Anura). *Jour. Herp.*, 24: 225–226.

Hailman, J. P., 1976. Oil droplets in the eyes of adult anuran amphibians: A comparative survey. *Jour. Morphol.*, 148: 453–468.

Hailman, J. P., and R. G. Jaeger, 1974. Phototactic responses to spectrally dominant stimuli and use of color vision by adult anuran amphibians: A comparative survey. *Anim. Behav.* 22: 757–795.

Hairston, N. G., Sr., 1987. *Community Ecology and Salamander Guilds.* Cambridge University Press, Cambridge, U.K..

Hall, R. J., and P. F. P. Henry, 1992. Assessing effects of pesticides on amphibians and reptiles: Status and needs. *Herp. Jour.*, 2: 65–71.

Halliday, T. R., and P. A. Verrell, 1988. Body size and age in amphibians and reptiles. *Jour. Herp.*, 22: 253–265.

Halpern, M., 1983. Nasal chemical senses in snakes. In J. P. Ewert, R. R. Capranica, and D. J. Ingle, eds., *Advances in Vertebrate Neuroethology.* NATO Adv. Stud. Inst. Ser. A, Life Sci., vol. 56. Plenum Press, New York and London.

Hamilton, W. J., Jr., 1948. The food and feeding behavior of the green frog, *Rana clamitans* Latreille, in New York state. *Copeia*, 1948: 203–207.

Hammen, C. S., and V. H. Hutchison, 1962. Carbon dioxide assimilation in the symbiosis of the salamander *Ambystoma maculatum* and the alga *Oophila amblystomatis. Life Sciences*, 10: 527–532.

Hardy, M. P., and J. N. Dent, 1988. Behavioral observations on the transfer of sperm from the male to the female red-spotted newt (*Notophthalmus viridescens*). *Copeia*, 1988: 789–792.

Harfenist, A., T. Power, K. L. Clark, and D. B. Peakall, 1989. A review and evaluation of the amphibian toxicological literature. Technical Report Series, no. 61, Can. Wildl. Service.

Harlan, R. A., and R. F. Wilkinson, 1981. The effects of progressive hypoxia and rocking activity on blood oxygen tension for hellbenders, *Cryptobranchus alleganiensis. Jour. Herp.*, 15: 383–387.

Harlow, H. J., 1977. Seasonal oxygen metabolism and cutaneous osmoregulation in the California newt, *Taricha torosa. Physiol. Zool.* 50: 231–236.

Harrison, R. G., 1969. Harrison stages and description of the normal development of the spotted salamander, *Ambystoma punctatum* (Linn.). In R. G. Harrison, ed., *Organization and Development of the Embryo.* Yale University Press, New Haven and London.

Harte, J., and E. Hoffman, 1989. Possible effects of acidic deposition on a Rocky Mountain population of the tiger salamander, *Ambystoma tigrinum. Conserv. Biol.*, 3: 149–158.

Hassinger, D. D., 1970. Notes on the thermal properties of frog eggs. *Herpetologica*, 26: 49–51.

Hayes, F. E., 1989. Antipredator behavior of recently metamorphosed toads (*Bufo a. americanus*) during encounters with garter snakes (*Thamnophis s. sirtalis*). *Copeia*, 1989: 1011–1015.

Hayes, M. P., 1994a. The spotted frog (*Rana pretiosa*) in western Oregon. Report for Oregon Department of Fish and Wildlife.

Hayes, M. P., 1994b. Current status of the spotted frog (*Rana pretiosa*) in western Oregon. Report to Oregon Department of Fish and Wildlife.

Hayes, M. P., and M. R. Jennings, 1988. Habitat correlates of distribution of the California red-legged frog (*Rana aurora draytonii*) and the foothill yellow-legged frog (*Rana boylii*): Implications for management, pp. 144–158. Symposium—Management of amphibians, reptiles and small mammals in North America, Flagstaff, Arizona, July 19–21, 1988.

Hayes, W. J., Jr., and E. R. Laws, Jr., eds., 1991. *Handbook of pesticide toxicology*, vols. 1–3. Academic Press, San Diego.

Hedlund, L., 1990. Courtship display in a natural population of crested newts, *Triturus cristatus*. *Ethology*, 85: 279–288.

Hendrickson, J. R., 1954. Ecology and systematics of salamanders of the genus *Batrachoseps*. *Univ. Calif. Publ. Zool.*, 54: 1–46.

Hensel, J. L., Jr., and E. D. Brodie, Jr., 1976. An experimental study of aposematic coloration in the salamander *Plethodon jordani*. *Copeia*, 1976: 59–65.

Hershey, J. L., and D. C. Forester, 1980. Sensory orientation in *Notophthalmus v. viridescens* (Amphibia: Salamandridae). *Can. J. Zool.*, 58: 266–276.

Hetherington, T. E., 1988a. Biomechanics of vibration reception in the bullfrog, *Rana catesbeiana*. *J. Comp. Physiol. (A)*, 163: 43–52.

Hetherington, T. E., 1988b. Metamorphic changes in the middle ear. In B. Fritzsch, M. J. Ryan, W. Wilczynski, T. E. Hetherington, and W. Walkowink, eds., *The Evolution of the Amphibian Auditory System*. John Wiley and Sons, New York.

Hetherington, T. E., and R. E. Lombard, 1981. Electromyography of the opercularis muscle of *Rana catesbeiana*. *Amer. Zool.*, 21: 1007 (abstr.).

Hetherington, T. E., and M. H. Wake, 1979. The lateral line system in larval *Ichthyophis* (Amphibia: Gymnophiona). *Zoomorphology*, 93: 209–225.

Heusser, H., 1960. Über die Beziehungen der Erdkröte (*Bufo bufo* L.) zu ihrem Laichplatz, II. *Behaviour*, 16: 94–109.

Heusser, H., 1968. Die Lebensweise der Erdkröte, *Bufo bufo* L.: Wanderungen und Sommerquartiere. *Rev. Suisse Zool.*, 75: 928–982.

Hews, D. K., 1988. Alarm response in larval western toads, *Bufo boreas*: Release of larval chemicals by a natural predator and its effect on predator capture efficiency. *Anim. Behav.*, 35: 125–133.

Hews, D. K., and A. R. Blaustein, 1985. An investigation of the alarm response of *Bufo boreas* and *Rana cascadae* tadpoles. *Behav. Neur. Biol.*, 43: 47–57.

Heyer, W. R., 1969. The adaptive ecology of the species groups of the genus *Leptodactylus* (Amphibia, Leptodactylidae). *Evolution*, 23: 421–428.

Heyer, W. R., 1976. Studies in larval amphibian habitat partitioning. *Smithsonian Contrib. Zool.*, 242: 1–27.

Heyer, W. R., M. A. Donnelly, R. W. McDiarmid, L. C. Hayek, and M. S. Foster, eds., 1994. *Measuring and Monitoring Biological Diversity: Standard Methods for Amphibians*. Smithsonian Institution Press, Washington, D.C., and London.

Higgins, G. M., and C. Sheard, 1926. Effects of ultraviolet radiation on the early larval development of *Rana pipiens*. *J. Exp. Zool.*, 46: 333–343.

Hileman, B., 1994. Environmental estrogens linked to reproductive abnormalities, cancer. *Chem. and Eng. News*, January 31, 1994, 19–23.

Hillman, S. S., 1980. Physiological correlates of differential dehydration tolerance in anuran amphibians. *Copeia*, 1980: 125–129.

Himstedt, W., 1972. Untersuchungen zum Farbensehen von Urodelen. *J. Comp. Physiol.* 81A: 229–238.

Himstedt, W., 1979. The significance of color signals in partner recognition of the newt *Triturus alpestris. Copeia*, 1979: 40–43.

Hodge, R. P., 1976. *Amphibians and Reptiles in Alaska, the Yukon and Northwest Territories*. Alaska Northwest Publishing Co., Anchorage.

Hoff, K. V., and S. D. Hillyard, 1991. Angiotensin 11 stimulates cutaneous drinking in the toad *Bufo punctatus. Physiol. Zool.*, 64: 1165–1172.

Hoff, K. V., and S. D. Hillyard, 1993. Toads taste sodium with their skin: Sensory function in a transporting epithelium. *J. Exp. Biol.*, 183: 347–351.

Hoppe, D. M., 1978. Thermal tolerance in tadpoles of the chorus frog *Pseudacris triseriata. Herpetologica*, 34: 318–321.

Hoppe, D. M., 1979. The influence of color on behavioral thermoregulation and hydroregulation. In E. H. Burtt, Jr., ed., *The Behavioral Significance of Color*. Garland Press, New York.

Houck, L. D., 1977. Life history patterns and reproductive biology of neotropical salamanders. In D. H. Taylor and S. I. Guttman, eds., *The Reproductive Biology of Amphibians*. Plenum Press, New York.

Houck, L. D., 1982. Male tail loss and courtship success in the plethodontid salamander *Desmognathus ochrophaeus. Jour. Herp.*, 16: 335–340.

Houck, L. D., S. J. Arnold, and A. R. Hickman, 1988. Tests for sexual isolation in plethodontid salamanders (genus *Desmognathus*). *Jour. Herp.*, 22: 186–191.

Houck, L.D., and K. Schwenk, 1984. The potential for long-term sperm competition in a plethodontid salamander. *Herpetologica*, 40: 410–415.

Houck, L. D., S. G. Tilley,, and S. J. Arnold, 1985. Sperm competition in a plethodontid salamander: Preliminary results. *Jour. Herp.*, 19: 420–423.

Howard, J. H., R. L. Wallace,, and J. R. Stauffer Jr., 1983. Critical thermal maxima in populations of *Ambystoma macrodactylum* from different elevations. *Jour. Herp.*, 17: 400–402.

Howard, R. D., 1978a. The evolution of mating strategies in bullfrogs, *Rana catesbeiana. Evolution*, 32: 850–871.

Howard, R. D., 1978b. The influence of male-defended oviposition sites on early embryo mortality in bullfrogs. *Ecology*, 59: 789–798.

Howard, R. D., 1980. Mating behavior, and mating success in woodfrogs *Rana sylvatica. Anim. Behav.*, 28: 705–716.

Howard, R. R., and E. D. Brodie, Jr. 1973. A Batesian mimetic complex in salamanders: Responses of avian predators. *Herpetologica*, 29: 33–41.

Huey, R. B., 1980. Sprint velocity of tadpoles (*Bufo boreas*) through metamorphosis. *Copeia*, 1980: 537–540.

Huheey, J. E., and R. A. Brandon, 1973. Rock-face populations of the mountain salamander, *Desmognathus ochrophaeus*, in North Carolina. *Ecol. Monogr.*, 43: 59–77.

Hurlbert, S. H., 1970. Predator responses to the vermilion-spotted newt (*Notophthalmus viridescens*). *Jour. Herp.*, 4: 47–55.

Hutchison, M. N, and L. R. Maxson, 1987. Biochemical studies on the relationships of the gastric-brooding frogs, genus *Rheobatrachus. Amphibia-Reptilia*, 8: 1–11.

Hutchison, V. H., 1961. Critical thermal maxima in salamanders. *Physiol. Zool.*, 34: 92–125.

Hutchison, V. H., and D. J. Erskine, 1981. Thermal selection, and prostaglandin E_1 fever in the salamander *Necturus maculosus. Herpetologica*, 37: 195–198.

Hutchison, V. H., and C. S. Hammen, 1958. Oxygen utilization in the symbiosis of embryos of the salamander, *Ambystoma maculatum*, and the alga, *Oophila amblysto-matis*. *Biol. Bull.*, 155: 483–489.

Hutchison, V. H., and L. G. Hill, 1978. Thermal selection of bullfrog tadpoles (*Rana catesbeiana*) at different stages of development and acclimation temperatures. *J. Thermal. Biol.*, 3: 57–60.

Hutchison, V. H., and K. Miller, 1979. Anaerobic capacity of amphibians. *Comp. Biochem. Physiol.*, 63A: 213–216.

Hutchison, V. H., and K. K. Spriestersbach, 1986. Diel and seasonal cycles of activity and behavioral thermoregulation in the salamander *Necturus maculosus*. *Copeia*, 1986: 612–618.

Inger, R. F., and H. K. Voris, 1988. Taxonomic status and reproductive biology of Bornean tadpole-carrying frogs. *Copeia*, 1988: 1060–1061.

Inger, R. F., H. K. Voris, and P. Walker, 1986. Larval transport in a Bornean ranid frog. *Copeia*, 1986: 523–525.

Ingram, G. J., M. Anstis, and C. J. Corben, 1975. Observations on the Australian lepto-dactylid frog, *Assa darlingtoni*. *Herpetologica*, 31: 425–429.

Jacobs, A. J., and D. H. Taylor, 1992. Chemical communication between *Desmognathus quadramaculatus* and *Desmognathus monticola*. *Jour. Herp.*, 26: 93–95.

Jacobson, S. K., 1985. Reproductive behavior and male mating success in two species of glass frogs (Centrolenidae). *Herpetologica*, 41: 396–404.

Jaeger, R. G., 1976. A possible prey-call window in anuran auditory perception. *Copeia*, 1976: 833–834.

Jaeger, R.G., 1981. Dear enemy recognition and the costs of aggression between salamanders. *Amer. Nat.*, 117: 962–974.

Jaeger, R. G., 1984. Agonistic behavior of the red-backed salamander. *Copeia*, 1984: 309–314.

Jaeger, R. G., and J. P. Hailman, 1976. Ontogenetic shift of spectral phototactic preferences in anuran tadpoles. *J. Comp. and Physiol. Psych.*, 90: 930–945.

Jaeger, R. G., and J. P. Hailman, 1981. Activity of neotropical frogs in relation to ambient light. *Biotropica*, 13: 59–65.

Jaeger, R. G., R. G. Joseph, and D. E. Barnard, 1981. Foraging tactics of a terrestrial salamander: Sustained yield in territories. *Anim. Behav.*, 29: 1100–1105.

Jaeger, R. G., and A. M. Rubin, 1982. Foraging tactics of terrestrial salamander: Judging prey profitability. *J. Anim. Ecol.*, 51: 167–176.

Jaeger, R. G., and J. K. Schwarz, 1991. Gradational threat postures by the red-backed salamander. *Jour. Herp.*, 1991: 112–114.

Jaeger, R. G., and S. E. Wise, 1991. A reexamination of the male salamander "sexy faeces hypothesis." *Jour. Herp.*, 25: 370–373.

Jameson, D. L., 1957. Population structure and homing responses in the Pacific tree frog. *Copeia*, 1957: 221–228.

Jameson, D. L., and S. Pequegnat, 1971. Estimation of relative viability and fecundity of color poymorphisms in anurans. *Evolution*, 25: 180–194.

Jamison, J. A., and R. N. Harris, 1992. The priority of linear over volumetric caudal regeneration in the salamander *Plethodon cinereus* (Caudata: Plethodontidae). *Copeia*, 1992: 235–237.

Jennings, W. B., D. F. Bradford, and D. F. Johnson, 1992. Dependence of the garter snake *Thamnophis elegans* on amphibians in the Sierra Nevada of California. *Jour. Herp.*, 26: 503–505.

John, K. R., and D. Fenster, 1975. The effects of partitions on the growth rates of crowded *Rana pipiens* tadpoles. *Amer. Midland Nat.*, 93: 123–130.

John-Alder, H. B., and P. J. Morin, 1990. Effects of larval density on jumping ability and stamina in newly metamorphosed *Bufo woodhousii fowleri. Copeia*, 1990: 856–860.

Johnson, C. R., 1972. Thermal relations and daily variation in the thermal tolerance in *Bufo marinus. Jour. Herp.*, 6: 35–38.

Johnson, C. R., and C. B. Schreck, 1969. Food and feeding of larval *Dicamptodon ensatus* from California. *Amer. Midland Nat.*, 81: 280–281.

Joly, J., 1966. Sur l'ethologie sexuelle de *Salamandra salamandra* (L.). *Z. Tierpsych.*, 23: 8–27.

Jones, L.L.C., 1985. *Ambystoma gracile gracile*: Winter activity. *Herp. Rev.*, 16: 26.

Jones, R. M., 1982. How toads breathe: Control of air flow to and from the lungs by the nares in *Bufo marinus. Respiration Physiol.*, 49: 251–265.

Jordan, O. R., W. W. Byrd, and D. E. Ferguson, 1968. Sun-compass orientation in *Rana pipiens. Herpetologica*, 24: 335–336.

Jørgensen, C. B., 1988. The role of endogenous factors in seasonal maturation in Temperate Zone female toads, *Bufo bufo. Jour. Herp.*, 22: 295–300.

Jørgensen, C. B., 1992. Growth and reproduction. In M. E. Feder and W. W. Burggren, eds., *Environmental Physiology of the Amphibians*, University of Chicago Press, Chicago and London.

Kagarise Sherman, C., and M. L. Morton, 1993. Population decline of Yosemite toads in the eastern Sierra Nevada of California. *Jour. Herp.*, 27: 186–198.

Kaplan, R.H., 1980a. The implications of ovum size variabilty for offspring fitness and clutch size within several populations of salamanders (*Ambystoma*). *Evolution*, 34: 51–64.

Kaplan, R. H., 1980b. Ontogenetic energetics in Ambystoma. *Physiol. Zool.*, 53: 43–56.

Kaplan, R. H., 1985. Maternal influences on offspring development in the California newt, *Taricha torosa. Copeia*, 1985: 1028–1035.

Kaplan, R. H., and P. W. Sherman, 1980. Intraspecific oophagy in California newts. *Jour. Herp.*, 14: 183–185.

Kasbohm, P., 1967. Der Einfluss des Lichtes auf die Temperatur-Adaptation bei *Rana temporaria. Helgoländer wiss. Meeresunters.*, 16: 157–178.

Kasperczyk, M., 1971. Comparative studies on colour sense in Amphibia (*Rana temporaria* L., *Salamandra salamandra* L. and *Triturus cristatus* Laur.). *Folia Biol. (Crakow)*, 19: 241–288.

Kats, L. B., 1988. The detection of certain predators via olfaction by small-mouthed salamander larvae (*Ambystoma texanum*). *Behav. Neur. Biol.*, 50: 126–131.

Kats, L. B., J. W. Petranka, and A. Sih, 1989. Antipredator defenses and the persistence of amphibian larvae with fishes. *Ecology*, 69: 1865–1870.

Kats, L. B., and A. Sih, 1992. Oviposition site selection and avoidance of fish by streamside salamanders (*Ambystoma barbouri*). *Copeia*, 1992: 468–473.

Kauer, J. S., 1974. Response patterns of amphibian olfactory bulb neurones to odour stimulation. *Jour. Physiol.*, 243: 695–715.

Kauer, J. S., and D. G. Moulton, 1974. Responses of olfactory bulb neurones to odor stimulation of small nasal areas in the salamander. *Jour. Physiol.*, 243: 717–737.

Kelleher, K. E., and J. R. Tester, 1969. Homing and survival in the Manitoba toad, *Bufo hemiophrys*, in Minnestoa. *Ecology*, 50: 1040–1048.

Kirk, J. J., 1988. Western spotted frog (*Rana pretiosa*) mortality following forest spraying of DDT. *Herp. Rev.*, 19: 51–53.

Kleeberger, S. R., and J. K. Werner, 1982. Home range and homing behavior of *Plethodon cinereus* in northern Michigan. *Copeia*, 1982: 409–415.

Kluger, M. J., 1977. Fever in the frog *Hyla cinerea. J. Thermal Biol.*, 2: 79–81.

Kluger, M. J., 1979. Fever in ectotherms: Evolutionary implications. *Amer. Zool.*, 19: 295–304.

Knopf, G. N., 1962. Paedogensis and metamorphic variation in *Ambystoma tigrinum mavortium. Southwest. Nat.*, 7: 75–76.

Kobelt, F., and K. E. Linsenmair, 1992. Adaptations of the reed frog *Hyperolius viridiflavus* (Amphibia: Anura: Hyperoliidae) to its arid environment. *J.Comp. Physiol. B.* 162: 314–326.

Kok, D., L. H. du Preez, and A. Channing, 1989. Channel construction by the African bullfrog: Another anuran parental care strategy. *Jour. Herp.*, 23: 435–437.

Kramer, D. C., 1973. Movements of western chorus frogs *Pseudacris triseriata triseriata* tagged with Co^{60}. *Jour. Herp.*, 7: 231–235.

Krupa, J. J., 1988. Fertilization efficiency in the great plains toad (*Bufo cognatus*). *Copeia*, 1988: 800–802.

Kruse, K. C., 1981a. Mating success, fertilization potential, and male body size in the American toad (*Bufo americanus*). *Herpetologica*, 37: 228–233.

Kuramoto, M., 1975. Embryonic temperature adaptation in development rate of frogs. *Physiol. Zool.*, 48: 360–366.

Labanick, G. M., 1984. Anti-predator effectiveness of autotomized tails of the salamander *Desmognathus ochrophaeus. Herpetologica*, 40: 110–118.

La Marca, E., and H. P. Reinthaler, 1991. Population changes in *Atelopus* species of the Cordillera de Mérida, Venezuela. *Herp. Rev.*, 22: 125–128.

Landreth, H. F., and Christensen, M. T., 1971. Orientation of the plains spadefoot toad, *Scaphiopus bombifrons*, to solar cues. *Herpetologica*, 27: 454–461.

Landreth, H. F., and D. E. Ferguson, 1967a. Newt orientation by sun-compass. *Nature* 215: 516–518.

Landreth, H. F., and D. E. Ferguson, 1967b. Sun-compass orientation. *Science*, 158: 1459–1461.

Landreth, H. F., and D. E. Ferguson, 1967c. Movements and orientation of the tailed frog, *Ascaphus truei. Herpetologica*, 23: 81–93.

Landreth, H. F., and D. E. Ferguson, 1968. The sun compass of Fowler's toad, *Bufo woodhousei fowleri. Behaviour*, 30: 27–43.

Lannoo, M. J., D. S. Townsend, and R. J. Wassersug, 1987. Larval life in the leaves: Arboreal tadpole types, with special attention to the morphology, ecology, and behavior of the oophagous *Osteopilus brunneus* (Hylidae) larva. *Fieldiana: Zoology*, 38.

Larsen, J. H., Jr., and J. T. Beneski, Jr., 1988. Quantitative analysis of feeding kinematics in dusky salamanders (*Desmognathus*). *Can. J. Zool.*, 66: 1309–1317.

Larsen, J. H., Jr., and D. J. Guthrie, 1975. The feeding system of terrestrial tiger sala-manders (*Ambystoma tigrinum melanostictum* Baird). *Jour. Morphol.*, 147: 137–154.

Larsen, L. O., 1976. Physiology of molting. In B. Lofts, ed., *Physiology of the Am-phibia*, vol. 3. Academic Press, New York and London.

Larsen, L. O., 1992. Feeding and digestion. In M. E. Feder and W. W. Burggren, eds., *Environmental Physiology of the Amphibians*. University of Chicago Press, Chicago and London.

Larsen, L. O., and J. N. Pedersen, 1982. The snapping response of the toad, *Bufo bufo*, towards prey dummies at very low light intensities. *Amphibia-Reptilia*, 2: 321–327.

Lauder, G. V., 1985. Aquatic feeding in lower vertebrates. In M. Hildebrand, D. M. Bramble, K. F. Liem, and D. B. Wake, eds., *Functional Vertebrate Morphol-ogy*. Cambridge University Press, Cambridge, U.K.

Lauder, G. V., and H. B. Shaffer, 1986. Functional design of the feeding mechanism in lower vertebrates: Unidirectional and bidirectional flow systems in the tiger sala-mander. *Zool. J. Linnean Soc.*, 88: 277–290.

Layne, J. R., Jr., and M. A. Romano, 1985. Critical thermal minima of *Hyla chrysoscelis, H. cinerea, H. gratiosa* and natural hybrids (*H. cinerea* x *H. gratiosa*). *Herpetologica*, 41: 216–221.

Lee, A. K., 1967. Studies in Australian Amphibia. II. Taxonomy, ecology, and evolu-tion of the genus *Heleioporus* Gray (Anura: Leptodactylidae). *Aust. J. Zool.*, 15: 367–439.

Lee, A. K., and E. H. Mercer, 1967. Cocoon surrounding desert-dwelling frogs. *Sci-ence*, 157: 87–88.

Lewis, D. L., G. T. Baxter, K. M. Johnson, and M. D. Stone, 1985. Possible extinction of the Wyoming toad, *Bufo hemiophreys baxteri*. *Jour. Herp.*, 19: 166–168.

Lewis, E. R., 1981a. Suggested evolution of tonotopic organization in the frog amphib-ian papilla. *Neurosci. Lett.*, 21: 131–136.

Lewis, E. R., 1981b. Evolution of inner-ear auditory apparatus of the frog. *Brain Res.*, 219: 149–155.

Lewis, E. R., 1984. On the frog amphibian papilla. *Scanning Electron Microsc.*, 1984: 1899–1913.

Lewis, E. R., R. A. Baird, E. L. Leverenz, and H. Koyama, 1982. Inner ear: Dye injec-tion reveals peripheral origin of specific sensitivities. *Science*, 215: 1641–1643.

Lewis, E. R., and P. M. Narins, 1985. Do frogs communicate with seismic signals? *Science*, 227: 187–189.

Licht, L. E., 1967. Growth inhibition in crowded tadpoles: Interspecific effects. *Ecol-ogy*, 48: 736–745.

Licht, L. E., 1969a. Palatability of *Rana* and *Hyla* eggs. *Amer. Midland Nat.*, 82: 296–298.

Licht, L. E., 1969b. Unusual aspects of anuran sexual behavior as seen in the red-legged frog, *Rana aurora aurora*. *Can. J. Zool.* 47: 505–509.

Licht, L. E., 1971. Breeding habits and embryonic thermal requirements of the frogs, *Rana aurora aurora* and *Rana pretiosa pretiosa*, in the Pacific northwest. *Ecology*, 52: 116–124.

Licht, L. E., 1973. Behavior and sound production by the northwestern salamander *Ambystoma gracile*. *Can. J. Zool.*, 51: 1055–1056.

Licht, L. E., 1976. Sexual selection in toads (*Bufo americanus*). *Can. J. Zool.*, 54: 1277–1284.

Licht, L. E., and J. P. Bogart, 1987. Comparative size of epidermal cell nuclei from shed skin of diploid, triploid, and tetraploid salamanders (genus *Ambystoma*). *Copeia*, 1987: 284–290.

Licht, P., and A. G. Brown, 1967. Behavioral thermoregulation and its role in the ecology of the red-bellied newt, *Taricha rivularis*. *Ecology*, 48: 599–611.

Lillywhite, H. B., 1970. Behavioral temperature regulation in the bullfrog, *Rana catesbeiana*. *Copeia*, 1970: 158–168.

Lillywhite, H. B., 1971a. Temperature selection by the bullfrog, *Rana catesbeiana*. *Comp. Biochem. Physiol.*, 40A: 213–227.

Lillywhite, H. B., 1971b. Thermal modulation of cutaneous mucus discharge as a determinant of evaporative water loss in the frog, *Rana catesbeiana*. *Z. Vergl. Physiol.*, 73: 84–104.

Lillywhite, H. B., 1974. How frogs regulate their body temperature. *Environ. Southwest*, 465: 3–6.

Lillywhite, H. B., and P. Licht, 1974. Movement of water over toad skin: Functional role of epidermal sculpturing. *Copeia*, 1974: 165–171.

Lillywhite, H. B., P. Licht, and P. Chelgren, 1972. The role of behavioral thermoregulation in the growth energetics of the toad, *Bufo boreas. Bull. Ecol. Soc. Amer.*, 53: 10.

Lindquist, S. B., and M. D. Bachmann, 1982. The role of visual and olfactory cues in the prey catching behavior of the tiger salamander, *Ambystoma tigrinum. Copeia*, 1982: 81–90.

Linke, R., G. Roth, and B. Rottluff, 1986. Comparative studies on the eye morphology of lungless salamanders, family Plethodontidae, and the effect of miniaturization. *Jour. Morph.*, 189: 131–143.

Littlejohn, M.J., 1965a. Premating isolation in the *Hyla ewingi* complex (Anura: Hylidae). *Evolution*, 19: 234–243.

Littlejohn, M. J., 1965b. Vocal communication in frogs. *Aust. Nat. Hist.*, 15: 52–55.

Littlejohn, M. J., 1977. Long-range acoustic communication in anurans: An integrated and evolutionary approach. In D. H. Taylor and S. I. Guttman, eds., *The Reproductive Biology of Amphibians*. Plenum Press, New York.

Lofts, B., ed., 1974. *Physiology of the Amphiba*, vol. 2, Academic Press, New York and London.

Lofts, B., ed., 1976. *Physiology of the Amphiba*, vol. 3. Academic Press, New York and London.

Loftus-Hills, J. J., and B. M. Johnstone, 1970. Auditory function, communication, and the brain-evoked response in anuran amphibians. *J. Acoust. Soc. Amer.*, 47: 1131–1138.

Loftus-Hills, J. J., and M. J. Littlejohn, 1971. Mating-call sound intensities of anuran amphibians. *J. Acoust. Soc. Amer.*, 49: 1327–1329.

Lombard, R. E., 1977. Comparative morphology of the inner ear in salamanders (Caudata: Amphibia). In M. K. Hecht and F. S. Szalay, eds., *Contributions to Vertebrate Evolution*, vol. 2. Karger, Basel.

Lombard, R. E., and I. R. Straughan, 1974. Functional aspects of anuran middle ear structures. *J. Exp. Biol.*, 61: 71–93.

Lombard, R. E., and D. B. Wake, 1976. Tongue evolution in the lungless salamanders, family Plethodontidae: 1, Introduction, theory and a general model of dynamics. *Jour. Morph.*, 148: 265–286.

Long, D. R., 1989. Energetics and reproduction in female *Scaphiopus multiplicatus* from western Texas. *Jour. Herp.*, 23: 176–179.

Lopez, C. H., and Brodie, E. D., Jr., 1977. The function of costal grooves in salamanders (Amphibia, Urodela). *Jour. Herp.*, 2: 372–374.

Lörcher, K., 1969. Vergleichende bio-akustiche Untersuchungen an der Rot-und Gelb-bauchunke, *Bombina bombina* (L.) und *Bombina v. variegata* (L.). *Oecologia*, 3: 84–124.

Lowcock, L. A., H. Griffith, and R. W. Murphy, 1991. The *Ambystoma laterale–jeffersonianum* complex in central Ontario: Ploidy structure, sex ratio, and breeding dynamics in a bisexual-unisexual community. *Copeia*, 1991: 87–105.

Lucas, E. A., and W. A. Reynolds, 1967. Temperature selection by amphibian larvae. *Physiol. Zool.*, 40: 159–171.

Luthardt, G., and G. Roth, 1979. The relationship between stimulus orientation and stimulus movement pattern in the prey catching behavior of *Salamandra salamandra. Copeia*, 1979: 442–447.

Luthardt-Laimer, G., 1983. Ontogeny of preferences to visual prey stimulus parameters in salamanders. *Jour. Herp.*, 17: 221–227.

Lutz, B., 1960. Fighting and an incipient notion of territory in male tree frogs. *Copeia*, 1960: 61–63.

Lutz, B., 1971. Venomous toads and frogs. In W. Bücherl and E. E. Buckley, *Venomous Animals and Their Venoms*, vol. 2, *Venomous Vertebrates*. Academic Press, New York.

Lynch, J. F., 1985. The feeding ecology of *Aneides flavipunctatus* and sympatric plethodontid salamanders in northwestern California. *Jour. Herp.*, 19: 328–352.

MacArthur, D. L., and J.W.T. Dandy, 1982. Physiological aspects of overwintering in the boreal chorus frog (*Pseudacris triseriata maculata*). *Comp. Biochem. Physiol.* 72A: 137–141.

Madison, D. M., 1969. Homing behavior of the red-cheeked salamander, *Plethodon jordani. Anim. Behav.*, 17: 25–39.

Madison, D. M., and C. R. Shoop, 1970. Homing behavior, orientation, and home range of salamanders tagged with tantalum-182. *Science*, 168: 1484–1487.

Mahoney, J. J., and V. H. Hutchison, 1969. Photoperiod acclimation and 24-hour variations in the critical thermal maxima of a tropical and a temperate frog. *Oecologia*, 2: 143–161.

Maina, J. N., and G.M.O. Maloiy, 1988. A scanning and transmission electron microscopic study of the lung of a caecilian *Boulengerula taitanus. Jour. Zool., London*, 215: 739–751.

Maiorana, V. C., 1974. Studies in the behavioral ecology of the plethodontid salamander *Batrachoseps altennatus*. Ph.D. dissertation, University of California, Berkeley.

Maiorana, V. C., 1977. Tail autotomy, functional conflicts and their resolution by a salamander. *Nature*, 265: 533–535.

Maiorana, V. C., 1978. Behavior of an unobservable species: Diet selection by a salamander. *Copeia*, 1978: 664–672.

Malvin, G. M., 1988. Microvascular regulation of cutaneous gas exchange in amphibians. *Amer. Zool.*, 28: 999–1007.

Maness, J. D., and V. H. Hutchison. 1980. Acute adjustment of thermal tolerance in vertebrate ectotherms following exposure to critical thermal maxima. *J. Thermal. Biol.*, 5: 225–233.

Manteuffel, G., L. Plasa, T. J. Sommer, and O. Wess, 1977. Involuntary eye movements in salamanders. *Naturwissenschaften*, 64: 533.

Marchisin, A., and J. D., Anderson, 1978. Strategies employed by frogs and toads (Amphibia, Anura) to avoid predation by snakes (Reptilia, Serpentes). *Jour. Herp.*, 12: 151–155.

Márquez-M. de Orense, R., and M. Tejedo-Madueño, 1990. Size-based mating pattern in the treefrog *Hyla arborea*. *Herpetologica*, 46: 176–182.

Marshall, C. H., L. S. Doyle, and R. H. Kaplan, 1990. Intraspecific and sex-specific oophagy in a salamander and a frog: Reproductive convergence of *Tarica torosa* and *Bombina orientalis*. *Herpetologica*, 46: 395–399.

Martin, D. L., 1991. Population census of a species of special concern: The Yosemite toad (*Bufo canorus*). Fourth Biennial Conf. of Research in California's National Parks. University of California, Davis, Sept. 10–12, 1991 (abstr.).

Martin, D. L., 1992. Sierra Nevada anuran survey: An investigation of amphibian population abundance in the National Forests of the Sierra Nevada of California. (Contributing scientists: W. E. Bros, D. L. Dondero, M. R. Jennings, and H. H. Welsh.) Prepared for the U.S. Forest Service, Report V.1.1.

Martin, J. B., N. B. Witherspoon, and M.H.A. Keenleyside, 1974. Analysis of feeding behavior in the newt *Notophthalmus viridescens*. *Can. J. Zool.*, 52: 277–281.

Martins, M., 1989. Deimatic behavior in *Pleurodema brachyops*. *Jour. Herp.*, 23: 305–307.

Martins, M., and C.F.B. Haddad, 1988. Vocalizations and reproductive behavior in the Smith frog, *Hyla faber* Wied (Amphibia: Hylidae). *Amphibia-Reptilia*, 9: 49–60.

Martof, B. S., 1953a. Territoriality in the green frog, *Rana clamitans*. *Ecology*, 34: 165–174.

Martof, B. S., 1953b. Home range and movements of the green frog, *Rana clamitans*. *Ecology*, 34: 529–543.

Marynick, S. P., 1971. Long term storage of sperm in *Desmognathus fuscus* from Louisiana. *Copeia*, 1971: 345–347.

Mason, J. R., M. D. Rabin, and D. A. Stevens, 1982. Conditioned taste aversions: Skin secretions used for defence by tiger salamanders, *Ambystoma tigrinum*. *Copeia*, 1982: 667–671.

Massey, A., 1990. Notes on the reproductive ecology of red-spotted newts (*Notophthalmus viridescens*). *Jour. Herp.*, 24: 106–107.

Mathis, A., 1989. Do seasonal spatial distributions in a terrestrial salamander reflect reproductive behavior or territoriality? *Copeia*, 1989: 788–791.

Matthews, G., 1983. Physiological characteristics of single green rod photoreceptors from toad retina. *J. Physiol., London*, 342: 347–359.

Mauger, D., 1988. Observation on calling behavior of bullfrogs in relation to male mating strategy. *Bull. Chi. Herp. Soc.*, 23: 57–59.

Mauger, D., 1989. Analysis of calling behavior of the bullfrog (*Rana catesbeiana*) in several northeastern Illinois populations. *Bull. Chi. Herp. Soc.*, 24: 208–215.

McAllister, K. R., and B. Leonard, 1991. Past distribution and current status of the spotted frog in western Washington. Washington Department of Wildlife, Wildlife Management, 1990 Progress Report.

McAllister, K. R., and W. P. Leonard, 1993. Searches for spotted frogs (*Rana pretiosa*) and other amphibians on National Forest lands in Washington, 1993. Unpubl. report, Washington Department of Wildlife, Olympia.

McAllister, K. R., W. P. Leonard, and R. M. Storm, 1993. Spotted frog (*Rana pretiosa*) surveys in the Puget Trough of Washington, 1989–1991. *Northwest. Nat.*, 74: 10–15.

McClanahan, L. L., Jr., 1972. Changes in body fluids of burrowed spadefoot toads as a function of soil water potential. *Copeia*, 1972: 209–216.

McClanahan, L. L., Jr., and V. H. Shoemaker, 1987. Behavior and thermal relations of the arboreal frog *Phyllomedusa sauvegei*. *Natl. Geogr. Research*, 3: 11–21.

McClanahan, L. L., Jr., V. H. Shoemaker, and R. Ruibal, 1976. Structure and function of the cocoon of a ceratophryd frog. *Copeia*, 1976: 179–185.

McDiarmid, R. W., 1978. Evolution of parental care in frogs. In G. M. Burghardt and M. Bekoff, eds., *The Development of Behavior: Comparative and Evolutionary Aspects*. Garland Press, New York.

McDiarmid, R. W., and M. S. Foster, 1987. Cocoon formation in another hylid frog, *Smilisca baudinii*. *Jour. Herp.*, 21: 352–355.

McFarland, W. N., 1955. Upper lethal temperatures in the salamander *Taricha torosa* as a function of acclimation. *Copeia*, 1955: 191–194.

McGavin, M., 1978. Recognition of conspecific odors by the salamander *Plethodon cinereus*. *Copeia*, 1978: 356–358.

McGregor, J. H., and W. R. Teska, 1989. Olfaction as an orientation mechanism in migrating *Ambystoma maculatum*. *Copeia*, 1989: 779–781.

McLachlan, J. A., R. R. Newbold, C. T. Teng, and K. S. Korach, 1992. Environmental estrogens: Orphan receptors and genetic imprinting. In T. Colborn and C. Clement, eds., *Chemically-induced Alterations in Sexual and Functional Development: The Wildlife/Human Connection*. Princeton Scientific Publishing Co., Princeton, N.J.

McLaren, I. A., and J. M. Cooley, 1972. Temperature adaptation of embryronic development rate among frogs. *Physiol. Zool.*, 45: 223–228.

McMahon, S. H., and D. I. Pav, 1982. Histological examination of the integument of fifteen species of plethodontid salamanders (Amphibia: Urodela: Plethodontidae). *J. Tenn. Acad. Sci.*, 57: 78–81.

McVey, M., T. Born, E. Hanson, and P. Trenhan, 1992. Biological populations as indicators of environmental change, eds. D. E. Hyatt and O. Gutenson. U.S. Environmental Protection Agency, Office of Policy, Planning, and Evaluation, Washington, D.C. (Draft.)

McVey, M. E., R. G. Zahary, D. Perry, and J. MacDougal, 1981. Territoriality and homing behavior in the poison dart frog (*Dendrobates pumilio*). *Copeia*, 1981: 1–8.

Meadows, D. H., D. L. Meadows, and J. Randers, 1992. *Beyond the Limits: Confronting Global Collapse, Envisioning a Sustainable Future*. Chelsea Green Publishing, Post Mills, Vt.

Melack, J. C., S. D. Cooper, and R. W. Holmes, 1987. Chemical and biological survey of lakes and streams located in the Emerald Lake watershed, Sequoia National Park. Final report to the California Air Resources Board, Sacramento, contract no. A3–096–32.

Melack, J. M., J. O. Sickman, F. V. Setaro, and D. Engle, 1993. Long-term studies of lakes and watersheds in the Sierra Nevada: Patterns and processes of surface-water acidification. Final report to California Air Resources Board, Sacramento, contract no. A932–060.

Merchant, H., 1972. Estimated population size and home range of the salamanders *Plethodon jordani* and *Plethodon glutinosus J. Wash. Acad. Sci.*, 62: 248–257.

Mitchell, S. L., 1990. The mating system genetically affects offspring perfomance in Woodhouse's toad (*Bufo woodhousei*). *Evolution*, 44: 502–519.

Moll, E. O., and H. M. Smith, 1967. Lizards in the diet of an American caecilian. *Nat. Hist. Misc.* (Chicago Acad. Sciences), 187: 1–2.

Möller, A., 1951. Die Struktur des Auges bei Urodelen verschiedener Körpergrösse. *Zool. Jahrb., Abt. Allg. Zool. Physiol. Tiere*, 62: 138–182.

Moodie, G.E.E., 1978. Observations on the life history of the caecilian *Typhlonectes compressicaudus* (Dumeril and Bibron) in the Amazon basin. *Can. J. Zool.*, 56: 1005–1008.

Moore, F. L., 1978. Effects of progesterone on sexual attractivity in female rough-skinned newts, *Taricha granulosa. Copeia*, 1978: 530–532.

Moore, J. A., 1939. Temperature tolerance and rates of development in the eggs of Amphibia. *Ecology*, 20: 459–478.

Moore, J. A., 1949a. Geographic variation of adaptive characters in *Rana pipiens* Schreber. *Evolution*, 3: 1–24.

Moore, J. A., 1949b. Patterns of evolution in the genus *Rana*. In G. Jepsen et al., eds., *Genetics, Paleontology, and Evolution*. Princeton University Press, Princeton, N.J.

Moore, J. A., ed., 1964. *Physiology of the Amphibia*, vols. 1–3. Academic Press, New York and London.

Morton, M. L., 1981. Seasonal changes in total body lipid and liver weight in the Yosemite toad. *Copeia*, 1981: 234–238.

Mosher, H. S., and F. A. Fuhrman, 1984. Occurrence and origin of tetrodotoxin. In E. P. Ragelis, ed., *Seafood Toxins.* Amer. Chem. Soc. Symposium Series, no. 262: 333–344.

Muntz, W.R.A., 1964. Vision in frogs. *Sci. Amer.*, 210: 110–119

Murphy, J. B., 1976. Pedal luring in the leptodactylid frog, *Ceratophrys calcarata* Boulenger. *Herpetologica*, 32: 339–341.

Murphy, J. B., H. Quinn, and J. A. Campbell, 1977. Observations on the breeding habits of the aquatic caecilian *Typhlonectes compressicaudus. Copeia*, 1977: 66–69.

Myers, C. W., and J. W. Daly, 1976. Preliminary evaluation of skin toxins and vocalizations in taxonomic and evolutionary studies of poison-dart frogs (Dendrobatidae). *Bull. Amer. Mus. Nat. Hist.*, 157: 173–262.

Myers, C. W., J. W. Daly, and B. Malkin, 1978. A dangerously toxic new frog (*Phyllobates*) used by Emberá indians of western Colombia, with discussion of blowgun fabrication and dart poisoning. *Bull. Amer. Mus. Nat. Hist.*, 161: 309–365.

Myhre, K., M. Cabanac, and G. Myhre, 1977. Fever and behavioral temperature regulation in the frog, *Rana esculenta. Acta Physiol. Scand.*, 101: 219–229.

Nace, G. W., 1970. The use of amphibians in biomedical research. In *Animal Models for Biomedical Research*, vol. 3. Proceedings of a Symposium. National Academy of Sciences, Washington, D.C.

Narins, P. M., 1976. Auditory processing of biologically meaningful sounds of the treefrog, *Eleutherodactylus coqui.* Ph.D. dissertation, Cornell University, Ithaca, New York.

Narins, P. M., 1992. Biological constraints on anuran acoustic communication: Auditory capabilities of naturally behaving animals. In D. B. Webster, R. R. Fay, and A. N. Popper, eds., *The Evolutionary Biology of Hearing.* Springer-Verlag, New York, Berlin, etc.

Narins, P. M., and R. R. Capranica, 1976. Sexual differences in the auditory system of the tree frog *Eleutherodactylus coqui. Science,* 192: 378–380.

Narins, P. M., and D. D. Hurley, 1982. The relationship between call intensity and function in the Puerto Rican coqui (Anura: Leptodactylidae). *Herpetologica,* 38: 287–295.

Neill, W. T., 1955. Posture of chilled newts (*Diemyctylus viridescens louisianensis*). *Copeia,* 1955:61.

Nevo, E., and H. Schneider, 1975. Mating call pattern of green toads in Israel and its ecological correlate. *J. Zool., London,* 178: 133–145.

Newman, R. A., 1988a. Adaptive plasticity in development of *Scaphiopus couchii* tadpoles in desert ponds. *Evolution,* 42: 774–783.

Newman, R. A., 1988b. Genetic variation for larval anuran (*Scaphiopus couchii*) development time in an uncertain environment. *Evolution,* 42: 763–773.

Newman, R. A., 1989. Developmental plasticity of *Scaphiopus couchii* tadpoles in an unpredictable environment. *Ecology,* 70: 1775–1787.

Nishikawa, K. C., 1989. "Organismal" vs. "mechanistic" biology. *Herpetologica,* 45: 473–479.

Nishikawa, K. C., 1990. Intraspecific spatial relationships of two species of terrestrial salamanders. *Copeia,* 1990: 418–426.

Nishikawa, K. C., and P. M. Service, 1988. A fluorescent marking technique for individual recognition of terrestrial salamanders. *Jour. Herp.,* 22: 351–353.

Noble, G. K., 1931. *The Biology of the Amphibia.* McGraw-Hill, New York; printed by Dover Publications, 1954.

Noble, G. K., and Aronson, L. R., 1942. The sexual behavior of Anura. I. The normal mating pattern of *Rana pipiens. Bull. Amer. Mus. Nat. Hist.,* 80: 127–142.

Noble, G. K., and Farris, E. J., 1929. The method of sex recognition in the wood-frog, *Rana sylvatica* Le Conte. *Amer. Mus. Novitates,* 363: 1–17.

Noguchi, T., D. F. Hwang, O. Arakawa, H. Sugita, Y. Deguchi, Y. Shida, and K. Hashimoto, 1987. *Vibrio alginolyticus,* a tetrodotoxin-producing bacterium in the intestine of the fish *Fugu vermicularis vermicularis. Marine Biology,* 94: 625–630.

Noguchi, T., J. Jeon, O. Arakawa, H. Sugita, Y. Deguchi, Y. Shida, and K. Hashimoto, 1986. Occurrence of tetrodotoxin and anhydrotetrodotoxin in *Vibrio* sp. isolated from the intestines of a xantid crab, *Atergatis floridus. Jour. Biochem.,* 99: 311–314.

Nowak, R. T., and E. D. Brodie, Jr., 1976. Rib penetration as an antipredator mechanism in *Pleurodeles waltl. Herp. Rev.,* 7: 94.

Nussbaum, R. A., E. D. Brodie, Jr., and R. M. Storm, 1983. *Amphibians and Reptiles of the Pacific Northwest.* University Press of Idaho, Moscow.

Nussbaum, R. A., and M. Wilkinson, 1989. On the classification and phylogeny of caecilians (Amphibia: Gymnophiona), a critical review. *Herp. Monogr.,* 3: 1–42.

Obert, H., 1977. Hormonal influences on calling and reproductive behavior in anurans.

In D. H. Taylor and S. I. Guttman, eds., *The Reproductive Biology of Amphibians.* Plenum Press, New York.

O'Hara, R. K., and A. R. Blaustein, 1981. An investigation of sibling recognition in *Rana cascadae* tadpoles. *Anim. Behav.*, 29: 1121–1126.

Oldham, R. S., 1967. Orienting mechanisms of the green frog, *Rana clamitans. Ecology* 48: 477–491.

Oldham, R. S., 1975. Ovulation induced by vocalization in members of the *Rana pipiens* complex. *Jour. Herp.*, 9: 248–249.

Oliver, J. A., 1951. "Gliding" in amphibians and reptiles, with a remark on an arboreal adaptation in the lizard, *Anolis carolinensis carolinensis* Voight. *Amer. Nat.*, 85: 171–176.

Oliver, J. A., 1955. *The Natural History of North American Amphibians and Reptiles.* D. Van Nostrand, Princeton, N.J.

Olson, L. J., B. J. Erickson, R. D. Hinsdill, J. A. Wyman, W. P. Porter, L. K. Binning, R. C. Bidgood, and E. V. Nordheim, 1987. Aldicarb immunomodulation in mice: An inverse dose-response to parts per billion levels in drinking water. *Arch. Environ. Contam. Toxicol.*, 16: 433–439.

Organ, J. A., 1958. Courtship and spermatophore of *Plethodon jordani metcalf. Copeia*, 1958: 251–259.

Organ, J. A., 1960. The courtship and spermatophore of the salamander *Plethodon glutinosus. Copeia*, 1960: 287–297.

Organ, J. A., 1968. Courtship behavior and spermatophore of the cave salamander, *Eurycea lucifuga* (Rafinesque). *Copeia*, 1968: 576–580.

Organ, J. A., and L. A. Lowenthal, 1963. Comparative studies of macroscopic and microscopic features of spermatophores of some plethodontid salamanders. *Copeia*, 1963: 659–669.

Organ, J. A., and D. J. Organ, 1968. Courtship behavior of the red salamander, *Pseudotriton ruber. Copeia*, 1968: 217–223.

Orr, L. P., and W. T. Maple, 1978. Competition avoidance mechanisms in salamander larvae of the genus *Desmognathus. Copeia*, 1978: 679–685.

Orton, G. L., 1953. The systematics of vertebrate larvae. *Syst. Zool.*, 2: 63–75.

Ovaska, K., 1988. Spacing and movements of the salamander *Plethodon vehiculum. Herpetologica*, 44: 377–386.

Ovaska, K., 1992. Short- and long-term movements of the frog *Eleutherodactylus johnstonei* in Barbados, West Indies. *Copeia*, 1992: 569–573.

Ovaska, K., and W. Hunte, 1992. Male mating behavior of the frog *Eleutherodactyus johnstonei* (Leptodactylidae) in Barbados, West Indies. *Herpetologica*, 48: 40–49.

Özeti, N., and D. B. Wake, 1969. The morphology and evolution of the tongue and associated structures in salamanders and newts (family Salamandridae). *Copeia*, 1969: 91–123.

Papenfuss, T., 1980. Sierra Nevada foothills amphibian and reptile survey. Prepared for the Bureau of Land Management, Folsom, Calif.

Passmore, N. I., 1981. Sound levels of mating calls of some African frogs. *Herpetologica*, 37: 116–171.

Passmore, N. I., and S. R. Telford, 1981. The effect of chorus organization on mate localization in the painted reed frog (*Hyperolius marmoratus*). *Behav. Ecol. Sociobiol.*, 9: 291–293.

Patla, D. A., and C. R. Peterson, 1993. The effects of habitat modification on a spotted frog population in Yellowstone National Park. Semiannual report to University of Wyoming National Park Service Research Center.

Pearson, O. P., and D. F. Bradford, 1976. Thermoregulation of lizards and toads at high altitudes in Peru. *Copeia*, 1976: 155–170.

Pearson, P. G., 1955. Population ecology of the spadefoot toad, *Scaphiopus h. holbrooki* (Harlan). *Ecol. Monogr.*, 25: 233–267.

Pearson, P. G., 1957. Further notes on the population ecology of the spadefoot toad. *Ecology*, 38: 580–586.

Pechmann, J.H.K., D. E. Scott, R. D. Semlitsch, J. P. Caldwell, L. J. Vitt, and J. W. Gibbons, 1991. Declining amphibian populations: The problem of separating human impacts from natural fluctuations. *Science*, 253: 892–895.

Pechmann, J.H.K., and H. M. Wilber, 1994. Putting declining amphibian populations in perspective: Natural fluctuations and human impacts. *Herpetologica*, 50: 65–84.

Penna, M., and A. Veloso, 1990. Vocal diversity in frogs of the South American temperate forest. *Jour. Herp.*, 24: 23–33.

Perrill, S. A., and R. E. Daniel, 1983. Multiple egg clutches in *Hyla regilla*, *H. cinerea* and *H. gratiosa*. *Copeia*, 1983: 513–516.

Perrill, S. A., and M. Magier, 1988. Male mating behavior in *Acris crepitans*. *Copeia*, 1988: 245–248.

Perrill, S. A., and W. J. Shepherd, 1989. Spatial distribution and male-male communication in the northern cricket frog, *Acris crepitans blanchardi*. *Jour. Herp.* 23: 237–243.

Peterson, C. R., E. D. Koch, and P. S. Corn, 1992. Monitoring amphibian populations in Yellowstone and Grand Teton National Parks. Final report to University of Wyoming National Park Research Service Center.

Petranka, J. W., 1987. *Notophthalmus viridescens dorsalis* (Broken-striped newt). *Behav. Herp. Rev.*, 18: 72–73.

Petranka, J. W., 1989a. Density-dependent growth and survival of larval *Ambystoma*: Evidence from whole-pond manipulations. *Ecology*, 70: 1752–1767.

Petranka, J. W., 1989b. Chemical interference competition in tadpoles. Does it occur outside laboratory aquaria? *Copeia*, 1989: 921–930.

Petranka, J. W., L. B. Kats, and A. Sih, 1987. Predator-prey interactions among fish and larval amphibians: Use of chemical cues to detect predatory fish. *Anim. Behav.*, 35: 420–425

Pfennig, D. W., 1990. 'Kin recognition' among spadefoot toad tadpoles: A side-effect of habitat selection? *Evolution*, 44: 785–798.

Phillips, C. A., and O. J. Sexton, 1989. Orientation and sexual differences during breeding migrations of the spotted salamander, *Ambystoma maculatum*. *Copeia*, 1989: 17–22.

Phillips, J. B., 1986. Magnetic compass orientation in the eastern red-spotted newt (*Notophthalmus viridesens*). *J. Comp. Physiol. (A)*, 158: 103–109.

Phillips, J. B., and K. Adler, 1978. Directional and discriminatory responses of salamanders to weak magnetic fields. In K. Schmidt-Koenig and W. T. Keeton, eds., *Animal Migration, Navigation, and Homing* (Symposium). Springer-Verlag, New York.

Pierce, B. A., 1985. Acid tolerance in amphibians. *BioSci.*, 35: 239–243.

Pinder, A. W., K. B. Storey, and G. R. Ultsch, 1992. Estivation and hibernation. In M. E. Feder and W. W. Burggren, eds., *Environmental Physiology of the Amphibians*. University of Chicago Press, Chicago and London.

Polls Pelaz, M., and C. Rougier, 1990. A comparative study of buccal volumes and the branchial skeleton of *Rana ridibunda* and *R. dalmatina* tadpoles. *Copeia*, 1990: 658–665.

Pool, T. B., and T. R. Hoage, 1973. The ultrastructure of secretion in the spermatheca of the salamander *Manculus quadridigitatus* (Holbrook). *Tissue and Cell*, 5: 303–313.

Porter, W. P., S. M. Green, M. L. Debbink, and I. Carlson, 1993. Ground water pesticides: Interactive effects of low concentrations of carbanates aldicarb and methomyl and the triazine metribuzin on thryroxine and somatotropin levels in white rats. *Jour. Tox. and Env. Health*, 40: 15–34.

Pough, F. H., 1974. Natural daily temperature acclimation of eastern red efts, *Notophthalmus v. viridescens* (Rafinesque) (Amphibia: Caudata). *Comp. Biochem. Physiol*, 47: 71–78.

Pough, F. H., 1983. Amphibians and reptiles as low energy systems. In W. P. Aspey and S. I. Lustick, eds., *Behavioral Energetics: The Cost of Survival in Vertebrates*. Ohio State University Press, Columbus.

Pough, F. H., W. E. Magnusson, M. J. Ryan, K. D. Wells, and T. L. Taigen, 1992. Behavioral energetics. In M. E. Feder and W.W. Burggren, eds., *Environmental Physiology of the Amphibians*. University of Chicago Press, Chicago and London.

Pough, F. H., and R. E. Wilson, 1970. Natural daily temperature stress, dehydration, and acclimation in juvenile *Ambystoma maculatum* (Shaw) (Amphibia: Caudata). *Physiol. Zool.*, 43: 194–205.

Pounds, J. A., and M. L. Crump, 1994. Amphibian declines and climate disturbance: The case of the Golden Toad and the Harlequin Frog. *Conserv. Biol.*, 8: 72–75.

Prattle, R. E., C. Schock, J. M. Creasey, and G. M. Hughes, 1977. Surpellic films, lung surfactant, and their cellular origin in newt, caecilian, and frog. *J. Zool., London*, 182: 125–136.

Price, R. M., and E. R. Meyer, 1979. An amplexus call made by the male American toad, *Bufo americanus americanus* (Amphibia, Anura, Bufonidae). *Jour. Herp.*, 13: 506–509.

Ptacek, M. B., 1992. Calling sites used by male gray treefrogs, *Hyla versicolor* and *Hyla chrysoscelis*, in sympatry and allopatry in Missouri. *Herpetologica*, 48: 373–382.

Putnam, R. W., and S. S. Hillman, 1977. Activity responses of anurans to dehydration. *Copeia*, 1977: 746–749.

Rabb, G. B., 1960. On the unique sound production of the Surinam Toad, *Pipa pipa*. *Copeia*, 1960: 368–369.

Rabb, G. B., 1973. Evolutionary aspects of reproductive behavior of frogs. In J. L. Vial, ed., *Evolutionary Biology of the Anurans*. University of Missouri Press, Columbia.

Radcliffe, C. W., D. Chiszar, K. Estep, J. B. Murphy, and H. M. Smith, 1986. Observations on pedal luring and pedal movements in leptodactylid frogs. *Jour. Herp.*, 20: 300–306.

Raloff, J., 1994. That feminine touch. *Science News*, 145: 56–58.

Rapaport, R., et al., 1985. "New" DDT imputs to North America: Atmospheric deposition. *Chemosphere*, 14: 1167–1173.

Rastogi, R. K., 1980. Importance of external factors in annual testicular cycles in anuran amphibia. *Gen. Comp. Endocrinol.*, 40: 309–310 (abstr.).

Ray, C., 1958. Vital limits and rates of desiccation in salamanders. *Ecology*, 39: 75–83.

Reagan, N. L., and P. A. Verrell, 1991. The evolution of plethodontid salamanders: Did terrestrial mating facilitate lunglessness? *Amer. Nat.*, 138: 1307–1313.

Regal, P. J., 1967. Voluntary hypothermia in reptiles. *Science*, 155: 1551–1553.

Regal, P. J., and C. Gans, 1976. Functional aspects of the evolution of frog tongues. *Evolution*, 30: 718–734.

Regier, H. A., and G. L. Baskerville, 1986. Sustainable redevelopment of regional ecosystems degraded by exploitive development. In W. C. Clark and R. E. Munn, eds., *Sustainable Development of the Biosphere*. Cambridge University Press, Cambridge, U.K.

Reno, H. W., F. R. Gehlbach, and R. A. Turner, 1972. Skin and aestivational cocoon of the aquatic amphibian *Siren intermedia* Le Conte. *Copeia*, 1972: 625–631.

Resetarits, W. J., Jr., and H. M. Wilbur, 1989. Choice of oviposition site by *Hyla chrysoscelis*: Role of predators and competitors. *Ecology*, 70: 220–228.

Resnick, L. E., and D. L. Jameson, 1963. Color polymorphism in Pacific tree frogs. *Science*, 142: 1081–1083.

Reynolds, W. W., and J. B. Covert, 1976. *Behavioral Fever in Aquatic Ectothermic Vertebrates: Drugs, Biogenic Amines and Temperature Regulation*. Proceedings of 3d International Pharmacology of Thermoregulation Symposium, Karger, Basel.

Richards, C. M., 1958. The inhibition of growth in crowded *Rana pipiens* tadpoles. *Physiol. Zool.*, 31: 138–151.

Richards, C. M., 1962. The control of tadpole growth by alga-like cells. *Physiol. Zool.*, 35: 285–296.

Robertson, J.G.M., 1986. Male territoriality, fighting and assessment of fighting ability in the Australian frog *Uperoleia rugosa*. *Anim. Behav.*, 34: 763–772.

Roble, S. M., 1985. Observations on satellite males in *Hyla chrysoscelis*, *Hyla picta*, and *Pseudacris triseriata*. *Jour. Herp.*, 19: 432–436.

Rome, L. C., E. D. Stevens, and H. B. John-Alder, 1992. The influence of temperature and thermal acclimation on physiological function. In M. E. Feder and W. W. Burggren, eds., *Environmental Physiology of Amphibians*. University of Chicago Press, Chicago and London.

Rose, F. L., 1966. Homing to nests by the salamander *Desmognathus auriculatus*. *Copeia*, 1966: 251–253.

Rosen, M., and R. E. Lemon, 1974. The vocal behavior of spring peepers, *Hyla crucifer*. *Copeia*, 1974: 940–950.

Ross, R. J., and J.J.B. Smith, 1978. Detection of substrate vibrations by salamanders: Inner ear sense organ activity. *Can. J. Zool.*, 56: 1156–1162.

Rossi, J. V., 1983. The use of olfactory clues by *Bufo marinus*. *Jour. Herp.*, 17: 72–73.

Roth, G., 1976. Experimental analysis of the prey catching behavior of *Hydromantes italicus* Dunn (Amphibia, Plethodontidae). *J. Comp. Physiol.*, 109: 47–58.

Roth, G., 1987. *Visual Behavior in Salamanders*. Springer-Verlag, New York.

Roudebush, R. E., and D. H. Taylor, 1987. Chemical communication between two species of desmognathine salamanders. *Copeia*, 1987: 744–748.

Ruben, J. A., and A. J. Boucot, 1989. The origin of the lungless salamanders (Amphibia: Plethodontidae). *Amer. Nat.*, 134: 161–169.

Ruben, J. A., N. L. Reagan, P. A. Verrell, and A. J. Boucot, 1993. Plethodontid sala-mander origins: A response to Beachy and Bruce. *Amer. Nat.*, 142: 1038–1051.

Ruibal, R., 1955. A study of altitudinal races in *Rana pipiens*. *Evolution*, 9: 322–338.

Ruibal, R., 1962a. The ecology and genetics of a desert population of *Rana pipiens*. *Copeia*, 1962: 189–195.

Ruibal, R., 1962b. The adaptive value of bladder water in the toad, *Bufo cognatus*. *Physiol. Zool.*, 35: 218–223.

Ruibal, R., and S. Hillman, 1981. Cocoon structure and function in the burrowing hylid frog, *Pternohyla fodiens*. *Jour. Herp.*, 15: 402–408.

Ruibal, R., L. Tevis, Jr., and V. Roig, 1969. The terrestrial ecology of the spadefoot toad *Scaphiopus hammondii*. *Copeia*, 1969: 571–584.

Ruibal, R., and E. Thomas, 1988. The obligate carnivorous larvae of the frog, *Lepidoba-trachus laevis* (Leptodactylidae). *Copeia*, 1988: 591–604.

Ryan, M. J., 1986. Neuroanatomy influences speciation rates among anurans. *Proc. Natl. Acad. Sci.*, 83: 1379–1382.

Ryan, M. J, M. D. Tuttle, and A. S. Rand, 1982. Bat predation and sexual advertisement in a neotropical anuran. *Amer. Nat.*, 119: 136–139.

Saidapur, S. K., R. D. Kanamadi, and N. U. Bhuttewadkar, 1989. Variations in the fat body mass in the male frog, *Rana cyanophlyctis*. *Jour. Herp.*, 23: 461–463.

St. John, A. D., 1982. The herpetology of Curry County, Oregon. Oregon. Dept. Fish and Wildl., Nongame Wildl. Prog. Tech. Rep. no. 82–2–04.

St. John, A. D., 1984. The herpetology of Jackson and Josephine Counties, Oregon. Oregon Dept. Fish and Wildl., Nongame Wildl. Prog. Tech. Rep. no. 84–2–05.

St. John, A. D., 1985a. The herpetology of the interior Umpqua River drainage, Douglas County, Oregon. Oregon Dept. Fish and Wildl., Nongame Wildl. Prog. Tech. Rep. no. 85–2–02.

St. John, A. D., 1985b. The herpetology of the Owyhee River drainage, Malheur County, Oregon. Oregon Dept. Fish and Wildl., Nongame Wildl. Prog., Tech. Rep. no. 85–5–03.

St. John, A. D., 1986. The herpetology of the Willamette Valley, Oregon. Oregon Dept. Fish and Wildl., Nongame Wildl. Prog. Tech. Rep. no. 86–1–02.

Salthe, S. N., 1963. The egg capsules in the Amphibia. *Jour. Morph.*, 113: 161–171.

Salthe, S. N., 1967. Courtship patterns and the phylogeny of the urodeles. *Copeia*, 1967: 100–117.

Salthe, S. N., 1969. Reproductive modes and the number and sizes of ova in the urode-les. *Amer. Midland Nat.*, 81: 467–490.

Salthe, S. N., and J. S. Mecham, 1974. Reproductive and courtship patterns. In B. Lofts, ed., *Physiology of the Amphibia*, vol. 2. Academic Press, New York.

Sanderson, I. T., 1937. *Animal Treasure*. Viking Press, New York.

Sarasin, P., and F. Sarasin, 1887–90. Ergebnisse Naturwissenschaftlichen Forschungen auf Ceylon in den Jahren 1884–1886. Zur Entwicklungsgeschichte u. Anat. der Cey-lonische Blindwühle *Ichthyophis glutinosus*. Keidels Verlag, Wiesbaden.

Savage, R. M., 1961. *The Ecology and Life History of the Common Frog (Rana tempo-raria temporaria)*. Sir Isaac Pitman and Sons, Ltd., London.

Scheuer, P. J., 1990. Some marine ecological phenomena: Chemical basis and biomedi-cal potential. *Science*, 248: 173–177.

Schmid, W. D., 1982. Survival of frogs in low temperature. *Science*, 215: 697–698.

Schmidt, A., and M. Wake, 1990. Olfactory and vomeronasal systems of caecilians (Amphibia: Gymnophiona). *Jour. Morph.*, 205: 255–268.

Schmuck, R., F. Kobelt, and K. E. Linsenmair, 1988. Adaptations of the reed frog *Hyperolius viridiflavus* (Amphibia, Anura, Hyperoliidae) to its arid environment. *J. Comp. Physiol. B*, 158: 537–546.

Schroeder, E. E., 1968. Movements of subadult green frogs, *Rana clamitans*. *Jour. Herp.*, 1: 119.

Schuett, G. W., and J. C. Gillingham, 1990. The function of scream calling in nonsocial vertebrates: Testing the predator attraction hypothesis. *Bull. Chi. Herp. Soc.*, 25: 137–142.

Schwalm, P. A., P. H. Starrett, and R. W. McDiarmid, 1977. Infrared reflectance in leaf-sitting neotropical frogs. *Science*, 196: 1225–1227.

Scott, N. J., Jr., and H. W. Campbell, 1992. A chronological bibliography, the history and status of studies of herpetological communities, and suggestions for future research. *Wildlife Res. Rep.*, 13: 221–239 (see p. 227—Energy Flow Studies).

Scott, N. J., Jr., and, R. A. Seigel, 1992. The management of amphibian and reptile populations: Specific priorities and methodological and theoretical constraints. In D. R. McCullough and R. H. Barrett, eds., *Wildlife 2001: Populations*. Elsevier Applied Science Pub. Ltd., Essex, England.

Scott, N. J., Jr., and A. Starrett, 1974. An unusual breeding aggregation of frogs, with notes on the ecology of *Agalychnis spurrelli* (Anura: Hylidae). *Bull. So. Calif. Acad. Sci.*, 73: 86–94.

Seale, D. B., 1980. Influence of amphibian larvae on primary production, nutrient flux, and competition in a pond ecosystem. *Ecology*, 61: 1531–1550.

Seale, D. B., 1982. Physical factors influencing oviposition by the woodfrog, *Rana sylvatica*, in Pennsylvania. *Copeia*, 1982: 627–635.

Semlitsch, R. D., 1981. Terrestrial activity and summer home range of the mole salamander (*Ambystoma talpoideum*). *Can. J. Zool.*, 59: 315–322.

Semlitsch, R. D., 1988. Allotropic distribution of two salamanders: Effects of fish predation and competitive interactions. *Copeia*, 1988: 290–298.

Sergeev, A. M., and K. S. Smirnov, 1939. The color of eggs of Amphibia. *Probl. Ecol. and Biocenology*, 5: 319–321 (English summary.)

Sever, D. M., 1976. Morphology of the mental hedonic gland clusters of plethodontid salamanders (Amphibia, Urodela, Plethodontidae). *Jour. Herp.*, 10: 227–239.

Sever, D. M., 1978. Male cloacal glands of *Plethodon cinereus* and *Plethodon dorsalis* (Amphibia: Plethodontidae). *Herpetologica*, 34: 1–20.

Sever, D. M., 1987. *Hemidactylium scutatum* and the phylogeny of cloacal anatomy in female salamanders. *Herpetologica*, 43: 105–116.

Sever, D. M., 1988a. The ventral gland in female salamander *Eurycea bislineata* (Amphibia: Plethodontidae). *Copeia*, 1988: 572–579.

Sever, D. M., 1988b. Male *Rhyacotriton olympicus* (Dicamptodontidae: Urodela) has a unique cloacal vent gland. *Herpetologica*, 44: 274–280.

Sever, D. M., 1989. Caudal hedonic glands in salamanders of the *Eurycea bislineata* complex (Amphibia: Plethodontidae). *Herpetologica*, 45: 322–329.

Sever, D. M., 1991. Comparative anatomy and phylogeny of the cloacae of salamanders (Amphibia: Caudata), I. Evolution at the family level. *Herpetologica*, 47: 165–193.

Sever, D. M., and L. D. Houck, 1985. Spermatophore formation in *Desmognathus ochrophaeus* (Amphibia: Plethodontidae). *Copeia*, 1985: 394–402.

Sever, D. M., P. A. Verrell, T. R. Halliday, M. Griffiths, and V. Waights, 1990. The cloaca and cloacal glands of the male smooth newt, *Triturus vulgaris vulgaris* (Linnaeus), with especial emphasis on the dorsal gland. *Herpetologica*, 46: 160–168.

Sexton, O. J., 1962. Apparent territorialism in *Leptodactylus insularum* Barbour. *Herpetologica*, 18: 212–214.

Sexton, O. J., and J. R. Bizer, 1978. Life history patterns of *Ambystoma tigrinum* in montane Colorado. *Amer. Midland Nat.*, 99: 101–118.

Seymour, R. S., 1972. Behavioral thermoregulation by juvenile green toads, *Bufo debilis*. *Copeia*, 1972: 572–575.

Seymour, R. S., 1973. Energy metabolism of dormant spadefoot toads (*Scaphiopus*). *Copeia*, 1973: 435–445.

Seymour, R. S., and A. K. Lee, 1974. Physiological adaptations of anuran amphibians to aridity: Australian prospects. *Aust. Zool.*, 18: 53–65.

Shaffer, H. B., 1984. Evolution in a paedomorphic lineage, I. An electrophoretic analysis of the Mexican ambystomatid salamanders. *Evolution*, 38: 1194–1206.

Shaffer, H. B., C. C. Austen, and R. B. Huey, 1991. The consequences of metamorphosis on salamander (*Ambystoma*) locomotor performance. *Physiol. Zool.*, 64: 212–231.

Shaffer, H. B., R. N. Fisher, and S. E. Stanley, 1994. Status report: The California tiger salamander *Ambystoma californiense*. Final Report for California Department of Fish and Game, Contract FG9422.

Shaffer, H. B., and G. V. Lauder, 1985. Patterns of variation in aquatic ambystomatid salamanders: Kinematics of the feeding mechanism. *Evolution*, 39: 83–92.

Sharpe, R. M., and N. E. Skakkebaek, 1993. Are oestrogens involved in falling sperm counts and disorders of the male reproductive tract? *Lancet*, 341: 1392–1395.

Sheffield, L. P., J. M. Law, and G. M. Burghart, 1968. On the nature of chemical food sign stimuli for newborn garter snakes. *Commun. Behav. Biol.*, 2: 7–12.

Shine, R., 1979. Sexual selection and sexual dimorphism in the Amphibia. *Copeia*, 1979: 297–306.

Shinn, E. A., and J. W. Dole, 1978. Evidence for a role for olfactory cues in the feeding response of leopard frogs, *Rana pipiens*. *Herpetologica*, 34: 167–172.

Shinn, E. A., and J. W. Dole, 1979a. Evidence for a role for olfactory cues in the feeding response of western toads, *Bufo boreas*. *Copeia*, 1979: 163–165.

Shinn, E. A., and J. W. Dole, 1979b. Lipid components of prey odors elicit feeding responses in western toads (*Bufo boreas*). *Copeia*, 1979: 275–278.

Shoemaker, V. H., M. A. Baker, and J. P. Loveridge, 1989. Effect of water balance on thermoregulation in waterproof frogs (*Chiromantis* and *Phyllomedusa*). *Physiol. Zool.*, 62: 133–146.

Shoemaker, V. H., S. S. Hillman, S. D. Hillyard, D. C. Jackson, L. L. McClanahan, P. C. Withers, and M. L. Wygota, 1992. Exchange of water, ions, and respiratory gases in terrestrial amphibians. In M. E. Feder and W. W. Burggren, eds., *Environmental Physiology of Amphibians*. University of Chicago Press, Chicago and London.

Shoop, C. R., 1968. Migratory orientation of *Ambystoma maculatum* movements near breeding ponds and displacements of migrating individuals. *Biol. Bull. Mar. Biol. Lab. Woods Hole*, 135: 230–238.

Silverstone, P. A., 1973. Observations on the behavior and ecology of a Colombian poison-arrow frog, the Kõkoe-Pá (*Dendrobates histrionicus* Berthold). *Herpetologica*, 29: 295–301.

Sinsch, U., 1987. Orientation behaviour of toads (*Bufo bufo*) displaced from the breeding site. *J. Comp. Physiol. A*, 161: 715–727.

Sinsch, U., 1988. Influence of temperature and nutrition on the diel calling activity of the marsupial frog, *Gastrotheca marsupiata. Verh. Deutsch. Zool. Ges.*, 81: 263–264.

Sinsch, U., 1989. Behavioral thermoregulation of the Andean toad (*Bufo spinulosus*) at high altitudes. *Oecologia* (Heidelberg), 80: 32–38.

Sinsch, U., 1992. Amphibians. In F. Papi, ed., *Animal Homing*. Chapman and Hall, London, New York, etc.

Sites, J. W., Jr., 1978. The foraging strategy of the dusky salamander, *Desmognathus fuscus* (Amphibia, Urodela, Plethodontidae): An empirical approach to predation theory. *Jour. Herp.*, 12: 373–383.

Sivak, J. G., and M. R. Warburg, 1980. Optical metamorphosis of the eye of *Salamandra salamandra. Can. J. Zool.*, 58: 2059–2064.

Slack, G., 1993. Magic frog leads anthropologist to new peptide. *Pacific Discovery*, 46: 4.

Sloan, A. J., 1964. Amphibians of San Diego County. *Occas. Papers San Diego Soc. Nat. Hist.*, 13: 1–40.

Smith-Gill, S. J., and K. A. Berven, 1980. In vitro fertilization and assessment of male reproductive potential using mammalian gonadotropin-releasing hormone to induce spermiation in *Rana sylvatica. Copeia*, 1980: 723–728.

Snyder, G. K., and W. W. Weathers, 1975. Temperature adaptation in amphibians. *Amer. Nat.*, 109: 93–101.

Sokol, O. M., 1975. The phylogeny of anuran larvae: A new look. *Copeia*, 1975: 1–23.

Soto, A. M., K. L. Chung, and C. Sonnenschein 1994. The pesticides encosulfan, toxaphene, and dieldrin have estrogen-sensitive cells. *Env. Health Persp.*, 102: 380–383.

Spearman, R.I.C., ed., 1977. *Comparative Biology of Skin*. Symposia of the Zoological Society of London, no. 39, Zool. Soc. London. Academic Press.

Spotila, J. R., 1972. Role of temperature and water in the ecology of lungless salamanders. *Ecol. Monogr.*, 42: 95–125.

Sprules, W. G., 1974a. The adaptive significance of paedogenesis in North American species of *Ambystoma* (Amphibia: Caudata): An hypothesis. *Can. J. Zool.*, 52: 393–400.

Sprules, W. G., 1974b. Environmental factors and the incidence of neoteny in *Ambystoma gracile* (Baird) (Amphibia: Caudata). *Can. J. Zool.*, 52: 1545–1552.

Starret, P. H., 1973. Evolutionary patterns in larval morphology. In J. L. Vial, ed., *Evolutionary Biology of the Anurans: Contemporary Research on Major Problems*. University of Missouri Press, Columbia.

Stebbins, R. C., 1945. Water absorption in a terrestrial salamander. *Copeia*, 1945: 25–28.

Stebbins, R. C., 1954. Natural history of the salamanders of the plethodontid genus *Ensatina. Univ. Calif. Publ. Zool.*, 54: 47–124.

Stebbins, R. C., and J. R. Hendrickson, 1959. Field studies of amphibians in Colombia, South America. *Univ. Calif. Publ. Zool.*, 56: 497–540.

Steinwascher, K., 1978. Interference and exploitation competition among tadpoles of *Rana utricularia. Ecology* 59: 1039–1046.

Stewart, M. M., 1985. Arboreal habitat use and parachuting by a subtropical forest frog. *Jour. Herp.*, 19: 391–401.

Stewart, M. M., and A. S. Rand, 1991. Vocalizations and the defense of retreat sites by male and female frogs, *Eleutherodactylus coqui. Copeia*, 1991: 1013–1024.

Stewart, M. M., and A. S. Rand, 1992. Diel variation in the use of aggressive calls by the frog *Eleutherodactylus coqui. Herpetologica*, 48: 49–56.

Stone, D.J.M., J. H. Bowie, M. J. Tyler, and J. C. Wallace, 1992. The structure of caerin 1.1, a novel antibiotic peptide from Australian frogs. *J. Chem. Soc., Chem. Commun.*, 1992: 1224–1225.

Stone, D.J.M., R. J. Waugh, J. H. Bowie, J. C. Wallace, and M. J. Tyler, 1993. Peptides from Australian frogs: The structures of the caerins from *Litoria caerulea. J. Chem. Research (S)*: 138.

Storer, T. I., R. L. Usinger, R. C. Stebbins, and J. W. Nybakken, 1979. *General Zoology.* McGraw-Hill, New York.

Storey, K. B., 1990. Life in a frozen state: Adaptive strategies for natural freeze tolerance in amphibians and reptiles. *Amer. J. Physiol.*, 258: R559–568.

Storey, K. B., and J. M. Storey, 1987. Persistence of freeze tolerance in terrestrially hibernating frogs after spring emergence. *Copeia*, 1987: 720–726.

Storm, R. M., 1960. Notes on the breeding biology of the red-legged frog (*Rana aurora aurora*). *Herpetologica*, 16: 251–259.

Storm, R. M., 1986. Current status of Oregon amphibians and reptiles—a brief review. Appendix 8 in Oregon nongame wildlife management plan. Oregon Dept. Fish and Wildl., Portland.

Straughan, I. R., 1973. Evolution of anuran mating calls: Bioacoustical aspects. In J. L. Vial, ed., *Evolutionary Biology of the Anurans.* University of Missouri Press, Columbia.

Straughan, I. R., and A. R. Main, 1966. Speciation and polymorphism in the genus *Crinia* Tschudi (Anura, Leptodactylidae) in Queensland. *Proc. R. Soc. Queensland*, 78: 11–28.

Stuart, J. N., and C. W. Painter, 1994. A review of the distribution and status of the boreal toad, *Bufo boreas boreas*, in New Mexico. *Bull. Chi. Herp. Soc.*, 29: 113–116.

Stumpel, A.H.P., 1987. Distrubution and present numbers of the tree frog *Hyla arborea* in Zealand Flanders, The Netherlands (Amphibia, Hylidae). *Bijdr. Dierkd.*, 57: 151–163.

Sullivan, B. K., 1984. Advertisement call variation and observations on breeding behavior of *Bufo debilis* and *B. punctatus. Jour. Herp.*, 18: 406–411.

Sullivan, B. K., 1985. Male calling behavior in response to playback of conspecific advertisement calls in two bufonids. *Jour. Herp.*, 19: 78–83.

Sweet, S. S., 1983. Mechanics of a natural extinction event: *Rana boylii* in southern California (abst.). Paper presented at 26th annual meeting of SSAR and 31st annual meeting of HL, University of Utah, Salt Lake City, Aug. 7–12, 1983.

Sweet, S. S., 1991 (revised 1992). Initial report on the ecology and status of the arroyo toad (*Bufo microscaphus californicus*) on the Los Padres National Forest of Southern

California, with management recommendations. Contract report to USDA, Forest Service, Los Padres National Forest, Goleta, Calif.

Sweet, S. S. 1993. Second report on the biology and status of the Arroyo Toad (*Bufo microscaphus californicus*) on the Los Padres National Forest of Southern California. Contract report to USDA, Forest Service, Los Padres National Forest, Goleta, Calif.

Taigen, T. L., and K. D. Wells, 1985. Energetics of vocalization by an anuran amphibian (*Hyla versicolor*). *J. Comp. Physiol.*, 155B: 163–170.

Taigen, T. L., K. D. Wells, and R. L. Marsh, 1985. The enzymatic basis of high metabolic rates in calling frogs. *Physiol. Zool.*, 58: 719–726.

Taylor, D. H., 1972. Extraoptic photoreception and compass orientation in larval and adult salamanders (*Ambystoma tigrinum*). *Anim. Behav.*, 20: 233–236.

Taylor, D. H., and K. Adler, 1973. Spatial orientation by salamanders using plane-polarized light. *Science*, 181: 285–287.

Taylor, D. H., and K. Adler, 1978. The pineal body: Site of extraocular perception of celestial cues for orientation in the tiger salamander (*Ambystoma tigrinum*). *J. Comp. Physiol.*, 124A: 359–361.

Taylor, D. H., and J. S. Auburn, 1978. Orientation of amphibians by linearly polarized light. In K. Schmidt-Koenig and W. T. Keeton, eds., *Animal Migration, Navigation, and Homing* (Symposium). Springer-Verlag, New York.

Taylor, D. H., and D. E. Ferguson, 1969. Solar cues and shoreline learning in the southern cricket frog, *Acris gryllus*. *Herpetologica*, 25: 147–149.

Taylor, D. H., and D. E. Ferguson, 1970. Extraoptic celestial orientation in the southern cricket frog *Acris gryllus*. *Science*, 168: 390–392.

Taylor, D. H., and S. I. Guttman, eds., 1977. *The Reproductive Biology of Amphibians*. Plenum Press, New York.

Test, F. H., 1954. Social aggressiveness in an amphibian. *Science*, 120: 140–141.

Test, F. H., and R. G. McCann, 1976. Foraging behavior of *Bufo americanus* tadpoles in response to high densities of micro-organisms. *Copeia*, 1976: 576–578.

Thomas, E. O., L. Tsang, and P. Licht, 1993. Comparative histochemistry of the sexually dimorphic skin glands of anuran amphibians. *Copeia*, 1993: 133–143.

Thuesen, E. V., and K. Kogura, 1989. Bacterial production of tetrodotoxin in four species of Chaetognatha. *Biol. Bull.*, 176: 191–194.

Thurow, G., 1976. Aggression and competition in eastern *Plethodon* (Amphibia, Urodela, Plethodontidae). *Jour. Herp.*, 10: 277–291.

Thurow, G. R., and H. J. Gould, 1977. Sound production in a caecilian. *Herpetologica*, 33: 234–237.

Tilley, S. G., 1972. Aspects of parental care and embryonic development in *Desmognathus ochrophaeus*. *Copeia*, 1972: 532–540.

Tilley, S. G., and J. S. Hausman, 1976. Allozymic variation and occurrence of multiple inseminations in populations of the salamander *Desmognathus ochrophaeus*. *Copeia*, 1976: 734–741

Tilley, S. G., B. L. Lundrigan, and L. P. Brower, 1982. Erythrism and mimicry in the salamander *Plethodon cinereus*. *Herpetologica*, 38: 409–417.

Toews, D., and D. MacIntyre, 1978. Respiration and circulation in an apodan amphibian. *Can. J. Zool.*, 56: 988–1004.

Toft, C. A., 1981. Feeding ecology of Panamanian litter anurans: Patterns in diet and foraging mode. *Jour. Herp.*, 15: 139–144.

Tomson, O. H., and D. E. Ferguson, 1972. Y-axis orientation in larvae and juveniles of three species of *Ambystoma. Herpetologica*, 28: 6–9.

Tillitt, D. E., G. T. Ankley, J. P. Giesy, J. P. Ludwig, H. Kurita-Matsuba, D. V. Weseloh, P. S. Ross, C. A. Bishop, L. Sileo, K. L. Stromborg, J. Larson, and T. J. Kubiak, 1992. Polychlorinated biphenyl residues and egg mortality in double-crested cormorants from the Great Lakes. *Env. Tox. Chem.*, 11: 1281– 1288.

Tordoff, W., 1971. Environmental factors affecting gene frequencies in montane populations of the chorus frog, *Pseudacris triseriata.* Ph.D. dissertation, Colorado State University, Fort Collins.

Tracy, C. R., C. R. Tracy, and J. S. Turner, 1992. Contrasting physiological abilities for heating and cooling in an amphibian (*Rana pipiens*) and a reptile (*Sauromalus obesus*). *Herpetologica*, 48: 57–60.

Trauth, S. E., 1983. Reproductive biology and spermathecal anatomy of the dwarf salamander (*Eurycea quadridigitata*) in Alabama. *Herpetologica*, 39: 9–15.

Trauth, S. E., 1984. Spermathecal anatomy and the onset of mating in the slimy salamander (*Plethodon glutinosus*) in Alabama. *Herpetologica*, 40: 314–321.

Travis, J., 1980. Phenotypic variation and the outcome of interspecific competition in hylid tadpoles. *Evolution*, 34: 40–50.

Tristram, D. A., 1977. Intraspecific olfactory communication in the terrestrial salamander *Plethodon cinereus. Copeia*, 1977: 597–600.

Trueb, L., and C. Gans, 1983. Feeding specializations of the Mexican burrowing toad *Rhinophrynus dorsalis* (Anura: Rhinophrynidae). *J. Zool., London*, 199: 189–208.

Turner, F. B., 1958. Life history of the western spotted frog in Yellowstone National Park. *Herpetologica*, 14: 96–100.

Turner, F. B., 1960. Population structure and dynamics of the western spotted frog, *Rana p. pretiosa* Baird and Girard, in Yellowstone Park, Wyoming. *Ecol. Monogr.*, 30: 251–278.

Turnipseed, G., and R. Altig, 1975. Population density and age structure of three species of hylid tadpoles. *Jour. Herp.*, 9: 287–291.

Tuttle, M. D., and M. J. Ryan, 1981. Bat predation and the evolution of frog vocalizations in the neotropics. *Science*, 214: 677–678.

Twitty, V. C., 1955. Field experiments on the biology and genetic relationships of the Californian species of *Triturus. J. Exp. Zool.*, 129: 129–148.

Twitty, V. C., 1959. Migration and speciation in newts. *Science*, 130: 1735–1743.

Twitty, V., D. Grant, and O. Anderson, 1967a. Home range in relation to homing in the newt *Taricha rivularis* (Amphibia: Caudata). *Copeia*, 1967: 649–653.

Twitty, V., D. Grant, and O. Anderson, 1967b. Initial homeward orientation after long distance displacement of the newt *Taricha rivularis. Proc. Natl. Acad. Sci.*, 57: 342–348.

Tyler, M. J., 1972. A new genus for the Australian leptodactylid frog *Crinia darlingtoni. Zool. Meded. Rijks Mus. Nat. Hist., Leiden*, 47: 193–201.

Tyler, M. J., 1976. A new genus and two new species of leptodactylid frogs from western Australia. *Rec. West. Aust. Mus.*, 4: 45–52.

Tyler, M. J., 1989. *Australian Frogs.* Viking O'Neil, New York.

Tyler, M. J., 1991. Declining amphibian populations—a global phenomenon? An Australian perspective. *Alytes*, 9: 43–50.

Tyler, M. J., and M. Davies, 1985. The gastric brooding frog *Rheobatrachus silus.* In

G. Grigg, R. Shine, and H. Ehmann, eds., *Biology of Australasian Frogs and Reptiles*. Surrey Beatty & Sons and Royal Zool. Soc., New South Wales.

Underwood, H. 1979. Extraretinal photoreception. In E. H. Burtt, Jr., ed., *The Behavioral Significance of Color*. Garland Press, New York.

Urbach, F., ed., 1969. *The Biological Effects of Ultraviolet Radiation, with Emphasis on the Skin*. Pergamon Press, Oxford and New York.

Valentine, B. D., and D. M. Dennis, 1964. A comparison of the gill-arch system and fins of three genera of larval salamanders, *Rhyacotriton*, *Gyrinophilus*, and *Ambystoma*. *Copeia*, 1964: 196–201.

Van Oordt, P.G.W.J., 1960. The influence of internal and external factors in the regulation of the spermatogenic cycle in amphibia. In E.J.W. Barrington, ed., *Cyclical Activity in Endocrine Systems* (Symposium). *Zool. Soc. Lond.*, no. 2.

Van Wijngaarden, R., and F. Bolaños, 1992. Parental care in *Dendrobates granuliferus* (Anura: Dendrobatidae), with a description of the tadpole. *Jour. Herp.*, 26: 102–105.

Verrell, P. A., 1985. Male mate choice for large, fecund females in the red-spotted newt, *Notophthalmus viridescens*: How is size assessed? *Herpetologica*, 41(4): 382–386.

Verrell, P. A., 1986. Male discrimination of larger, more fecund females in the smooth newt, *Triturus vulgaris*. *Jour. Herp.*, 20: 416–422.

Verrell, P. A., 1988. Intrinsic male mating capacity is limited in the plethodontid salamander, *Desmognathus ochrophaeus*. *Jour. Herp.*, 22: 394–400.

Verrell, P. A., 1989. The sexual strategies of natural populations of newts and salamanders. *Herpetologica*, 45: 265–282.

Verrell, P. A., 1990. A note on the courtship of the broken-striped newt, *Notophthalmus viridenscens dorsalis* (Harlan). *Jour. Herp.*, 24: 215–217.

Verrell, P. A., 1991. Proximity preference in female smooth newts, *Triturus vulgaris vulgaris*: Do they reveal complex mating decisions? *Copeia*, 1991: 835–836.

Vertucci, F. A., and P. S. Corn, 1993. Declines of amphibian populations in the Rocky Mountains are not due to episodic acidification. *Bull. Ecol. Soc. Amer.*, 74; Supplement: 470 (abstr.).

Vestal, E. H., 1941. Defensive inflation of the body in *Bufo boreas halophilus*. *Copeia*, 1941: 183.

Vial, J. L., ed., 1973. *Evolutionary Biology of the Anurans*. University of Missouri Press, Columbia.

Vial, J. L., and L. Saylor, 1993. The status of amphibian populations: A compilation and analysis. International Union for Conservation of Nature and Natural Resources. Species Survival Commission. Declining Amphibian Populations Task Force. Corvallis, Oregon, Center for Analysis of Environmental Change.

Villolobos, M., P. León, S. K. Sessions, and J. Kezer, 1988. Enucleated erythrocytes in plethodontid salamanders. *Herpetologica*, 44: 243–250.

Vitt, L. J., J. P. Caldwell, H. M. Wilbur, and D. C. Smith, 1990. Amphibians as harbingers of decay. *BioSci.*, 40: 418.

Volpe, E. P., 1953. Embryonic temperature adaptations and relationships in toads. *Physiol. Zool.*, 26: 344–354.

Volpe, E. P., 1957a. Embryonic temperature tolerance and rate of development in *Bufo valliceps*. *Physiol. Zool.*, 30: 164–176.

Volpe, E. P., 1957b. Embryonic temperature adaptions in highland *Rana pipiens*. *Amer. Nat.*, 41: 303–309.

Wagner, W. E., Jr., 1989. Social correlates of variation in male calling behavior in Blanchard's cricket frog, *Acris crepitans blanchardi*. *Ethology*, 82: 27–45.

Wagner, W. E., Jr., 1992. Deceptive or honest signalling of fighting ability? A test of alternative hypotheses for the function of changes in call dominant frequency by male cricket frogs. *Anim. Behav.*, 44: 449–462.

Wagner, W. E., Jr., and B. K. Sullivan, 1992. Chorus organization in the Gulf Coast toad (*Bufo valliceps*): Male and female behavior and the opportunity for sexual selection. *Copeia*, 1992: 647–658.

Wake, D. B., 1991. Declining amphibian populations. *Science*, 253: 860.

Wake, D. B., and I. G. Dresner, 1967. Functional morphology and evolution of tail autonomy in salamanders. *Jour. Morph.*, 122: 265–306.

Wake, M. H., 1974. The comparative morphology of the caecilian lung. *Anat. Rec.*, 178 (2): 483.

Wake, M. H., 1976. The development and replacement of teeth in viviparous caecilians. *Jour. Morph.*, 148: 33–63.

Wake, M. H., 1977a. Fetal maintenance and its evolutionary significance in the Amphibia: Gymnophiona. *Jour. Herp.*, 11: 379–386.

Wake, M. H., 1977b. The reproductive biology of caecilians: An evolutionary perspective. In D. H. Taylor and S. I. Guttman, eds., *The Reproductive Biology of Amphibians*. Plenum Press, New York.

Wake, M. H., 1978a. Comments on the ontogeny of *Typhlonectes obesus*, particularly its dentition and feeding. *Papéis Avulsos de Zoologia, S. Paulo*, 32: 1–13.

Wake, M. H., 1978b. The reproductive biology of *Eleutherodactylus jasperi* (Amphibia, Anura, Leptodactylidae), with comments on the evolution of live-bearing systems. *Jour. Herp.*, 12: 121–133.

Wake, M. H., 1980a. Reproduction, growth, and population structure of the Central American caecilian *Dermophis mexicanus*. *Herpetologica*, 36: 244–256.

Wake, M. H., 1980b. Morphological information on caecilian eye function. *Amer. Zool.*, 20: 287.

Wake, M. H., 1981. Structure and function of the male Mullerian gland in caeclians (Amphibia: Gymnophiona) with comments on its evolutionary significance. *Jour. Herp.*, 15: 17–22.

Wake, M. H., 1982. Diversity within a framework of constraints: Reproductive modes in the Amphibia. In D. Mossakowski and G. Roth, eds., *Environmental Adaptation and Evolution: A Theoretical and Empirical Approach*. Gustav-Fischer-Verlag, Stuttgart and New York.

Wake, M. H., 1983. *Gymnopis multiplicata, Dermophis mexicanus*, and *Dermophis parviceps* (Soldas, Suelda con Suelda, Dos Cabezas, Caecilians). In D. H. Janzen, ed., *Costa Rican Natural History*. University of Chicago Press, Chicago.

Wake, M. H., 1985. The comparative morphology and evolution of the eyes of caecilians (Amphibia, Gymnophiona). *Zoomorphology*, 105: 277–295.

Wake, M. H., 1986. Caecilians. In T. R. Halliday and K. Adler, eds., *The Encyclopaedia of Reptiles and Amphibians*. Facts on File, New York.

Wake, M. H., and G. Z. Wurst, 1979. Tooth crown morphology in caeclians (Amphibia: Gymnophiona). *Jour. Morph.*, 159: 331–340.

Waldman, B., 1981. Sibling recognition in toad tadpoles: The role of experience. *Z. Tierpsychol.*, 56: 341–358.

Waldman, B., 1982. Sibling association among schooling toad tadpoles: Field evidence and implications. *Anim. Behav.*, 30: 700–713.

Waldman, B., 1985. Olfactory basis of kin recognition in toad tadpoles. *J. Comp. Physiol.*, 156A: 565–577.

Waldman, B., and M. J. Ryan, 1983. Thermal advantages of communal egg mass deposition in wood frogs (*Rana sylvatica*). *Jour. Herp.*, 17: 70–72.

Walls, S. C., A. Mathis, R. G. Jaeger, and W. F. Gergits, 1989. Male salamanders with high-quality diets have faeces attractive to females. *Anim. Behav.*, 38: 546–548.

Walls, S. C., and R. E. Roudebush, 1991. Reduced aggression toward siblings as evidence of kin recognition in cannibalistic salamanders. *Amer. Nat.*, 138: 1027–1038.

Warburg, M. R., 1965. Studies on the water economy of some Australian frogs. *Aust. J. Zool.*, 13: 317–330.

Warburg, M. R., 1967. On thermal and water balance of three central Australian frogs. *Comp. Biochem. Physiol.*, 20: 27–43.

Ward, D., and O. J. Sexton, 1981. Anti-predator role of salamander egg membranes. *Copeia*, 1981: 724–726.

Wassersug, R. J., 1972. The mechanism of ultraplankton entrapment in anuran larvae. *Jour. Morph.*, 137: 279–287.

Wassersug, R. J., 1975. The adaptive significance of the tadpole stage with comments on the maintenance of complex life cycles in anurans. *Amer. Zool.*, 15: 405–417.

Wassersug, R. J., 1980. Internal oral features of larvae from eight anuran families: Functional, systematic, evolutionary and ecological considerations. *Univ. Kansas Mus. Nat. Hist., Misc. Publ.*, 68.

Wassersug, R. J., 1984. The *Pseudohemisus* tadpole: A morphological link between microhylid (Orton Type 2) and ranoid (Orton Type 4) larvae. *Herpetologica*, 40: 138–149.

Wassersug, R. J., and W. E. Duellman, 1984. Oral structures and their development in egg-brooding hylid frog embryos and larvae: Evolutionary and ecological implications. *Jour. Morph.*, 182: 1–37.

Wassersug, R. J., and C. M. Hessler, 1971. Tadpole behavior: Aggregation in larval *Xenopus laevis*. *Anim. Behav.*, 19: 386–389.

Wassersug, R. J., A. M. Lum, and M. J. Potel, 1981. An analysis of school structure for tadpoles (Anura: Amphibia). *Behav. Ecol. Sociobiol.*, 9: 15–22.

Wassersug, R. J., and W. F. Pyburn, 1987. The biology of the Pe-ret' toad, *Otophryne robusta* (Microhylidae) with special consideration of its fossorial larvae and systematic relationships. *Zool. J. Linn. Soc.*, 91: 137–169.

Wassersug, R. J., and K. Rosenberg, 1979. Surface anatomy of branchial food traps of tadpoles a comparative study. *Jour. Morph.*, 159: 393–426.

Weathers, W. W., and G. K. Snyder, 1977. Relation of oxygen consumption to temperature and time of day in tropical anuran amphibians. *Aust. J. Zool.*, 25: 19–24.

Weiss, B. A., B. H. Stuart, and W. F. Strother, 1973. Auditory sensitivity in the *Rana catesbeiana* tadpole. *Jour. Herp.*, 7: 211–214.

Wells, K. D., 1976a. The evolution of courtship behavior in frogs. *Herp. Rev.*, 7: 73–74.

Wells, K. D., 1976b. Territorial behavior of the green frog (*Rana clamitans*). Ph.D. dissertation, Cornell University, Ithaca, New York.

Wells, K. D., 1977a. Territoriality and male mating success in the green frog (*Rana clamitans*). *Ecology*, 58: 750–762.

Wells, K. D., 1977b. The social behavior of anuran amphibians. *Anim. Behav.*, 25: 666–693.

Wells, K. D., 1978a. Territoriality in the green frog (*Rana clamitans*): Vocalizations and agonistic behavior. *Anim. Behav.*, 26: 1051–1063.

Wells, K. D., 1978b. Courtship and parental behavior in a Panamanian poison-arrow frog (*Dendrobates auratus*). *Herpetologica*, 34: 148–155.

Wells, K. D., 1980. Social behavior and communication of a dendrobatid frog (*Colostethus trinitatis*). *Herpetologica*, 36: 189–199.

Wells, K. D., 1981. Territorial behavior of the frog *Eleutherodactylus urichi* in Trinidad. *Copeia*, 1981: 726–728.

Wells, K. D., 1989. Vocal communication in a neotropical treefrog, *Hyla ebraccata*: Response of males to graded aggressive calls. *Copeia*, 1989: 461–466.

Wells, K. D., and K. M. Bard, 1988. Parental behavior of an aquatic-breeding tropical frog, *Leptodactylus bolivianus*. *Jour. Herp.*, 22: 361–364.

Wells, K. D., and B. J. Greer, 1981. Vocal responses to conspecific calls in a neotropical hylid frog, *Hyla ebraccata*. *Copeia*, 1981: 615–624.

Wells, K. D., and J. J. Schwartz, 1982. The effect of vegetation on the propagation of calls in the neotropical frog *Centrolenella fleischmanni*. *Herpetologica*, 38: 449–455.

Werner, J. K., 1969. Temperature-photoperiod effects on spermatogenesis in the salamander *Plethodon cinereus*. *Copeia*, 1969: 592–602.

Werner, J. K., and M. B. McCune, 1979. Seasonal changes in anuran populations in a northern Michigan pond. *Jour. Herp.*, 13: 101–104.

Wever, E. G., 1978. Sound transmission in the salamander ear. *Proc. Natl. Acad. Sci.*, 75: 529–530.

Wever, E. G., and C. Gans, 1976. The caecilian ear: Further observations. *Proc. Natl. Acad. Sci.*, 73: 3744–3746.

Weygoldt, P., 1980. Complex brood care and reproductive behavior in captive poison-arrow frogs, *Dendrobates pumilio* O. Schmidt. *Behav. Ecol. Sociobiol.*, 7: 329–332.

Weygoldt, P., 1989. Changes in the composition of mountain stream frog communities in the Atlantic Mountains of Brasil: Frogs as indicators of environmental deteriorations? *Stud. Neotrop. Fauna and Environ.*, 243: 249–255.

Whitford, W. G., and V. H. Hutchison, 1963. Cutaneous and pulmonary gas exchange in the spotted salamander, *Ambystoma maculatum*. *Biol. Bull.*, 124: 344–354.

Whitford, W. G., and V. H. Hutchison, 1966. Cutaneous and pulmonary gas exchange in ambystomatid salamanders. *Copeia*, 1966: 573–577.

Whitford, W. G., and K. H. Meltzer, 1976. Changes in O_2 consumption, body water and lipid in burrowed desert juvenile anurans. *Herpetologica*, 32: 23–25.

Whittow, G. C., ed., 1970. *Comparative Physiology of Thermoregulation*. vol. 1, *Invertebrates and Nonmammalian Vertebrates*. Academic Press, New York and London.

Wickler, W., 1968. *Mimicry in Plants and Animals*. World University Library. McGraw-Hill, New York.

Wickler, W., and U. Seibt, 1974. Rufen und Antworten bei *Kassina senegalensis*, *Bufo regularis* und anderen Anuran. *Z. Tierpsychol.*, 34: 524–537.

Wiewandt, T. A., 1969. Vocalization, aggressive behavior, and territoriality in the bullfrog, *Rana catesbeiana*. *Copeia*, 1969: 276–285.

Wilbur, H. M., 1977. Interactions of food level and population density in *Rana sylvatica*. *Ecology*, 58: 206–209.

Wilbur, H. M., D. I. Rubenstein, and L. Fairchild, 1978. Sexual selection in toads: The roles of female choice and male body size. *Evolution*, 32: 264–270.

Wilczynski, W., 1992. The nervous system. In M. E. Feder and W. W. Burggren, eds., *Environmental Physiology of Amphibians*. University of Chicago Press, Chicago and London.

Wilson, E. O and F. M. Peter, 1988. *Biodiversity*. National Academy Press, Washington, D.C.

Winokur, R. M., and S. Hillyard, 1992. Pelvic cutaneous musculature in toads of the genus *Bufo. Copeia*, 1992: 760–769.

Wissinger, S. A., and H. H. Whiteman, 1992. Fluctuation in a Rocky Mountain population of salamander anthropogenic acidification or natural variation? *Jour. Herp.*, 26: 377–391.

Wood, S. C., R. E. Weber, G.M.O. Maloiy, and K. Johansen, 1975. Oxygen uptake and blood respiratory properties of the caecilian *Boulengerula taitanus. Respir. Physiol.*, 24: 355–363.

Woodward, B. D., 1982b. Sexual selection and nonrandom mating patterns in desert anurans (*Bufo woodhousei, Scaphiopus couchi, S. multiplicatus* and *S. bombifrons*). *Copeia*, 1982: 351–355.

Woodward, B. D., 1986. Paternal effects on juvenile growth in *Scaphiopus multiplicatus* (the New Mexico spadefoot toad). *Amer. Nat.*, 128: 58–65.

Woodward, B. D., 1987. Interactions between Woodhouse's toad tadpoles (*Bufo woodhouseii*) of mixed sizes. *Copeia*, 1987: 380–386.

Woolbright, L. L., 1985. Patterns of nocturnal movement and calling by the tropical frog *Eleutherodactylus coqui. Herpetologica*, 41: 1–9.

Wygoda, M., 1984. Low cutaneous evaporative water loss in arboreal frogs. *Physiol. Zool.*, 57: 329–337.

Wygoda, M. L., 1987. Cutaneous and subcutaneous adipose tissue in anuran amphibians. *Copeia*, 1987: 1031–1035.

Wygoda, M., 1989. A comparative study of heating rates in arboreal and nonarboreal frogs. *Jour. Herp.*, 23: 141–145.

Wygoda, M. L., and A. A. Williams, 1991. Body temperature in free-ranging green tree frogs (*Hyla cinerea*): A comparison with "typical" frogs. *Herpetologica*, 43: 328–335.

Wyman, R. L., and J. H. Thrall, 1972. Sound production by the spotted salamander, *Ambystoma maculatum. Herpetologica*, 28: 210–212.

Xavier, F., 1977. An exceptional reproductive strategy in Anura: *Nectoprhynoides occidentalis* Angel (Bufonidae), an example of adaptation to terrestrial life by viviparity. In: M. K. Hect, P. C. Goody, and B. M. Hect, eds., *Major Patterns in Vertebrate Evolution*. NATO Advanced Study Institutes Series, Ser. A, Life Sciences, 14.

Xavier, F., 1978. *Nectophrynoides liberiensis*, a new species (Anura: Bufonidae) from the Nimba ridge, Liberia, I. Description of the species. *Bull. Soc. Zool. France*, 103: 431–442.

Xavier, F., 1986. La reproduction des Nectophyrynoides. In P. P. Grassé and M. Delsol, eds., *Traité de zoologie*, 14: 497–513.

Xavier, F., M. Zuber-Vogeli, and Y. Le Quang Trong, 1970. Recherchés sur l'activité endocrine de l'ovaire de *Nectophrynoides occidentalis* Angel (Amphibien anoure vivipare). *Gen. Comp. Endocr.*, 15: 425–431.

Yasumoto, T., H. Nagai, D. Yasumura, T. Michishita, A. Endo, M. Yotsu, and Y. Kotaki, 1986. Interspecies distribution and possible origin of tetrodotoxin. In C. Y. Kao and S. R. Levinson, eds., *Tetrodotoxin, Saxitoxin, and the Molecular Biology of the Sodium Channel*. Annals N.Y. Acad. Sciences, vol. 479, 1–14.

Yasumoto, T., M. Yotsu, A. Endo, M. Murata, and H. Naoki, 1989. Interspecies distribution and biogenetic origin of tetrodotoxin and its derivatives. *Pure Appl. Chem.*, 61: 505–508.

Yasumoto, T., M. Yotsu, M. Murata, and H. Naoki, 1988. New tetrodotoxin analogues from the newt *Cynops ensicauda*. *J. Amer. Chem. Soc.*, 110: 2344–2345.

Yoon, D., 1977. The effect of introduced fish on the amphibian life in Westfall Meadow. *Yosemite Nature Notes*, 46: 69–70.

Yotsu, M., T. Yamazaki, Y. Meguro, A. Endo, M. Murata, H. Naoki, and T. Yasumoto, 1987. Production of tetrodotoxin and its derivatives by *Pseudomonas* sp. isolated from the skin of a pufferfish. *Toxicon*, 25: 225–228.

Youth, H., 1994a. Flying into trouble. *World Watch*, 7:10–19.

Youth, H., 1994b. Birds are in decline. In L. R. Brown, H. Hane, and D. M. Roodman (ed. L. Starke), *Vital Signs*, 1994. W. W. Norton and Co., New York and London.

Zalisko, E. J., R. A. Brandon, and J. Martan, 1984. Microstructure and histochemistry of salamander spermatophores (Ambystomatidae, Salamandridae and Plethodontidae). *Copeia*, 1984: 739–747.

Zasloff, M., 1987. Magainins, a class of antimicrobial peptides from *Xenopus* skin: Isolation characterization of two active forms, and partial c DNA sequence of a precursor. *Proc. Natl. Acad. Sci.*, 84: 5449–5453.

Zeller, E., 1891. Über den Copulation sact von *Salamandra maculosa*. *Zoolog. Anzeiger* (XIV Jahrg.), 371: 292–293.

Zimmerman, B. L., and J. P. Bogart, 1988. Ecology and calls of four species of Amazonian forest frogs. *Jour. Herp.*, 22: 97–108.

Zug, G. R., 1972. Anuran locomotion: Structure and function, I. Preliminary observations on relation between jumping and osteometrics of appendicular and postaxial skeleton. *Copeia*, 1974: 613–624.

Zug, G. R., 1978. Anuran locomotion: Structure and function, II. Jumping performance of semiaquatic, terrestrial, and arboreal frogs. *Smithsonian Contrib. Zool.*, 276.

Zweifel, R. G., 1968. Reproductive biology of anurans of the arid southwest, with emphasis on adaptation of embryos to temperature. *Bull. Amer. Mus. Nat. Hist.*, 140: 1–64.

Zweifel, R. G., 1977. Upper thermal tolerances of anuran embryos in relation to stage of development and breeding habits. *Amer. Mus. Novitates*, 2617: 1–20.

Zylberberg, L., and M. W. Wake, 1990. Structure of the scales of *Dermophis* and *Microcaecilia* (Amphibia: Gymnophiona) and a comparison to dermal ossifications of other vertebrates. *Jour. Morph.*, 206: 25–43.

Index

acclimation, 95
acclimatization, 97
Acris, 132
Acris crepitans, 5, 82, 108, 135, 161
Acris crepitans blanchardi, 84
Acris gryllus, 82, 108
activity rhythms and pineal complex, 100
advertisement calls, 80–82
African Bullfrog: cocoons, 104, 107; guarding
    eggs and nest sites, 195–197
African Clawed Frog, 20, 183; lateral line sys-
    tem, 73–74; tadpole schooling and behavior,
    186; tadpole structure and habits, 184; sound
    production method, 77–78
African foam-nest frogs, 94
African Hairy Frog, 23–24
African Leaf-folding Frog: advertisement call,
    81; satellite behavior, 161
African live-bearing toads, 6–7
Afrixalis delicatus, 81, 161, 197
Agalychnis moreletii, 90
Agalychnis spurrelli, 30
Agile Frog tadpoles, 193
Alpine Newt: color vision, 52; sexual visual
    signals, 146
Alpine Salamander, 6, 204
Alteromonas sp. bacteria, 12
Alytes cisternasii, 198
Alytes muletensis, 198
Alytes obstetricans, 198
Ambystoma, 72, 119, 143, 175
Ambystoma barbouri, 170
Ambystoma californiense, 46, 177, 232–233
Ambystoma gracile, 77, 94, 120, 150, 162, 164,
    177
Ambystoma jeffersonianum, 136, 162
Ambystoma laterale, 98
Ambystoma macrodactylum, 99
Ambystoma maculatum, 24, 77, 128, 136, 138,
    149–150, 152, 162
Ambystoma mexicanum, 149
Ambystoma opacum, 23, 128, 136, 178, 188,
    195
Ambystoma talpoideum, 136, 190
Ambystoma tigrinum, 2, 42, 53, 55, 60–61,

100, 116, 134, 143, 149, 152, 162, 164, 177,
    233–234
Ambystoma tigrinum diaboli, 177
Ambystoma tigrinum mavortium, 177
American Toad, 13; mating success, 85; palata-
    bility of eggs, 120; signaling release, 71; tad-
    pole schooling and behavior, 186–187;
    tongue, 59
Amolops, 152, 181
Amphibia class, 3
amphibians:
    as bio-indicators, 238–241
    breathing, 17–25
    characteristics, 239–240
    diploid, 15–16
    direct development of eggs, 6
    dormant (estivating), 107
    foot structure variations, 28
    larval, 17–18
    life cycles, 6–9
    limbs and locomotion, 26–32
    major groups, 3–4
    modes of reproduction, 6–9
    natural history overview, 9–16
    oviparous, 6
    ovoviviparous, 7–9
    place in nature, 4–6
    polyploid, 15–16
    primary predators of invertebrates
        (as), 5
    skin, 10–16
    strictly aquatic, 6
    tails, 33–36
    viviparous, 6–7
amphibious, 6
Amphiuma, 26, 74
Amphiuma means, 74
Anax junius, 120
Andean Toad, 91
Andelman, Sandy, xiii
Anderson Salamander, 117
Anderson, Stanley, xiii
Andrias, 6, 8, 23
Andrias davidianus, 3
Andrias japonicus, 3